THE
Adams-Jefferson
LETTERS

The Institute of Early American History and Culture is sponsored jointly by the College of William and Mary and Colonial Williamsburg, Incorporated. Publication of this book has been assisted by a grant from the Lilly Endowment, Inc.

THOMAS JEFFERSON

Portrait by Mather Brown, painted in London, 1786
(See p. vii)

THE
Adams-Jefferson
LETTERS

*The Complete Correspondence
Between Thomas Jefferson
and Abigail and John Adams*

*

EDITED BY

LESTER J. CAPPON

IN TWO VOLUMES

Vol. II, 1812-1826

PUBLISHED FOR
*The Institute of Early American History and Culture
at Williamsburg, Virginia*
by The University of North Carolina Press • Chapel Hill

CONTENTS

VOLUME II

v

ILLUSTRATIONS

Volume Two

tion "was a bold experiment, ... on the health of an octogenary. ... Successive coats of thin grout plastered on the naked head and kept there an hour, would have been a severe trial of a young and hale man." Charles Henry Hart, *Browere's Life Masks of Great Americans* (N.Y., 1899), 39–45. (Courtesy of the New York State Historical Association, Cooperstown, New York)

JOHN ADAMS   *facing page 464*

After completing the likeness of Jefferson, Browere proceeded to Quincy, where he made a mask of John Adams at the age of ninety. Adams authorized his son "to say that the moulds were made ... without injury, pain or inconvenience." Charles Henry Hart, *Browere's Life Masks of Great Americans* (N.Y., 1899), 51–52. (Courtesy of the New York State Historical Association, Cooperstown, New York)

UNIVERSITY OF VIRGINIA   *facing page 465*

This drawing was made by a Mr. Williams in 1824. It first appeared as a vignette in the upper left-hand corner of the Herman Böyë map of Virginia (1826), as engraved by H. S. Tanner. John H. B. Latrobe, who visited the University in 1832, regarded the vignette as "a very accurate one." Edwin M. Betts, "Groundplans and Prints of the University of Virginia, 1822–1826," American Philosophical Society, *Proceedings*, 90, no. 2 (May 10, 1946), 89–90. (Courtesy of the American Philosophical Society)

THE
Adams-Jefferson
LETTERS

9

"Whether you or I were right Posterity must judge"

DURING THE SUMMER of 1811 Edward Coles, secretary to President Madison, and his brother John were traveling through the northern states, armed with letters of introduction from the President to various statesmen they hoped to meet. John Adams was of course on their list. Cordially received by Mr. and Mrs. Adams, the Coles brothers found their host in a reminiscent mood and they spent the better part of two days talking with him about the history of the United States and especially his presidential administration. As Adams warmed to the subject, he voiced his grievances against Jefferson and recalled events culminating in the election of 1800 and the last days of the Federalist regime.

Edward Coles, a neighbor of Jefferson in Albemarle County, had heard some of these same incidents retold from a different point of view; in particular he gave Adams the Jefferson version of how the President-elect in 1801 had carefully selected the proper time to call on President Adams before the last session of the Federalist Congress and how the tense emotion at the opening of their conference had given way gradually to amicable conversation. The narrative as retold by Coles was accurate according to Adams's own recollection. He admitted that he had been sensitive about their meeting, but he added, "I never heard before that Mr. Jefferson had given a second thought as to the proper time for making the particular visit described." Adams went on to express admiration for the character of his old friend and strong disapproval of the scurrilous attacks upon him in the newspapers of that day. "I always loved Jefferson," Adams exclaimed, "and still love him." [1]

When Jefferson heard the details of Coles's visit, he was deeply moved. There was one friend to whom he turned without hesitation to unburden himself—the same person to whom, earlier that year, he had sent his correspondence of 1804 with Mrs. Adams. "This is enough for me," he wrote Dr. Benjamin Rush concerning Adams's outburst of affection. "I only needed this knowledge to revive towards him all the affections of the most cordial moments of our lives. . . . I knew him to be always an honest man, often a great one, but sometimes incorrect and precipitate in his judgments; and it is known to those who have ever heard me speak of Mr. Adams, that I have ever done him justice myself, and defended him when assailed by others, with the single exception as to political opinions." [2] Thus in early December 1811 Adams and Jefferson were on the eve of reconciliation, but it had taken two years of well-planned, persistent efforts on the part of their mutual friend Dr. Rush.

Rush, two and a half years younger than Jefferson, was a fellow signer of the Declaration of Independence. Although he won both fame and notoriety through his medical theories and practice, his reputation as a teacher had made Philadelphia the medical center of the nation. He carried on a wide correspondence on scientific and other "philosophical" matters, and like Adams and Jefferson, he had a keen sense of national consciousness. As these friends of his grew older and retired from public life, Rush regarded them increasingly as the personification of the American Republic, of its principles and ideals. The prolonged estrangement of the two former Presidents was to Rush both a personal and a national misfortune. In 1809 he thought he had found a way of healing the breach. [3]

During his stimulating correspondence with Adams on a variety of subjects, Rush had urged him to write a history of his life and times for the enlightenment of the American people, but Adams had rejected the proposal. [4] Now, in October 1809, Rush, assuming a casual

1. TJ to Benjamin Rush, Dec. 5, 1811, Ford, IX, 300n.; Edward Coles to Henry S. Randall, May 11, 1857, Randall, *Jefferson*, III, 639-40.

2. TJ to Rush, Dec. 5, 1811, Ford, IX, 300n. See above, Chap. 8, 268.

3. L. H. Butterfield has written the best account of "The Dream of Benjamin Rush: The Reconciliation of John Adams and Thomas Jefferson," *Yale Review*, 40 (1950-51), 297-319.

4. Rush to JA, July 11, Aug. 22, 1806, April 1, Aug. 14, 1809, Butterfield, ed., *Letters of Rush*, II, 922, 927, 1000-1, 1013-14.

air, recounted a dream he hoped would come true. He was reading in a history of the United States that the two ex-Presidents had renewed their friendship in November of that year. It had come about through a letter from Adams congratulating Jefferson on his domestic happiness in retirement from public office. With Jefferson's cordial reply their correspondence was resumed and continued during the remainder of their lives; and, according to the dream, "these gentlemen sunk into the grave nearly at the same time. . . ." [5] Adams assured Rush that the dream put him in good spirits, but "it is not History. It may be Prophecy." [6] It was indeed prophetic, but Rush's feeler for reconciliation was rebuffed.

A year later, Rush tried a more direct approach through Jefferson, with an allusion to the "patriotic years" of 1774-76, "your early attachment to Mr. Adams, and his to you." "I have ardently wished a friendly and epistolary intercourse might be revived between you. . . . Human nature will be a gainer by it. I am sure an advance on your side will be a cordial to the heart of Mr. Adams." [7] It was at this juncture that Jefferson forwarded to Rush his unsatisfactory exchange of letters with Mrs. Adams and professed to "the same good opinion of Mr. Adams which I ever had." (At his wife's request John Adams had already read them in 1804, without comment.)[8] After reviewing the issues between Adams and himself, Jefferson asked Rush to "judge for yourself whether they admit a revival of that friendly intercourse for which you are so kindly solicitous." [9] Rush realized he had failed again, but the reply from Monticello nourished his hope that the way to an accord would yet be found.

When Edward Coles proved to be the accidental messenger of good will in 1811, Rush acted promptly on Jefferson's warm response by quoting at length from it in a letter to Adams and concluding: "And now, my dear friend, permit me again to suggest to you to receive the olive branch which has thus been offered to you by the hand of a man who still loves you. Fellow laborers in erecting the great fabric of American independence! . . . embrace—embrace each

5. Rush to JA, Oct. 17, 1809, *ibid.*, 1021-22.
6. JA to Rush, Oct. 25, 1809, *ibid.*, 1023*n*.
7. Rush to TJ, Jan. 2, 1811, *ibid.*, 1075-76.
8. AA to TJ, Oct. 25, 1804, postscript dated Nov. 19, 1804, above, 282.
9. TJ to Rush, Jan. 16, 1811, Ford, IX, 295-99.

other!" [10] The next day Rush informed Jefferson hopefully of his second effort to revive their friendship. [11]

Undoubtedly Adams had made up his mind about writing to Jefferson when he replied to Rush in a half-comic, half-serious vein and left the issue apparently unresolved. He might keep Rush in doubt a while longer, but the doctor had not tricked him. "I perceive plainly enough, Rush, that you have been teasing Jefferson to write to me, as you did me some time ago to write to him. . . . When there has been no war, there can be no room for negotiations of peace." He and Jefferson were in agreement concerning the Constitution and forms of government in general; they differed on measures of administration and other details. Rush seemed to imply that Adams had considered Jefferson as an enemy. "This is not so; I have always loved him as a friend." Rush's exhortation was so hyper-solemn that Adams "had some inclination to be ludicrous." "But why do you make so much ado about nothing? Of what use can it be for Jefferson and me to exchange letters? . . . Time and chance, however, or possibly design, may produce ere long a letter between us." [12]

Adams carried out his "design" a week later when he informed Jefferson that he was mailing him "two Pieces of Homespun lately produced in this quarter." Wishing Jefferson "many happy New Years," [13] the statesman of Quincy expressed his esteem for the statesman of Monticello and thus opened the second and richer period of their correspondence. The prospect of receiving some homespun from Massachusetts prompted Jefferson to begin his reply with a short essay on domestic manufactures in Virginia, a practical subject of deep concern to a practical-minded man who advocated economic independence to fortify his country's political independence in a world at war. However, this was a letter chiefly of reminiscence, of personal matters rather than public affairs, a letter of "recollections very dear to my mind." Jefferson wrote eagerly and saluted his old friend "with unchanged affections and respect." [14] The next day, to his delight, he received the "homespun"—the two-volumed *Lectures*

10. Rush to JA, Dec. 16, 1811, Butterfield, ed., *Letters of Rush*, II, 1110.
11. Rush to TJ, Dec. 17, 1811, *ibid.*, 1111-12.
12. JA to Rush, Dec. 25, 1811, *Works*, X, 10-12. In a letter to Rush, Aug. 28, 1811, JA had referred, almost inadvertently, to TJ as "my friend." *Ibid.*, IX, 638, 639.
13. JA to TJ, Jan. 1, 1812, below, 290.
14. TJ to JA, Jan. 21, 1812, below, 290-92.

on Rhetoric and Oratory by John Quincy Adams, to whom as a youth in Paris, almost thirty years before, he had become strongly attached.[15]

The correspondence of the two former Presidents was resumed amid the mounting national and international tension which culminated in the War of 1812. The controversies with Great Britain over neutral rights and impressment of American sailors had not changed fundamentally since Jefferson's presidency, but the Republican party had split over the power of the national government vis-à-vis the states, and the Federalists of commercial New England were threatening disunion. "The Union is still to me an Object of as much Anxiety," declared Adams, "as ever Independence was. To this I have sacrificed my Popularity in New England"—and so did his son John Quincy Adams.[16] The elder Adams had never been a party man. He put the interests of the nation first, whether he opposed Federalist Hamilton or Republican Burr. President Jefferson had combatted the Essex Junto of Massachusetts, proponents of a confederacy of the eastern states.[17] In their exchange of letters during the winter and spring of 1812, Adams and Jefferson were in agreement on what they opposed, despite their frank discussion of political differences. At Monticello on June 11 Jefferson was "taking for granted that the doors of Congress will re-open with a Declaration of war."[18] On June 18 Congress reached that decision.

Even in retirement Adams could not view the political scene, currently or in retrospect, with the detachment that Jefferson achieved. Charges of corruption against the Republican Presidents Adams treated with contempt, even though he told Jefferson, "in the Measures of Administration I have neither agreed with you or Madison." As for non-importation, non-intercourse, embargoes, the structure of the judiciary, or the neglect of the Navy, "whether you or I were right Posterity must judge."[19] In the conflict with the Barbary states, Jefferson had been the first to propose a navy,[20] but Adams was the more consistent advocate. And now, with the nation at war, "if only a few Frigates had been ordered to be built!"[21] By May 1813 the little

15. TJ to JA, Jan. 23, 1812, below, 292.
16. JA to TJ, Feb. 3, 1812, below, 295; Bemis, *John Quincy Adams*, Chap. VII.
17. TJ to JA, April 20, 1812, JA to TJ, May 3, 1812, below, 300, 303.
18. TJ to JA, below, 308.
19. JA to TJ, May 1, 1812, 301.
20. See above, Chap. 4, 128, 142.
21. JA to TJ, June 28, 1812, below, 311.

American Navy had won some victories—by the frigates *Constitution* and *United States*, by the sloop-of-war *Wasp*—"which must be more gratifying to you than to most men," wrote Jefferson to Adams. "If I have differed with you on this ground, it was not on the principle, but the time." [22] Luckily time had not run out.

Because Adams was extremely sensitive about his political career, one incident of the past, unexpectedly brought to light, put his renewed friendship with Jefferson to a severe test. In 1798 Adams had addressed the young men of Philadelphia in response to a pledge they made to defend their country in the quasi-war with France. During the course of his remarks, "without wishing to damp the ardor of curiosity, or influence the freedom of inquiry," he predicted that "after the most industrious and impartial researches, the longest liver of you will find no principles, institutions, or systems of education more fit, in general, to be transmitted to your posterity, than those you have received from your ancestors." [23] Writing to Joseph Priestley after the Republicans came into power, Jefferson criticized the Federalist regime for its bigotry and backward look to "the education of our ancestors.... President [Adams] himself declaring that we were never to expect to go beyond them in real Science.' " [24] Jefferson also condemned the Alien Act, passed by the Federalist Congress, as a "Libel on Legislation." When in 1813 Adams read these sharp criticisms in the appendix to the *Memoirs of the Late Reverend Theophilus Lindsey* (1812), the English Unitarian, he demanded ("in the French sense of the word," which softened it to a request) proof and explanation.[25] Paraphrasing Jefferson's words, Adams declaimed, "Oh! Mr. Jefferson! What a wave of Public Opinion has rolled over the Universe?" [26]

Jefferson was greatly embarrassed by the publication, without permission, of his private letters to Priestley. Indictment of the party in power before 1801 was not directed personally at Adams, explained his former adversary. Adams's pithy phrases were too quotable to omit. Nevertheless, argued Jefferson, "you possess, yourself, too much

22. TJ to JA, May 27, 1813, below, 324; see also JA to TJ, June 11, 1813, below, 328-29.

23. "To the Young Men of the City of Philadelphia, the District of Southwark, and the Northern Liberties, Pennsylvania," May 7, 1798, *Works*, IX, 188.

24. TJ to Priestley, March 21, 1801, Ford, VIII, 21-22; quoted in JA to TJ, June 10, 1813, below, 327.

25. JA to TJ, May 29, June 10 and 14, 1813, below, 325-26, 326-27, 329-30.

26. JA to TJ, June 14, 1813, below, 330.

science, not to see how much is still ahead of you, unexplained and unexplored." [27] In accepting these explanations in good grace Adams could not resist giving advice: "Checks and Ballances, Jefferson, however you and your Party may have ridiculed them, are our only Security, for the progress of Mind, as well as the Security of Body." And he had stressed the importance of *general principles* in advising the young men of Philadelphia.[28] Jefferson, however, maintained the philosophical point of view, that "the same political parties which now agitate the U.S. have existed thro' all time" and "that every one takes his side in favor of the many, or of the few...." [29]

Although the veteran statesmen did not succeed in excluding political issues from their letters, they derived most pleasure from discussing scientific, historical, and religious subjects. Each man sought information and speculation from the other in a bombardment of ideas. Discovery of prophets in every era, argued Adams, suggested false prophets who have confounded mankind, whether in Biblical or modern times, whether in international relations or among the Indian tribes.[30] Jefferson needed no prodding to launch into a survey of Indian antiquities; happily he analyzed the historical sources available and commented on conflicting hypotheses. Adams ridiculed the far-fetched analogies drawn by some writers to determine the origin of the American Indians and their language.[31] Jefferson contributed first-hand knowledge of the Indians in Virginia, Adams about those in Massachusetts. They also exchanged historical data and queries on their native colonies. As for religion, both were advocates of freedom of the mind and would not minimize the spiritual tyranny that still threatened where it did not prevail over their own generation.[32]

By the summer of 1813 their accord was re-established, despite a few old wounds exposed and irritated. But their mutual friend who had brought about the rapprochement died on April 19. As Adams and Jefferson mourned Rush's death, they took count of the surviving signers of the Declaration of Independence.[33] Besides themselves, only six were still alive.

27. TJ to JA, June 15, 1813, below, 332.
28. JA to TJ, June 25 and 28, 1813, below, 334, 338-40.
29. TJ to JA, June 27, 1813, below, 335, 337.
30. JA to TJ, Feb. 10, 1812, and TJ to JA, April 20, 1812, below, 297, 298-99.
31. TJ to JA, June 11, 1812, and JA to TJ, June 28, 1812, Jan. 26, 1813, below, 305-8, 308-11.
32. JA to TJ, Feb. 10, 1812, June 25, 1813, below, 297-98, 333-34. See also, Chap. 10.
33. Butterfield, ed., *Letters of Rush*, II, 992; TJ to JA, May 27, 1813, below, 323.

Adams to Jefferson

Quincy January 1st. 1812.

DEAR SIR

As you are a Friend to American Manufactures under proper restrictions, especially Manufactures of the domestic kind, I take the Liberty of sending you by the Post a Packett containing two Pieces of Homespun [34] lately produced in this quarter by One who was honoured in his youth with some of your Attention and much of your kindness.

All of my Family whom you formerly knew are well. My Daughter Smith is here and has successfully gone through a perilous and painful Operation, which detains her here this Winter, from her Husband and her Family at Chenango: [35] where one of the most gallant and skilful Officers of our Revolution is probably destined to spend the rest of his days, not in the Field of Glory, but in the hard Labours of Husbandry.

I wish you Sir many happy New Years and that you may enter the next and many succeeding Years with as animating Prospects for the Public as those at present before Us. I am Sir with a long and sincere Esteem your Friend and Servant

JOHN ADAMS

Jefferson to Adams

Monticello Jan. 21. 1812.

DEAR SIR

I thank you before hand (for they are not yet arrived) for the specimens of homespun you have been so kind as to forward me by post. I doubt not their excellence, knowing how far you are advanced in these things in your quarter. Here we do little in the fine way, but in coarse and midling goods a great deal. Every family in the country is a manu-

34. JA sent TJ a copy of John Quincy Adams's *Lectures on Rhetoric and Oratory*, 2 vols. (Cambridge, [Mass.], 1810), prepared while he was professor at Harvard College, 1806-9. Bemis, *John Quincy Adams*, 132-33.

35. Colonel William Stephens Smith's farm was at Lebanon, Madison County, New York, in the Chenango Valley. In 1812 he was elected to Congress as a Federalist and served from 1813 until his death in 1816. Curtis, "Smith, William Stephens," *DAB*, XVII, 368-69.

factory within itself, and is very generally able to make within itself all the stouter and midling stuffs for it's own cloathing and household use. We consider a sheep for every person in the family as sufficient to clothe it, in addition to the cotton, hemp and flax which we raise ourselves. For fine stuff we shall depend on your Northern manufactures. Of these, that is to say, of company establishments, we have none. We use little machinery. The Spinning Jenny and loom with the flying shuttle can be managed in a family; but nothing more complicated. The economy and thriftiness resulting from our household manufactures are such that they will never again be laid aside; and nothing more salutary for us has ever happened than the British obstructions to our demands for their manufactures. Restore free intercourse when they will, their commerce with us will have totally changed it's form, and the articles we shall in future want from them will not exceed their own consumption of our produce.

A letter from you calls up recollections very dear to my mind. It carries me back to the times when, beset with difficulties and dangers, we were fellow laborers in the same cause, struggling for what is most valuable to man, his right of self-government. Laboring always at the same oar, with some wave ever ahead threatening to overwhelm us and yet passing harmless under our bark, we knew not how, we rode through the storm with heart and hand, and made a happy port. Still we did not expect to be without rubs and difficulties; and we have had them. First the detention of the Western posts: [36] then the coalition of Pilnitz,[37] outlawing our commerce with France, and the British enforcement of the outlawry. In your day French depredations: in mine English, and the Berlin and Milan decrees: now the English orders of council, and the piracies they authorise: when these shall be over, it will be the impressment of our seamen, or something else: and so we have gone on, and so we shall go on, puzzled and prospering beyond example in the history of man. And I do believe we shall continue to growl, [i.e., grow] to multiply and prosper until we exhibit an association, powerful, wise and happy, beyond what has yet been seen by men.   As for France and England, with all their pre-eminence in science, the one is a den of robbers, and the other of pirates. And if science produces no better fruits than tyranny, murder, rapine and destitution of national morality, I would rather wish our country to be ignorant, honest and estimable as our neighboring savages are.

But whither is senile garrulity leading me? Into politics, of which I have taken final leave. I think little of them, and say less. I have given up newspapers in exchange for Tacitus and Thucydides, for Newton and Euclid; and I find myself much the happier. Sometimes indeed I look back to

36. See above, Chap. 2, 62, n. 49, and Bemis, *Jay's Treaty*, 3-20.
37. See R. R. Palmer, *A History of the Modern World* (N. Y., 1952), 364.

former occurrences, in remembrance of our old friends and fellow laborers, who have fallen before us. Of the signers of the Declaration of Independence I see now living not more than half a dozen on your side of the Potomak, and, on this side, myself alone.[38] You and I have been wonderfully spared, and myself with remarkable health, and a considerable activity of body and mind. I am on horseback 3. or 4. hours of every day; visit 3. or 4. times a year a possession I have 90 miles distant,[39] performing the winter journey on horseback. I walk little however; a single mile being too much for me; and I live in the midst of my grandchildren, one of whom has lately promoted me to be a great grandfather.[40] I have heard with pleasure that you also retain good health, and a greater power of exercise in walking than I do. But I would rather have heard this from yourself, and that, writing a letter, like mine, full of egotisms, and of details of your health, your habits, occupations and enjoyments, I should have the pleasure of knowing that, in the race of life, you do not keep, in it's physical decline, the same distance ahead of me which you have done in political honors and atchievements. No circumstances have lessened the interest I feel in these particulars respecting yourself; none have suspended for one moment my sincere esteem for you; and I now salute you with unchanged affections and respect.

TH: JEFFERSON

Jefferson to Adams

Monticello Jan. 23. 12.

DEAR SIR

The messenger who carried my letter of yesterday to the Post-office brought me thence, on his return, the two pieces of homespun which had been separated by the way from your letter of Jan. 1. A little more

38. Ten signers of the Declaration, including JA and TJ, were alive in 1812: Elbridge Gerry (d. 1814) and Robert Treat Paine (d. 1814) of Massachusetts, William Ellery (d. 1820) of Rhode Island, William Floyd (d. 1821) of New York, Benjamin Rush (d. 1813) and George Clymer (d. 1813) of Pennsylvania, Thomas McKean (d. 1817) of Delaware, and Charles Carroll (d. 1832) of Maryland.

39. Poplar Forest, in Bedford County, Va., which TJ had acquired in 1774 from his father-in-law's estate. He built an octagon house there while he was president. Malone, Jefferson, I, 441-42; Paul Wilstach, Jefferson and Monticello (N. Y., 1925), 159-60.

40. TJ's first great-grandchild was John Warner Bankhead (b. 1810), eldest child of Charles Lewis Bankhead and Mrs. Anne Cary Randolph Bankhead, first-born of Thomas Mann Randolph and Mrs. Martha Jefferson Randolph. Walter L. Zorn, The Descendants of the Presidents of the United States (2d rev. edn.; Monroe, Mich., 1955), 32.

sagacity of conjecture in me, as to their appellation, would have saved you the trouble of reading a long dissertation on the state of real homespun in our quarter. The fact stated however will not be unacceptable to you: and the less when it is considered as a specimen only of the general state of our whole country and of it's advance towards an independance of foreign supplies for the necessary manufactures.

Some extracts from these volumes which I had seen in the public papers had prepared me to recieve them with favorable expectations. These have not been disappointed; for I have already penetrated so far into them as to see that they are a mine of learning and taste, and a proof that the author of the inimitable reviews of Ames and Pickering [41] excels in more than one character of writing. The thanks therefore which I had rendered by anticipation only in my letter, I reiterate in this Postscript on a knolege of their high merit, and avail myself of the occasion it furnishes of repeating the assurances of my sincere friendship and respect.

Th: Jefferson

Adams to Jefferson

Quincy February 3. 1812

Dear Sir

Sitting at My Fireside with my Daughter Smith, on the first of February My Servant brought me a Bundle of Letters and Newspapers from the Post Office in this Town: one of the first Letters that struck my Eye had the Post Mark of Milton 23. Jany. 1812. Milton is the next Town to Quincy and the Post Office in it is but three Miles from my House. How could the Letter be so long in coming three miles? Reading the Superscription, I instantly handed the Letter to Mrs. Smith. Is that not Mr. Jeffersons hand? Looking attentively at it, she answered it is very like it. How is it possible a Letter from Mr. Jefferson, could get into the Milton Post office? Opening the Letter I found it, indeed from Monticello in the hand and with the Signature of Mr. Jefferson: but this did not much diminish my Surprize. How is it possible a Letter can come from Mr. Jefferson to me in seven or Eight days? I had no Expectation of an Answer, thinking

41. *American Principles: a Review of the Works of Fisher Ames, compiled by a Number of His Friends* (Boston, 1809). J. Q. Adams's authorship of this anonymous work, originally published in the Boston *Patriot*, April-June 1809, in a series of letters, was well known. Bemis, *John Quincy Adams*, 152-53.

the Distance so great and the Roads so embarrassed under two or three Months. This History would not be worth recording but for the Discovery it made of a Fact, very pleasing to me, vizt. that the Communication between Us is much easier, surer and may be more frequent than I had ever believed or suspected to be possible.

The Material of the Samples of American Manufacture which I sent you was not Wool nor Cotton, nor Silk nor Flax nor Hemp nor Iron nor Wood. They were spun from the Brain of John Quincy Adams and consist in two Volumes of his Lectures on Rhetorick and oratory, delivered when he was Professor of that Science in our University of Cambridge. A Relation of mine, a first Cousin of my ever honoured, beloved and revered Mother, Nicholas Boylston, a rich Merchant of Boston, bequeathed by his Will a Donation for establishing a Professorship, and John Quincy Adams, having in his Veins so much of the Blood of the Founder, was most earnestly solicited to become the first Professor. The Volumes I sent you are the Fruit of his Labour during the short time he held that office. But it ought to be remembered that he attended his Duty as a Senator of the United States during the same Period. It is with some Anxiety submitted to your Judgment.

Your Account of the flourishing State of Manufactures in Families in your Part of the Country is highly delightful to me. I wish the Spirit may spread and prevail through the Union. Within my Memory We were much in the same Way in New England: but in later Times We have run a gadding abroad too much to seek for Eatables, Drinkables and Wearables.

Your Life and mine for almost half a Century have been nearly all of a Piece, resembling in the whole, mine in The Gulph Stream, chaced by three British Frigates, in a Hurricane from the North East and a hideous Tempest of Thunder and Lightning, which cracked our Mainmast, struck three and twenty Men on Deck, wounded four and killed one.[42] I do not remember that my Feelings, during those three days were very different from what they have been for fifty Years.

What an Exchange have you made? Of Newspapers for Newton! Rising from the lower deep of the lowest deep of Dulness and Bathos to the Contemplation of the Heavens and the heavens of Heavens. Oh that I had devoted to Newton and his Fellows that time which I fear has been wasted on Plato and Aristotle, Bacon (Nat) Acherly, Bolin[g]broke, De Lolme, Harrington, Sidney, Hobbes, Plato Redivivus,[43] Marchmont, Nedham,

42. On JA's voyage to France in the *Boston* frigate in Feb. 1778. JA, "Diary," *Works*, III, 98-100.

43. By Henry Nevill, an English republican closely allied with James Harrington. Zera S. Fink, *The Classical Republicans* ... (Evanston, Ill., 1945), 129-32.

with twenty others upon Subjects which Mankind is determined never to Understand, and those who do Understand them are resolved never to practice, or countenance.

Your Memoranda of the past, your Sense of the present and Prospect for the Future seem to be well founded, as far as I see. But the Latter i.e. the Prospect of the Future, will depend on the Union: and how is that Union to be preserved? Concordia Res parvae crescunt, Discordia Maximae dilabuntur.[44] Our Union is an immense Structure. In Russia, I doubt not, a Temple or Pallace might be erected of Wood, Brick or Marble, which should be cemented only with Ice. A sublime and beautiful Building it might be; surpassing St. Sophia, St. Peters, St. Pauls, Notre Dame or St. Genevieve. But the first Week, if not the first day of the *Debacle* would melt all the Cement and Tumble The Glass and Marble, the Gold and Silver, the Timber and the Iron into one promiscuous chaotic or anarchic heap.

I will not at present point out the precise Years Days and Months when; nor the Names of the Men by whom this Union has been put in Jeopardy. Your Recollection can be at no more loss than mine.

Cobbets, Callenders, Peter Markoes, Burrs and Hamiltons may and have passed away. But Conquerors do not so easily disappear. Battles and Victories are irresis[t]able by human Nature. When a Man is once acknowledged by the People in the Army and the Country to be the Author of a Victory, there is no longer any Question. He is undoubtedly a great and good Man. Had Hamilton, [or] Burr obtained a recent Victory, neither You, nor Jay nor I should have stood any Chance against them or either of them more than a Swallow or a Sparrow.

The Union is still to me an Object of as much Anxiety as ever Independence was. To this I have sacrificed my Popularity in New England and yet what Treatment do I still receive from the Randolphs and Sheffeys of Virginia. By the Way are not these Eastern Shore Men? My Senectutal Loquacity has more than retaliated your "Senile Garrulity."

I have read Thucidides and Tacitus, so often, and at such distant Periods of my Life, that elegant, profound and enchanting as is their Style, I am weary of them. When I read them I seem to be only reading the History of my own Times and my own Life. I am heartily weary of both; i.e. of recollecting the History of both: for I am not weary of Living. Whatever a peevish Patriarch might say, I have never yet seen the day in which I could say I have had no Pleasure; or that I have had more Pain than Pleasure.

44. "Small communities grow great through harmony, great ones fall to pieces through discord." Sallust, *Jugurtha*, X.

Gerry, Paine, and J. Adams, R. R. Livingston,[45] B. Rush and George Clymer and yourself, are all that I can recollect, of the Subscribers to Independence who remain. Gerry is acting a decided and a splendid Part. So daring and so hazardous a Part; but at the same time so able and upright, that I say: "God save the Governor:" and "prosper long our noble Governor."

I walk every fair day, sometimes 3 or 4 miles. Ride now and then but very rarely more than ten or fifteen Miles. But I have a Complaint that Nothing but the Ground can cure, that is the Palsy; a kind of Paralytic Affection of the Nerves, which makes my hands tremble, and renders it difficult to write at all and impossible to write well.

I have the Start of you in Age by at least ten Years: but you are advanced to the Rank of a Great Grandfather before me. Of 13 Grand Children I have two, William and John Smith, and three Girls, Caroline Smith, Susanna and Abigail Adams, who might have made me Great Grand Children enough. But they are not likely to employ their Talents very soon. They are all good Boys and Girls however, and are the solace of my Age. I cordially reciprocate your Professions of Esteem and Respect. Madam joins and sends her kind Regards to your Daughter and your Grand Children as well as to yourself.

JOHN ADAMS

P. S. I forgot to remark your Preference to Savage over civilized life. I have Something to say upon that Subject. If I am in an Error, you can set me Right, but by all I know of one or the other I would rather be the poorest Man in France or England, with sound health of Body and Mind, than the proudest King, Sachem or Warriour of any Tribe of Savages in America.

Adams to Jefferson

Quincy Feb. 10 1812

DEAR SIR

I have received with great pleasure your favour of the 23 of January. I suspected that the Sample was left at the Post Office and that you would soon have it. I regret the shabby Condition in which you found it: but it

45. Robert R. Livingston was a member of the committee to draft the Declaration of Independence, but the New York delegation in Congress, for lack of instructions, was excused from voting on its adoption and he was absent when it was signed. Robert C. Hayes, "Livingston, Robert R.," *DAB*, XI, 321.

was the only Copy I had, and I thought it scarcely worth while to wait till I could get a Sett properly bound.

The Dissertation on the State of real homespun was a feast to me, who delight in every Information of that kind. In a moral œconomical and political point of View, it ought to be considered by every American Man Woman and child as a most precious Improvement in the Condition and prosperity of our Country.

Although you and I are weary of Politicks, You may be surprised to find me making a Transition to such a Subject as Prophecies. I find that Virginia produces Prophets, as well as the Indiana Territory. There have been lately sent me from Richmond two Volumes, one written by Nimrod Hewes and the other by Christopher Macpherson; both, upon Prophecies, and neither, ill written. I should apprehend that two such Mulattoes might raise the Devil among the Negroes in that Vicinity: for though they are evidently cracked, they are not much more irrational than Dr. Towers who wrote two ponderous Vollumes, near twenty years ago to prove that The French Revolution was the Commencement of the Millenium, and the decapitation of The King of France but the beginning of a Series, immediately to follow, by which all The Monarchies were to be destroyed and succeeded by universal Republicanism over all Europe; nor than Dr. Priestly who told me soberly, cooly and deliberately that though he knew of Nothing in human Nature or in the History of Mankind to justify the Opinion, Yet he fully believed upon the Authority of Prophecy that the French Nation would establish a free Government and that the King of France who had been executed, was the first of the Ten Horns of the great Beast, and that all the other Nine Monarks were soon to fall off after him; nor than The Reverend Mr. Faber who has lately written a very elegant and learned Volume to prove that Napoleon is Antichrist; nor than our worthy Friend Mr. Joseph Wharton of Philadelphia, who in consequence of great Reading and profound Study has long since settled his opinion, that the City of London is or is to be the Head Quarters of Antichrist; Nor than the Prophet of the Wabash [Tenskwatawa], of whom I want to know more than I do, because I learn that the Indians the Sons of the Forrest are as Superstitious as any of the great learned Men aforesaid, and as firm believers in Witchcraft as all Europe and America were in the Seventeenth Century and as frequently punish Witches by splitting their Sculls with the Tomahawk, after a solemn Tryal and Adjudication by the Sachems and Warriours in Council.

The Crusades were commenced by the Prophets and every Age since, when ever any great Turmoil happens in the World, has produced fresh Prophets. The Continual Refutation of all their Prognostications by Time and Experience has no Effect in extinguishing or damping their Ardor.

I think these Prophecies are not only unphilosophical and inconsistent with the political Safety of States and Nations; but that the most sincere and sober Christians in the World ought upon their own Principles to hold them impious, for nothing is clearer from their Scriptures than that Their Prophecies were not intended to make Us Prophets.

Pardon this strange Vagary. I want only to know something more than I do about the Richmond and Wabash Prophets.

Called to Company and to dinner I have only time to repeat the Assurances of the Friendship and Respect of

JOHN ADAMS

Jefferson to Adams

Monticello Apr. 20. 12.

DEAR SIR

I have it now in my power to send you a piece of homespun in return for that I recieved from you.[46] Not of the fine texture, or delicate character of yours, or, to drop our metaphor, not filled as that was with that display of imagination which constitutes excellence in Belles lettres, but a mere sober, dry and formal piece of Logic. Ornari res ipsa negat.[47] Yet you may have enough left of your old taste for law reading to cast an eye over some of the questions it discusses. At any rate accept it as the offering of esteem and friendship.

You wish to know something of the Richmond and Wabash prophets. Of Nimrod Hewes I never before heard. Christopher Macpherson I have known for 20. years. He is a man of color, brought up as a bookkeeper by a merchant, his master, and afterwards enfranchised. He had understanding enough to post up his ledger from his journal, but not enough to bear up against Hypochondriac affections and the gloomy forebodings they inspire. He became crazy, foggy, his head always in the clouds, and rhapsodising what neither himself nor any one else could understand. I think he told me he had visited you personally while you were in the

46. *The Proceedings of the Government of the United States, in maintaining the Public Right to the Beach of the Mississippi, Adjacent to New-Orleans, against the Intrusion of Edward Livingston.* Prepared for the Use of Counsel, by Thomas Jefferson (N. Y., 1812); reprinted in H[enry] A. Washington, ed., *The Writings of Thomas Jefferson* (Washington, D.C., 1853-54), VIII, 503-604. Livingston had acquired alluvial lands in New Orleans as payment for legal fees, but he was dispossessed of them by the United States as sovereign of the soil. He brought action in the federal court in New Orleans to recover damages, without success. William S. Carpenter, "Livingston, Edward," *DAB*, XI, 310.

47. "The subject itself refuses to be embellished."

administration, and wrote you letters, which you have probably forgotten in the mass of the correspondencies of that crazy class, of whose complaints, and terrors, and mysticisms, the several presidents have been the regular depositories. Macpherson was too honest to be molested by anybody, and too inoffensive to be a subject for the Mad-house; altho', I believe, we are told in the old Book that 'every man that is mad, and maketh himself a prophet, thou shouldest put him in prison and in the stocks.'

The Wabash prophet [Tenskwatawa] is a very different character, more rogue than fool, if to be a rogue is not the greatest of all follies. He arose to notice while I was in the administration, and became of course a proper subject of enquiry for me. The enquiry was made with diligence. His declared object was the reformation of his red brethren, and their return to their pristine manner of living. He pretended to be in constant communication with the great spirit, that he was instructed by him to make known to the Indians that they were created by him distinct from the Whites, of different natures, for different purposes, and placed under different circumstances, adapted to their nature and destinies: that they must return from all the ways of the Whites to the habits and opinions of their forefathers. They must not eat the flesh of hogs, of bullocks, of sheep etc. the deer and buffalo having been created for their food; they must not make bread of wheat, but of Indian corn. They must not wear linen nor woollen, but dress like their fathers in the skins and furs of wild animals. They must not drink ardent spirits; and I do not remember whether he extended his inhibitions to the gun and gunpowder, in favor of the bow and arrow. I concluded from all this that he was a visionary, inveloped in the clouds of their antiquities, and vainly endeavoring to lead back his brethren to the fancied beatitudes of their golden age. I thought there was little danger of his making many proselytes from the habits and comforts they had learned from the Whites to the hardships and privations of savagism, and no great harm if he did. We let him go on therefore unmolested. But his followers increased till the English thought him worth corruption, and found him corruptible. I suppose his views were then changed; but his proceedings in consequence of them were after I left the administration, and are therefore unknown to me; nor have I ever been informed what were the particular acts on his part which produced an actual commencement of hostilities on ours.[48] I have no doubt however that his subsequent proceedings are but a chapter apart, like that of [John]

48. Indian resistance, led by Tecumseh and his brother, the Prophet, against American expansion west of Ohio, culminated in the Battle of Tippecanoe, Nov. 7, 1811. Although General William Henry Harrison's "victory" was greatly exaggerated, it did end the possibility of an Indian confederacy. Glenn Tucker, *Poltroons and Patriots* ... (N. Y., [1954]), I, Chap. VII.

Henry and L[or]d Liverpool [Robert Jenkinson], in the Book of the Kings of England.

Of this mission of Henry your son had got wind, in the time of the embargo, and communicated it to me. But he had learned nothing of the particular agent, altho', of his workings, the information he had obtained appears now to have been correct. He stated a particular which Henry has not distinctly brought forward, which was that the Eastern States were not to be required to make a formal act of separation from the Union, and to take a part in the war against it; a measure deemed much too strong for their people: but to declare themselves in a state of neutrality, in consideration of which they were to have peace and free commerce, the lure most likely to ensure popular acquiescence. Having no indications of Henry as the intermediate in this negociation of the Essex junto,[49] suspicions fell on Pickering and his nephew Williams in London. If he was wronged in this, the ground of the suspicion is to be found in his known practices and avowed opinions, as of that of his accomplices in the sameness of sentiment and of language with Henry, and subsequently by the fluttering of the wounded pidgeons.

This letter, with what it encloses, has given you enough, I presume, of law and the prophets. I will only add to it therefore the homage of my respects to Mrs. Adams, and to yourself the assurances of affectionate esteem and respect.

TH: JEFFERSON

Adams to Jefferson

Quincy May 1. 1812

DEAR SIR

Yesterday, I received from the Post Office, under an envellope inscribed with your hand, but without any letter, a very learned and ingenious Pamphlet, prepared by you for the Use of your Counsel, in the case of Edward Livingston against you. Mr. Ingersol of Philadelphia, two or three Years ago sent me two large Pamphlets upon the same Subject. Neddy is a naughty lad as well as a saucy one. I have not forgotten his lying Villany in his fictitious fabricated Case of a Jonathan Robbins who never existed. His Suit against you, I hope has convinced you of his Character.

49. A group of the rich and well born of Essex County, Mass., organized in 1778 on behalf of a state constitution; ten years later they supported the United States Constitution. As New England Federalists they bitterly opposed President Jefferson's policies and the War of 1812. Henry Adams, ed., *Documents Relating to New-England Federalism, 1800-1815* (Boston, 1877), 108-14 *passim*, 149, 151, 152, 203, 369, 371.

What has become of his defalcation and plunder of the Publick? I rejoice however that you have been plagued by this fellow; because it has stimulated you to a Research that cannot fail to be of great Use to your Country. You have brought up to the View of the young Generation of Lawyers in our Country Tracts and Regions of legal Information of which they never had dreamed: but which will become, every day more and more necessary for our Courts of Justice to investigate.

Good God! Is a President of U. S. to be Subject to a private Action of every Individual? This will soon introduce the Axiom that a President can do no wrong; or another equally curious that a President can do no right.

I have run over this Pamphlet with great pleasure but must read it with more Attention. I have uniformly treated the Charges of Corruption, which I have read in Newspapers and Pamphlets and heard from the Pulpit against you and Mr. Madison with contempt and Indignation. I believe in the Integrity of both, at least as undoubtingly as in that of Washington. In the Measures of Administration I have neither agreed with you or Mr. Madison. Whether you or I were right Posterity must judge. I have never approved of Non Importations, Non Intercourses, or Embargoes for more than Six Weeks. I never have approved and never can approve of the Repeal of the Taxes, the Repeal of the Judiciary System, or the Neglect of the Navy. You and Mr. Madison had as good a right to your Opinions as I had to mine, and I must acknowledge the Nation was with you. But neither your Authority nor that of the Nation has convinced me. Nor, I am bold to pronounce will convince Posterity.

I wrote you on the third of February and on the 10th. of February but have received no answer, which makes me suspect some Accident in the Post Office or in the transportation of the Mail. The Embargo and the fatal Vote against an Augmentation of the Navy have knock'd out Gerry. Even Henry's dear bought disclosures have operated against the Administration. There is something in this Country too deep for me to sound. The escape of Governor Blount, of Aaron Burr, of John Smith, and now the coldness and Indifference about Henrys Communications, are beyond the reach of my Sagacity. So is the Language of John Randolph and Major Sheffey. What do these ignorant Boys mean by the "Profligacy of John Adams's Administration?" Randolph and Sheffey accuse John Adams of Profligacy!

Our old Friend Clinton is gone, and I suppose has left as many Millions as Washington or Franklin. And yet his Administration has not been profligate.

I am still as I ever have been and ever shall be with great Esteem and regard your Friend and Se[r]vant

JOHN ADAMS

Adams to Jefferson

Quincy. May 3. 1812

DEAR SIR

I wrote you on the first of this Month acknowledging the receipt of your "Proceedings" etc. and now repeat my thanks for it. It is as masterly a pamphlet as ever I have read; and every way worthy of the Mind that composed and the pen which commited it to writing. There is witt and fancy and delicate touches of Satyr enough in it to make it entertaining while the profusion of learning, the close reasoning and accurate Criticism must have required a Patience of Investigation that at your Age is very uncommon.

On the second of the Month your letter of the 20. of April was sent me from the Post Office. How it was seperated from the pamphlet I know not. I thank you for the Account of the Wabash Prophet. Macpherson, parson Austin and Abraham Brown made themselves sufficiently known to me when I was in the Government. They all assumed the Character of Ambassadors extraordinary from The Almighty: but as I required miracles in proof of their Credentials, and they did not perform any, I never gave publick Audience to either of them.

Though I have long acknowledged your Superiority in most branches of Science and Litterature, I little thought of being compelled to confess it in Biblical Knowledge. I had forgotten the custom of putting Prophets in the Stocks, and was obliged to have recourse to the concordance to discover Jer. 29. 26 for your Text, and found at the same time [from] Jer. 20. 2. 3 that Jeremiah himself had been put in the Stocks. It may be thought impiety by many, but I could not help wishing that the ancient practice had been continued down to more modern times and that all the Prophets at least from Peter the Hermit, to Nimrod Hews inclusively, had been confined in the Stocks and prevented from spreading so many delusions and shedding so much blood. Could you believe that the mad rant of Nimrod, which was sent to me by Christopher [Macpherson] with his own and which I lent to a Neigbour in whose house it was seen and read by some Visitors, spread a great deal of terror and a serious Apprehension that one third of the human race would be destroyed on the fourth day of the next month? As my neighbours are far from being remarkably superstitious, I could not have believed what has appeared in experience.

The transition from one set of crazy people to another is not unnatural.

There were two Gentlemen in the Senate of The United States together for several Years, who became very intimate Friends and uncommonly fond of each other. These were Mr. Pickering and Mr. Hillhouse. They were understood by the Circle in Boston, who were in the Confidence of the former, to be perfectly united in Opinion. The latter made no Secret of his Opinion, that an Amputation and a Surgical Operation as he called it, was become necessary and he made a motion in Senate, for an Amendment of the Constitution which was indeed a total Alteration of it to as absurd and as arbitrary an Aristocracy as ever was imagined. This plan he published in a Pamphlet. P.'s friends in Boston at first gave out that he perfectly concurred with H. in this project, and I heard some of them say, that they went along with them throughout. I immediately wrote an Examination of it,[50] and put it into the hands of the Anthologists for publication: but as I had made pretty free with some of their favourites they declined printing it. But that Manuscript or Something else put them so out of conceit of it, that they immediately hushed it into Oblivion. This project of a new constitution, which you must remember, was supposed to be intended for the Arm or the Leg, or the head or the Tail that was to be cut off by the chirurgical operation. I have heard that Mr. P. once on his Journey to the Senate of U. S. carried with him from his friends in Boston a project of a Division by the Potomac, the Delaware or the Hudson, i.e. as far as they could succeed, and communicated it to Gen. Hamilton who could not see his way clear, and to Mr. King, who liked it as little.[51] That there is a Party in New England, encouraged by more or less of kindred Spirits in every State in the Union, who wish to urge the Nation to a War with France and to shelter themselves and their Commerce under the Wings of the British Navy at almost any rate there can be little doubt.

I have long opposed these People in all such Projects: but the national Government by Embargoes, Non importations, Non Intercourses, and above all by the Opposition to any naval Power, have been constantly playing popularity into their hands and the consequence will soon be, if

50. James Hillhouse's pamphlet, *Propositions for Amending the Constitution of the United States* (New Haven, 1810), was examined by John Adams in his "Review of the Propositions for Amending the Constitution submitted by Mr. Hillhouse to the Senate of the United States, in 1808," but the manuscript was not published until 1851, in *Works*, VI, 523-50. The *Propositions* included annual election of representatives, three-year terms for senators, and a one-year term for the president who was to be chosen by lot from the retiring senators.

51. Pickering propagandized for a northern confederacy of the commercial states; a member of the House of Representatives from Massachusetts, he opposed the War of 1812 as destructive of American commerce; and he supported the Hartford Convention of 1814. Adams, ed., *Documents Relating to New-England Federalism*, 147-48, 339 ff., 389 ff., 414; Tucker, *Poltroons and Patriots*, II, Chap. XXXV.

it is not already, that I and my Sons and all my Friends will be hated throughout New England worse than Burr ever was or Bonaparte. If these measures are persisted in, there will be a Convulsion as certainly as there is a Sky over our heads.

My better half charges me to present you her ancient respect and regards with those of your old friend

JOHN ADAMS

Adams to Jefferson

Quincy May 21. 1812

DEAR SIR

Samuel B. Malcom Esqr. is not wholly a Stranger to you. He was three Years in my family in the Character of my private Secretary, and I believe his conduct appeared to you, as it invariably did to me, ingenuous, candid faithful and industrious. His Friends in New York were among the most respectable; his Education was public and his Studies in the Law and introduction to the Bar regular.

Congress has erected a new district of which Utica the place of his residence is the centre, and Mr. Malcom aspires to be the Judge. I believe there is no Objection to his morals, politicks, or legal qualifications. If you could find it consistent to intimate any thing in his favour to Mr. Monroe, or Mr. Madison you would oblige him and me.[52] He possesses a landed Estate, but I suppose, like all other landed Estates that I know, [it] is productive of a very small revenue, after the labour and taxes are paid.

The Embargo and the Vote against any Augmentation of the Navy, more than the Taxes and the Threats or prospect of War, have raised a Storm in Massachusetts and New York which has hurled Gerry out of his Chair and electrified and revolutionised all the subsequent Elections. How far the Hurricane or the Earthquake will extend I know not: but if it should not essentially hazard Mr. Madisons Election I fear it will embarrass if not parrallyze his Administration.

Though Mr. Gerry is not too old for the most arduous Service, he is one of the earliest and oldest Legislators in the Revolution and has devoted himself his fortune and his family in the Service of his Country. I

52. TJ forwarded Malcom's application to President Madison, stating "I barely remember such a person as the secretary of Mr. Adams" and calling him "a strong federalist." TJ to Madison, May 30, 1812, Thomas Jefferson Randolph, ed., *Memoir, Correspondence, and Miscellanies, from the Papers of Thomas Jefferson* (Charlottesville, Va., 1829), IV, 175.

feel for his Situation; and if he is not in some Way or other supported the strongest Pillar of the present best System will fall and great will be the fall of it. The strongest Pillar I mean on this side of Pensilvania. His failure will dishearten and discourage the cause in this quarter of the Union and do incalculable Injury to the Nation.

In one of your letters you mentioned the confused traditions of Indian Antiquities. Is there any Book that pretends to give any Account of these Traditions, or how can one acquire any idea of them? Have they any order of Priesthood among them, like the Druids, Bards or Minstrells of the Celtic nations etc.?

If I had not lived through the War of 1745, the War of 1755 and the War of 1775, I believe I should be now too anxious for a determined Philosopher on Account of the State of the Nation. But in all dangers and in all Vicissitudes I believe I shall never cease, as I have never ceased to be your Friend

JOHN ADAMS

Jefferson to Adams

Monticello June 11. 1812.

DEAR SIR

By our post preceding that which brought your letter of May 21, I had recieved one from Mr. Malcolm on the same subject with yours, and by the return of the post had stated to the President my recollections of him. But both of your letters were probably too late; as the appointment had been already made, if we may credit the newspapers.

You ask if there is any book that pretends to give any account of the traditions of the Indians, or how one can acquire an idea of them? Some scanty accounts of their traditions, but fuller of their customs and characters are given us by most of the early travellers among them. These you know were chiefly French. Lafitau, among them, and Adair an Englishman, have written on this subject; the former two volumes, the latter one, all in 4to [quarto]. But unluckily Lafitau had in his head a preconcieved theory on the mythology, manners, institutions and government of the antient nations of Europe, Asia, and Africa, and seems to have entered on those of America only to fit them into the same frame, and to draw from them a confirmation of his general theory. He keeps up a perpetual parallel, in all those articles, between the Indians of America, and the antients of the other quarters of the globe. He selects therefore all the facts, and adopts all the falsehoods which favor his theory, and very gravely retails such absurdities as zeal for a theory could alone swallow. He was a man of much classical and scriptural reading, and has rendered his book not un-entertaining. He resided five years among the Northern Indians, as a Missionary, but collects his matter much more from the writings of others, than from his own observation.

Adair too had his kink. He believed all the Indians of America to be descended from the Jews: the same laws, usages; rites and ceremonies, the same sacrifices, priests, prophets, fasts and festivals, almost the same religion, and that they all spoke Hebrew. For altho he writes particularly of the Southern Indians only, the Catawbas, Creeks, Cherokees, Chickasaws and Choctaws, with whom alone he was personally acquainted, yet he generalises whatever he found among them, and brings himself to believe that the hundred languages of America, differing fundamentally every one from every other, as much as Greek from Gothic, have yet all one common prototype. He was a trader, a man of learning, a self-taught Hebraist, a strong religionist, and of as sound a mind as Don Quixot in whatever did not touch his religious chivalry. His book contains a great deal of real instruction on it's subject, only requiring the reader to be constantly on his guard against the wonderful obliquities of his theory.

The scope of your enquiry would scarcely, I suppose, take in the three folio volumes of Latin of De Bry. In these fact and fable are mingled together, without regard to any favorite system. They are less suspicious therefore in their complexion, more original and authentic, than those of Lafitau and Adair. This is a work of great curiosity, extremely rare, so as never to be bought in Europe, but on the breaking up, and selling some antient library. On one of these occasions a bookseller procured me a copy, which, unless you have one, is probably the only one in America.

You ask further, if the Indians have any order of priesthood among them, like the Druids, Bards or Minstrels of the Celtic nations? Adair alone, determined to see what he wished to see in every object, meta-morphoses their Conjurers into an order of priests, and describes their sorceries as if they were the great religious ceremonies of the nation. Lafitau calls them by their proper names, Jongleurs, Devins, Sortileges; De Bry praestigiatores, Adair himself sometimes Magi, Archimagi, cunning men, Seers, rain makers, and the modern Indian interpreters, call them Conjurers and Witches. They are persons pretending to have communications with the devil and other evil spirits, to foretel future events, bring down rain, find stolen goods, raise the dead, destroy some, and heal others by enchantment, lay spells etc. And Adair, without departing from his parallel of the Jews and Indians, might have found their counterpart, much more aptly, among the Soothsayers, sorcerers and wizards of the Jews, their Jannes and Jambres, their Simon Magus, witch of Endor, and the young damsel whose sorceries disturbed Paul so much; instead of placing them in a line with their High-priest, their Chief priests, and their magnificent hierarchy generally.   In the solemn ceremonies of the Indians, the persons who direct or officiate, are their chiefs, elders and warriors, in civil ceremonies or in those of war; it is the Head of the Cabin, in their private or particular feasts or ceremonies; and sometimes the Matrons, as in their Corn feasts. And, even here, Adair might have kept up his parallel, with ennobling his Conjurers. For the antient Patriarchs, the Noahs, the Abrahams, Isaacs and Jacobs, and, even after the consecration of Aaron, the Samuels and Elijahs, and we may say further every one for himself, offered sacrifices on the altars. The true line of distinction seems to be, that solemn ceremonies, whether public or private, addressed to the Great Spirit, are conducted by the worthies of the nation, Men, or Matrons, while Conjurers are resorted to only for the invocation of evil spirits. The present state of the several Indian tribes, without any public order of priests, is proof sufficient that they never had such an order. Their steady habits permit no innovations, not even those which the progress of science offers to increase the comforts, enlarge the understanding, and improve the morality of mankind. Indeed so little idea have they of a regular order of priests, that they mistake ours for their Conjurers, and call them by that name.

So much in answer to your enquiries concerning Indians, a people with whom, in the very early part of my life, I was very familiar, and acquired impressions of attachment and commiseration for them which have never been obliterated. Before the revolution they were in the habit of coming often, and in great numbers to the seat of our government, where I was very much with them. I knew much the great Outassete [i.e., Outacity], the warrior and orator of the Cherokees. He was always the guest of my father, on his journeys to and from Williamsburg. I was in his camp when he made his great farewell oration to his people, the evening before his departure for England. The moon was in full splendor, and to her he seemed to address himself in his prayers for his own safety on the voyage, and that of his people during his absence. His sounding voice, distinct articulation, animated action, and the solemn silence of his people at their several fires, filled me with awe and veneration, altho' I did not understand a word he uttered. That nation, consisting now of about 2000. wariors, and the Creeks of about 3000. are far advanced in civilisation. They have good Cabins, inclosed fields, large herds of cattle and hogs, spin and weave their own clothes of cotton, have smiths and other of the most necessary tradesmen, write and read, are on the increase in numbers, and a branch of the Cherokees is now instituting a regular representative government. Some other tribes were advancing in the same line. On those who have made any progress, English seductions will have no effect. But the backward will yeild, and be thrown further back. These will relapse into barbarism and misery, lose numbers by war and want, and we shall be obliged to drive them, with the beasts of the forest into the Stony mountains. They will be conquered however in Canada. The possession of that country secures our women and children for ever from the tomahawk and scalping knife, by removing those who excite them: and for this possession, orders I presume are issued by this time; taking for granted that the doors of Congress will re-open with a Declaration of war. That this may end in indemnity for the past, security for the future, and compleat emancipation from Anglomany, Gallomany, and all the manias of demoralized Europe, and that you may live in health and happiness to see all this, is the sincere prayer of Yours affectionately.

TH: JEFFERSON

Adams to Jefferson

Quincy, June 28 1812

DEAR SIR

I know not what, unless it were the Prophet of Tippacanoe [Tenskwatawa], had turned my Curiosity to inquiries after the metaphisical Science of the Indians, their ecclesiastical Establishments and theological Theories: but your Letter, written with all the Accuracy perspicuity and Elegance of your Youth and middle Age, as it has given me great Satisfaction, deserves my best Thanks.

It has given me Satisfaction, because, while it has furnished me with Information *where* all the Knowledge is to be obtained, that Books afford: it has convinced me that I shall never know much more of the Subject than I do now. As I have never aimed at making any Collection of Books upon this Subject I have none of those you have abridged in so concise a manner. Lafitau, Adair and De Bry were known to me only by Name.

The various Ingenuity which has been displayed in Inventions of hypotheses to account for the original Population of America; and the immensity of learning profusely expended to support them, have appeared to me, for a longer time than I can precisely recollect, what the Physicians call the Litteræ nihil Sanantes.[53] Whether Serpents Teeth were sown here and sprung up Men; whether Men and Women dropped from the Clouds

53. "Writings correcting nothing."

upon this Atlantic Island; whether the Almighty created them here, or whether they immigrated from Europe, are questions of no moment to the present or future happiness of Man. Neither Agriculture, Commerce, Manufactures, Fisheries, Science, Litterature, Taste, Religion, Morals, nor any other good will be promoted, or any Evil averted, by any discoveries that can be made in answer to those questions.

The Opinions of the Indians and their Usages, as they are represented in your obliging letter of the 11. June, appear to me to resemble the Platonizing Philo, or the Philonizing Plato, more than the Genuine System of Judaism.

The philosophy both of Philo and Plato are at least as absurd. It is indeed less intelligible.

Plato borrowed his doctrines from Oriental and Egyptian Philosophers, for he had travelled both in India and Egypt.

The Oriental philosophy, immitated and adopted in part if not the whole by Plato and Philo was

1. One God the good.

2. The Ideas, the thought, the Reason, the Intellect, the Logos, the Ratio, of God.

3. Matter, the Universe, the Production of the Logos, or contemplations of God. This Matter was the Source of Evil.

Perhaps, the three powers of Plato, Philo, the Egyptians and Indians, can not be distinctly made out, from your account of the Indians, but

1. The great Spirit, the good, who is worshiped by the Kings, Sachems and all the great Men in their solem Festivals as the Author, the Parent of Good.

2. The Devil, or the Source of Evil. They are not metaphisicians enough as yet to suppose it, or at least to call it matter, like the Wiseacres of Antiquity, and like Frederic the Great, who has written a very silly Essay on the Origin of Evil, in which he ascribes it all to Matter, as if this was an original discovery of his own.

The Watchmaker has in his head an Idea of the System of a Watch before he makes it. The Mechanician of the Universe had a compleat idea of the Universe before he made it: and this Idea, this Logos, was almighty or at least powerful enough to produce the World, but it must be made of Matter which was eternal. For creation out of Nothing was impossible. And Matter was unmanageable. It would not, and could not be fashioned into any System, without a large mixture of Evil in it; for Matter was essentially evil.

The Indians are not Metaphisicians enough to have discovered This *Idea*, this Logos, this intermediate Power between good and Evil, God and Matter. But of the two Powers The Good and the Evil, they seem to have a full Conviction; and what Son or Daughter of Adam and Eve has not?

This Logos of Plato seems to resemble if it was not the Prototype of the *Ratio and its Progress* of Manilius The Astrologer; of the *Progress of the Mind* of Condorcet; and the Age of Reason of Tom. Payne.

I could make a System too. The seven hundred Thousand Soldiers of Zingis, when the whole or any part of them went to battle, they sett up a howl, which resembled nothing that human Imagination has conceived, unless it be the Supposition that all the Devils in Hell were let loose at once to set up an infernal Scream, which terrified their Ennemies and never failed to obtain them Victory. The Indian Yell resembles this: and therefore America was peopled from Asia.

Another System. The Armies of Zingis, sometimes two or three or four hundred Thousands of them, surrounded a Province in a Circle, and marched towards the Centre, driving all the wild Beasts before them, Lyons, Tigers, Wolves, Bears, and every living thing, terrifying them with their Howls and Yells, their Drums, Trumpetts, etc., till they terrified and tamed enough of them to Victual the whole Army. Therefore the Scotch Highlanders who practice the same thing in miniature, are emigrants from Asia. Therefore the American Indians, who, for anything I know, practice the same custom, are emigrants from Asia or Scotland.

I am weary of contemplating Nations from the lowest and most beastly degradations of human Life, to the highest Refinement of Civilization: I am weary of Philosophers, Theologians, Politicians, and Historians. They are immense Masses of Absurdities, Vices and Lies. Montesquieu had sense enough to say in Jest, that all our Knowledge might be comprehended in twelve Pages in Duodecimo: and, I believe him, in earnest. I could express my Faith in shorter terms. He who loves the Workman and his Work, and does what he can to preserve and improve it, shall be accepted of him.

I also have felt an Interest in the Indians and a Commiseration for them from my Childhood. Aaron Pomham the Priest and Moses Pomham the King of the Punkapaug and Neponsit Tribes, were frequent Visitors at my Fathers house at least seventy Years ago. I have a distinct remembrance of their Forms and Figures. They were very aged, and the tallest and stoutest Indians I have ever seen. The titles of King and Priest, and the names of Moses and Aaron were given them no doubt by our Massachusetts Divines and Statesmen. There was a numerous Family in this Town, whose Wigwam was within a Mile of this House. This Family were frequently at my Fathers house, and I in my boyish Rambles used to call at their Wigwam, where I never failed to be treated with Whortle Berries, Blackberries, Strawberries or Apples, Plumbs, Peaches, etc., for they had planted a variety of fruit Trees about them. But the Girls went out to Service and the Boys to Sea, till not a Soul is left. We scarcely see an

Indian in a year. I remember the Time when Indian Murders, Scalpings, Depredations and conflagrations were as frequent on the Eastern and Northern Frontier of Massachusetts as they are now in Indiana, and spread as much terror. But since the Conquest of Canada, all this has ceased; and I believe with you that another Conquest of Canada will quiet the Indians forever and be as great a Blessing to them as to Us.

The Instance of Aaron Pomham made me suspect that there was an order of Priesthood among them. But according to your Account, the Worship of the good Spirit was performed by the Kings, Sachems, and Warriors, as among the ancient Germans, whose highest Rank of Nobility were Priests. The Worship of the Evil Spirit by the Conjurers, Jongleurs, Praestigiatores.

We have War now in Earnest. I lament the contumacious Spirit that appears about me. But I lament the cause that has given too much Apology for it: the total Neglect and absolute Refusal of all maritime Protection and Defence.

Money, Mariners, and Soldiers would be at the Public Service, if only a few Frigates had been ordered to be built. Without this our Union will be a brittle China Vase, a house of Ice or a Palace of Glass. I am, Sir, with an affectionate Respect, yours.

JOHN ADAMS

Adams to Jefferson

Quincy October 12. 1812

DEAR SIR

I have a Curiosity to learn Something of the Character Life and death of a Gentleman, whose name was Wollaston,[54] who came from England with a Company of a few dozens of Persons in the year 1622, took possession of an height on Massachusetts Bay, built houses there for his People, and after looking about him and not finding the face of Nature smiling enough for him, went to Virginia to seek a better Situation, leaving the Government of his little band, in the hands of Thomas Morton. As I have not found any Account of him after his departure from his little flock, in any History or record of New England, I should be very much obliged to you, for any information you can give me, of any notice that remains of him in Virginia.

54. Little is known about Captain Wollaston beyond William Bradford's *Of Plymouth Plantation, 1620-1647*. See edition by Samuel Eliot Morison (N. Y., 1952), 204-5.

My curiosity has been stimulated by an event of singular Oddity. John Quincy Adams, at Berlin, purchased at an Auction a Volume, containing three Pamphlets bound together; Woods Prospect, Wonder working Providence of Zions Saviour in New England, and "The New English Canaan, or New Canaan, containing an Abstract of New England, composed in three Books; the first Book setting forth the Original of the natives, their manners and customs, together with their tractable nature and love towards the English. The second Book setting forth the natural Endowments of the Country, and what Staple Commodities it yeildeth. The third Book setting forth, what people are planted there, their prosperity, what remarkable accidents have happened since the first planting of it, together with their tenents and practice of their Church.

"Written by Thomas Morton of Cliffords Inne Gentleman, upon ten years knowledge and experiment of the Country." "Printed at Amsterdam by Jacob Frederick Stam, in the Year 1637." The Book is dedicated to The Commissioners of the privy Councell, for the Government of all his Majesties foreign Provinces.

To add a trifle to the whimsical Circumstances attending the A[d]ventures of this Volume, there are a few Words in manuscript on a blank leaf, which, had I seen them in any other place, I should have sworn were in the hand Writing of my Father.

The design of the Writer appears to have been to promote two Objects: 1. to spread the fame and exaggerate the Advantages of New England; 2. to destroy the Characters of the English Inhabitants, and excite the Government to suppress the Puritans, and send over Settlers in their Stead, from among the Royalists and the disciples of Archbishop Laud.

That such a Work had been written, has been known by tradition, and I have enquired for it, more than half a Century: but have never been able to learn that any Copy of it ever was seen in this Country. The Berlin Adventurer is I believe the only one in America.[55] It is possible however that some straggling Copy of it may be in Virginia, and if you have ever seen or heard of it, I shall be obliged to you for the information.

I know not whether you have in your library, extensive and well chosen as it is, any of our New England Histories. If you have and feel any inclination to know any Thing of this Cliffords Inn man, this incendiary instrument of spiritual and temporal domination, you may find it in Neals Hist. New England III., 1. Hutchinson 8. 31., Winthrops Journal 20. 27. 321. 352., 2 Belknaps Biography 332.

He hints at his Objects in his Preface: "I have observed how diverse

55. Morton's *The New English Canaan* was reported extremely rare in 1825 by James Savage, noted antiquarian scholar; he said the only extant copy was JA's. From this copy Charles Francis Adams prepared the 1883 edition (Boston).

Persons not so well affected to the Weal public in mine Opinion, out of respect to their own private ends, have laboured to keep, both the practice of the People there, and the real worth of that eminent Country, concealed from public Knowledge, both which I have abundantly in this discourse laid open."

Sir Christopher Gardiner, Knight, as he calls him, tho he was only a Cavalier of St. Iago de Compostella, a Roman Catholick and another Tool of Archbishop Laud as well as a Companion and fellow labourer in the pious Work of destroying the first Planters of Plymouth and Massachusetts: writes in laudem Authoris, and in the despicable Verse of that Age:

> This Work a matchless mirror is that shows
> The humors of the Seperatists, and those
> So truly personated by thy Pen,
> I was amaz'd to see it.
> Nothing but Opposition, 'gainst the Right
> Of sacred Majesty Men; full of Spight
> Goodness abusing, turning Virtue out
> Of doors, to whipping, Stocking, and full bent
> To plotting mischief 'gainst the innocent
> Burning their Houses, as if ordained by fate
> In Spight of Law to be made ruinate.

Another "In laudem Authoris, by F. C. Armiger" shows the high Church and high State Principles of this group of Laudians and their inveterate hatred of that Opposition to Priestcraft and Kingcraft which animated the first Settlers of New England:

> But that I rather pitty I confesse
> The Practice of their Church, I could expresse
> Myself a Satyrist, whose smarting fanges
> Should strike it with a Palsy, and the Pangs
> Beget a fear, to tempt the Majesty,
> Of those, our mortal Gods, will they defy
> The thundering Jove, like children they desire,
> Such is their Zeal, to sport themselves with fire
> So have I seen an angry fly presume
> To strike a burning taper, and consume
> His feeble Wings. Why in an Air so milde
> Are they so monstrous grown up? and so vilde?
> That Savages can of themselves espy
> Their Errors, brand their names with infamy
> What is their Zeale for blood, like Cyrus thirst
> Will they be over head and ears accurst

A cruel Way to found a Church On? Noe
T'is not their Zeal, but fury blinds them so.
And pricks their malice on, like fire to joyne
And offer up the Sacrifice of Kain;
Jonas! thou hast done well, to call these men
Home, to repentance, with thy painful Pen.

Then comes the Authors prologue in a similar Strain of Panegyrick upon his New English Canaan and of Phillippic against the Inhabitants.

If Art and Industry should do as much
As Nature hath for Canaan, not such
Another place, for benefit and rest
In all the Universe can be possess'd
The more We prove it by discovery
The more delight each Object to the Eye
Discovers etc.

In page 15 is a high wrought Eulogium of Sir Ferdinand Gorges to whom he ascribes all the Glory of discovering and Settling in fine Country situated in the middle of the Golden mean, the temperate Zone.

Then he discovers the wondrous Wisdom and love of God, in sending his Minister, the plague, among the Indians, to sweepe away by heaps the Savages, and in giving Sir Ferdinando length of days, to see the same performed, after his enterprize was begun, for the propagation of the Church of Christ, i. e., as I understand him, the Church of Archbishop Laud and Sir Ferdinando Gorges.

In Chapter 2. p. 17. He says, "In the Year since the Incarnation of Christ 1622, it was my Chance to be landed in the parts of New England, where I found two Sorts of People, the one Christians, the other Infidels; these I found most full of humanity and more friendly than the other: as shall hereafter be made apparent in due course, by their several Actions from time to time, after my Arrival among them."

In no part of the Work has he said any thing of Mr. Wollaston, his Commander in Chief, to whom he was only second, in command of the Party. But it was of Wollaston I was most interested to enquire. I knew enough of Morton, and was therefore much disappointed in perusing the Book.

The Original Indian Name of the Spot possest by the Party was Passonagesset, but the People of the Company changed it to Mount Wollaston by which Name it has been called to this day. Morton, however, after the departure of his Leader for Virginia, chose to alter the Name, and call it Mare Mount from its Position near the Sea and commanding the prospect of Boston Harbour and Massachusetts Bay. In his 132 page He gives us a History of the Ceremonies instituted by him in honor of this important Nomination. Several Songs were composed to be sung. A Pine Tree, Eighty feet long, was erected with a pair of Bucks Horns nailed on the Top. On May Day this mighty May Pole was drawn to its appointed Place on the Summit of the Hill by the help of Savages males and females, with Sound of Guns Drums, Pistols and other Instruments of Musick. A Barrel of excellent Beer was brewed, and a Case of Bottles, (of Brandy I suppose) with other good Chear, and English Men and Indians Sannups and Squaws, danced and sang and revelled round the Maypole till Bacchus and Venus, I suppose, were satiated. The Seperatists called it an Idol, the Calf of Horeb, Mount Dagon, threatening to make it a woeful mount and not a merry Mount.

It is whimsical that this Book, so long lost, should be brought to me, for this Hill is in my Farm. There are curious Things in it, about the Indians and the Country. If you have any Inclination, I will send you more of them. Yours as Usual

JOHN ADAMS

Jefferson to Adams

Monticello Dec. 28. 12.

DEAR SIR

An absence of 5. or 6. weeks, on a journey I take three or four times a year,[56] must apologize for my late acknolegement of your favor of Oct. 12. After getting thro the mass of business which generally accumulates during my absence, my first attention has been bestowed on the subject of your letter. I turned to the passages you refer to in Hutchinson and Winthrop, and with the aid of their dates, I examined our historians to see if Wollaston's migration to this state was noticed by them. It happens unluckily that Smith and Stith, who alone of them go into minute facts, bring their histories, the former only to 1623, and the latter to 1624. Wollaston's arrival in Massachusets was in 1625, and his removal to this state was 'some time' after. Beverley and Keith, who come lower down, are merely superficial, giving nothing but those general facts which every one knew as well as themselves. If our public records of that date were not among those destroyed by the British on their invasion of this state, they may possibly have noticed Wollaston. What I possessed in this way have

56. To Poplar Forest. See above, 292, n. 39.

been given out to two gentlemen the one engaged in writing our history,[57] the other in collecting our antient laws,[58] so that none of these resources are at present accessible to me. Recollecting that Nathaniel Morton in his New England's Memorial, gives with minuteness the early annals of the colony of New Plimouth, and occasionally interweaves the occurrences of that on Massachusetts bay, I recurred to him, and, under the year 1628, I find he notices both Wollaston and Thomas Morton, and gives with respect to both, some details which are not in Hutchinson or Winthrop. As you do not refer to him, and so possibly may not have his book, I will transcribe from it the entire passage, which will prove at least my desire to gratify your curiosity as far as the materials within my power will enable me.

Extract from Nathaniel Morton's New England's Memorial, pa. 93. to 99. anno 1628.[59] 'Whereas about three years before this time there came over one Captain * Wollaston, a man of considerable parts, and with him 3. or 4. more of some eminency, who brought with them a great many servants, with provisions and other requisites, for to begin a plantation, and pitched themselves in a place within the Massachusetts-bay, which they called afterwards by their Captain's name, Mount Wollaston; which place is since called by the name of Braintry. And amongst others that came with him, there was one Mr. Thomas Morton, who it should seem had some small adventure of his own or other men's amongst them, but had little respect, and was slighted by the meanest servants they kept. They having continued sometime in New England, and not finding things to answer their expectation, nor profit to arise as they looked for, the said Capt. Wollaston takes a great part of the servants, and transports them to Virginia, and disposed of them there, and writes back to one Mr. Rasdale, one of his chief partners (and accounted their merchant) to bring another part of them to Virginia likewise, intending to put them off there, as he had done the rest; and he with the consent of the said Rasdale, appointed

57. Louis H. Girardin, who with Skelton Jones completed the fourth volume of John Daly Burk's History of Virginia (Petersburg, Va., 1804-16). Edward A. Wyatt IV, John Daly Burk, Patriot-Playwright-Historian, in Southern Sketches, ed. by J. D. Eggleston, 1st ser., 7 (1936), 22.

58. William Waller Hening, comp., The Statutes at Large ... of Virginia, 13 vols. (Richmond and Philadelphia, 1809-23).

59. Nathaniel Morton, New Englands Memoriall (Cambridge, Mass., 1669), based on William Bradford's history of Plymouth Plantation, was eclipsed by the publication of the Bradford manuscript, ed. by Charles Deane (Boston, 1856). The excerpt quoted by TJ is from Bradford, Of Plymouth Plantation, 1620-1647, ed. by Morison, 204-10.

* [TJ's note:] This gentleman's name is here occasionally used, and altho' he came over in the year 1625, yet these passages in reference to Morton fell out about this year, and therefore referred to this place.

one whose name was Filcher [i.e., Fitcher] to be his Lieutenant, and to govern the remainder of the plantation, until he or Rasdale should take further order thereabout.

But the aforesaid Morton (having more craft than honesty) having been a petty-fogger at Furnivals-inn; he, in the others absence, watches an opportunity (commons being put hard among them) and got some strong drink and other junkets, and made them a feast, and after they were merry, he began to tell them he would give them good counsel; you see (saith he) that many of your fellows are carried to Virginia, and, if you stay still until Rasodales return, you will also be carried away and sold for slaves with the rest; therefore I would advise you to thrust out Lieutenant Filcher, and I, having a part in the plantation, will recieve you as my partners and consociates, so may you be free from service, and we will converse, plant, trade and live together as equals (or to the like effect). This counsel was easily followed, so they took opportunity, and thrust Lieutenant Filcher out of doors, and would not suffer him to come any more amongst them, but forced him to seek bread to eat, and other necessaries amongst his neighbors, till he would get passage for England. (See the sad effect of want of good government.)

After this they fell to great licentiousness of life, in all prophaneness, and the said Moreton became lord of misrule, and maintained (as it were) a school of atheism, and after they had got some goods into their hands, and got much by trading with the Indians, they spent it as vainly, in quaffing and drinking both wine and strong liquors in great excess (as some have reported) ten pounds worth in a morning, setting up a Maypole, drinking and dancing about it, and frisking about it, like so many fairies, or furies rather, yea and worse practices, as if they had anew revived and celebrated the feast of the Romans goddess Flora, or the beastly practices of the mad Bacchanalians. The said Morton likewise to shew his poetry, composed sundry rythmes and verses, some tending to lasciviousness, and others to the detraction and scandal of some persons names, which he affixed to his idle, or idol May-pole; they changed also the name of their place, and instead of calling it Mount Wolloston, they called it the Merry mount, as if this jollity would have lasted always. But this continued not long, for shortly after that worthy gentleman Mr. John Endicot, who brought over a patent under the broad seal of England for the government of the Massachusetts, visiting those parts, caused that May-pole to be cut down, and rebuked them for their prophaness, and admonished them to look to it that they walked better; so the name was again changed and called Mount Dagon.

Now to maintain this riotous prodigality and profuse expence, the said

Morton thinking himself lawless, and hearing what gain the fishermen made of trading of pieces, powder and shot; he as head of this consortship, began the practice of the same in these parts: and first he taught the Indians how to use them, to charge and discharge 'em, and what proportion of powder to give the piece, according to the size or bigness of the same, and what shot to use for fowl, and what for deer; and having instructed them, he imployed some of them to hunt and fowl for him; so as they became somewhat more active in that imployment than any of the English, by reason of their swiftness of foot, and nimbleness of body, being also quick sighted, and by continual exercise, well knowing the haunt of all sorts of game; so as when they saw the execution that a piece would do, and the benefit that might come by the same, they became very eager after them, and would not stick to give any price they could attain to for them; accounting their bows and arrows but baubles in comparison of them.

And here we may take occasion to bewail the mischief which came by this wicked man, and others like unto him; in that notwithstanding laws for the restraint of selling ammunition to the natives, that so far base covetousness prevailed, and doth still prevail, as that the Salvages become amply furnished with guns, powder, shot, rapiers, pistols, and also well skilled in repairing of defective arms: yea some have not spared to tell them how gunpowder is made, and all the materials in it, and that they are to be had in their own land; and would (no doubt, in case they could attain to the making of Saltpeter) teach them to make powder; and what mischief may fall out unto the English in these parts thereby, let this pestilent fellow Morton (aforenamed) bear a great part of the blame and guilt of it to future generations. But lest I should hold the reader too long in the relation of the particulars of his vile actings; when as the English that then lived up and down about the Massachusetts, and in other places, percieving the sad consequences of his trading, so as the Indians became furnished with the English arms and ammunition, and expert in the improving of them, and fearing they should at one time or another get a blow thereby; and also taking notice, that if he were let alone in his way, they should keep no servants for him, because he would entertain any, how vile soever, sundry of the chief of the stragling plantations met together, and agreed by mutual consent to send to Plimouth, who were then of more strength to join with them, to suppress this mischief: who considering the particulars proposed to them to join together to take some speedy course to prevent (if it might be) the evil that was accrewing towards them; and resolved first to admonish him of his wickedness respecting the premises, laying before him the injury he did to their common safety, and that his acting concerning the same, was against the

King's proclamation: but he insolently persisted on in his way, and said, the king was dead, and his displeasure with him, and threatened them that if they come to molest him, they should look to themselves; so that they saw there was no way but to take him by force: so they resolved to proceed in such a way, and obtained of the Governor of Plimouth, to send Capt. Standish and some other aid with him, to take the sd. Morton by force, the which accordingly was done; but they found him to stand stifly on his defence, having made fast his doors, armed his consorts, set powder and shot ready upon the table; scoffed and scorned at them, and he and his complices being filled with strong drink, were desperate in their way: but he himself coming out of doors to make a shot at Capt. Standish, he stepping to him, put by his piece and took him, and so little hurt was done; and so he was brought prisoner to Plimouth, and continued in durance till an opportunity of sending him for England, which was done at their common charge, and letters also with him, to the honourable council for New England, and returned again into the country in some short time, with less punishment than his demerits deserved (as was apprehended.) The year following he was again apprehended, and sent for England, where he lay a considerable time in Exeter goal: for besides his miscarriage here in New England, he was suspected to have murthered a man that had ventured monies with him, when he came first into New England; and a warrant was sent over from the Lord Chief justice to apprehend him, by virtue whereof, he was by the Governor of Massachusetts sent into England, and for other of his misdemeanours amongst them in that government, they demolished his house, that it might no longer be a roost for such unclean birds. Notwithstanding he got free in England again, and wrote an infamous and scurrilous book against many godly and chief men of the country, full of lies and slanders, and full fraught with prophane calumnies against their names and persons, and the ways of god. But to the intent I may not trouble the reader any more with mentioning of him in this history: in fine sundry years after he came again into the country, and was imprisoned at Boston, for the aforesaid book and other things, but denied sundry things therein, affirming his book was adulterated. And soon after being grown old in wickedness; at last ended his life at Piscataqua. But I fear I have held the reader too long about so unworthy a person, but hope it may be useful to take notice how wickedness was beginning, and would have further proceeded, had it not been prevented timely.'

So far Nathaniel Morton. The copy you have of Thomas Morton's New English Canaan, printed in 1637 by Stam at Amsterdam, was a second edition of that 'infamous and scurrilous book against the godly.'

The 1st. had been printed in 1632 by Charles Green in a 4to [quarto] of 188. pages, and is the one alluded to by N. Morton.[60] Both of them made a part of the American library given by White Kennett in 1713 to the Society for the propagation of the gospel in foreign parts. This society, being a chartered one, still, as I believe, existing, and probably their library also, I suppose that these and the other books of that immense collection, the catalogue of which occupies 275. pages 4to.[61] are still to be found with them. If any research I can hereafter make should ever bring to my knolege any thing more of Wollaston, I shall not fail to communicate it to you. Ever, and affectionately your's

TH: JEFFERSON

Adams to Jefferson

Quincy January 26. 1813.

DEAR SIR

I thank you for your rich present of Dec. 28th. The Pettifogger of Furnivals Inn, or of Cliffords Inn, scarcely deserves the pains you have taken to enquire into his Biography. My Curiosity is selfish, personal and local. The Character of the Miscreant, however, is not wholly contemptible. It marks the Complextion of the Age in which he lived. How many such Characters could You and I enumerate, who in our times have had a similar influence on Society!

The fellow was not wholly destitute of Learning, tho' all he had, was not worth much. I promised you some more Samples of his Erudition. His 2. Chapter is "Of the original of the Natives." Moreton, Nathaniel, the Ancestor of Our Perez, the Husband of Philenia, was mistaken. It was not in 1625 but 1622 that Wollaston and Tom Moreton arrived. All our History and Traditions conspire to confirm the Assertion of the latter in this Chapter, that he arrived in 1622. After a Philipic against the Puri-

60. TJ was mistaken about this early edition. The work was written before the close of 1635 and was first printed in Amsterdam in 1637. It was supposed for years, however, that there was a copy of the book of the imprint and date cited here. For an explanation, see Harvard University Library, *Library Bulletin*, Nos. 9 and 10, 1878-79, 196, 244, and Thomas Morton, *New English Canaan*, ed. by C. F. Adams, 99 ff.

61. [White Kennett], *Bibliothecae Americanae Primordia. An Attempt towards laying the Foundation of an American Library, in Several Books, Papers, and Writings, Humbly given to the Society for the Propagation of the Gospel in Foreign Parts ...By a Member of the said Society* (London, 1713). The collection, however, has been partially dispersed. E. Millicent Sowerby, comp., *Catalogue of the Library of Thomas Jefferson* (Washington, D.C., 1952), I, 217-18.

tans and a Panegiric, on the Indians, he enquires Whence the latter proceeded? He finds that they Use "very many Words both of greek and latin; as "En Unimia" to express in earnest, or con amore. "Pascopan, Greedy gut" for "pasco signifies to feed, and Pan is all." "Pasco nantum" quasi "Pasco nondum," "half starved, or not eating as yet." "Equa coge, set it upright" "Mona, an Island," "quasi monon, i. e., alone." "Cos, a Whetstone." "Hame, an instrument to take fish." "Many places retain the name of Ham, as Pantneket, and Matta Pan" "So that it may be thought that these People have, heretofore had the name of Pan, in great reverence, and it may be, have worshipped Pan the great God of the Heathens": "howsoever they do Use no manner of Worship at all now." "It is most likely, descended from People bred towards the Tropick of Cancer, for they retain the memory of some Starrs on that part of the cœlestial globe; as the North Starr, which they call Maske, which in their language signifies, a Bear." "They divide the Winds into Eight parts" "have had some litterature among them, which time hath cancelled" But what traces of it, he perceived, Mr. Morton further saith not. He then reprobates the conjecture, that they came from Tartary over the frozen Sea. "But it may be granted that they might come of the scattered Trojans" "For after that Brutus who was the fourth from Æneas left Latium, upon the conflict had with the Latines etc. this People were dispersed etc. but by reason of their conversation with the Grecians and Latins, had a mixed Language that participated with both." "When Brutus did depart from Latium" etc. "being put to Sea, might encounter a Storm, that would carry them out of Sight of Land and then they might sayle, God knoweth Whither; and so might put upon this coast as well as any other." "Compass, I believe they had none; Sayles they might have." For "Daedalus had Sayles, and Icarus his Son had Sayles" etc. "oars, without question" etc. "For the Use of Compass there is no mention, at that time, About Saul's time, the first King of Israel." "Yet the Loadstone and Compasse, were known in Solomons time etc." "for he sent Ships to fetch the Gold of Ophir." "It is held by Cosmographers to be three Years Voyage from Hierusalem to Ophir." "And it is conceived that such a Voyage could not have been performed, without the Help of the Loadstone and Compass." "Therefore, since I have had the Approbation of Sir Christopher Gardiner Knight, an able Gentleman, that lived among them (the Indians) and of David Tompson, a Scottish Gentleman, that likewise was conversant with them; both Scollers and Travellers, that were diligent in taking notice of these Things, as men of good Judgment" etc. "Now I am bold to conclude that the Original of the Natives of New England may be well conjectured to be from the scattered Trojans after such time as Brutus departed from Latium."

Such is the Learning, such the Sagacity, such the critical discriminating Judgment of Thomas Moreton.

I wonder that the *Houra* of Zingis, the Bonaparte of Asia, has never been Urged as a Proof that our Indians are descended from some of his Soldiers or Subjects, or from some of the Nations who learned the Art of War from him when he scattered and drove so many of them, the Lord knows where. The Indian Yell, is said to be the most horrible Sound that human Voices can produce, and the most intimidating to an Enemy. The same is said of the Asiatic Houra. Neither Nations, nor wild Beasts could resist it. Indeed, when Zingis's Army of seven hundred thousand men were drawn up in the Periphery of a circle, of one hundred miles in diameter, and marched from all points to the Centre, driving all the beasts before them with Drums trumpets and all their Instruments of Musick added to their hideous houra, no wonder the brutes were frightened out of all their Strength and ferocity. Nothing can be conceived like it, even in Imagination, unless we suppose all the Beasts and Birds in Noahs Ark sett to roaring, howling, barking, braying, chattering, cackling, and all the Women shrieking and screaming at once. Miltons millions of rebellious Angels, when they "clash'd on their sounding Shields the din of War" could not have produc'd a harsher dissonance or more tremendous Crash. This practise of hunting in Circles is said to be, or to have not long since been, in Use in the Highlands of Scotland. Has any such Usage ever been known among any of our Tribes of Indians?

I will not teaze you, with any more of Morton lore, at present nor of my own. Hereafter I may send a little more from him,[62] with repeated Assurances of the regard of your old Friend

JOHN ADAMS

62. In an incomplete draft of a letter, JA to TJ, Quincy, Feb. 2, 1813, JA gave "some Account of Tom Moreton's New Canaan, which is infinitely more entertaining and instructive to me, than our Friend Condorcets 'NEW HEAVEN' was almost 30 years ago, or than Swedenborgs 'NEW JERUSALEM' is now. In his Third Chapter is a curious History. Before the English came to New Plymouth, Frenchmen had been here, who had given Some 'distast' to the Natives, who set upon them, killed many, burned their Ship, at Peddocks Island So called in Memory of Leonard Peddock, who first landed there. N.B. This Island is well known, at this day and is called by all of Us *Petticks Island* without knowing why. 'Many wild Anckies haunted there.' Your Researches, in natural History may enable you to say what are Anckies. Unless they be wild Geese, I know no more about them than I do about Yankies. Of these Frenchmen, who came to trade in Beaver, and misbehaved, some were killed and the rest taken Prisoners. These Prisoners, were distributed among Five Sachems, Lords of Several Adjoining Territories, kept for Sport and to fetch Wood and Water. One of these five Frenchmen outliving the rest, learned their Language and rebuked them for their blody deed, saying that God would be angry for it, and in his displeasure destroy them; but the Savages replyed They were *so many that God could not kill them*...."

Jefferson to Adams

Monticello May 27. 13.

Another of our friends of 76. is gone, my dear Sir, another of the Co-signers of the independance of our country. And a better man, than Rush, could not have left us, more benevolent, more learned, of finer genius, or more honest. We too must go; and that ere long. I believe we are under half a dozen at present; I mean the signers of the Declaration. Yourself, Gerry, Carroll, and myself are all I know to be living. I am the only one South of the Patomac. Is Robert Treat Payne, or Floyd living? It is long since I heard of them, and yet I do not recollect to have heard of their deaths.[63]

Moreton's deduction of the origin of our Indians from the fugitive Trojans, stated in your letter of Jan. 26. and his manner of accounting for the sprinckling of their Latin with Greek, is really amusing. Adair makes them talk Hebrew. Reinold Foster derives them from the soldiers sent by Kouli Khan to conquer Japan. Berewood [i.e., Brerewood] from the Tartars, as well as our bears, wolves, foxes etc. which he says 'must of necessity fetch their beginning from Noah's ark, which rested, after the deluge, in Asia, seeing they could not proceed by the course of nature, as the unperfect sort of living creatures do, from putrefaction.' Bernard Romans is of opinion that God created an original man and woman in this part of the globe. Doctr. Barton thinks they are not specifically different from the Persians; but, taking afterwards a broader range, he thinks 'that in all the vast countries of America, there is but one language, nay that it may be proven, or rendered highly probable, that all the languages of the earth bear some affinity together.' This reduces it to a question of definition, in which every one is free to use his own. To wit, what constitutes identity, or difference in two things? (in the common acceptation of *sameness*.) All languages may be called the same, as being all made up of the same primitive sounds, expressed by the letters of the different alphabets. But, in this sense, all things on earth are the same, as consisting of matter. This gives up the useful distribution into genera and species, which we form, arbitrarily indeed, for the relief of our imperfect memories. To aid the question, from whence are our Indian tribes descended? some have gone into their religion, their morals, their manners, customs, habits, and physical forms. By such helps it may be learnedly proved that our trees and plants of every kind are descended from those of Europe; be-

63. See above, 292, n. 38.

cause, like them they have no locomotion, they draw nourishment from the earth, they clothe themselves with leaves in spring, of which they divest themselves in autumn for the sleep of winter etc. Our animals too must be descended from those of Europe, because our wolves eat lambs, our deer are gregarious, our ants hoard etc. But when, for convenience, we distribute languages, according to common understanding, into Classes originally different, as we chuse to consider them, as the Hebrew, the Greek, the Celtic, the Gothic; and these again into genera, or families, as the Icelandic, German, Swedish, Danish, English; and these last into species, or dialects, as English, Scotch, Irish, we then ascribe other meanings to the terms 'same' and 'different.' In some one of these senses, Barton, and Adair, and Foster, and Brerewood, and Moreton, may be right, every one according to his own definition of what constitutes 'identity.' Romans indeed takes a higher stand, and supposes a separate creation. On the same unscriptural ground, he had but to mount one step higher, to suppose no creation at all, but that all things have existed without beginning in time, as they now exist, and may for ever exist, producing and reproducing in a circle, without end. This would very summarily dispose of Mr. Morton's learning, and shew that the question of Indian origin, like many others pushed to a certain height, must recieve the same answer, 'Ignoro.'

You ask if the usage of hunting in circles has ever been known among any of our tribes of Indians? It has been practised by them all; and is to this day, by those still remote from the settlement of the whites. But their numbers not enabling them, like Genghis Kahn's 700,000. to form themselves into circles of 100. miles diameter, they make their circle by firing the leaves fallen on the ground, which gradually forcing the animals to a center, they there slaughter them with arrows, darts, and other missiles. This is called firehunting, and has been practised in this state within my time, by the white inhabitants. This is the most probable cause of the origin and extension of the vast prairies in the Western country, where the grass having been of extraordinary luxuriance, has made a conflagration sufficient to kill even the old, as well as the young timber.

I sincerely congratulate you on the successes of our little navy; which must be more gratifying to you than to most men, as having been the early and constant advocate of wooden walls. If I have differed with you on this ground, it was not on the principle, but the time. Supposing that we cannot build or maintain a navy, which will not immediately fall into the same gulph which has swallowed, not only the minor navies, but even those of the great second rate powers of the sea. Whenever these can be resuscitated, and brought so near to a balance with England that we can turn the scale, then is my epoch for aiming at a navy. In the mean time one competent to keep the Barbary states in order, is necessary; these being the only smaller powers disposed to quarrel with us. But I respect too much the weighty opinions of others to be unyielding on this point, and acquiesce with the prayer 'quod felix faustumque sit ["may this be favorable and auspicious"],' adding ever a sincere one for your health and happiness.

TH. JEFFERSON

Adams to Jefferson

Quincy May 29. 1813.

DEAR SIR

To leave the Pettifogger of Fu[r]nivals Inn, or Cliffords Inn, his Archbishop Laud, and his Chevalier of St. Iago of Compostella, Sir Christopher Gardiner, for the present; Paulo Multo majora canamus.[64]

There has been put into my hands, within a few days a gross Volume in octavo, of 544 Pages, with the Title of "Memoirs of the late reverend Theophilus Lindsey, M. A." including a brief "Analysis of his Works; together with Anecdotes and Letters of eminent Persons, his Friends and Correspondents: also a general View of the progress of the Unitarian doctrine in England and America. By Thomas Belsham, Minister of the Chapel in Essex Street [London, 1812]."

Whether you have seen this Work, I know not. But this I know, the Author, and his Friends ought to have sent you a Copy of it; and therefore I conclude they have.

With Lindsey, Disney, Price, Priestley, Jebb, Kippis etc. and their Connections, whom I could name, I was much Acquainted in London from 1785 to 1788. These Characters, with Cappe, Farmer, and a multitude of others, figure in this Work. The Religion, the Philosophy, the Morality, the Politicks which these People teach, have been Objects of my anxious Attention for more than Three Score Years, as I could demonstrate to you, if I could give you a brief Sketch of my Life. But my Life has been too trifling and my Actions too insignificant for me to write or the Public to read. In my wandering romantic Life, with my incessant Res angusta Domi,[65] and my numerous unfortunate Family, of Children and Grand Children without the honour, which you have attained of being a great grandfather, tho' I have a near prospect of it; it has been impossible for me to pursue such Inquiries with any thing like Learning.

64. "Come let us sing of much greater themes." Virgil, *Eclogues*, IV, 1.
65. "Narrow circumstances at home (poverty)." Juvenal, *Satires*, III, 164; *Multis Satires*, VI, 357.

What may be the Effect, of these "Memoirs" in the U. S. if they should become public I know not; and I will add I care not, for I wish every Subject to be discussed at all Events. The human Mind is awake: Let it not Sleep. Let it however consider. Let it think, Let it pause.

This Work must produce a noise in U. S.   Fiat Justitia ["Let justice be done"]. The 12th. Article in the Appendix is "Letters from Dr. Priestley to Mr. Lindsey: and from Thomas Jefferson Esq. President of the United States to Dr. Priestley. p. 525. The first Letter from you is dated March 21. 1801. at Washington. The second April 9. 1803 at Washington.[66] Dr. Priestleys Letter to Mr. Lindsey, containing remarks upon Mr. Jeffersons Letter is dated Northumberland April 23. 1803.

I wish to know, if you have seen this Book. I have much to say on the Subject. And you may depend upon it, I will discuss the Subject with as much Candour, as much Friendship, as much Freedom, as Price, Priestley, Lindsey, Cappe or Farmer ever displayed in their Controversies. I have not time to enlarge at present.

I will only Add, have you seen the Naval History by Mr. Clark,[67] published by Mathew Carey at Philadelphia? I wish I had time and Eyes and fingers to write much to you on this Subject.

I lament the death of my dear Friend of 38 Years, Dr. Benjamin Rush, much the more since I have seen Lindseys Memoirs. I am, with unalterable Esteem and Affection your old Friend

JOHN ADAMS

Adams to Jefferson

Quincy June 10. 1813.

DEAR SIR

In your Letter to Dr. Priestley of March 21. 1801, you ask "What an Effort of Bigotry in politics and religion have We gone through! The barbarians really flattered themselves, they should be able to bring back the times of Vandalism, when ignorance put every thing into the hands of power and priestcraft. All Advances in Science were proscribed as innovations; they pretended to praise and encourage education, but it was to be the education of our ancestors; We were to look backwards, not forwards,

66. Reprinted in Ford, VIII, 21-23, 224-25. See also TJ to Benjamin Rush, April 21, 1803, *ibid.*, 223-24.

67. Benjamin Rush to JA, Feb. 15, March 16, April 10, 1813, Butterfield, ed., *Letters of Rush*, II, 1183, 1190, 1191, concerning Thomas Clark, *Sketches of the Naval History of the United States* ... (Philadelphia, 1813).

for improvement; *the President himself* declaring, in one of his Answers to addresses, that We were never to expect to go beyond them in real Science." [68] I shall stop here. Other parts of this Letter, may hereafter be considered if I can keep the Book long enough: but only four Copies have arrived in Boston, and they have spread terror, as yet, however in secret.

"The President himself declaring, that "We were never to expect to go beyond them in real Science". This Sentence shall be the theme of the present Letter.

I would ask, what President is meant? I remember no such Sentiment in any of Washingtons Answers to addresses. I, myself must have been mean'd. Now I have no recollection of any such Sentiment ever issued from my Pen, or my tongue, or of any such thought in my heart for, at least sixty Years of my past life. I should be obliged to you, for the Words of any Answer of mine, that you have thus misunderstood. A man of 77 or 78 cannot commonly be expected to recollect promptly every passage of his past life, or every trifle he has written. Much less can it be expected of me, to recollect every Expression of every Answer to an Address, when for six months together, I was compelled to answer Addresses of all Sorts from all quarters of the Union. My private Secretary has declared that he has copied fifteen Answers from me in one morning. The greatest Affliction, distress, confusion of my Administration arose from the necessity of receiving and Answering those Addresses. Richard Cromwells Trunk, did not contain so many of the Lives and Fortunes of the English Nati[on] as mine of those in the United States. For the hon[or] of my Country I wish these Addresses and Answers [to be] annihilated. For my own Character and repu[tation I] wish every Word of every Address and every Answer were published.[69]

The Sentiment, that you have attributed to me in your letter to Dr. Priestley I totally disclaim and demand in the French sense of the word demand of you the proof. It is totally incongruous to every principle of my mind and every Sentiment of my heart for Threescore Years at least.

You may expect, many more expostulations from one who has loved and esteemed you for Eight and thirty Years.

John Adams

When this Letter was ready to go, I recd your favour of May 27th. came to hand, I can only thank you for it, at present.

68. This letter is reprinted in Ford, VIII, 21-23; for TJ's explanation see TJ to JA, June 15, 1813, below, 331-32.
69. Some words or portions of words, missing at ends of lines in the MS, are supplied by conjecture. For JA's quotation from his address, see JA to TJ, June 28, 1813, below, 339.

Adams to Jefferson

Quincy June 11. 1813

DEAR SIR

I received yesterday your favour of may 27th. I lament with you the loss of Rush. I know of no Character living or dead, who has done more real good in America. Robert Treat Paine still lives, at 83 or 84, alert drol and witty though deaf. Floyd I believe, yet remains. Paine must be very great; Philosopher and Christian; to live under the Afflictions of his Family. Sons and Daughters with Genius and qualities and Connections and prospects the most pleasing, have been signally unfortunate. A Son, whose name was altered, from Thomas to Robert Treat has left a Volume of Prose and Verse, which will attract the Attention of Posterity to his Father, more than his Signature of Independence. It is the History of a Poet, in Genius Excentricity, Irregularity Misfortune and Misery, equal to most in Johnsons Lives.

To your ignoro, I add non curo. I should as soon suppose that the Prodigal Son, in a frolic with one of his Girls made a trip to America in one of Mother Careys Eggshels, and left the fruits of their Amours here, as believe any of the grave hypotheses and solemn reasonings of Philosophers or Divines upon the Subject of the peopling of America. If my Faith in Moses or Noah depended on any of these Speculations, I woul[d] give it up.

I sincerely thank you for your congratulations on the Successes of our Navy. I wish to write you more, than my paralyttic Fingers will justify or tollerate up[on] this Subject. I believe, but am not certain, that you was present in Congress on the 5th. of October 1775, when it appears by the Journal, the first foundation of an American Navy was laid. I wish to know, whether you recollect the Opposition that was made to the Appointment of that Committee, to their report, and to the Adoption [of] the Resolution. Do you retain any recollection of the Speeches of Edward Rutledge, Robert Treat Paine, or any other Member, on that Occasion? [70] It is, to be sure, a question of idle curiosity. But the curiosity is very strong.

I have another Curiosity, more ardent still. I have ever believed that you were the Author of the Essay towards a Navy when you was Secretary of State. I have reason to suspect that Hamilton was averse to that Measure. That you were always for a Navy to compell the Barbary Powers to

70. Adams served on the Navy committee with Silas Deane and John Langdon. See the entry for Oct. 5, 1775, in the *Journals of the Continental Congress, 1774-1789* (Washington, 1905), III, 277-79. For Adams's views on "the true origins and foundations of the American Navy," see his "Autobiography," *Works*, III, 7-12.

peace, I distinctly remember in many of our personal Conversations in Europe; and I have carefully preserved very strong Letters from You full of arguments for such a Navy. If I am mistaken in ascribing to you the measures taken in Washingtons Administration, looking towards a Navy, I wish you to correct my Error.[71] Till that is done I shall sincerely believe myself orthodox. The Mail approaches, and I must cease with Assurances of respect and Esteem

JOHN ADAMS

P. S. We must have a Navy now to command The Lakes, if it costs Us 100 Ships of the Line; whatever becomes of the Ocean.

J. A.

Adams to Jefferson

Quincy June 14. 1813

DEAR SIR

In your Letter to Dr. Priestley of March 21. 1801, you "tender him, the protection of those laws which were made for the wise and good, like him; and disclaim the legitimacy of that Libel on legislation, which, under the form of a Law, was for Sometime placed among them". This Law, I presume was, the Alien Law, as it was called.

As your name is subscribed to that law, as Vice President, and mine as President, I know not why you are not as responsible for it as I am. Neither of Us were concerned in the formation of it. We were then at War with France: French Spies then swarmed in our Cities and in the Country. Some of them were, intollerably, turbulent, impudent and seditious. To check these was the design of this law. Was there ever a Government, which had not Authority to defend itself against Spies in its own Bosom? Spies of an Ennemy at War? This Law was never executed by me, in any Instance.

But what is the conduct of our Government now? Aliens are ordered to report their names and obtain Certificates once a month: and an industrious Scotchman, at this moment industriously labouring in my Garden is

71. In his reply TJ did not comment on the early United States Navy, probably because he overlooked the question among the many that JA had asked him on diverse subjects. When JA reverted to the development of the Navy nine years later (Oct. 15, 1822), TJ replied in considerable detail on Nov. 1. See below, 582-83, 584-85.

TJ had advocated a navy as early as 1786 to bring the Barbary pirates to terms (TJ to JA, July 11, 1786, above, 142), while he was minister to France, and he adhered to this policy as secretary of state. Hamilton also favored a navy. Washington's attitude reflected the agreement in his cabinet. Freeman, *Washington*, VII, 158-59, 346-47, 420.

obliged to walk once a month to Boston, eight miles at least, to renew his Certificate from the Marshall. And a fat organist is ordered into the Country. etc. etc. etc. All this is right. Every Government has by the Law of Nations a right to make prisoners of War, of every Subject of an Enemy.[72] But a War with England differs not from a War with France. The Law of Nations is the same in both.

I cannot write Volumes in a single Sheet: but these Letters of yours require Volumes from me.

"The mighty Wave of public Opinion, which has rolled over!" This is, in your Style, and sometimes in mine, with less precision, and less delicacy. Oh! Mr. Jefferson! What a Wave of public Opinion has rolled over the Universe? By the Universe here, I mean our Globe. I can yet say there is nothing new Under the Sun, in my Sense. The Reformation rolled a Wave of public Opinion over the Globe, as wonderful as this; A War of thirty Years, was necessary to compose this Wave. The Wars of Charlemaigne rolled a Wave. The Crusades rolled a Wave, more mountainous than the French Revolution. Only one hundred Years ago, a Wave was rolled; when Austria England and Holland in Alliance, contended against France, for the dominion or rather the Alliance of Spain.

Had "The Clock run down," I am not so sanguine, as you, that the Consequence would have been as you presume. I was determined in all Events to retire. You and Mr. Madison are indebted to Bayard, for an Evasion of the Contest.[73] Had the voters for Burr, addressed the Nation, I am not sure that your Convention would have decided in your Favour. But what Reflections does this suggest? What Pretensions had Aaron Burr to be President or Vice President?

What "a Wave" has rolled over Christendom for 1500 years? What a Wave has rolled over France for 1500 Years supporting in Power and Glory the Dinasty of Bourbon? What a Wave supported the House of Austria? What a Wave has supported the Dinasty of Mahomet, for 1200 Years? What a Wave supported the House of Hercules, for so many Ages in more remote Antiquity? These waves are not to be slighted. They are less resistable than those in the Gulph Stream in an hurricane. What a Wave has the French Revolution spread? And what a Wave is our Navy of five Frigates raising?

If I can keep this book, "Memoirs of Lindsey," I shall have more to say. Meantime I remain your Friend

JOHN ADAMS

72. During the War of 1812, Congress amended "An act respecting alien enemies," which had been passed during Adams's administration. See *U. S. Stat. at L.*, I, 577-78 (July 6, 1798) and II, 781 (July 6, 1812).

73. For Bayard's role in the election of 1800, see Morton Borden, *The Federalism of James A. Bayard* (N. Y., 1955), Chap. VII.

Jefferson to Adams

Monticello June 15. 13.

Dear Sir

I wrote you a letter on the 27th. of May, which probably would reach you about the 3d. inst. and on the 9th. I recieved yours of the 29th. of May. Of Lindsay's Memoirs I had never before heard, and scarcely indeed of himself. It could not therefore but be unexpected that two letters of mine should have any thing to do with his life. The name of his editor was new to me, and certainly presents itself, for the first time, under unfavorable circumstances. Religion, I suppose, is the scope of his book: and that a writer on that subject should usher himself to the world in the very act of the grossest abuse of confidence, by publishing private letters which passed between two friends, with no views to their ever being made public, is an instance of inconsistency, as well as of infidelity of which I would rather be the victim than the author. By your kind quotation of the dates of my two letters I have been enabled to turn to them. They had compleatly evanished from my memory. The last is on the subject of religion, and by it's publication will gratify the priesthood with new occasion of repeating their Comminations against me. They wish it to be believed that he can have no religion who advocates it's freedom. This was not the doctrine of Priestley, and I honored him for the example of liberality he set to his order. The first letter is political. It recalls to our recollection the gloomy transactions of the times, the doctrines they witnessed, and the sensibilities they excited. It was a confidential communication of reflections on these from one friend to another, deposited in his bosom, and never meant to trouble the public mind. Whether the character of the times is justly portrayed or not, posterity will decide. But on one feature of them they can never decide, the sensations excited in free yet firm minds, by the terrorism of the day. None can concieve who did not witness them, and they were felt by one party only. This letter exhibits their side of the medal. The Federalists no doubt have presented the other, in their private correspondences, as well as open action. If these correspondencies should ever be laid open to the public eye, they will probably be found not models of comity towards their adversaries. The readers of my letter should be cautioned not to confine it's view to this country alone. England and it's alarmists were equally under consideration. Still less must they consider it as looking personally towards you. You happen indeed to be quoted because you happened to express, more pithily than had been done by themselves, one of the mottos of the party. This was in your answer to the address of the young men of Philadelphia. [See Selection of patriotic addresses. pa. 198.] [74] One of the questions you know on which our parties took different sides, was on the improvability of the human mind, in science, in ethics, in government etc. Those who advocated reformation of institutions, pari passu, with the progress of science, maintained that no definite limits could be assigned to that progress. The enemies of reform, on the other hand, denied improvement, and advocated steady adherence to the principles, practices and institutions of our fathers, which they represented as the consummation of wisdom, and akmé of excellence, beyond which the human mind could never advance. Altho' in the passage of your answer alluded to, you expressly disclaim the wish to influence the freedom of enquiry, you predict that that will produce nothing more worthy of transmission to posterity, than the principles, institutions, and systems of education recieved from their ancestors. I do not consider this as your deliberate opinion. You possess, yourself, too much science, not to see how much is still ahead of you, unexplained and unexplored. Your own consciousness must place you as far before our ancestors, as in the rear of our posterity. I consider it as an expression lent to the prejudices of your friends; and altho' I happened to cite it from you, the whole letter shews I had them only in view. In truth, my dear Sir, we were far from considering you as the author of all the measures we blamed. They were placed under the protection of your name, but we were satisfied they wanted much of your approbation. We ascribed them to their real authors, the Pickerings, the Wolcotts, the Tracys, the Sedgwicks, et id genus omne ["and all of their kind"], with whom we supposed you in a state of Duresse. I well remember a conversation with you, in the morning of the day on which you nominated to the Senate a substitute for Pickering, in which you expressed a just impatience under 'the legacy of Secretaries which Gen. Washington had left you' and whom you seemed therefore to consider as under public protection. Many other incidents shewed how differently you would have acted with less impassioned advisers; and subsequent events have proved that your minds were not together. You would do me great injustice therefore by taking to yourself what was intended for men who were then your secret, as they are now your open enemies. Should you write on the subject, as you propose, I am sure we shall see you place yourself farther from them than from us.

As to myself, I shall take no part in any discussions. I leave others to judge of what I have done, and to give me exactly that place which they shall think I have occupied. Marshall has written libels on one side; others, I suppose, will be written on the other side; and the world will sift both,

74. TJ's note.

and separate the truth as well as they can. I should see with reluctance the passions of that day rekindled in this, while so many of the actors are living, and all are too near the scene not to participate in sympathies with them. About facts, you and I cannot differ; because truth is our mutual guide. And if any opinions you may express should be different from mine, I shall recieve them with the liberality and indulgence which I ask for my own, and still cherish with warmth the sentiments of affectionate respect of which I can with so much truth tender you the assurance.

Th: Jefferson

Adams to Jefferson

Quincy June 25. 1813

DEAR SIR

Your favour of the 15th came to me Yesterday, and it is a pleasure to discover that We are only 9 days apart.

Be not surprised or alarmed. Lindsays Memoirs will do no harm to you or me. You have right and reason to feel and to resent the breach of Confidence. I have had enough of the same kind of Treachery and Perfidy practiced upon me, to know how to sympathize with you. I will agree with you, in unquallified censure of such Abuses. They are the worst Species of Tyrany over private Judgment and free Enquiry. They suppress the free communication of Soul to Soul.

There are critical moments, when Faction, whether in Church or State, will stick at nothing. Confidence of Friendship the most sacred, is but a cobweb tie. How few! Oh how few are the exceptions! I could name many Cases of the rule, but will mention but one. Do you remember Tenche Coxe?

You must have misunderstood me, when you understood that I "proposed to write on the Subject," if you meant, to the Public. I have written enough and too much. I have no thought, in this correspondence, but to satisfy you and myself. If our Letters should be shewn to a friend or two, in confidence; and if that confidence should be betrayed: your Letters will do you no dishonour. As to mine I care not a farthing. My Reputation has been so much the Sport of the public for fifty Years, and will be with Posterity, that I hold it, a bubble, a Gossameur, that idles in the wanton Summers Air. Now for your Letter.

During the three Years, that I resided in England, I was somewhat acquainted with Lindsay, Disnay, Farmer, Price, Priestley, Kippis, Jebb, Vaughans, Bridgen, Brand Hollis, etc. etc. etc., even Dr. Towers was not personally unknown to me. A Belsham was once introduced to me, probably the Author of Lindsays Memoirs. I had much conversation with him. Whether he is a Brother of Belsham the Historian, I know not. Lindsay was a singular Character, unless Jebb was his parrallel. Unitarianism and Biblical Criticism were the great Characteristicks of them all. All were learned, scientific, and moral. Lindsay was an heroic Christian Philosopher. All professed Friendship for America, and these were almost all, who pretended to any such Thing.

I wish You could live a Year in Boston, hear their Divines, read their publications, especially the Repository. You would see how spiritual Tyranny and ecclesiastical Domination are beginning in our Country: at least struggling for birth.

Now, for your political Letter. No, I have not done with spiritual Pride, in high places and in low. I would trust these liberal Christians in London and in Boston, with Power, just as soon as I would Calvin or Cardinal Lorrain; just as soon as I would the Quakers of Pensylvania; just as soon as I would Methodists or Moravians; just as soon as I would Rochefoucault and Condorcet; just as soon as I would the Œconomists of France; just as soon as I would Bolingbroke and Voltaire, Hume and Gibbon; nay just as soon as I would Robespierre or Brissot. I can go no higher, unless I add the League and the Fronde in France, or Charles the first and Archbishop Laud in England and Ireland.

Let me say, however, by the Way, that I fully believe, that Priestley is only guilty of an indiscretion, very pardonable, in this thing. Lindsay is perfectly innocent. Belsham has done the wrong. I cannot but contrast his Conduct with that of Disney, who found among the Papers of Brand Hollis Letters from me and my Wife, which We had both forgotten. He wrote to Us and asked leave to publish them. Neither of Us recollected a Word of them for We had no Copies. We both left to his discretion to publish what he pleased and he has done it. I expected much more nonsense and extravagance in mine than appears, for I wrote to Hollis without reserve.

Checks and Ballances, Jefferson, however you and your Party may have ridiculed them, are our only Security, for the progress of Mind, as well as the Security of Body. Every Species of these Christians would persecute Deists, as soon as either Sect would persecute another, if it had unchecked and unballanced Power. Nay, the Deists would persecute Christians, and Atheists would persecute Deists, with as unrelenting Cruelty, as any Christians would persecute them or one another. Know thyself, human Nature!

I am not sure, that I am yet ready to return to Politicks.

Upon the whole, I think this is enough for one Letter. Politicks shall be adjourned to a future day. Not a very distant one, however.

JOHN ADAMS

Jefferson to Adams

῎Ιδαν ἐς πολύδενδρον ἀνὴρ ὑλητόμος ἐλθὼν
Παπταίνει, παρέοντος ἅδην, ποθεν ἄρξεται ἔργῳ·
Τί πρᾶτον καταλεξῶ; ἐπεὶ πάρα μυρία εἰπῆν. [75]

Monticello June 27. 13.

And I too, my dear Sir, like the wood-cutter of Ida, should doubt where to begin, were I to enter the forest of opinions, discussions, and contentions which have occurred in our day. I should exclaim with Theocritus, Τί πρᾶτον καταλεξῶ; ἐπεὶ πάρα μυρία ειπῆν. [76] But I shall not do it. The summum bonum with me is now truly Epicurean, ease of body and tranquility of mind; and to these I wish to consign my remaining days. Men have differed in opinion, and been divided into parties by these opinions, from the first origin of societies; and in all governments where they have been permitted freely to think and to speak. The same political parties which now agitate the U.S. have existed thro' all time. Whether the power of the people, or that of the ἄριστοι ["aristocrats"] should prevail, were questions which kept the states of Greece and Rome in eternal convulsions; as they now schismatize every people whose minds and mouths are not shut up by the gag of a despot. And in fact the terms of whig and tory belong to natural, as well as to civil history. They denote the temper and constitution of mind of different individuals. To come to our own country, and to the times when you and I became first acquainted, we well remember the violent parties which agitated the old Congress, and their bitter contests. There you and I were together, and the Jays, and the Dickinsons, and other anti-independants were arrayed against us. They cherished the monarchy of England; and we the rights of our countrymen. When our present government was in the mew, passing from Confederation to Union, how bitter was the schism between

75. "A woodcutter, having come onto heavily wooded Ida, looked all around, doubtful at first where he should begin his task. 'What first shall I gather?' he said, gazing at the thousands of trees." Theocritus 17.9.

76. " 'What first shall I gather?' he said, gazing at the thousands of trees."

the Feds and Antis. Here you and I were together again. For altho' for a moment, separated by the Atlantic from the scene of action, I favored the opinion that nine states should confirm the constitution, in order to secure it, and the others hold off, until certain amendments, deemed favorable to freedom, should be made, I rallied in the first instant to the wiser proposition of Massachusets, that all should confirm, and then all instruct their delegates to urge those amendments. The amendments were made, and all were reconciled to the government. But as soon as it was put into motion, the line of division was again drawn, we broke into two parties, each wishing to give a different direction to the government; the one to strengthen the most popular branch, the other the more permanent branches, and to extend their permanence. Here you and I separated for the first time: and as we had been longer than most others on the public theatre, and our names therefore were more familiar to our countrymen, the party which considered you as thinking with them, placed your name at their head; the other, for the same reason, selected mine. But neither decency nor inclination permitted us to become the advocates of ourselves, or to take part personally in the violent contests which followed. We suffered ourselves, as you so well expressed it, to be the passive subjects of public discussion. And these discussions, whether relating to men, measures, or opinions, were conducted by the parties with an animosity, a bitterness, and an indecency, which had never been exceeded. All the resources of reason, and of wrath, were exhausted by each party in support of it's own, and to prostrate the adversary opinions. One was upbraided with recieving the Antifederalists, the other the old tories and refugees into their bosom. Of this acrimony the public papers of the day exhibit ample testimony in the debates of Congress, of state legislatures, of stump-orators, in addresses, answers, and newspaper essays. And to these without question may be added the private correspondences of individuals; and the less guarded in these, because not meant for the public eye, not restrained by the respect due to that; but poured forth from the overflowings of the heart into the bosom of a friend, as a momentary easement of our feelings. In this way, and in answers to addresses, you and I could indulge ourselves. We have probably done it, sometimes with warmth, often with prejudice, but always, as we believed, adhering to truth. I have not examined my letters of that day. I have no stomach to revive the memory of it's feelings. But one of these letters, it seems, has got before the public, by accident and infidelity, by the death of one friend to whom it was written, and of his friend to whom it was communicated, and by the malice and treachery of a third person, of whom I had never before heard, merely to make mischief, and in the same Satanic spirit, in which the same enemy had intercepted and published, in 1776, your letter animadverting on Dickinson's character.[77] How it happened that I quoted you in my letter to Dr. Priestly, and for whom, and not for yourself, the strictures were meant, has been explained to you in my letter of the 15th. which had been committed to the post 8. days before I received yours of the 10th. 11th. and 14th. That gave you the reference which these asked to the particular answer alluded to in the one to Priestley.

The renewal of these old discussions, my friend, would be equally useless and irksome. To the volumes then written on these subjects, human ingenuity can add nothing new: and the rather, as lapse of time has obliterated many of the facts. And shall you and I, my dear Sir, like Priam of old, gird on the 'arma, diu desueta, trementibus aevo humeris ["arms, long unused, upon the trembling shoulders of an old man"]'? Shall we, at our age, become the Athletae of party, and exhibit ourselves, as gladiators, in the Arena of the newspapers? Nothing in the universe could induce me to it. My mind has been long fixed to bow to the judgment of the world, who will judge me by my acts, and will never take counsel from me as to what that judgment shall be. If your objects and opinions have been misunderstood, if the measures and principles of others have been wrongfully imputed to you, as I believe they have been, that you should leave an explanation of them, would be an act of justice to yourself. I will add that it has been hoped you would leave such explanations as would place every saddle on it's right horse, and replace on the shoulders of others the burthens they shifted on yours.

But all this, my friend, is offered, merely for your consideration and judgment; without presuming to anticipate what you alone are qualified to decide for yourself. I mean to express my own purpose only, and the reflections which have led to it. To me then it appears that there have been differences of opinion, and party differences, from the first establishment of governments, to the present day; and on the same question which now divides our own country: that these will continue thro' all future time: that every one takes his side in favor of the many, or of the few, according to his constitution, and the circumstances in which he is placed: that opinions, which are equally honest on both sides, should not affect personal esteem, or social intercourse: that as *we* judge between the Claudii

77. JA to General James Warren, president of the Massachusetts Provincial Congress, July 24, 1775. While he was a member of the Continental Congress, JA, disgusted with John Dickinson's desire for reconciliation with Great Britain, referred to him in this letter, though not by name, as "a certain great fortune and piddling genius, whose fame has been trumpeted so loudly." The carrier of the letter was captured by the British and it was promptly published in Boston by General Gage and soon circulated in the colonies and in England. Although JA lost Dickinson's friendship, he felt that the letter helped the cause of independence. JA, "Diary," *Works*, II, 411-12; John Quincy Adams and Charles Francis Adams, *The Life of John Adams* (Philadelphia, 1871), I, 249-52.

and the Gracchi, the Wentworths and the Hampdens of past ages, so, of those among us whose names may happen to be remembered for awhile, the next generations will judge, favorably or unfavorably, according to the complexion of individual minds, and the side they shall themselves have taken: that nothing new can be added by you or me to what has been said by others, and will be said in every age, in support of the conflicting opinions on government: and that wisdom and duty dictate an humble resignation to the verdict of our future peers. In doing this myself, I shall certainly not suffer moot questions to affect the sentiments of sincere friendship and respect, consecrated to you by so long a course of time, and of which I now repeat sincere assurances.

TH: JEFFERSON

Adams to Jefferson

Quincy June 28th. 1813

DEAR SIR

It is very true, that "the denunciations of the Priesthood are fulminated against every Advocate for a compleat Freedom of Religion. Comminations, I believe, would be plenteously pronounced, by even the most liberal of them, against Atheism, Deism; against every Man who disbelieved or doubted the Resurrection of Jesus or the Miracles of the New Testament. Priestley himself would denounce the man who should deny The Apocalyps, or the Prophecies of Daniel. Priestley and Lindsay both have denounced as Idolaters and Blasphemers, all the Trinitarians and even the Arrians. Poor weak Man, when will thy Perfection arrive? Perfectibility, I shall not deny: for a greater Character than Priestley or Godwin has said, "Be ye perfect" etc. For my part, I cannot deal damnation round the land on all I judge the Foes of God or Man. But I did not intend to say a Word on this Subject, in this Letter. As much of it as you please hereafter: but let me now return to Politicks.

With some difficulty I have hunted up, or down, "the Address of the Young men of the City of Philadelphia, the District of South wark, and the Northern Liberties:" and the Answer.

The Addressers say, "Actuated by *the same principles* on which our forefathers atchieved their independence, the recent Attempts of a foreign Power to derogate from the dignity and rights of our country, awaken our liveliest Sensibility, and our strongest indignation." Huzza, my brave Boys! Could Thomas Jefferson or John Adams hear these Words, with insensibility, and without Emotion? These Boys afterwards add "We regard our Liberty and Independence, as the richest portion given Us by our Ancestors." And, who were these Ancestors? Among them were Thomas Jefferson and John Adams. And I very cooly believe that no two Men among those Ancestors did more towards it than those two. Could either hear this like Statues? If, one hundred Years hence, Your Letters and mine should see the light, I hope the Reader will hunt up this Address and read it all: and remember that We were then engaged or on the point of engaging in a War with France. I shall not repeat the Answer, till We come to the paragraph upon which you cr[i]ticised to Dr. Priestley though every Word of it is true and I now rejoice to see it recorded; and though I had wholly forgotten it.

The Paragraph is "Science and Morals are the great Pillars on which this Country has been raised to its present population, Oppulence and prosperity, and these alone, can advance, support and preserve it." "Without wishing to damp the Ardor of curiosity, or influence the freedom of inquiry, I will hazard a prediction, that after the most industrious and impartial Researches, the longest liver of you all, will find no Principles, Institutions, or Systems of Education, more fit, IN GENERAL to be transmitted to your Posterity, than those you have received from you[r] Ancestors." [78]

Now, compare the paragraph in the Answer, with the paragraph in the Address, as both are quoted above: and see if We can find the Extent and the limits of the meaning of both.

Who composed that Army of fine young Fellows that was then before my Eyes? There were among them, Roman Catholicks, English Episcopalians, Scotch and American Presbyterians, Methodists, Moravians, Anababtists, German Lutherans, German Calvinists Universalists, Arians, Priestleyans, Socinians, Independents, Congregationalists, Horse Protestants and House Protestants, Deists and Atheists; and "Protestans qui ne croyent rien ["Protestants who believe nothing"]." Very few however of several of these Species. Never the less all Educated in the *general Principles* of Christianity: and the general Principles of English and American Liberty.

Could my Answer be understood, by any candid Reader or Hearer, to recommend, to all the others, the general Principles, Institutions or Systems of Education of the Roman Catholicks? Or those of the Quakers? Or those of the Presbyterians? Or those of the Menonists? Or those of the Methodists? or those of the Moravians? Or those of the Universalists? or those of the Philosophers? No.

The *general Principles,* on which the Fathers Atchieved Independence,

78. *Works,* IX, 188.

were the only Principles in which that beautiful Assembly of young Gentlemen could Unite, and these Principles only could be intended by them in their Address, or by me in my Answer. And what were these *general Principles?* I answer, the general Principles of Christianity, in which all those Sects were United: And the *general Principles* of English and American Liberty, in which all those young Men United, and which had United all Parties in America, in Majorities sufficient to assert and maintain her Independence.

Now I will avow, that I then believed, and now believe, that those general Principles of Christianity, are as eternal and immutable, as the Existence and Attributes of God; and that those Principles of Liberty, are as unalterable as human Nature and our terrestrial, mundane System. I could therefore safely say, consistently with all my then and present Information, that I believed they would never make Discoveries in contradiction to these *general Principles.* In favour of these *general Principles* in Phylosophy, Religion and Government, I could fill Sheets of quotations from Frederick of Prussia, from Hume, Gibbon, Bolingbroke, Reausseau and Voltaire, as well as Neuton and Locke: not to mention thousands of Divines and Philosophers of inferiour Fame.

I might have flattered myself that my Sentiments were sufficiently known to have protected me against Suspicions of narrow thoughts, contrasted Sentiments, biggotted, enthusiastic or superstitious Principles civil political philosophical, or ecclesiastical. The first Sentence of the Preface to my Defence of the Constitutions, Vol. 1, printed in 1787, is in these Words: "The Arts and Sciences, in general, during the three or four last centuries, have had a regular course of *progressive* improvement. The Inventions in Mechanic Arts, the discoveries in natural Philosophy, navigation and commerce, and the Advancement of civilization and humanity, have occasioned Changes in the condition of the World and the human Character, which would have astonished the most refined Nations of Antiquity." etc.[79] I will quote no farther; but request you to read again that whole page, and then say whether the Writer of it could be suspected of recommending to Youth, "to look backward, instead of forward" for instruction and Improvement.

This Letter is already too long. In my next I shall consider "The Terrorism of the day." Meantime, I am as ever, your Friend

JOHN ADAMS

79. *Ibid.,* IV, 283.

10

"Belief... the assent of the mind
to an intelligible proposition"

✳ JUNE 1813 – DECEMBER 1813 ✳

I HAVE GIVEN UP NEWSPAPERS," Jefferson informed Adams on the
resumption of their correspondence in 1812, "in exchange for
Tactitus and Thucydides, for Newton and Euclid." Adams, with his
New England background, found most pleasure in "Theological and
Ecclesiastical Instructors." [1] The major interest of Jefferson in historical and scientific questions, of Adams in theological and religious, is
characteristic of each, as their wide-ranging minds were characteristic
of the Enlightenment. The intensive reading and worldly experience
of each enriched the reflections of the other. Much of that experience
had been in politics, which Jefferson had gladly abandoned but which
Adams followed more closely through his son John Quincy. Both of
the veteran statesmen were very much aware of current develop-
ments in the world at large, but they could view them with greater
detachment as their years of retirement lengthened.

In 1813 events of great import for the future of republican government could hardly be ignored. In America a war of uncertain outcome
was testing the nation's ability to maintain independence and the
union of the states. As Adams recalled past political crises in his life
and took stock of the current threats of disunion, he found "more
real Terrorism in New England than there ever was in Virginia," [2]
when the Kentucky and Virginia Resolutions of 1798 had stirred the
South. In Europe, Napoleon's ambition and appetite for power, an
outcome of the French Revolution, in Adams's judgment, had en-

1. TJ to JA, Jan. 21, 1812, above, 291; JA to TJ, July 18, 1813, below, 362.
2. JA to TJ, June 30, 1813, below, 348.

veloped the Continent in flames for a decade and the final result was still in doubt. How different the outcome of the American Revolution!

When the two diplomats were colleagues in Europe before the collapse of the *ancien régime*, Jefferson had encouraged Adams in his desire to compose a treatise on aristocracy. This became Adams's medium for developing his concept of balanced government in which aristocracy played a significant but often misunderstood role. "I . . . have been writing Upon that Subject ever since," he declared, quoting the ancient Greek poets to re-enforce his position: " 'Nobility in Men is worth as much as it is in Horses Asses or Rams, but the meanest blooded Puppy, in the World, if he gets a little money, is as good a man as the best of them.' Yet Birth and Wealth together," according to Adams, "have prevailed over Virtue and Talents in all ages." [3] The French Revolution and the course of events in the American Republic had supplied fresh clinical data for his thesis.

As memories of vital issues of the past and present flooded his mind, Adams wrote a series of letters in close succession, reviewing the occasion for composing his *Defence of the Constitutions* and elaborating on his theory of balanced government.[4] The existence of the "well born" in every society, the real meaning of "Gentleman," could not be ignored or discarded; but aristocracy might be controlled. "The five Pillars of Aristocracy, are Beauty, Wealth, Birth, Genius and Virtues." What chance, asked Adams, had Talents (Genius) and Virtues in competition with the first three attributes? [5]

This question called forth one of Jefferson's most famous letters—his essay on natural and artificial aristocracy and the form of government "which provides the most effectually for a pure selection of these natural aristoi into the offices of the government." [6] It provoked, in turn, Adams's counterpart on the natural aristocracy, asking what talents, physical or intellectual, material or moral, might not assert influence in society and eventually dominate it.[7] Jefferson, the optimist, had confidence in the ability of citizens of a republic to "elect the real good and wise," to separate "the aristoi from the pseudo-aristoi." He cited what the revolution in Virginia had accomplished,

3. JA to TJ, July 9, 1813, below, 351, 352.
4. JA to TJ, July 9, 13, and 15, 1813, below, 350-52, 354-56, 357-58.
5. JA to TJ, Aug. [14?], Sept. 2, 1813, below, 365-66, 371.
6. TJ to JA, Oct. 28, 1813, below, 389.
7. JA to TJ, Nov. 15, 1813, below, 398.

what his proposed system of public education might further attain, and what the American example, along with the liberating influence of science, had already meant to European peoples. Adams, skeptical of man as a rational creature, found no assurance that the natural aristocracy, established by law and honor, would not also secure legal sanction as an hereditary class, succumb to political corruption, and become a venal artificial aristocracy. To Adams such an aristocracy was "a subtle Venom that diffuses itself unseen," "a Phœnix that rises again out of its own Ashes." He would "chain it ... and place ... on each side of it" "a Watchful Centinel," consisting of the co-ordinate branches of his balanced government.[8] Although Jefferson's remedy of free elections prevailed as political democracy became unrestricted, Adams's argument that economic and social conditions affect political functions became more widely accepted by later generations.

The two statesmen were neither seeking controversy nor avoiding it, for they agreed that "we ought not to die before we have explained ourselves to each other."[9] With the historical perspective of the revolutionary era, their philosophical discussions ran as easily to religion as to government and from the one subject to the other and back again. Both thought that corruption in government had its parallel in the hierarchies established in the name of religion; dogmatic assertions in a maze of fine-spun theological argument overpowered men's minds and obscured fundamental principles. Although they agreed that complete freedom of religion was an inviolable principle, they discussed religious issues chiefly within the framework of the prevailing faith and subscribed to the fundamentals of Jesus's teachings, "the most sublime and benevolent code of morals which has ever been offered to man."[10]

While Adams was the tireless reader of theological works, it was Jefferson with his scientific bent who sought to organize and systematize his thoughts on religion. Not that he expected to write a treatise on the subject—his friend Dr. Joseph Priestley had provided that—but the corruptions of Christianity ought to be refuted. "I am a Christian," he confessed to Rush, "in the only sense he [Jesus] wished any one to be; sincerely attached to his doctrines, in preference to all others;

8. JA to TJ, Dec. 19, 1813, below, 409.
9. JA to TJ, July 15, 1813, and TJ to JA, Oct. 28, 1813, below, 358, 391.
10. JA to TJ, July 16, 1813, and TJ to JA, Oct. 12, 1813, below, 359-60, 383-86.

ascribing to himself every *human* excellence; and believing he never claimed any other." [11] Shortly before, Jefferson had received a copy of Priestley's *Socrates and Jesus Compared*. To the author he confided the outline (quoted in Adams's letter of July 16, 1813) of the "Christian system" as compared with the precepts of the ancient philosophers and those of the Jews.[12] With this outline in mind Jefferson prepared a more detailed, though still brief, Syllabus of an Estimate of the Merit of the Doctrines of Jesus, Compared with Those of Others.[13]

In 1813 Jefferson sent his Syllabus to Adams. It was not concerned with the divinity of Christ, but the implication of unbelief was clear. Since Jesus himself left no written words, "the committing to writing of his life and doctrines fell on the most unlettered and ignorant men," recording from memory long after the events. Only fragments of what he said were handed down, perverted or disfigured by the corruptions of "schismatising followers" or willfully destroyed by bigots for the same purpose. Jefferson advised going back to the "simple evangelists" and selecting "the very words only of Jesus," as he had already done in compiling The Philosophy of Jesus of Nazareth.[14] Adams noted with approval Jefferson's conclusions concerning the moral and ethical doctrines of Jesus, including his confirmation of the deism of the Jews—"their belief of one only God." [15] Jefferson's comparative study provided a firm relativist approach to combat the absolutism characteristic of most theologians of the period: let historical criticism be applied to Christianity in the same spirit that religious freedom is desired by all men. Adams had found the essence of Christian devotion and piety in the Greek exhortation (as Adams rendered it): "It is our duty and our privilege to address the Throne of thy grace." [16] Jefferson agreed with Adams's "outline of the theism of the three religions when you say that the principle of the Hebrew was the fear, of the Gentile the honor, and of the Christian the love of God." [17]

But Adams and Jefferson were unmistakable vestiges of the vanished Age of Enlightenment, nurturer of revolution, victim of war. Jeffer-

11. TJ to Rush, April 21, 1803, Ford, VIII, 223*n*.
12. TJ to Priestley, April 9, 1803, *ibid.*, 224-25*n*.
13. "Syllabus of an Estimate of the Merit of the Doctrines of Jesus, Compared with Those of Others," *ibid.*, 223-28.
14. See below, 384, n. 71.
15. "Syllabus," Ford, VIII, 228.
16. JA to TJ, [Oct. 4], 1813, below, 380.
17. TJ to JA, Oct. 12, 1813, and JA to TJ, Sept. 22, 1813, below, 385, 380.

son, always reticent about his own religion, observed that "if thinking men would have the courage to think for themselves, and to speak what they think, it would be found they do not differ in religious opinions, as much as is supposed." [18] "The Life and Morals of Jesus of Nazareth" were his guide. And belief he supposed "to be the assent of the mind to an intelligible proposition." [19] For Adams, whose testimony derived strength from its spontaneity, "The love of God and his Creation, delight, Joy, Tryumph, Exultation in my own existence, ... are my religion." "Ask me not, then, whether I am a Catholic or Protestant, Calvinist or Arminian. As far as they are Christians, I wish to be a fellow-disciple with them all." [20]

In religion as in the science of politics the two retired statesmen could turn philosophers without effort. But their frank discussion of religion, it should be remembered, was confined to their private correspondence. Their sharp condemnation of the priestcraft, their ridicule of the mystical Trinity as untenable by rational men, and their use of historical criticism to distinguish fact from "revelation" would have raised public furor. Under the aegis of the Enlightenment, freedom of thought won least recognition in the field of religion and theology. To Adams and Jefferson the achievement of religious freedom in most of the states during the Revolution and the adoption of the First Amendment to the Constitution of the United States had done more, they hoped, than establish a grudging toleration. They insisted on the ultimate truth "that Almighty God hath created the mind free." [21]

By the second decade of the nineteenth century the conservative reaction to rational religion was well advanced in America. Resurgent evangelism was spawning such organizations as the American Tract Society (1814) and the American Bible Society (1816) [22] to propagate the gospel by prescription rather than by exchange of opinions. Adams and Jefferson would have to find what encouragement they could in the substantial minority of free thinkers who provided the nucleus for a countervailing growth of liberal thought.

18. TJ to JA, Aug. 22, 1813, below, 368.
19. *Ibid.*
20. JA to TJ, Sept. 14, 1813, below, 374; JA to Benjamin Rush, Jan. 21, 1810, *Works*, IX, 627.
21. Preamble to TJ's "Act for establishing Religious Freedom," passed by the General Assembly of Virginia in 1786, Jefferson's *Notes on the State of Virginia*, ed. by William Peden (Chapel Hill, 1955), 223.
22. JA to TJ, Nov. 4, 1816, and TJ to JA, Nov. 25, 1816, below, 493-94, 496.

Adams to Jefferson

Quincy June 30th. 1813

DEAR SIR

Before I proceed to the Order of the day, which is the terrorism of a former day: I beg leave to correct an Idea that some readers may infer from an expression in one of your Letters. No sentiment or expression in any of my Answers to Addresses were obtruded or insinuated by any Person about me. Every one of them was written with my own hand. I alone am responsable for all the Mistakes and Errors in them. To have called Council to deliberate upon such a Mass of [writings] would have taken all the time; and the Business of the State must have been suspended. It is true, I was sufficiently plagued by Ps. and Ts. and Ss.[23] These however, were but Puppets danced upon the Wires of two Jugglers behind the Scene: and these Jugglers were Hamilton and Washington. How you stare at the name of Washington! But to return, *for the present* to

"The Sensations excited, in free yet firm Minds by the Terrorism of the day." You say, "none can conceive them who did not witness them, and they were felt by one party only".

Upon this Subject I despair of making myself understood by Posterity, by the present Age, and even by you. To collect and arrange the documents illustrative of it, would require as many Lives as those of a Cat. You never felt the Terrorism of Chaises Rebellion in Massachusetts.[24] I believe You never felt the Terrorism of Gallatins Insurrection in Pensilvania: [25] You certainly never reallized the Terrorism of Fries's,[26] most outragious Riot and Rescue, as I call it, Treason, Rebellion as the World and great Judges and two Juries pronounced it. You certainly never felt the Terrorism, excited by Genet, in 1793, when ten thousand People in the Streets of Philadelphia, day after day, threatened to drag Washington

23. I.e., "the Pickerings, . . . the Tracys, the Sedgwicks." TJ to JA, June 15, 1813, above, 331.

24. On Shays's Rebellion see above, Chap. 5.

25. As representative in Congress from western Pennsylvania, Albert Gallatin led the opposition to Hamilton's whiskey tax in 1792, but he was also opposed to violence and his peace policy won out in the Whiskey Rebellion of 1794. Henry Adams, *The Life of Albert Gallatin* (Philadelphia, 1880), 88-89, 123-40.

26. Fries Rebellion occurred in Bucks and Northampton counties, Pa., in 1799. Farmers, led by John Fries, gave armed resistance to a federal tax on land and houses, and women poured scalding water on the assessors. The rebellion was put down by federal troops; Fries was tried for treason and sentenced to be hanged, but President John Adams pardoned him. W. W. H. Davis, *The Fries Rebellion* (Doylestown, Pa., 1899).

out of his House, and effect a Revolution in the Government, or compell it to declare War in favour of the French Revolution, and against England. The coolest and the firmest Minds, even among the Quakers in Philadelphia, have given their Opinions to me, that nothing but the Yellow Fever, which removed Dr. Hutchinson and Jonathan Dickenson Sargent from this World, could have saved the United States from a total Revolution of Government. I have no doubt You was fast asleep in philosophical Tranquility, when ten thousand People, and perhaps many more, were parading the Streets of Philadelphia, on the Evening of my Fast Day; [27] When even Governor Mifflin himself, thought it his Duty to order a Patrol of Horse And Foot to preserve the peace; when Markett Street was as full as Men could stand by one another, and even before my Door; when some of my Domesticks in Phrenzy, determined to sacrifice their Lives in my defence; when all were ready to make a desperate Salley among the multitude, and others were with difficulty and danger dragged back by the others; when I myself judged it prudent and necessary to order Chests of Arms from the War Office to be brought through bye Lanes and back Doors: determined to defend my House at the Expence of my Life, and the Lives of the few, very few Domesticks and Friends within it. What think you of Terrorism, Mr. Jefferson? Shall I investigate the Causes, the Motives, the Incentives to these Terrorisms? Shall I remind you of Phillip Freneau, of Loyd? of Ned Church? of Peter Markoe[?] of Andrew Brown? of Duane? of Callender? of Tom Paine? of Greenleaf, of Cheetham, of Tennison at New York? of Benjamin Austin at Boston? [28] But above all; shall I request you, to collect the circular Letters from Members of Congress in the middle and southern States to their Constituents? I would give all I am worth for a compleat Collection of all those circular Letters. Please to recollect Edward Livingstones motions and Speeches and those of his Associates in the case of Jonathan Robbins.[29]

The real terrors of both Parties have allways been, and now are, The fear that they shall loose the Elections and consequently the Loaves and Fishes; and that their Antagonists will obtain them. Both parties have excited artificial Terrors and if I were summoned as a Witness to say upon Oath, which Party had excited, Machiavillialy, the most terror, and which had really felt the most, I could not give a more sincere Answer, than in the vulgar Style "Put Them in a bagg and shake them, and then see which comes out first."

27. President John Adams proclaimed April 25, 1799, as a fast day, that God "would withhold us from unreasonable discontent, from disunion, faction, sedition, and insurrection...." *Works*, IX, 172-74.

28. All of the foregoing were Republican writers and editors, vehement in their denunciation of the Federalists.

29. See JA to TJ, May 1, 1812, above, 300-1.

Where is the Terrorism, now, my Friend? There is now more real Terrorism in New England than there ever was in Virginia. The Terror of a civil War, a La Vendee, a division of the States etc. etc. etc. How shall We conjure down this damnable Rivalry between Virginia, and Massachusetts? Virginia had recourse to Pensilvania and New York, Massachusetts has now recourse to New York. They have almost got New Jersey and Maryland, and they are aiming at Pennsylvania.[30] And all this in the midst of a War with England, when all Europe is in flames.

I will give you a hint or two more, on the Subject of Terrorism. When John Randolph in the House and Stephens Thompson Mason in the Senate were treating me, with the Utmost Contempt, when Ned Livingston was threatening me with Impeachment for the murder of Jonathan Robbins *the native of Danvers in Connecticutt*. When I had certain Information, that the daily Language in an Insurance Office in Boston, was, even from the Mouth of Charles Jarvis, "We must go to Philadelphia, and dragg that John Adams from his Chair."

I tha[n]k God that Terror never Yet seized on my mind. But I have had more excitements to it, from 1761 to this day than any other Man. Name the other if you can. I have been disgraced and degraded and I have a right to complain. But as I always expected it, I have always submitted to it; perhaps often with too much tameness.

The amount of all the Speeches of John Randolph in the House for two or three Years is, that himself and myself, are the only two honest and consistent Men in the United States. Himself, eternally in Opposition to Government, and myself as constantly in favour of it. He is now in Correspondence with his Friend Quincy. What will come of it, let Virginia and Massachusetts Judge. In my next, you may find Something, upon "Correspondencies" Whigg and Tory; Federal and democratic; Virginian and Novanglian; English and French; Jacobinic and despotic, etc.

Mean time, I am as ever Your Friend,

JOHN ADAMS

30. In the election of 1808 Pennsylvania and New York went heavily Republican; in 1812 most of New York, New Jersey, and Maryland voted Federalist, as did certain sections of Pennsylvania. By 1816 all these states were back in the Republican ranks. Charles O. Paullin, *Atlas of the Historical Geography of the United States* (Washington, 1932), pl. 102.

Adams to Jefferson

Quincy July [3] 1813

DEAR SIR

Correspondences! The Letters of Bernard and Hutchinson, and Oliver and Paxton etc. were detected and exposed before The Revolution. There are I doubt not, thousands of Letters, now in being, but still concealed, (from their Party to their Friends,) which will, one day see the light. I have wondered for more than thirty Years that so few have appeared: and have constantly expected that a Tory History of the Rise and progress of the Revolution would appear. And wished it. I would give more for it than for Marshall, Gordon, Ramsay and all the rest. Private Letters of all Parties will be found analogous to the Newspapers Pamph[l]ets and Historians of the Times. Gordon's and Marshall's Histories were written to make money: and fashioned and finished, to sell high in the London Market. I should expect to find more Truth in a History written by Hutchinson, Oliver or Sewell. And I doubt not, such Histories will one day appear. Marshall's is a Mausolaeum, 100 feet square at the base, and 200 feet high. It will be as durable, as the monuments of the Washington benevolent Societies. Your Character in History may be easily foreseen. Your Administration, will be quoted by Philosophers, as a model, of profound Wisdom; by Politicians, as weak, superficial and short sighted. Mine, like Popes Woman [31] will have no Character at all. The impious Idolatry to Washington, destroyed all Character. His Legacy of Ministers, was not the worst part of the Tradgedy. Though by his own express confession to me, and by Pickerings confession to the World, in his Letters to Sullivan: two of them, at least were fastened upon him by Necessity, because he could get no other. The Truth is, Hamiltons Influence over him was so well known, that no Man fit for the Office of State or War would accept either. He was driven to the Necessity of appointing such as would accept. And this necessity was, in my Opinion the real Cause of his retirement from office: for you may depend upon it, that retirement was not voluntary.[32]

My Friend! You and I have passed our Lives, in serious Times. I know

31. "Most Women have no Characters at all." See "Of the Characters of Women: an Epistle to a Lady," F. W. Bateson, ed., *Alexander Pope, Epistles to Several Persons (Moral Essays)*, (London and New Haven, 1951), 45.

32. President Washington made it a practice to consult his cabinet, but following TJ's resignation as secretary of state, Hamilton was Washington's chief adviser, even after he left the cabinet. The best account of these official and personal relationships is in Charles, *Origins of the American Party System*, Chaps. I-II.

not whether We have ever seen any moments more serious than the present. The Northern States are now retaliating, upon the Southern States, their conduct from 1797 to 1800. It is a mortification to me, to see how servile Mimicks they are. Their Newspapers, Pamphlets, hand Bills, and their Legislative Proceedings, are copied from the Examples sett them, especially by Virginia and Kentucky. I know not which Party has the most unblushing Front, the most lying Tongue, or the most impudent and insolent not to say the most seditious and rebellious Pen.

If you desire explanations on any of the Points in this Letter you shall have them. This Correspondence I hope will be concealed as long as Hutchinsons and Olivers. But I should have no personal Objection to the Publication of it in the national Intelligencer. I am, and shall be for Life Your Friend

JOHN ADAMS

Adams to Jefferson

Quincy July 9 1813

Lord! Lord! What can I do, with so much Greek? When I was of your Age, young Man, i. e. 7 or 8 or 9 Years ago I felt, a kind of pang of Affection, for one of the flames of my Youth, and again paid my Addresses to Isocrates and Dionissius Hallicarnassensis etc. etc. etc. I collected all my Lexicons and Grammers and sat down to περι συνθεσεως ονοματων[33] etc. In this Way I amused myself for sometime: but I found, that if I looked a Word to day, in less than a Week I had to look it again. It was to little better purpose, than writing Letters on a pail of Water.

Whenever I sett down to write to you, I am precisely in the Situation of the Wood Cutter on Mount Ida: I can not see Wood for Trees. So many Subjects crowd upon me that I know not, with which to begin. But I will begin, at random with Belsham,[34] who is, as I have no doubt, a Man of merit. He had no malice against you, nor any thought of doing mischief: nor has he done any, though he has been imprudent. The Truth is the Dissenters of all Denominations in England and especially the Unitarians, are cowed, as We used to say at Colledge. They are ridiculed, insulted, persecuted. They can scarcely hold their heads above water. They catch at Straws and Shadows to avoid drowning. Priestley sent your Letter to Linsay, and Belsham printed it from the

33. "Concerning the treatment of words." Dion. Hal. wrote a treatise by this name on composition.

34. See JA to TJ, May 29, June 25, 1813, above, 325, 334.

same motive, i.e., to derive some countenance from the Name of Jefferson. Nor has it done harm here. Priestley says to Linsay "You see he is almost one of Us, and He hopes will soon be altogether such as We are." Even in our New England I have heard a high Federal Divine say, your Letters had increased his respect for you.

"The same political parties which now agitate U. S. have existed through all time." Precisely. And this is precisely the complaint in the preface to the first volume of my defence. While all other Sciences have advanced, that of Government is at a stand; little better understood; little better practiced now than 3 or 4 thousand Years ago. What is the Reason? I say Parties and Factions will not suffer, or permit Improvements to be made. As soon as one Man hints at an improvement his Rival opposes it. No sooner has one Party discovered or invented an Amelioration of the Condition of Man or the order of Society, than the opposite Party, belies it, misconstrues it, misrepresents it, ridicules it, insults it, and persecutes it. Records are destroyed. Histories are annihilated or interpolated, or prohibited sometimes by Popes, sometimes by Emperors, sometimes by Aristocratical and sometimes by democratical Assemblies and sometimes by Mobs.

Aristotle wrote the History and description of Eighteen hundred Republicks, which existed before his time. Cicero wrote two Volumes of discour[s]es on Government, which, perhaps were worth all the rest of his Works. The Works of Livy and Tacitus etc that are lost, would be more interesting than all that remain. Fifty Gospells have been destroyed, and where are St. Lukes World of Books that had been written? If you ask my Opinion, who has committed all the havoc? I will answer you candidly; Ecclesiastical and Imperial Despotism has done it, to conceal their Frauds.

Why are the Histories of all Nations, more ancient than the Chr[is]tian Æra, lost? Who destroyed the Alexandrian Library? I believe that Christian Priests, Jewish Rabbies Grecian Sages and Roman Emperors had as great a hand in it as Turks and Mahomitans.

Democrats, Rebells and Jacobins, when they possessed a momentary Power, have shewn a disposition, both to destroy and to forge Records, as vandalical, as Priests and Despots. Such has been and such is the World We live in.

I recollect, near 30 years ago to have said car[e]lesly to You, that I wished I could find time and means to write something upon Aristocracy.[35] You seized upon the Idea, and encouraged me to do it, with all that friendly warmth that is natural and habitual to you. I soon began, and have been writing Upon that Subject ever since. I have been so un-

35. See TJ to JA, Feb. 6, 1787, and JA to TJ, March 1, 1787, above, 170, 177.

fortunate as never to be able to make myself understood. Your "ἄριστοι ["aristocrats"]" are the most difficult Animals to manage, of anything in the whole Theory and practice of Government. They will not suffer themselves to be governed. They not only exert all their own Subtilty Industry and courage, but they employ the Commonalty, to knock to pieces every Plan and Model that the most honest Architects in Legislation can invent to keep them within bounds. Both Patricians and Plebeians are as furious as the Workmen in England to demolish labour-saving Machinery.

But who are these "ἄριστοι"? Who shall judge? Who shall select these choice Spirits from the rest of the Congregation? Themselves? We must first find out and determine who themselves are. Shall the congregation choose? Ask Xenophon. Perhaps hereafter I may quote you Greek. Too much in a hurry at present, english must suffice. Xenophon says that the ecclesia, always chooses the worst Men they can find, because none others will do their dirty work.[36] This wicked Motive is worse than Birth or Wealth. Here I want to quote Greek again. But the day before I received your Letter of June 27. I gave the Book to George Washington Adams[37] going to the Accadamy at Hingham. The Title is ΗΘΙΚΗ ΠΟΙΗΣΙΣ a Collection of Moral Sentences from all the most Ancien[t] Greek Poets.[38] In one of the oldest of them I read in greek that I cannot repeat, a couplet the Sense of which was

"Nobility in Men is worth as much as it is in Horses Asses or Rams: but the meanest blooded Puppy, in the World, if he gets a little money, is as good a man as the best of them." Yet Birth and Wealth together have prevailed over Virtue and Talents in all ages. The Many, will acknowledge no other "αριστοι". Your Experience of this Truth, will not much differ from that of your old Friend

JOHN ADAMS

Adams to Jefferson

Quincy July 12. 1813

DEAR SIR

I forgot in my last to remark a very trifling Inaccuracy in yours of June 27th. The Letter intercepted in Hichbournes Trunk[39] which was reported to glance at Mr. Dickenson, was not in 1776. It was in the month

36. This statement was attributed to Xenophon in JA's time, but it was later recognized as from the unknown author of *Treatise of the Old Oligarch.*

37. JA's grandson, the son of John Quincy Adams, who died in 1829. Bemis, *John Quincy Adams,* 276.

38. "Moralia ex Poetis," compiler unknown.

39. See above, Chap. 9, 337, n. 77.

of June 1775. Had it been June 1776, the English would not have printed it. The Nation had then too maturely reflected on the necessity of Independence, and was too ripe and too hot for a Proclamation of it. Neither Mr. Dickenson, nor any of his Friends would have dared to express the smallest resentment of it, out of their own gloomy circles. The Penns the Allens the Chews and the Willings, in other Words the Proprietary Gentlemen of Pensilvania, I mean those of them who had not ran away to the English, would have been silent. The Quakers, instead of producing my Letters and reading and recording them in their General Meeting, and holding me up to the detestation of their whole Society as the most odious of Men aiming, or at least having in contemplation the Possibility of Independence in any case whatsoever, would have concealed and dissimulated their hypocritical cant. The Pembertons, (even Israel,) the Drinkers, the Shoemakers and all the rest would have been silent. The Spirit would not have moved one of them to open his Lips.[40]

In June 1776 my Friends would not have put on long faces and lamented my imprudence. None of them would have wondered, as some of them did in 1775, that a Man of Forty Years of Age, and of considerable Experience in business, and in life should have been guilty of such an Indiscretion. Others would not have said "it was a premature declaration of Independence," and Joseph Reed, soon afterwards private Secretary of General Washington, and after that Governor of Pennsylvania, would not have said to me, as he did, "I look upon the Interception and publication of that Letter, as an Act of the Providence of God, to excite the Attention of the people to their real Situation, and to shew them, what they must come to."

You say, "it has been hoped, I would leave such explanations as would place every Saddle on its right Horse, and replace on the Shoulders of others, the burthens they shifted on yours."

Hoped! by whom? They know not what they hope! I have already "replaced on the Shoulders of Franklin, burthens he shifted on mine.["] [41]

40. The attitude in Pennsylvania toward revolution and independence changed considerably during 1775-76. By the beginning of 1776 opposition to the king and abrogation of the colonial charter were getting increasing support, although internal disputes complicated the problem of independence. Many Quakers were disowned by the meetings for joining the Revolutionary movement and as late as June 1776 that sect officially opposed war with England and abrogation of the charter. Charles J. Stille, *The Life and Times of John Dickinson, 1732-1808* (Philadelphia, 1891), 169 ff.; Isaac Sharpless, *A History of Quaker Government in Pennsylvania* (Philadelphia, 1900), II, Chap. VI.

41. Disagreement and ill feeling developed between JA and Franklin on three occasions in France: in 1778-79 when they were commissioners to negotiate a loan; in 1780 when there seemed some prospect of negotiating a peace treaty; and in 1782-83 during the negotiation of the peace treaty, when Franklin disapproved the desire of JA and John Jay to make a separate peace with France.

Shall I "replace on the shoulders of WASHINGTON the burthens that a bastard Bratt of a Scotch Pedlar placed on his Shoulders, and he shifted on mine? ["] [42]

How many Gauntletts am I destined to run? How many Martyrdoms must I suffer?

Be they more or less, I have enjoyed a happy Life, and I would not exchange Life, Character or Fortune with any of them.

There are few Men now living, if any, who know more of me than you do. Yet you know but little of the Life I have led, the hazards I have run, or the "light Afflictions for a moment" I have endured.

I will conclude this grave solemn Letter with a merry Story: but as true as it is diverting.

In my Youth I was acquainted with one of our New England Nobility, Representative, Counsellor, Colonel, Judge, John Chandler of Worcester, of whom I could tell you twenty, humerous and instructive Anecdotes. He was a good, tho a rapid and free Character. He had great Influence in our Legislature. Upon some Occasion there was a complaint against him As a Justice of the Peace in the County of Worcester. He arrived in Boston and the Counsell sent for him, and interrogated him and threatened him. When he came down from the Counsell Chamber, one of his Brother Representatives asked him, "what can the matter be?" "God damn them," said Chandler, "they talk of uncreating their Creator."

If you do not understand this, and wish an explanation, You shall have it. Not to say too much at once.

JOHN ADAMS

Adams to Jefferson

Quincy July 13th. 1813

DEAR SIR

Let me allude, to one circumstance more, in one of your Letters to me, before I touch upon the Subject of Religion in your Letters to Priestley.

The first time, that you and I differed in Opinion on any material

42. Alexander Hamilton, who during the war fever against France, 1798-99, inveigled Washington into demanding that Hamilton be appointed second in command; if President Adams did not comply, Washington would resign as commander-in-chief. Stephen G. Kurtz, *The Presidency of John Adams: The Collapse of Federalism, 1795-1800* (Philadelphia, 1957), 325-27; Charles, *Origins of American Party System,* 48-49.

Question; was after your Arrival from Europe; and that point was the french Revolution.

You was well persuaded in your own mind that the Nation would succeed in establishing a free Republican Government: I was as well persuaded, in mine, that a project of such a Government, over five and twenty millions people, when four and twenty millions and five hundred thousands of them could neither write nor read: was as unnatural irrational and impracticable; as it would be over the Elephants Lions Tigers Panthers Wolves and Bears in the Royal Menagerie, at Versailles. Napoleon has lately invented a Word, which perfectly expresses my Opinion at that time and ever since. He calls the Project Ideology. And John Randolph, tho he was 14 years ago, as wild an Enthusiast for Equality and Fraternity, as any of them; appears to be now a regenerated Proselite to Napoleons Opinion and mine, that it was all madness.

The Greeks in their Allegorical Style said that the two Ladies Αριστοκρατια ["Aristocracy"] and δημοκ[ρ]ατια ["democracy"], always in a quarrel, disturbed every neighbourhood with their brawls. It is a fine Observation of yours that "Whig and Torey belong to Natural History." Inequalities of Mind and Body are so established by God Almighty in his constitution of Human Nature that no Art or policy can ever plain them down to a Level. I have never read Reasoning more absurd, Sophistry more gross, in proof of the Athanasian Creed,[43] or Transubstantiation, than the subtle labours of Helvetius and Rousseau to demonstrate the natural Equality of Mankind. Jus cuique ["Justice for everyone"]; the golden rule; do as you would be done by; is all the Equality that can be supported or defended by reason, or reconciled to common Sense.

It is very true, as you justly observe, I can say nothing new on this or any other Subject of Government. But when La Fayette harrangued You and me, and John Quincy Adams, through a whole evening in your Hotel in the Cul de Sac, at Paris; and develloped the plans then in Operation to reform France: though I was as silent as you was, I then thought I could say something new to him. In plain Truth I was astonished at the Grossness of his Ignorance of Gover[n]ment and History, as I had been for Years before at that of Turgot, Rochefaucault, Condorcet and Franklin. This gross Ideology of them all, first suggested to me the thought and the inclination which I afterwards hinted to you in London, of writing Something upon Aristocracy. I was restrained for years by many fearful considerations. Who and what was I? A Man of no name or consideration in Europe. The manual Exercise of Writing was painful and distressing to

43. The belief in the Trinity, upheld by Athanasius, later Bishop of Alexandria, against Arius at the Council of Nicaea in 325, the first ecumenical council of the Christian Church.

me, almost like a blow, on the elbow or the knee; my Style was habitually negligent, unstudied, unpolished; I should make Enemies of all the French Patriots, the Dutch Patriots, the English Republicans, Dissenters, Reformers, call them what you will; and what came nearer home to my bosom than all the rest, I knew, I should give offence to many, if not all of my best Friends in America, and very probably destroy all the little Popularity I ever had, in a Country where Popularity had more Omnipotence than the British Parliament assumed. Where should I get the necessary Books? What Printer or Bookseller would undertake to print such hazardous Writings?

But when the French Assembly of Notables met, and I saw that Turgots "Government in one Centre and that Center the Nation" a Sentence as misterious or as contradictory as the Athanasian Creed, was about to take place; and when I saw that Shaises Rebellion was breaking out in Massachusetts, and when I saw that even my obscure Name was often quoted in France as an Advocate for simple Democracy; when I saw that the Sympathies in America had caught the French flame: I was determined to wash my own hands as clean as I could of all this foulness. I had then strong forebodings that I was sacrificing all the honours and Emoluments of this Life; and so it has happened: but not in so great a degree as I apprehended.

In Truth my "defence of the Constitutions" and "Discourses on Davila," [44] laid the foundation of that immense Unpopula[ri]ty, which fell like the Tower of Siloam upon me. Your steady defence of democratical Principles, and your invariable favourable Opinion of the french Revolution laid the foundation of your Unbounded Popularity.

Sic transit Gloria Mundi.

Now, I will forfeit my Life, if you can find one Sentence in my Defence of the Constitutions, or the Discourses on Davila, which by a fair construction, can favour the introduction of hereditary Monarchy or Aristocracy into America.

They were all written to support and strengthen the Constitutions of the United States.

The Woodcutter on Ida, though he was puzzled to find a Tree to chop, at first, I presume knew how to leave off, when he was weary; But I never know when to cease, when I begin to write to you

JOHN ADAMS

44. See above, Chap. 7.

Adams to Jefferson

Quincy July 15th 1813

Never mind it, my dear Sir, if I write four Letters to your one; your one is worth more than my four.

It is true that I can say and have said nothing new on the Subject of Government. Yet I did say in my Defence and in my Discourses on Davila, though in an uncouth Style, what was new to Lock, to Harrington, to Milton, to Hume to Montesquieu to Reauseau, to Turgot, Condorcet, to Rochefaucault, to Price to Franklin and to yourself; and at that time to almost all Europe and America. I can prove all this by indisputable Authorities and documents. Writings on Government had been not only neglected, but discountenanced and discouraged, through out all Europe, from the Restoration of Charles the Second in England, till the french Revolution commenced. The English Commonwealth, the Fate of Charles 1st, and the military despotism of Cromwell had sickened Mankind with disquisitions on Government to such a degree, that there was scarcely a Man in Europe who had looked into the Subject. David Hume had made himself, so fashionable with the Aid of the Court and Clergy, A theist as they call'd him, and by his elegant Lies against the Republicans and gaudy daubings of the Courtiers, that he had nearly laughed into contempt Rapin Sydney and even Lock. It was ridiculous and even criminal in almost all Europe to speak of Constitutions, or Writers upon the Principles or the Fabricks of them. In this state of Things my poor, unprotected, un-patronised Books appeared; and met with a Fate, not quite so cruel as I had anticipated. They were At last how[ev]er overborne by Misrepresen-tations and will perish in Obscurity, though they have been translated into German as well as french. The three Emperors of Europe, the Prince Regents, and all the ruling Powers would no more countenanc[e] or tolerate such Writings, than the Pope, the Emperor of Haiti, Ben. Austin or Tom Paine.

The Nations of Europe, appeared to me, when I was among them, from the begining of 1778, to 1785 i.e. to the commencement of the Troubles in France, to be advancing by slow but sure Steps towards an Amelioration of the condition of Man, in Religion and Government, in Liberty, Equal-ity, Fraternity Knowledge Civilization and Humanity. The French Revo-lution I dreaded; because I was sure it would, not only arrest the progress of Improvement, but give it a retrograde course, for at least a Century, if not many Centuries. The French Patriots Appeared to me like young

Schollars from a Colledge or Sailors flushed with recent pay or prize Money, mounted on wild Horses, lashing and speerring, till they would kill the Horses and break their own Necks.

Let me now ask you, very seriously my Friend, Where are now in 1813, the Perfection and perfectability of human Nature? Where is now, the progress of the human Mind? Where is the Amelioration of Society? Where the Augmentations of human Comforts? Where the diminutions of human Pains and Miseries? I know not whether the last day of Dr. Young can exhibit; to a Mind unstaid by Phylosophy and Religion, for I hold there can be no Philosophy without Religion; more terrors than the present State of the World.

When? Where? and how? is the present Chaos to be arranged into Order?

There is not, there cannot be, a greater Abuse of Words than to call the Writings of Calender, Paine, Austin and Lowell [45] or the Speeches of Ned. Livingston and John Randolph, Public Discussions. The Ravings and Rantings of Bedlam, merit the Character as well; and yet Joel Barlow [46] was about to record Tom Paine as the great Author of the American Revolution! If he was; I desire that my name may be blotted out forever, from its Records.

You and I ought not to die, before We have explained ourselves to each other.

I shall come to the Subject of Religion, by and by. Your Friend

JOHN ADAMS

I have been looking for some time for a space in my good Husbands Letters to add the regards of an old Friend, which are still cherished and preserved through all the changes and v[ic]issitudes which have taken place since we first became acquainted, and will I trust remain as long as

A ADAMS

45. John Lowell's *The Antigallican; or The Lover of His Own Country* (Philadelphia, 1797), includes "extracts from letters written during the late war by a person [John Adams] in a high official station abroad."

46. Barlow, one of the original "Hartford Wits," developed from a Federalist into a liberal democrat and was made a citizen of France. His *Advice to the Privileged Orders* (London, 1792) presents the theory of the responsibility of the state. After living abroad for more than a decade, he returned to the United States in 1805. He worked on a history of the United States for TJ, but it was never completed.

Adams to Jefferson

Quincy July 16. 1813

DEAR SIR

Your Letters to Priestley, have encreased my Grief if that were possible, for the loss of Rush. Had he lived, I would have stimulated him to insist on your promise to him to write him on the Subject of Religion. Your Plan, I admire.

In your Letter to Priestley of March 21. 1801, dated at Washington you call "The Christian Philosophy, the most sublime and benevolent, but the most perverted System that ever shone on Man." [47] That it is the most sublime and benevolent, I agree. But whether it has been more perverted than that of Mosse, of Confucius, of Zoroaster, of Sanchoniathan of Numa, of Mahomet of the Druids, of the Hindoos etc. etc. etc. I cannot as yet determine; because I am not sufficiently acquainted with those Systems or the History of their Effects to form a decisive Opinion of the result of the Comparison.

In your Letter dated Washington April 9. 1803, You say "In consequence of some conversations with Dr. Rush in the Years 1798-99, I had promised some day to write him a Letter giving him my View of the Christian System. I have reflected often on it since, and even sketched the Outlines in my own mind. I should first take a general View of the moral doctrines of the most remarkable of the ancient Philosophers, of whose Ethicks We have sufficient information to make an estimate; say of Pythagoras, Epicurus, Epictetus Socrates, Cicero, Seneca, Antoninus. I should do justice to the branches of Morality they have treated well, but point out the importance of those in which they are deficient. I should then take a view of the Deism and Ethicks of the Jews, and shew in what a degraded State they were, and the necessity they presented of a reformation. I should proceed to a view of the Life, Character, and doctrines of Jesus, who sensible of the incorrectness of their Ideas of the Deity, and of morality, and endeavoured to bring them to the Principles of a pure Deism, and juster Notions of the Attributes of God; to reform their moral doctrines to the Standard of reason, justice and Philanthropy and to inculcate the belief of a future State. This View would purposely omit the question of his Divinity, and even of his Inspiration. To do him Justice, it would be necessary to remark the disadvantages his doctrines have to encounter, not having been committed to Writing by himself, but by the

47. Ford, VIII, 21-22.

most unlettered of Men, by memory, long after they had heard them from him, when much was forgotten, much misunderstood, and presented in very paradoxical Shapes. Yet such are the fragments remaining, as to show a master workman, and that his System of Morality was the most benevolent and sublime, probably that has been ever taught, and more perfect than those of any of the ancient Philosophers. His Character and Doctrines, have received still greater injury from those who pretend to be his special Disciples, and who have disfigured and sophisticated his Actions and precepts from views of personal interest, so as to induce the unthinking part of Mankind, to throw off the whole System in disgust, and to pass sentence, as an Impostor, on the most innocent, the most benevolent, the most eloquent and sublime Character, that ever has been exhibited to Man. This is the Outline."! [48]

"Sancte Socrate! Ora pro nobis ["Holy Socrates! Pray for us"]."! Erasmus. Priestley in his Letter to Lindssey inclosing a Copy of your letter to him says "He is generally considered as an Unbeliever: if so, however, he cannot be far from Us, and I hope in the Way to be not only almost, but altogether what We are. He now attends publick worship very regularly, and his moral Conduct was never impeached."

Now, I see not, but you are as good a Christian as Priestley and Lindsey. Piety and Morality were the End and Object of the Christian System according to them, and according to You. They believed in the Resurrection of Jesus, in his Miracles, and in his inspiration: but what inspiration? Not all that is recorded in the New Testament, nor the old. They have not yet told Us, how much they believe, nor how much, they doubt or disbelieve. They have not told Us, how much Allegory how much Parable, they find, nor how they explain them all, in the old Testament or the new.

John Quincy Adams, has written for Years, to his two Sons, Boys of 10 and 12, a Series of Letters, in which he pursues a plan more extensive than yours, but agreeing in most of the essential points. I wish these Letters could be preserved in the Bosoms of his Boys: but Women and Priests will get them: and I expect, if he makes a peace he will be obliged to retire like a Jay [49] to study Prophecies to the End of his Life.

I have more to say, upon this Subject of Religion.

JOHN ADAMS

48. *Ibid.*, 224-25.
49. After his retirement from public life, following his governorship of New York, 1795-1800, John Jay became increasingly interested in religious and church activities and became president of the American Bible Society in 1821. Samuel F. Bemis, "Jay, John," *DAB*, X, 9.

Adams to Jefferson

Quincy. July 18th. 1813

DEAR SIR

I have more to say, on Religion. For more than sixty Years I have been attentive to this great Subject. Controversies, between Calvinists and Arminians, Trinitarians and Uniterians, Deists and Christians, Atheists and both, have attracted my Attention, whenever the singular Life I have lead would admit, to all these questions. The History of this little Village of Quincy, if it were worth recording would explain to you, how this happened. I think, I can now say I have read away Bigotry, if not Enthusiasm.

What does Priestly mean, by an Unbeliever? When he applies it to you? How much did he "unbelieve," himself? Gibbon had him right, when he denominated his Creed, "Scanty." We are to understand, no doubt, that he believed The Resurrection of Jesus, some of his Miracles. His Inspiration, but in what degree? He did not believe in the Inspiration of the Writings that contain his History. Yet he believed in the Apocalyptic Beast, and he believed as much as he pleased in the Writings of Daniel and John. This great, excellent and extraordinary Man, whom I sincerely loved esteemed and respected, was really a Phenomenon; a Comet in the System, like Voltaire Bolingbroke and Hume. Had Bolingbroke or Voltaire taken him in hand, what would they have made of him and his Creed?

I do not believe you have read much of Priestleys "Corruptions of Christianity." His History of early Opinions of Jesus Christ. His Predestination, his No Soul System or his Controversy with Horseley.[50]

I have been a diligent Student for many Years in Books whose Titles you have never seen. In Priestleys and Lindsay Writings; in Farmer, Cappe, in Tuckers or Edwards Searches, Light of Nature pursued; in Edwards and Hopkins, and lately in Ezra Styles Ely; his reverend and learned Panegyrists and his elegant and spirited Opponents. I am not wholly uninformed of the Controversies in Germany and the learned Researches of Universities and Professors; in which the Sanctity of the Bible and the

50. Priestley's best known theological work was *History of the Corruptions of Christianity* (London, 1782). His four-volume *History of Early Opinions Concerning Jesus Christ* (London, 1786), rejecting the doctrine of the infallibility of Christ, "has brought me more antagonists," he wrote, "and I now write a pamphlet annually in defence of the Unitarian doctrine against all my opponents." *Memoirs of the Rev. Joseph Priestley to the Year 1795.* Written by Himself with a Continuation, to the Time of His Decease, by His Son, Joseph Priestley (Reprinted from the American edn.; London, 1809), 88.

Inspiration of its Authors are taken for granted or waived; or admitted, or not denied. I have also read Condorcets Progress of the human mind.

Now, what is all this to you? No more, than if I should tell you that I read Dr. Clark and Dr. Waterland and Emlyn, and Lelands View or Review of the Deistical Writers more than fifty Years ago, which is a litteral Truth.

I blame you not for reading Euclid and Newton, Thucidides and Theocritus: for I believe you will find as much entertainment and Instruction in them as I have found, in my Theological and Ecclesiastical Instructors: Or even as I have found in a profound Investigation of the Life Writings and Doctrines of Erastus, whose Disciples were Milton, Harrington, Selden, St. John, the Chief Justice, Father of Bolingbroke, and others the choicest Spirits of their Age: or in La Harpes History of the Philosophy of the 18th Century, or in Van der Kemps vast Map of the Causes of the Revolutionary Spirit, in the same and preceeding Centuries. These Things are to me, at present, the Marbles and Nine Pins of old Age: I will not say the Beads and Prayer Books.

I Agree with you, as far as you go. Most cordially and I think solidly. How much farther I go, how much more I believe than You, I may explain in a future Letter.

Thus much I will say at present, I have found so many difficulties, that I am not astonished at your stopping where you are. And so far from sentencing you to Perdition, I hope soon to meet you in another Country.

JOHN ADAMS

Adams to Jefferson

Quincy, July 22, 1813

DEAR SIR

Dr. Priestley, in a letter to Mr. Lindsay Northumberland Nov. 4. 1803 says

"As you were pleased with my comparison of Socrates and Jesus, I have begun to carry the same comparison to all the heathen Moralists, and I have all the books that I want for the purpose, except Simplicius and Arrian on Epictetus, and them I hope to get from a Library in Philadelphia: lest however I should fail there, I wish you or Mr. Belsham would procure and send them from London. While I am capable of any thing I can not be idle, and I do not know that I can do any thing better. This too is an Undertaking that Mr. Jefferson recommends to me."

In another Letter dated Northumberland Jan. 16. 1804 Dr. Priestley says to Mr. Lindsey "I have now finished and transcribed for the Press, my comparison of the Grecian Philosophers, with those of Revelation, and with more ease and more to my own Satisfaction, than I expected. They who liked my pamphlet entitled "Socrates and Jesus compared," will not, I flatter myself dislike this work. It has the same Object and completes the Scheme. It has increased my own sense of the unspeakable value of Revelation, and must, I think, that of every person, who will give due attention to the Subject". I have now given You all that relates to yourself in Priestleys Letters.

This was possibly and not improbably, the last Letter this great, this learned, indefatigable, most excellent and extraordinary Man, ever wrote: for on the fourth of February 1804, he was released from his labours and Sufferings. Peace, Rest, Joy and Glory to his Soul! For I believe he had one; and one of the greatest.

I regret; oh how, I lament, that he did not live, to publish this Work! It must exist in Manuscript. Cooper must know Something of it. Can you learn from him where it is, and get it printed? I hope you will still perform your promise to Dr. Rush.

If Priestley had lived, I should certainly have corresponded with him. His Friend Cooper, who unfortunately for him and me, and you, had as fatal an influence over him as Hamilton had over Washington; and whose rash hot head led Priestley into all his Misfortunes and most [of] his Errors in Conduct, could not have prevented explanations between Priestley and me.

I should propose to him a thousand, a million Questions. And no M[an] was more capable or better disposed to answer them candidly than Dr. Priestley. Scarcely any thing that has happened to me, in my curious Life has made a deeper Impression upon me, than that such a learned ingenious scientific and talented Madcap as Cooper, could have had influence enough to make Priestley my Enemy.

I will not yet, communicate to you, more than a Specimen, of the Questions I would have asked Priestley.

One is, learned and scientific Sir! You have written largely about matter and Spirit, and have concluded, there is no human Soul. Will you please to inform me, what matter is? and what Spirit is? Unless We know the meaning of Words, We cannot reason in, or about Words. I shall never send you all my Questions that I would put to Priestley; because they are innumerable: but I may hereafter send you two or three. I am in perfect Charity Your old Friend

JOHN ADAMS

Adams to Jefferson

Quincy Aug. 9 13.

I believe I told you in my last, that I had given you all in Lindseys Memoirs, that interested you. But I was mistaken. In Priestleys Letter to Lindsey Decr. 19. 1803, I find this Paragraph

"With the Work I am now composing I go on much faster and better than I expected; so that in two or three months, if my health continue as it now is, I hope to have it ready for the Press; though I shall hardly proceed to print it, till We have dispatched the Notes. It is upon the same plan with that of Socrates and Jesus compared, considering all the more distinguished of the Grecian Sects of Philosophy, till the establishment of Christianity in the Roman Empire. If you liked that Pamphlet, I flatter myself you will like this. I hope it is calculated to show, in a peculiarly striking Light, the great Advantage of Revelation, and that it will make an impression on candid Unbelievers, if they will read. But I find few that will trouble themselves to read any thing, on the Subject; which considering the great magnitude and interesting nature of the Subject, is a proof of a very improper State of mind unworthy of a rational Being."

I send you this extract for several reasons. 1st. because you sett him upon this Work. 2dly. because I wish you to endeavour to bring it to light and get it printed. 3ly. Because I wish it may stimulate You, to pursue Your own plan which you promised to Dr. Rush.[51] I have not seen any Work which expressly compares the Morality of the old Testament with that of the New in all their Branches: nor either with that of the ancient Philosop[h]ers. Comparisons with the Chinese, the East Indians, the Affricans, the West Indians etc would be more difficult; with more ancient Nations, impossible. The Documents are destroyed.

JOHN ADAMS

51. TJ's Syllabus of the Doctrine of Jesus. See TJ to JA, Aug. 22, 1813, below, 369, n. 58.

Adams to Jefferson

Quincy   August   [14?]   1813

κριοὺς μὲν καὶ ὄνους διζήμεθα, Κύρνε, καί ἵππους
εὐγενέας· καί τις βούλεται ἐξ ἀγαθῶν
κτήσασθαι. γῆμαι δὲ κακὴν κακοῦ οὐ μελεδαίνει
ἐσθλὸς ἀνήρ, ἤν οἱ χρήματα πολλὰ διδῶ.

Behold my translation
"My Friend Curnis, When We want to purchace, Horses, Asses or
Rams, We inquire for the Wellborn. And every one wishes to procure,
from the good Breeds. A good Man, does not care to marry a Shrew, the
Daughter of a Shrew; unless They give him, a great deal of Money with
her."
What think you, of my translation? Compare it with that of Grotius,
and tell me, which, is nearest to the Original in letter and in Spirit.
Grotius renders it

Nobilitas asinis et equis simul, arietibusque
Dat pretium: nec de semine degeneri
Admissura placet. sed pravæ e Sanguine pravo,
Si dos sit, præsto est optima conditio.

This flower of Greek Poetry, is extracted, from the

ΘΕΟΓΝΙΔΟΣ ΜΕΓΑΡΕΩΣ ΠΑΡΑΙΝΕΣΕΙΣ [52]

Theognis lived five hundred and forty four Years before Jesus Christ.
Has Science or Morals, or Philosophy or Criticism or Christianity, advanced or improved, or enlightened Mankind upon this Subject, and
shewn them, that the Idea of the "Well born" is a prejudice, a Phantasm,
a Point no point, a Gape Fly away, a dream? I say it is the Ordonance of
God Almighty, in the Constitution of human nature, and wrought into the
Fabrick of the Universe. Philosophers and Politicians, may nibble and
quibble, but they never will get rid of it. Their only resource is, to controul it. Wealth is another Monster to be subdued. Hercules could not
subdue both or either. To subdue them by regular approaches by a regular
Seige, and strong fortifications, was my Object in writing on Aristocracy,
as I proposed to you in Grovenor Square.
If you deny any one of these Positions, I will prove them to demonstration by Examples drawn from your own Virginia, and from every other

52. "Works of Theognis."

State in the Union, and from the History of every Nation civilized and savage, from all We know of the time of the Creation of the World.

Whence is the derivation of the Words Generous, Generously, Generosity etc? Johnson says "Generous. a. Generosus Latin, Not of mean Birth; of good extraction. Noble of mind. Magnanimous, Open of Heart Liberal, munificent. Strong, vigorous." And he might have added, Couragious, heroic, patriotic.

Littleton happens to be at hand. Generosus— εὐγενὴς, γενναῖος Nobilis, ex præclaro genere ortus: qui a genere non deflectit.
Born of a noble Race, a Gentleman born. See his Examples.[53]

What is the Origin of the Word Gentleman?

It would be a curious critical Speculation for a learned Idler to pursue this Idea, through all Languages.

We may call this Sentiment a prejudice, because We can give what names We please, to such things as We please; but in my Opinion it is a part of the Natural History of Man: and Politicians and Philosophers may as well project to make The Animal live with out Bones or Blood, as Society can pretend to establish, a free Government without Attention to it.

Quincy August 16. 1813. I can proceed no farther, with this Letter, as I intended.

Your Friend, my only Daughter,[54] expired, Yesterday Morning in the Arms of Her Husband her Son, her Daughter, her Father and Mother, her Husbands two Sisters and two of her Nieces, in the 49th. Year of her Age, 46 of which She was the healthiest and firmest of Us all: Since which, She has been a monument to Suffering and to Patience.

JOHN ADAMS

Jefferson to Abigail Adams

Monticello Aug. 22.13.

DEAR MADAM

A kind note at the foot of Mr. Adams's letter of July 15. reminds me of the duty of saluting you with friendship and respect; a duty long suspended by the unremitting labors of public engagement, and which ought to have been sooner revived, since I am become proprietor of my own time. And yet so it is, that in no course of life have I been ever more closely pressed by business than in the present. Much of this proceeds

53. Adam Littleton, *A Latin Dictionary in Four Parts* (London, 1703).
54. Mrs. William Stephens (Abigail Adams) Smith.

from my own affairs; much from the calls of others; leaving little time for indulgence in my greatest of all amusements, reading. Doctr. Franklin used to say that when he was young, and had time to read, he had not books; and now when he had become old and had books, he had no time. Perhaps it is that, when habit has strengthed our sense of duties, they leave no time for other things; but when young, we neglect them, and this gives us time for any thing. However I will now take time to ask you how you do, how you have done? and to express the interest I take in whatever affects your happiness. I have been concerned to learn that, at one time you suffered much and long from rheumatism, and I can sympathise with you the more feelingly, as I have had more of it myself latterly than at any former period; and can form a truer idea of what it is in it's higher degrees. Excepting for this, I have enjoyed general health; for I do not consider as a want of health the gradual decline and increasing debility which are the natural diathesis of age. This last comes on me fast. I am not able to walk much; tho' I still ride without fatigue; and take long and frequent journies to a distant possession.[55]

I have compared notes with Mr. Adams on the score of progeny, and find I am ahead of him, and think I am in a fair way to keep so. I have 10½ grandchildren, and 2¾ great-grand-children; and these fractions will ere long become units. I was glad to learn from Mr. Adams that you have a grandson far enough advanced in age and acquirements to be reading Greek. These young scions give us comfortable cares, when we cease to care about ourselves. Under all circumstances of health or sickness, of blessing or affliction, I tender you assurances of my sincere affection and respect; and my prayers that the hand of time and of providence may press lightly on you, till your own wishes shall withdraw you from all mortal feeling.

TH: JEFFERSON

Jefferson to Adams

Monticello Aug. 22. 13.

DEAR SIR

Since my letter of June 27. I am in your debt for many; all of which I have read with infinite delight. They open a wide field for reflection; and offer subjects enough to occupy the mind and the pen indefinitely. I must follow the good example you have set; and when I have not time to take up every subject, take up a single one.

Your approbation of my outline to Dr. Priestly is a great gratification

55. Poplar Forest, in Bedford County, Va.

to me; and I very much suspect that if thinking men would have the courage to think for themselves, and to speak what they think, it would be found they do not differ in religious opinions, as much as is supposed. I remember to have heard Dr. Priestly say that if all England would candidly examine themselves, and confess, they would find that Unitarianism was really the religion of all: and I observe a bill is now depending in parliament for the relief of Anti-Trinitarians. It is too late in the day for men of sincerity to pretend they believe in the Platonic mysticisms that three are one, and one is three; and yet the one is not three, and the three are not one: to divide mankind by a single letter into ὁμοουσians and ὁμοιουσians ["consubstantialists and like-substantialists"]. But this constitutes the craft, the power and the profit of the priests. Sweep away their gossamer fabrics of factitious religion, and they would catch no more flies. We should all then, like the quakers, live without an order of priests, moralise for ourselves, follow the oracle of conscience, and say nothing about what no man can understand, nor therefore believe; for I suppose belief to be the assent of the mind to an intelligible proposition.

It is with great pleasure I can inform you that Priestly finished the comparative view of the doctrines of the Philosophers of antiquity, and of Jesus, before his death; and that it was printed soon after; [56] and, with still greater pleasure, that I can have a copy of his work forwarded from Philadelphia, by a correspondent there, and presented for your acceptance, by the same mail which carries you this, or very soon after. The branch of the work which the title announces is executed with learning and candor, as was every thing Priestly wrote: but perhaps a little hastily; for he felt himself pressed by the hand of death. The Abbé Batteux had in fact laid the foundation of this part, in his Causes premieres; with which he has given us the originals of Ocellus, and Timaeus, who first committed the doctrines of Pythagoras to writing; [57] and Enfield, to whom the Doctor refers, had done it more copiously. But he has omitted the important branch, which in your letter of Aug. 9. you say you have never seen executed, a comparison of the morality of the old testament with that of the new. And yet no two things were ever more unlike. I ought not to have asked him to give it. He dared not. He would have been eaten alive by his intolerant brethren, the Cannibal priests. And yet this was really the most interesting branch of the work.

Very soon after my letter to Doctr. Priestley, the subject being still in

56. *The Doctrines of Heathen Philosophy Compared with Those of Revelation* (Northumberland, Pa., 1804).

57. The works attributed to Ocellus and Timaeus in the eighteenth century are now thought by classical scholars to be spurious and were suspect by the mid-nineteenth century. Anthon's *Classical Dictionary* (N. Y., 1867); *Oxford Classical Dictionary* (Oxford, 1949).

my mind, I had leisure, during an abstraction from business, for a day or two while on the road, to think a little more on it, and to sketch more fully than I had done to him, a Syllabus of the matter which I thought should enter into the work. I wrote it to Dr. Rush; and there ended all my labor on the subject; himself and Dr. Priestley being the only depositories of my secret.[58] The fate of my letter to Priestley, after his death, was a warning to me on that of Dr. Rush; and at my request his family was so kind as to quiet me by returning my original letter and Syllabus. By this you will be sensible how much interest I take in keeping myself clear of religious disputes before the public, and especially of seeing my Syllabus disembowelled by the Aruspices of the modern Paganism. Yet I enclose it *to you* with entire confidence, free to be perused by yourself and Mrs. Adams, but by no one else; and to be returned to me.

You are right in supposing, in one of yours, that I had not read much of Priestley's Predestination, his No-soul system, or his controversy with Horsley. But I have read his Corruptions of Christianity, and Early opinions of Jesus, over and over again; and I rest on them, and on Middleton's writings, especially his letters from Rome, and to Waterland, as the basis of my own faith. These writings have never been answered, nor can be answered, by quoting historical proofs, as they have done. For these facts therefore I cling to their learning, so much superior to my own.

I now fly off in a tangent to another subject. Marshal, in the 1st. vol. of his history, C. 3, pa. 180. ascribes the petition to the king of 1774. (1 Journ. Congr. 67.) to the pen of Richard Henry Lee.[59] I think myself certain it was not written by him, as well from what I recollect to have heard, as from the internal evidence of style. His was loose, vague, frothy, rhetorical. He was a poorer writer than his brother Arthur; and Arthur's standing may be seen in his Monitor's letters, to ensure the sale of which they took the precaution of tacking to them a new edition of the Farmer's

58. During the evenings of 1798-99 in Philadelphia TJ and Dr. Rush sometimes discussed the Christian religion, and TJ promised to set forth his views, one day or other. In August 1800 Rush reminded TJ of his promise, but the pressure of public duties interfered. Then, in April 1803 during a short visit to Monticello, TJ received a copy of Dr. Priestley's *Socrates and Jesus Compared* from the author. This moved TJ that same month to write his Syllabus of an Estimate of the Merit of the Doctrines of Jesus, Compared with Those of Others, which he sent in confidence to Rush. These views, TJ stated, "are the result of a life of inquiry and reflection, and very different from that anti-Christian system imputed to me by those who know nothing of my opinions." Rush to TJ, Aug. 22, 1800, May 5, 1803, Butterfield, ed., *Letters of Rush*, II, 820, 864n.; TJ to Priestley, April 9, 1803, and TJ to Rush, April 21, 1803, and "Syllabus," Ford, VIII, 223-28.

59. John Marshall, *The Life of George Washington*, 5 vols. (Philadelphia, 1804-7). John Dickinson, citing the Journals of Congress to prove his authorship, so informed Marshall, and his claim is generally accepted. Stille, *Dickinson*, 143n.; Edmund C. Burnett, *The Continental Congress* (N. Y., 1941), 51.

letters; like Mezentius who 'mortua jungebat corpora vivis ["bound dead bodies to the living"].' You were of the committee, and can tell me who wrote this petition: and who wrote the Address to the inhabitants of the colonies ib. 45.[60]

Of the papers of July 1775 I recollect well that Mr. Dickinson drew the petition to the king, ib. 149.[61] I think Robt. R. Livingston drew the address to the Inhabitants of Great Britain. ib. 152. Am I right in this? [62] And who drew the Address to the people of Ireland, ib. 180.? [63] On these questions, I ask of your memory to help mine. Ever and affectionately your's.

TH: JEFFERSON

P.S. Miss Lomax, daughter of one of our friends of 1776, lately dead, now here on a visit, asks permission to consign to you a memorial of the family respect for you: not done with the pencil, the burine or the chissel, but with the only instrument habitual to her, the humble scissars. You will find it inclosed.

Adams to Jefferson

Quincy Sept. 2. 1813

Οὐδὲ γυνὴ κακοῦ ανδρὸς ἀναίνεται εἶναι ἄκοιτις
Πλουσίου, ἀλλ᾽ ἀφνεὸν βούλεται ἀντ᾽ ἀγαθοῦ.
Χρήματα γὰρ τιμῶσι· καὶ εκ κακοῦ ἐσθλὸς ἔγημε
Καὶ κακὸς ἐξ ἀγαθοῦ· πλοῦτος ἔμιξ γένος.

Grotius renders this into latin, thus.

> Nec dedignatur ditemque malumque maritum
> femina: divitiæ præ probitate placent.
> In pretio pretium est: genus et prænobile, vili,
> Obscurum claro, miscet avaritia.

I should render the Greek into English thus.

60. Written by Richard Henry Lee. Worthington C. Ford, ed., *Journals of the Continental Congress, 1774-1789* (Washington, 1904-37), I, 62*n.*, 90*n.*
61. This was Dickinson's last opportunity to try reconciliation. TJ, "Autobiography," Ford, I, 17; Burnett, *Continental Congress*, 85.
62. Livingston's authorship cannot be proved, although he was a member of the committee to draft the address, which JA thought was puerile, juvenile, and petty. Ford, ed., *Journals of Continental Congress*, II, 80; Lynn Montross, *The Reluctant Rebels* (N. Y., 1950), 82.
63. This address was prepared by a committee composed of James Duane, William Livingston, John Adams, and Samuel Adams. Ford, ed., *Journals of Continental Congress*, II, 80.

Nor does a Woman disdain to be the Wife of a bad rich Man. But She prefers a Man of Property before a good Man. For Riches are honoured; and a good Man marries from a bad Family, and a bad Man from a good one. Wealth mingles all races.

Now please to tell me, whether my translation has not hit the Sense of Theognis, as exactly as that of Grotius.

Tell me also, whether Poet, Orator, Historian or Philosopher can paint the Picture of every City, County or State in our pure, uncorrupted, un-adulterated, uncontaminated federal Republick; or in France England Holland, and all the rest of Chri[s]tendom or Mahometanism, in more precise Lines or Colures.?

Another translation of the whole Passage of Theognis.

> Arietes quidem et Asinos quaerimus, Cyrne, et Equos
> Generosos, et quisque vult ex bonis,:
> Admittere: ducero autem malam (filiam) mali non renuit
> Generosus Vir, Si ei pecunias multas dederit.
> Nulla (femina) mali viri recusat esse Uxor
> Divitis; Sed divitem vult pro bono
> Opes quidem æstimant, et ex malo (natam) bonus ducet
> Et malus ex bono ortam. Divitiæ mixent genus.[64]

Now, my Friend, who are the ἄριστοι ["aristocrats"]? Philosophy may Answer "The Wise and Good." But the World, Mankind, have by their practice always answered, "the rich the beautiful and well born." And Philosophers themselves in marrying their Children prefer the rich the handsome and the well descended to the wise and good.

What chance have Talents and Virtues in competition, with Wealth and Birth? and Beauty?

> Haud facile emergunt, quorum Virtutibus obstant [i.e., obstat]
> Res Angusta Domi.

> > One truth is clear,; by all the World confess'd
> > Slow rises worth, by Poverty oppress'd.

The five Pillars of Aristocracy, are Beauty Wealth, Birth, Genius and Virtues. Any one of the three first, can at any time over bear any one or both of the two last.

Let me ask again, what a Wave of publick Opinion, in favour of Birth has been spread over the Globe, by Abraham, by Hercules, by Mahomet, by Guelphs, Ghibellines, Bourbons, and a miserable Scottish Chief Steuart? By Zingis by, by, by, a million others? And what a Wave will be spread

64. JA earlier quoted the first four lines in his letter of Aug. [14?], 1813; see above, 365. For TJ's quotation from Theognis, see his letter of Oct. 28, 1813, below, 388, 390.

by Napoleon and by Washington? Their remotest Cousins will be sought and will be proud, and will avail themselves of their descent. Call this Principle, Prejudice, Folly Ignorance, Baseness, Slavery, Stupidity, Adulation, Superstition or what you will. I will not contradict you. But the Fact, in natural, moral, political and domestic History I cannot deny or dispute or question.

And is this great Fact in the natural History of Man? This unalterable Principle of Morals, Philosophy, Policy domestic felicity, and dayly Experience from the Creation; to be overlooked, forgotten neglected, or hypocritically waived out of Sight; by a Legislator? By a professed Writer upon civil Government, and upon Constitutions of civil Government?

Thus far I had written, when your favour of Aug. 22 was laid on my table, from the Post Office. I can only say at present that I can pursue this idle Speculation no farther, at least till I have replied to this fresh proof of your friendship and Confidence. Mrs. A. joins in cordial Thanks, with

JOHN ADAMS

You may laugh at the introduction of Beauty, among the Pillars of Aristocracy. But Madame Barry says Le veritable Royauté est la B[e]autee ["true royalty is beauty"], and there is not a more certain Truth. Beauty, Grace, Figure, Attitude, Movement, have in innumerable Instances prevailed over Wealth, Birth, Talents Virtues and every thing else, in Men of the highest rank, greatest Power, and sometimes, the most exalted Genius, greatest Fame, and highest Merit.

Adams to Jefferson

Quincy Sept. 14. 1813

DEAR SIR

I owe you a thousand thanks for your favour of Aug. 22 and its Enclosures, and for Dr. Priestley's "Doctrines of heathen Philosophy compared with those of Revelation". Your Letter to Dr. Rush, and the Syllabus, I return inclosed with this, according to your Injunction; though with great reluctance. May I beg a copy of both? They will do you no harm: me and others much good. I hope you will pursue your plan, for I am confident you will produce a Work much more valuable than Priestleys; tho' that is curious and considering the expiring Powers with which it was written, admirable.

The Bill in Parliament for the relief of Antitrinitarians [65] is a great Event; and will form an Epoch in Ecclesiastical History. The Motion was made by my Friend [William] Smith of Clapham, a Friend of the Belshams. I should be very happy to hear, that the Bill is passed.

The human Understanding is a revelation from its Maker which can never be disputed or doubted. There can be no Scepticism, Pyrrhonism or Incredulity or Infidelity here. No Prophecies, no Miracles are necessary to prove this celestial communication. This revelation has made it certain that two and one make three; and that one is not three; nor can three be one. We can never be so certain of any Prophecy, or the fullfillment of any Prophecy; or of any miracle, or the design of any miracle as We are, from the revelation of nature i.e. natures God that two and two are equal to four. Miracles or Prophecies might frighten Us out of our Witts; might scare us to death; might induce Us to lie; to say that We believe that 2 and 2 make 5. But We should not believe it. We should know the contrary.

Had you and I been forty days with Moses on Mount Sinai and admitted to behold, the divine Shekinah, and there told that one was three and three, one: We might not have had courage to deny it, but We could not have believed it. The thunders and Lightenings and Earthqu[ak]es and the transcendant Splendors and Glories, might have overwhelmed Us with terror and Amazement: but We could not have believed the doctrine. We should be more likely to say in our hearts, whatever We might say with our Lips, This is Chance. There is no God! No Truth. This is all delusion, fiction and a lie: or it is all Chance. But what is Chance? It is motion; it is Action; it is Event; it is Phenomenon, without Cause. Chance is no cause att all. It is nothing. And Nothing has produced all this Pomp and Splendor; and Nothing may produce Our eternal damnation in the flames of Hell fire and Brimstone for what We know, as well as this tremendous Exhibition of Terror and Falshood.

God has infinite Wisdom, goodness and power. He created the Universe. His duration is eternal, a parte Ante, and a parte post. His presence is as extensive as Space. What is Space? an infinite, spherical Vaccuum. He created this Speck of Dirt and the human Species for his glory: and with the deliberate design of making, nine tenths of our Species miserable forever, for his glory. This is the doctrine of Christian Theologians in general: ten to one.

Now, my Friend, can Prophecies, or miracles convince You, or Me, that infinite Benevolence, Wisdom and Power, created and preserves, for

65. The act of 1813 placed Unitarians on an equal basis with other Dissenters by repeal of provisions in the Toleration Act of 1689 which had made denial of the Trinity illegal.

a time, innumerable millions to make them miserable, forever; for his own Glory? Wretch! What is his Glory? Is he ambitious? does he want promotion? Is he vain? tickled with Adulation? Exulting and tryumphing in his Power and the Sweetness of his Vengeance? Pardon me, my Maker, for these Aweful Questions. My Answer to them is always ready: I believe no such Things. My Adoration of the Author of the Universe is too profound and too sincere. The Love of God and his Creation; delight, Joy, Tryumph, Exultation in my own existence, 'tho but an Atom, a Molecule Organique, in the Universe; are my religion. Howl, Snarl, bite, Ye Calvinistick! Ye Athanasian Divines, if You will. Ye will say, I am no Christian: I say Ye are no Christians: and there the Account is ballanced. Yet I believe all the honest men among you, are Christians in my Sense of the Word.

When I was at Colledge I was a mighty Metaphis[ic]ian. At least I thought myself such; and such Men as Lock, Hemenway, and West thought me so too: for We were forever disputing, though in great good humour.

When I was sworn as an Attorney in 1758, in Boston, 'tho I lived in Braintree; I was in a low state of Health; thought in great danger of a Consumption; living on Milk, Vegetable Pudding and Water. Not an Atom of Meat or a drop of Spirit. My next Neighbour, my Cousin my Friend Dr. Savil was my Physician. He was anxious for me, and did not like to take upon himself the sole Responsability of my recovery. He invited me to a ride. I mounted my Horse and rode with him to Hingham, on a visit to Dr. Ezekiel Hersey, a Physician of great fame: who felt my pulse, looked in my Eyes, heard Savil describe my regimen and course of Medicine; and then pronoun[c]ed his Oracle "Persevere, and as sure as there is a God in Heaven you will recover." He was an everlasting Talker, and ran out, into History, Philosophy Metaphysicks, etc and frequently put questions to me, as if he wanted to sound me, and see if there was any thing in me, besides Hectic fever. I was young, and then very bashful; however saucy I may have sometimes been since. I gave him very modest and very diffident Answers. But when he got upon Metaphysicks, I seemed to feel a little bolder, and ventured into some thing like Argument with him. I drove him up, as I thought, into a Corner, from which he could not escape. Sir, it will follow from what you have now advanced, that the Universe, as distinct from God is both infinite and eternal. "Very true, said Dr. Hearsey: Your inference is just; the Consequence is inevitable; and I believe the Universe to be, both eternal and infinite." Here I was brought up! I was defeated. I was not prepared for this Answer. This was 55 Years ago.

When I was in England from 1785, to 1788 I may say, I was intimate with Dr. Price. I had much conversation with him at his own House, at my houses, and at the houses and Tables of many Friends. In some of our most unreserved Conversations, when We have been alone, he has repeatedly said to me "I am inclined to believe that the Universe, is eternal and infinite. It seems to me that an eternal and infinite Effect, must necessarily flow from an eternal and infinite Cause; and an infinite Wisdom Goodness and Power, that could have been induced to produce a Universe in time, must have produced it from eternity." "It seems to me, the Effect must flow from the Cause."

Now, my Friend Jefferson, suppose an eternal self existent Being existing from Eternity, possessed of infinite Wisdom, Goodness and Power, in absolute total Solitude, Six thousand Years ago, conceiving the benevolent project of creating a Universe! I have no more to say, at present.

It has been long, very long a settled opinion in my Mind that there is now, never will be, and never was but one being who can Understand the Universe. And that it is not only vain but wicked for insects to pretend to comprehend it.

JOHN ADAMS

Adams to Jefferson

Quincy Septr. 15. 1813

DEAR SIR

My last Sheet, would not admit an Observation that was material to my design.

Dr. Price was "inclined to think" that infinite Wisdom and Goodness, could not permit infinite Power, to be inactive, from Eternity: but that, an infinite and eternal Universe, must have necessarily flowed from these Attributes.

Plato's System was "Αγαθος ["good"]" was eternal, Self existent etc. His Ideas, his Word, his Reason, his Wisdom, his Goodness, or in one Word, his "Logos," was omnipotent and produced the Universe from all Eternity.

Now! As far as You and I can understand Hersey, Price and Plato, are they not of one Theory? of one mind? What is the difference? I own, an eternal Solitude of a Self existent Being infinitely wise, powerful and good, is to me, altogether incomprehensible, and incredible. I could as soon believe the Athanasian Creed.

You will ask me "What conclusion, I draw from all this?" I answer, I drop into myself, and acknowledge myself to be a Fool. No Mind, but one, can see through, the immeasurable System. It would be Presumption and Impiety in me to dogmatize, on such Subjects. My duties, in my little infinitessimal Circle I can understand and feel. The Duties of a Son, a Brother, a Father, a Neighbour, a Citizen, I can see and feel: But I trust the Ruler with his Skies.

Si quid novisti rectius, istis

Candidus imperti, si non, his Utere mecum.[66]

This World is a mixture of the Sublime and the beautiful, the base and contemptible, the whimsical and ridiculous, (According to our narrow Sense; and triffling Feelings). It is a Riddle and an Enigma. You need not be surprised then, if I should descen[d] from these Heights, to an egregious Trifle. But, first let me say. I asked you in a former Letter, how far advanced We were in the Science of Aristocracy, since Theognis's Stalions Jacks and Rams? Have not Chancellor Livingston and Major General Humphreys introduced an hereditary Aristocracy of Merino Sheep? How shall We get rid of this Aristocracy? It is intailed upon Us forever. And an Aristocracy of Land Jobbers and Stock jobbers, is equally and irremediably entailed upon Us, to endless generations.

Now for the Odd; the whimsical; the frivolous. I had scarcely sealed my last Letter to you, upon Theognis's doctrine of well born, Stallions, Jacks and Rams; when they brought me from the Post Office a Packett, without Post Mark, without Letter, without name date or place. Nicely sealed, was a printed Copy of Eighty or Ninety Pages in large full Octavo,[67] intitled

Section first

Aristocracy. I gravely composed my risible Muscles and read it through. It is, from beginning to End an Attack upon me by name for the doctrines of Aristocracy in my 3 Volumes of "Defence" etc. The Conclusion of the whole is that an Aristocracy of Bank Paper, is as bad as the Nobility of France or England. I, most assuredly will not controvert this point, with this man. Who he is, I cannot conjecture: The Honourable John Taylor of Virginia, of all men living or dead first Occurred to me.

Is it Oberon? Is it queen Mab, that reigns and sports with Us little Beings? I thought my Books as well as myself were forgotten. But behold! I am to become a great Man in my expiring moments. Theognis and Plato,

66. "If you know anything better than these maxims, candidly share them; if not, with me adopt these." Horace, *Epistulae*, 1. 6. 67.

67. John Taylor, *An Inquiry into the Principles and Policy of the Government of the United States* ... (Fredericksburg, Va., 1814), first conceived in 1794 as an answer to JA's *Defence of the Constitutions of the United States*. Taylor denied the existence of a "natural aristocracy" and maintained that democracy was endangered by consolidation and the creation of an aristocracy of "paper and patronage." Charles A. Beard, *Economic Origins of Jeffersonian Democracy* (N. Y., 1915), Chap. XI.

and Hersey, and Price and Jefferson and I, must go down to Posterity together; and I know not, upon the whole, where to wish for better company. I wish to add Vanderkemp, who has been here to see me, after an interruption of 24 Years. I could and ought to add many others but the Catalogue would be too long. I am, as ever,

JOHN ADAMS

P. S. Why is Plato associated with Theognis etc? Because no Man ever expressed so much terror of the Power of Birth. His Genius could invent no remedy or precaution against it; but a Community of Wives; a confusion of Families, a total extinction of all Relations of Father, Son and Brother. Did the French Revolutionists contrive much better, against the influence of Birth?

Abigail Adams to Jefferson

Quincy Sepbr 20th 1813

DEAR SIR

Your kind and Friendly Letter found me in great affliction for the loss of my dear and only daughter, Mrs. Smith.

She had been with me only three weeks having undertaken a journey from the State of N. York, desirious once more to see her parents, and to close her days under the paternal roof.

She was accompanied by her son and daughter, who made every exertion to get her here, and gratify which seemed the only remaining wish she had, so helpless and feeble a state as she was in. It is wonderfull how they accomplished it. Two years since, she had an opperation performed for a cancer in her breast. This she supported, with wonderfull fortitude, and we flatterd ourselves that the cure was effectual, but it proved otherways. It soon communicated itself through the whole mass of the Blood, and after severe sufferings, terminated her existance.

You sir, who have been called to seperations of a similar kind, can sympathize with your bereaved Friend. I have the consolation of knowing that the Life of my dear daughter was pure, her conduct in prosperity and adversity, exemplary, her patience and resignation becomeing her religion. You will pardon by [i.e., my] being so minute, the full Heart loves to pour out its sorrows, into the Bosom of sympathizing Friendship.

A lively only daughter of her Mother, lives to console me.

"who in her youth, has all that Age required"
"And with her prudence, all that youth admired"

You called upon me to talk of myself, and I have obeyed the summons from the assurrance you gave me, that you took an interest in what ever affected my happiness.

> "Greif has changed me since you saw me last,
> "And carefull hours, with times deformed hand"
> "hath written strange defections o'er my face"

But altho, time has changed the outward form, and political "Back wounding calumny" for a period interrupted the Friendly intercourse and harmony which subsisted, it is again renewed, purified from the dross.

With this assurance I beg leave to subscribe myself your Friend

ABIGAIL ADAMS

Adams to Jefferson

Quincy Septr. 22 1813

DEAR SIR

Considering all things, I admire Dr. Priestleys last Effort for which I am entirely indebted to you. But as I think it is extreamly imperfect, I beg of you to pursue the investigation, according to your promise to Dr. Rush, and according to your Syllabus. It may be presumptuous in me to denominate any Thing of Dr. Priestley imperfect: but I must avow, that among all the vast Exertions of his Genius, I have never found one, that is not imperfect; and this last is egregiously so. I will instance at present in one Article. I find no notice of Cleanthes: one of whose Sayings alone ought to have commanded his Attention. He compared "Philosophers to Instruments of Musick, which made a Noise, without Understanding it, or themselves." He was ridiculed by his Brother Philosophers, and called "An Ass". He owned, he was the "Ass of Zeno: and the only one whose back and Shoulders were stout enough to carry his Burthens." Why has not Priestley, quoted more from Zeno, and his Disciples? Were they too Christian? though he lived two Centuries and an half before Christ?

If I did not know, it would be sending Coal to Newcastle, I would, with all my dimness of Eyes and trembling of Fingers copy in Greek the Hymn of Cleanthes and request you to compare it, with any Thing of Moses of David of Soloman.

Instead of those ardent oriental Figures, which are so difficult to understand We find that divine Simplicity, which constitutes the Charm of Grecian Eloquence in prose and verse.

Pope had read, if Priestley had not, the

ΚΛΕΑΝΘΟΥΣ ΥΜΝΟΣ ΕΙΣ ΔΙΑ

Κύδιστ' ἀθανάτων, πολυώνυμε, παγκρατὲς αἰεὶ
Ζεῦ, φύσεως ἀρχηγέ, νόμου μέτα πάντα κυβερνῶν
Χαῖρε.

"Most glorious of immortal beings! though denominated by innumerable names and titles, always omnipotent,! Beginning and End of Nature! governing the Universe by fixed Laws! Blessed be thy name!" What think you, of this translation? Is it too Jewish? or too Christian? Pope did not think it was either: for the first Sentence in his Universal prayer is more Jewish and more christian still. If it is not a litteral translation, it is a close paraphrase, of this Simple Verse of Cleanthes.

> Father of all! in every Age,
> In every clime ador'd
> By Saint by Savage and by Sage
> Johovah, Jove, or Lord.[68]

But it may be said, for it has been said, that Pope, was a Deist and Swift too, as well as Bolingbroke. What will not Men say? But is the Existence, the Omnipotence, the Eternity, the Alpha and Omega, and the Universal Providence of one Supream Being, governing by fixed Laws, asserted by St John in his Gospel, or in the Apocalypse, whether his or not, in clearer or more precise terms?

Can you conjecture, a reason why Grotius has not translated this Hymn? Were Grotius and Priestley both afraid that The Stoicks would appear too much like Unitarian Jews and Christians.

Duport has translated, the Sentence thus

> Magne Pater Divum, cui nomina multa, Sed una
> Omnipotens semper Virtus, tu Jupiter Auctor
> Naturæ, certa qui singula lege gubernas,
> Rex, Salve!

Bougainville, has translated it

> Pere, et Maitre des Dieux, Auteur de la Nature,
> Jupiter, O Sagesse! O loi sublime et pure!
> Unite souveraine a qui tous les mortels
> Sous mille noms divers elevent des Autels;

68. These are the opening lines from Pope's "The Universal Prayer"; Norman Ault and John Butt, eds., *Alexander Pope, Minor Poems* (London and New Haven, 1954), 145.

Je t'adore, nos coeurs te doivent leur homage,
Nous sommes tes enfans, ton ombre, ton image:
Et tout ce qui respire animé par tes mains,
A celébrer ta gloire invite les humains.
Beni sois a jamais!

I am so aukward in Italian, that I am ashamed to quote that Language to you: but Pompeius a Gentleman of Verona, h[as] translated it thus: and you will understand it.

O glorioso fra gli eterni, in guise
Molte nomato, onnipossente ognora,
Tu che, tutto con legge governando,
De la natura sei principio e duce,
Salve, O Giove.

It appears to me, that the great Principle of the Hebrews was the *Fear* of God; that of the Gentiles, *Honour* the Gods, that of Christians, the *Love* of God. Could the quiveration of my nerves and the inflammation of my Eyes be cured and my Age diminished by 20 or 30 Years: I would attend you in these researches, with infinitely more Pleasure, than I would be George the 4th. Napoleone, Alexander, or Madison. But only a few Hours; a few moments remain for Your Old Friend

JOHN ADAMS

Adams to Jefferson

Quincy Sept. [i.e., Oct. 4] 1813

Σὲ γὰρ πάντεσσι θέμις θνητοῖσι προσαυδᾶν

"It is not only permitted but enjoined upon all Mortals to address you". Why should not our Divines translate it
"It is our duty and our priviledge to address the Throne of thy grace and pray for all needed lawfull Blessings temporal and spiritual."
Θεμις was the Goddess of honesty, Justice, Decency, and right; the Wife of Jove, another name for Juno. She presided over all oracles, deliberations and Counsells. She commanded all Mortals to pray to Jupiter, for all lawful Benefits and Blessings.
Now, is not this, (so far forth) the Essence of Christian devotion? Is not this Christian Piety? Is it not an Acknonowledgement [sic] of the

existence of a Supream Being? of his universal Providence? of a righteous Administration of the Government of the Universe? And what can Jews, Christians or Mahometans do more?

Priestley, the heroic Priestley, would not have dared to answer or to ask these questions; tho' he might have answered them, consistently enough with the Spirit of his System.

I regret that Grotius has not translated this Hymn: and cannot account for his Omission of it. Duport translates, the above line, only by "Te nempe licet mortalibus ægris cunctis compellare." Where he finds his ægris ["sick"], I know not. No such Idea, is in the greek. All Mortalls, sick or well, have a right and it is their duty to pray, as far as I can understand the Greek.

Bougainville translates it

["]Et tout ce qui respire animé par tes mains, à celebrer tu gloire, invite les humains. Beni sois a jamais." This translation is Christian with a witness. None but a Jew, a Mahometan or a Christian, could ever have translated that simple line in this manner. Yet the Idea, the Sentiment translated into Christianity is very well: well enough.

The Gentleman of Verona Gironomo Pompei, translates it thus. After Salve O Giove, for "Χαῖρε." "pero che gli nomin tutte, dritto è ben, che a te volgan le parole." Now tell me, what resemblance of the Greek you can find in this Italian Version.

In this manner are the most ancient Greek Theologians rendered and transmitted to our Youth, by the Christians.

Ἐκ σοῦ γὰρ γένος ἐσμὲν, ἰῆς μίμημα λαχόντες
Μοῦνον, ὅσα ζωει τε καὶ ἕρπει θνήτ᾽ ἐπὶ γαῖαν. [69]

I presume is the phrase quoted by Saint Paul, when he says to the Atheneans, "One of your own Poets have said We are all his Offspring." Acts. 17th. 28. "For in him We live and move and have our being; as certain also of your own Poets have said, for We are also his Offspring." "Forasmuch then as We are the Offspring of God, We ought not to think that the Godhead is like unto Silver or Gold, or Stone graven by Mans device." This reasoning is irresistable. For what can be more mad, than to represent the eternal almighty omnipresent Cause and Principle of the Universe, by Statues and Pictures, by Coins or Medals?

Duport renders these two lines by "Omnes tua namque Propago

Nos sumus, æternæ quasi imago vocis et echo
Tantum, quotquot humi spirantes repimus."

69. "For we are of your race, being only a copy of your voice,
    How ever many a mortal lives or creeps on the earth."

Bougainville translates them thus

> Nous sommes tes enfans, ton Ombre ton image:
> Et tout ce qui respire animé par tes mains,
> A celebrer ta gloire invite les humains.
> Beni sois a jamais.

Pompei renders them

> Che siam tua Stirpe, e solo noi, fra quanti
> Vivon mortali e muovon su la terra,
> Lo imitar de la voce abbiam sortito.

Moses says, Genesis. 1. 27. ["]God created man in his own image." What then is the difference between Cleanthes and Moses? Are not the Being and Attributes of the Supream Being: The Resemblance, the Image the Shadow of God in the Intelligence, and moral qualities of Man, and the Lawfulness and duty of Prayer, as clear[l]y asserted by Cleanthes as by Moses? And did not the Chaldeans, the Egyptians the Persians the Indians, the Chinese, believe all this, as well as the Jews and Greeks?

Alexander appears to have behaved to the Jews, as Napoleon did to the Mahometans in the Pyramid of Grand Cairo. Ptolomy the greatest of his Generals, and a greater Man than himself was so impressed with what he learned in Judea, that he employed 70 learned Men to translate the Hebrew Scriptures into Greek, nearly 300 Years before Christ. He sent learned Men to collect Books from all Nations and deposited them in the Alexandrian Library. Will any Man make me believe that Caesar that Pompey, that Cicero, that Seneca, that Tacitus, that Dionisius Hallicarnarnassensis, that Plutarch, had never seen nor heard of the Septuagint? Why, might not Cleanthes, have seen the Septuagint? [70] The Curiosity of Pompey to see, the interiour of the temple shews that the System of the Jews, was become an Object of Speculation. It is impossible to believe, that the Septuagint, was unknown and unheard of by Greeks or Romans at that time, at least by the great Generals Orators Historians Phylosophers and Statesmen, who looked through the then known World, for information of every thing. On the other hand how do We know how much Moses Samuel Joshua David Solomon and Esdrass, Daniel Ezekiel, Isaiah and Jeremiah learned in Babilon Egypt and Persia? The Destruction of the Library at Alexandria, is all the Answer We can obtain to these Questions. I believe that Jews Grecians Romans and Christians all conspired, or connived At that Savage Catastrophy.

70. C. A. Muses, ed., *The Septuagint Bible ... in the Translation of Charles Thomson, Secretary of the Continental Congress ... 1774-1789* (Indian Hills, Colorado, 1954), xviii-xxiv.

I believe Cleanthes to be as good a Christian as Priestley.

But enough of my School Boy criticisms and crude Philosophy, problematical History and heretical Divinity for the present.

JOHN ADAMS

Jefferson to Adams

Monticello Oct. 12. 13.

DEAR SIR

Since mine of Aug. 22. I have recieved your favors of Aug. 16. Sep. 2. 14. 15. and—and Mrs. Adams's of Sep. 20. I now send you, according to your request a copy of the Syllabus. To fill up this skeleton with arteries, with veins, with nerves, muscles and flesh, is really beyond my time and information. Whoever could undertake it would find great aid in Enfield's judicious abridgment of Brucker's history of Philosophy, in which he has reduced 5. or 6. quarto vols. of 1000. pages each of Latin closely printed, to two moderate 8 vos. [octavos] of English, open, type.

To compare the morals of the old, with those of the new testament, would require an attentive study of the former, a search thro' all it's books for it's precepts, and through all it's history for it's practices, and the principles they prove. As commentaries too on these, the philosphy of the Hebrews must be enquired into, their Mishna, their Gemara, Cabbala, Jezirah, Sohar, Cosri, and their Talmud must be examined and understood, in order to do them full justice. Brucker, it should seem, has gone deeply into these Repositories of their ethics, and Enfield, his epitomiser, concludes in these words. 'Ethics were so little studied among the Jews, that, in their whole compilation called the Talmud, there is only one treatise on moral subjects. Their books of Morals chiefly consisted in a minute enumeration of duties. From the law of Moses were deduced 613. precepts, which were divided into two classes, affirmative and negative, 248 in the former, and 365 in the latter. It may serve to give the reader some idea of the low state of moral philosophy among the Jews in the Middle age, to add, that of the 248. affirmative precepts, only 3. were considered as obligatory upon women; and that, in order to obtain salvation, it was judged sufficient to fulfill any one single law in the hour of death; the observance of the rest being deemed necessary, only to increase the felicity of the future life. What a wretched depravity of sentiment and manners must have prevailed before such corrupt maxims could have obtained credit! It is impossible to collect from these writings a consistent series of moral Doctrine.' Enfield, B. 4. chap. 3. It was the reformation of

this 'wretched depravity' of morals which Jesus undertook. In extracting
the pure principles which he taught, we should have to strip off the
artificial vestments in which they have been muffled by priests, who have
travestied them into various forms, as instruments of riches and power to
them. We must dismiss the Platonists and Plotinists, the Stagyrites and
Gamalielites, the Eclectics the Gnostics and Scholastics, their essences and
emanations, their Logos and Demi-urgos, Aeons and Daemons male and
female, with a long train of Etc. Etc. Etc. or, shall I say at once, of
Nonsense. We must reduce our volume to the simple evangelists, select,
even from them, the very words only of Jesus, paring off the Amphibolo-
gisms into which they have been led by forgetting often, or not understanding, what had fallen from him, by giving their own misconceptions
as his dicta, and expressing unintelligibly for others what they had not
understood themselves. There will be found remaining the most sublime
and benevolent code of morals which has ever been offered to man. I have
performed this operation for my own use, by cutting verse by verse out
of the printed book, and arranging, the matter which is evidently his, and
which is as easily distinguishable as diamonds in a dunghill. The result is
an 8vo. [octavo] of 46. pages of pure and unsophisticated doctrines,[71] such
as were professed and acted on by the *unlettered* apostles, the Apostolic
fathers, and the Christians of the 1st. century. Their Platonising successors
indeed, in after times, in order to legitimate the corruptions which they
had incorporated into the doctrines of Jesus, found it necessary to disavow
the primitive Christians, who had taken their principles from the mouth of
Jesus himself, of his Apostles, and the Fathers cotemporary with them.
They excommunicated their followers as heretics, branding them with
the opprobrious name of Ebionites or Beggars.

For a comparison of the Graecian philosophy with that of Jesus, materials might be largely drawn from the same source. Enfield gives a history, and detailed account of the opinions and principles of the different
sects. These relate to
the gods, their natures, grades, places and powers;
the demi-gods and daemons, and their agency with man;
the Universe, it's structure, extent, production and duration;
the origin of things from the elements of fire, water, air and earth;
the human soul, it's essence and derivation;
the summum bonum and finis bonorum; with a thousand idle dreams and

71. The Philosophy of Jesus of Nazareth (text in Randall, *Jefferson*, III, 654-55),
which TJ was planning as early as 1804; see TJ to Priestley, Jan. 29, 1804, Ford, VIII,
294, and Rush to TJ, Aug. 29, 1804, Butterfield, ed., *Letters of Rush*, II, 886. In 1819
or later TJ prepared the more elaborate The Life and Morals of Jesus of Nazareth
Extracted textually from the Gospels in Greek, Latin French and English. See Introduction by Cyrus Adler to facsimile edn. [Washington, 1904], 12-18.

fancies on these and other subjects the knolege of which is withheld from man, leaving but a short chapter for his moral duties, and the principal section of that given to what he owes himself, to precepts for rendering him impassible, and unassailable by the evils of life, and for preserving his mind in a state of constant serenity.

Such a canvas is too broad for the age of seventy, and especially of one whose chief occupations have been in the practical business of life. We must leave therefore to others, younger and more learned than we are, to prepare this euthanasia for Platonic Christianity, and it's restoration to the primitive simplicity of it's founder. I think you give a just outline of the theism of the three religions when you say that the principle of the Hebrew was the fear, of the Gentile the honor, and of the Christian the love of God.

An expression in your letter of Sep. 14. that 'the human understanding is a revelation from it's maker' gives the best solution, that I believe can be given, of the question, What did Socrates mean by his Daemon? He was too wise to believe, and too honest to pretend that he had real and familiar converse with a superior and invisible being. He probably considered the suggestions of his conscience, or reason, as revelations, or inspirations from the Supreme mind, bestowed, on important occasions, by a special superintending providence.

I acknolege all the merit of the hymn of Cleanthes to Jupiter, which you ascribe to it. It is as highly sublime as a chaste and correct imagination can permit itself to go. Yet in the contemplation of a being so superlative, the hyperbolic flights of the Psalmist may often be followed with approbation, even with rapture; and I have no hesitation in giving him the palm over all the Hymnists of every language, and of every time. Turn to the 148th. psalm, in Brady and Tate's version.[72] Have such conceptions been ever before expressed? Their version of the 15th. psalm is more to be esteemed for it's pithiness, than it's poetry. Even Sternhold,[73] the leaden Sternhold, kindles, in a single instance, with the sublimity of his original, and expresses the majesty of God descending on the earth, in terms not unworthy of the subject.

'The Lord descended from above   And bowed the heav'ns most high;
And underneath his feet he cast   The darkness of the sky.
On Cherubim and Seraphim   Full royally he rode;
And on the wings of mighty winds   Came flying all abroad.[']

Psalm xviii. 9. 10.

72. N. Tate and N. Brady, *A New Version of the Psalms of David, Fitted to the Tunes in Churches* (London, 1696, and later edns.).
73. Thomas Sternhold, J. Hopkins, and others, *The Whole Book of Psalmes Collected into Englysche Meter* (London, 1564, and later edns.).

The Latin versions of this passage by Buchanan and by Johnston,[74] are but mediocres. But the Greek of Duport [75] is worthy of quotation.

Ουρανον αγκλινας κατεβη· ὑπο ποσσι δ᾽ ἑοισιν
Αχλυς αμφι μελαινα χυθη και νυξ ερεβεννη.
Ριμφα ποτᾶτο Χερουβῳ οχευμενος, ωσπερ εφ᾽ ἱππῳ.
῾Ιπτατο δε πτερυγεσσι πολυπλαγκτου ανεμοιο.

The best collection of these psalms is that of the Octagonian dissenters of Liverpool, in their printed Form of prayer; but they are not always the best versions. Indeed bad is the best of the English versions; not a ray of poetical genius having ever been employed on them. And how much depends on this may be seen by comparing Brady and Tate's XVth. psalm with Blacklock's Justum et tenacem propositi virum ["a man just and steadfast of purpose"] of Horace, quoted in Hume's history, Car. 2. ch. 65. A translation of David in this style, or in that of Pompei's Cleanthes, might give us some idea of the merit of the original. The character too of the poetry of these hymns is singular to us. Written in monostichs, each divided into strophe and antistrophe, the sentiment of the 1st. member responded with amplification or antithesis in the second.

On the subject of the Postscript of yours of Aug. 16. and of Mrs. Adams's letter, I am silent. I know the depth of the affliction it has caused, and can sympathise with it the more sensibly, inasmuch as there is no degree of affliction, produced by the loss of those dear to us, which experience has not taught me to estimate. I have ever found time and silence the only medecine, and these but assuage, they never can suppress, the deep-drawn sigh which recollection for ever brings up, until recollection and life are extinguished together. Ever affectionately yours

TH: JEFFERSON

P.S. Your's of Sep—just recieved

74. George Buchanan, ed., Psalmorum Davidis paraphrasis poetica, nunc primum edita (Paris, 1566); Arthur Johnston, Paraphrasis poetica Psalmorium Davidis (Aberdeen, 1637).
75. James Duport, Δαβιδης ᾽Εμμετρος, sive metaphrasis libri Psalmorum Graecis versibus contexta (London, 1712).

Jefferson to Adams

Monticello Oct. 28. 13.

DEAR SIR

According to the reservation between us, of taking up one of the subjects of our correspondence at a time, I turn to your letters of Aug. 16. and Sep. 2.

The passage you quote from Theognis, I think has an Ethical, rather than a political object. The whole piece is a moral *exhortation*, παραίνεσις, and this passage particularly seems to be a reproof to man, who, while with his domestic animals he is curious to improve the race by employing always the finest male, pays no attention to the improvement of his own race, but intermarries with the vicious, the ugly, or the old, for considerations of wealth or ambition. It is in conformity with the principle adopted afterwards by the Pythagoreans, and expressed by Ocellus in another form. Περι δε τῆς ἐκ τῶν αλληλων ανθρωπων γενεσεως etc.— ουχ ἡδονης ενεκα ἡ μιξις. Which, as literally as intelligibility will admit, may be thus translated. 'Concerning the interprocreation of men, how, and of whom it shall be, in a perfect manner, and according to the laws of modesty and sanctity, conjointly, this is what I think right. First to lay it down that we do not commix for the sake of pleasure, but of the procreation of children. For the powers, the organs and desires for coition have not been given by god to man for the sake of pleasure, but for the procreation of the race. For as it were incongruous for a mortal born to partake of divine life, the immortality of the race being taken away, god fulfilled the purpose by making the generations uninterrupted and continuous. This therefore we are especially to lay down as a principle, that coition is not for the sake of pleasure.' But Nature, not trusting to this moral and abstract motive, seems to have provided more securely for the perpetuation of the species by making it the effect of the oestrum implanted in the constitution of both sexes. And not only has the commerce of love been indulged on this unhallowed impulse, but made subservient also to wealth and ambition by marriages without regard to the beauty, the healthiness, the understanding, or virtue of the subject from which we are to breed. The selecting the best male for a Haram of well chosen females also, which Theognis seems to recommend from the example of our sheep and asses, would doubtless improve the human, as it does the brute animal, and produce a race of veritable αριστοι [“aristocrats”]. For experience proves that the moral and physical qualities of man, whether good or evil, are transmissible in a certain degree from father to son. But I suspect that the equal rights of men will rise up against this privileged Solomon, and oblige us to continue acquiescence under the Ἀμαυρωσις γενεος ἀστων ["the degeneration of the race of men"] which Theognis complains of, and to content ourselves with the accidental aristoi produced by the fortuitous concourse of breeders. For I agree with you that there is a natural aristocracy among men. The grounds of this are virtue and talents. Formerly bodily powers gave place among the aristoi. But since the invention of gunpowder has armed the weak as well as the strong with missile death, bodily strength, like beauty, good humor, politeness and other accomplishments, has become but an auxiliary ground of distinction. There is also an artificial aristocracy founded on wealth and birth, without either virtue or talents; for with these it would belong to the first class. The natural aristocracy I consider as the most precious gift of nature for the instruction, the trusts, and government of society. And indeed it would have been inconsistent in creation to have formed man for the social state, and not to have provided virtue and wisdom enough to manage the concerns of the society. May we not even say that that form of government is the best which provides the most effectually for a pure selection of these natural aristoi into the offices of government? The artificial aristocracy is a mischievous ingredient in government, and provision should be made to prevent it's ascendancy. On the question, What is the best provision, you and I differ; but we differ as rational friends, using the free exercise of our own reason, and mutually indulging it's errors. *You* think it best to put the Pseudo-aristoi into a separate chamber of legislation where they may be hindered from doing mischief by their coordinate branches, and where also they may be a protection to wealth against the Agrarian and plundering enterprises of the Majority of the people. I think that to give them power in order to prevent them from doing mischief, is arming them for it, and increasing instead of remedying the evil. For if the coordinate branches can arrest their action, so may they that of the coordinates. Mischief may be done negatively as well as positively. Of this a cabal in the Senate of the U. S. has furnished many proofs. Nor do I believe them necessary to protect the wealthy; because enough of these will find their way into every branch of the legislation to protect themselves. From 15. to 20. legislatures of our own, in action for 30. years past, have proved that no fears of an equalisation of property are to be apprehended from them.

I think the best remedy is exactly that provided by all our constitutions, to leave to the citizens the free election and separation of the aristoi from the pseudo-aristoi, of the wheat from the chaff. In general they will elect the real good and wise. In some instances, wealth may corrupt, and birth blind them; but not in sufficient degree to endanger the society.[76]

It is probable that our difference of opinion may in some measure be produced by a difference of character in those among whom we live. From what I have seen of Massachusets and Connecticut myself, and still more from what I have heard, and the character given of the former by yourself, [vol. 1. pa. 111.] [77] who know them so much better, there seems to be in those two states a traditionary reverence for certain families, which has rendered the offices of the government nearly hereditary in those families. I presume that from an early period of your history, members of these families happening to possess virtue and talents, have honestly exercised them for the good of the people, and by their services have endeared their names to them.

In coupling Connecticut with you, I mean it politically only, not morally. For having made the Bible the Common law of their land they seem to have modelled their morality on the story of Jacob and Laban. But altho' this hereditary succession to office with you may in some degree be founded in real family merit, yet in a much higher degree it has proceeded from your strict alliance of church and state. These families are canonised in the eyes of the people on the common principle 'you tickle me, and I will tickle you.' In Virginia we have nothing of this. Our clergy, before the revolution, having been secured against rivalship by fixed salaries, did not give themselves the trouble of acquiring influence over the people. Of wealth, there were great accumulations in particular families, handed down from generation to generation under the English law of entails. But the only object of ambition for the wealthy was a seat in the king's council. All their court then was paid to the crown and it's creatures; and they Philipised in all collisions between the king and people. Hence they were unpopular; and that unpopularity continues attached to their names. A Randolph, a Carter, or a Burwell must have great personal superiority over a common competitor to be elected by the people, even at this day.

At the first session of our legislature after the Declaration of Independance, we passed a law abolishing entails. And this was followed by one abolishing the privilege of Primogeniture, and dividing the lands of intestates equally among all their children, or other representatives. These laws, drawn by myself, laid the axe to the root of Pseudo-aristocracy. And had another which I prepared been adopted by the legislature, our work

76. The foregoing is TJ's most explicit statement concerning natural aristocracy. Cf. his "Autobiography," Ford, I, 49-50, 68-69.

77. TJ's note, referring to JA's Defence.

would have been compleat. It was a Bill for the more general diffusion of learning.[78] This proposed to divide every county into wards of 5. or 6. miles square, like your townships; to establish in each ward a free school for reading, writing and common arithmetic; to provide for the annual selection of the best subjects from these schools who might recieve at the public expence a higher degree of education at a district school; and from these district schools to select a certain number of the most promising subjects to be compleated at an University, where all the useful sciences should be taught. Worth and genius would thus have been sought out from every condition of life, and compleatly prepared by education for defeating the competition of wealth and birth for public trusts.

My proposition had for a further object to impart to these wards those portions of self-government for which they are best qualified, by confiding to them the care of their poor, their roads, police, elections, the nomination of jurors, administration of justice in small cases, elementary exercises of militia, in short, to have made them little republics, with a Warden at the head of each, for all those concerns which, being under their eye, they would better manage than the larger republics of the county or state. A general call of ward-meetings by their Wardens on the same day thro' the state would at any time produce the genuine sense of the people on any required point, and would enable the state to act in mass, as your people have so often done, and with so much effect, by their town meetings. The law for religious freedom,[79] which made a part of this system, having put down the aristocracy of the clergy, and restored to the citizen the freedom of the mind, and those of entails and descents nurturing an equality of condition among them, this on Education would have raised the mass of the people to the high ground of moral respectability necessary to their own safety, and to orderly government; and would have compleated the great object of qualifying them to select the veritable aristoi, for the trusts of government, to the exclusion of the Pseudalists: and the same Theognis who has furnished the epigraphs of your two letters assures us that 'ουδεμιαν πω, Κυρν' ἀγαθοι πολιν ὤλεσαν ἀνδρες ["Curnis, good men have never harmed any city"]'. Altho' this law has not yet been acted on but in a small and inefficient degree, it is still considered as before the legislature, with other bills of the revised code, not yet taken up, and I have great hope that some patriotic spirit will, at a favorable moment, call it up, and make it the key-stone of the arch of our government.

78. "A Bill for the More General Diffusion of Knowledge," No. 79 in the "Catalogue of Bills Prepared by the Committee of Revisors," Boyd, II, 526-35 and *n*.

79. "An ACT for establishing RELIGIOUS FREEDOM, passed in the Assembly of Virginia in the beginning of the year 1786," in TJ, *Notes on the State of Virginia*, ed. by Peden (1955), 223-25.

With respect to Aristocracy, we should further consider that, before the establishment of the American states, nothing was known to History but the Man of the old world, crouded within limits either small or overcharged, and steeped in the vices which that situation generates. A government adapted to such men would be one thing; but a very different one that for the Man of these states. Here every one may have land to labor for himself if he chuses; or, preferring the exercise of any other industry, may exact for it such compensation as not only to afford a comfortable subsistence, but wherewith to provide for a cessation from labor in old age. Every one, by his property, or by his satisfactory situation, is interested in the support of law and order. And such men may safely and advantageously reserve to themselves a wholsome controul over their public affairs, and a degree of freedom, which in the hands of the Canaille of the cities of Europe, would be instantly perverted to the demolition and destruction of every thing public and private. The history of the last 25. years of France, and of the last 40. years in America, nay of it's last 200. years, proves the truth of both parts of this observation.

But even in Europe a change has sensibly taken place in the mind of Man. Science had liberated the ideas of those who read and reflect, and the American example had kindled feelings of right in the people. An insurrection has consequently begun, of science, talents and courage against rank and birth, which have fallen into contempt. It has failed in it's first effort, because the mobs of the cities, the instrument used for it's accomplishment, debased by ignorance, poverty and vice, could not be restrained to rational action. But the world will recover from the panic of this first catastrophe. Science is progressive, and talents and enterprize on the alert. Resort may be had to the people of the country, a more governable power from their principles and subordination; and rank, and birth, and tinsel-aristocracy will finally shrink into insignificance, even there. This however we have no right to meddle with. It suffices for us, if the moral and physical condition of our own citizens qualifies them to select the able and good for the direction of their government, with a recurrence of elections at such short periods as will enable them to displace an unfaithful servant before the mischief he meditates may be irremediable.

I have thus stated my opinion on a point on which we differ, not with a view to controversy, for we are both too old to change opinions which are the result of a long life of inquiry and reflection; but on the suggestion of a former letter of yours, that we ought not to die before we have explained ourselves to each other. We acted in perfect harmony thro' a long and perilous contest for our liberty and independance. A constitution has been acquired which, tho neither of us think perfect, yet both consider as competent to render our fellow-citizens the happiest and the securest on whom the sun has ever shone. If we do not think exactly alike as to it's imperfections, it matters little to our country which, after devoting to it long lives of disinterested labor, we have delivered over to our successors in life, who will be able to take care of it, and of themselves.

Of the pamphlet on aristocracy which has been sent to you, or who may be it's author, I have heard nothing but thro' your letter. If the person you suspect [80] it may be known from the quaint, mystical and hyperbolical ideas, involved in affected, new-fangled and pedantic terms, which stamp his writings. Whatever it be, I hope your quiet is not to be affected at this day by the rudeness of intemperance of scribblers; but that you may continue in tranquility to live and to rejoice in the prosperity of our country until it shall be your own wish to take your seat among the Aristoi who have gone before you. Ever and affectionately yours.

TH: JEFFERSON

P.S. Can you assist my memory on the enquiries of my letter of Aug. 22.?

Adams to Jefferson

Quincy November 12. 1813

DEAR SIR

As I owe you more for your Letters of Oct. 12. and 28 than I shall be able to pay, I shall begin with the P.S. to the last.

I am very sorry to say, that I cannot "assist your memory in the Enquiries of your letter of August 22d." I really know not who was the compositor of any one of the Petitions or Addresses you enumerate. Nay farther I am certain I never did know. I was so shallow a polititian, that I was not aware of the importance of those compositions. They all appeared to me, in the circumstances of the Country like childrens play at marbles or push pin, or rather like misses in their teens emulating each other in their pearls, their braceletts their Diamond Pins and brussells lace.

In the Congress of 1774 there was not one member, except Patrick Henry, who appeared to me sensible of the Precipice or rather the Pinnacle on which he stood, and had candour and courage enough to acknowledge it. America is in total Ignorance, or under infinite deception concerning that Assembly. To draw the characters of them all would require a volume and would now be considered as a caracatura print. One third Tories, another Whigs and the rest mongrels.

80. John Taylor of Caroline.

There was a little Aristocracy, among Us, of Talents and Letters. Mr. Dickinson was primus inter pares; the Bell Weather; the leader of the Aristocratical flock. Billy, alias Governor Livingstone, and his Son in law Mr. Jay, were of this priviledged order. The credit of most if not all those compositions was often if not generally given to one or the other of these choice Spirits. Mr. Dickenson however was not on any of the original Committees. He came not into Congress till Oct. 17. He was not appointed till the 15th by his Assembly. [*Journals of Congress, containing Their Proceedings*] Vol. 1. 30. Congress adjourned 27. Oct. though our correct Secretary has not recorded any final Adjournment or dissolution. Mr. Dickenson was in Congress but ten days. The business was all prepared arranged and even in a manner finished before his Arrival.

R. H. Lee was the Chairman of the Committee for preparing "the loyal and dutiful Address to his Majesty." Johnson and Henry were acute Spirits and understood the Controversy very well; though they had not the Advantages of Education like Lee and John Rutledge. The Subject had been near a month under discussion in Congress and most of the materials thrown out there. It underwent another deliberation in committee; after which they made the customary compliment to their Chairman, by requesting him to prepare and report a draught, which was done, and after examination, correction, amelioration or pejoration, as usual reported to Congress. Oct. 3. 4. and 5th were taken up in debating and deliberating on matters proper to be contained in the Address to his Majesty. Vol. 1. 22. October 21. The Address to the King was after debate recommitted and Mr. John Dickenson added to the Committee. The first draught was made and all the essential materials put together by Lee, it might be embellished and seasoned Afterward with some of Mr. Dickenson piety; but I know not that it was. Neat and handsome as the composition is, having never had any confidenc[e] in the Utility of it, I never have thought much about it since it was adopted. Indeed I never bestowed much Attention on any of those Addresses; which were all but repetitions of the same Things: the same facts and Arguments. Dress and ornament rather than Body, Soul or Substance. My thoughts and cares were nearly monopolized by the Theory of our Rights and Wrongs, by measures for the defence of the country; and the means of governing our Selves.
Please to turn over [to see N. B. at end of letter].

I was in a great Error, no doubt, and am ashamed to confess it; for those things were necessary to give Popularity to Our cause both at home and abroad. And to shew my Stupidity in a stronger light the reputation of any one of those compositions, has been a more splendid distinction than any aristocratical Starr or garter, in the Escutchion of every man who has enjoyed it. Very sorry that I cannot give you more Satisfactory information, And more so that I cannot at present give more Attention to your two last excellent Letters I am as Usual affectionately yours

JOHN ADAMS

N.B. I am almost ready to believe that John Taylor of Caroline, or of Hazel Wood Port Royal, Virginia, is the Author of 630 pages of printed Octavo, upon my Books, that I have received. The Style answers every characteristic, that you have intimated.

Within a Week I have received, and looked into his Arator.[81] They must spring from the same brain as Minerva issued from the head of Jove; or rather as Venus rose from the froth of the Sea.

There is however a great deal of good Sense in Arator. And there is some in his "Aristocracy."

Adams to Jefferson

Quincy Nov. 14. 1813

DEAR SIR

Accept my thanks for the comprehensive Syllabus, in your favour of Oct. 12.

The Psalms of David, in Sublimity beauty, pathos and Originality, or in one Word, in poetry, are superiour to all the Odes Hymns and Songs in any language. But I had rather read them in our prose translation, than in any version I have seen. His Morality, however, often shocks me, like Tristram Shandy's execrations.

Blacklocks translation of Horace's "Justum" is admirable; superiour to Addisons. Could David be translated as well; his Superiority would be universally acknowledged. We cannot compare the Sybbiline Poetry. By Virgils Pollio [82] we may conjecture, there was Prophecy as well as Sublimity. Why have those Verses been annihilated? I suspect platonick Christianity, pharisaical Judaism, or machiavilian Politicks, in this case; as in all other cases of the destruction of records and litterary monuments. The Auri sacra fames, et dominandi sæva cupido.[83]

81. *Arator; Being a Series of Agricultural Essays, Practical and Political:* in Sixty-one Numbers. By a Citizen of Virginia (Georgetown, D.C., 1813), explaining Taylor's methods of scientific agriculture.
82. The phrasing of Virgil's Pollio (Fourth Eclogue) parallels that of Isaiah, chapter 11. This similarity, along with its contents, led the early Church fathers to believe that Virgil prophesied the birth of Christ.
83. "The horrible hunger of gold, and the savage lust of power." Virgil, *Aen.,* III, 57.

Among all your researches in Hebrew History and Controversy have you ever met a book, the design of which is to prove, that the ten Commandments, as We have them in our Catechisms and hung up in our Churches, were not the Ten Commandments written by the Finger of God upon tables, delivered to Moses on mount Sinai and broken by him in a passion with Aaron for his golden calf, nor those afterwards engraved by him on Tables of Stone; but a very different Sett of Commandments?

There is such a book by J. W. Goethens Schristen.[84] Berlin 1775-1779. I wish to see this Book.

You will see the Subject and perceive the question in Exodus 20. 1-17. 22-28. chapter 24. 3 etc. ch. 24. 12. ch. 25. 31 ch. 31. 18. ch. 31. 19. ch. 34. 1. ch. 34. 10 etc.

I will make a Covenant with all this People. Observe that which I command this day.

1

Thou shall not adore any other God. Therefore take heed, not to enter into covenant, with the Inhabitants of this country; neither take for your Sons, their daughters in marriage. They would allure thee to the Worship of false Gods. Much less shall you in any place, erect Images.

2

The Feast of unleavened bread, shall thou keep. Seven days, shall thou eat unleavened bread, at the time of the month Abib; to remember that about that time, I delivered thee from Egypt.

3

Every first born of the mother is mine; the male of thine herd, be it Stock or flock. But you shall replace the first born of an Ass with a Sheep. The first born of your Sons shall you *redeem*. No Man shall appear before me with empty hands.

4

Six days shall thou labour: the seventh day, thou shall rest from ploughing and gathering.

84. JA misread the f in *Schriften* for a long *s* and took the title for part of the author's name (*Goethens* was a possessive form already obsolescent). One of the earliest collected editions of Goethe's *Writings,* unauthorized by him, was first issued by C. F. Himberg in 3 vols. (Berlin, 1775). A fourth volume (1779) included two tracts on religious subjects, in part an early application of historical criticism to the Old Testament. The derivation of JA's translation of Goethe's selection from Exodus 34: 10-27 has not been determined.

5

The Feast of Weeks shall thou keep, with the firstlings of the Wheat Harvest: and the Feast of Harvesting, at the end of the year.

6

Thrice, in every year, all male persons shall appear before the Lord. Nobody shall invade your Country, as long as you obey this Command.

7

Thou shall not sacrifice the blood of a Sacrifice of mine, upon leavened bread.

8

The Sacrifice of the Passover shall not remain, till the next day.

9

The Firstlings of the produce of your land, thou shall bring to the House of the Lord.

10

Thou shall not boil the kid, while it is yet sucking.

And the Lord spake to Moses: Write these Words; as, after these Words I made with you, and with Israel a Covenant.

I know not whether Goethens translated or abridged from the Hebrew, or whether he used any translation Greek, Latin, or German. But he differs in form and Words, somewhat from our Version. Exod. 34. 10. to 28. The Sense seems to be the same. The Tables were the evidence of the covenant, by which the Almighty attached the People of Israel to himself. By these laws they were seperated from all other nations, and were reminded of the principal Epochas of their History.

When and where originated our Ten Commandments? The Tables and The Ark were lost. Authentic Copies, in few, if any hands; the ten Precepts could not be observed, and were little remembered.

If the Book of Deuteronomy was compiled, during or after the Babilonian Captivity, from Traditions, the Error or Amendment might come in there.

But you must be weary, as I am at present, of Problems, Conjectures, and paradoxes, concerning Hebrew, Grecian and Christian and all other Antiquities; but while We believe that the finis bonorum will be happy, We may leave learned men to this disquisitions and Criticisms.

I admire your Employment, in selecting the Philosophy and Divinity of Jesus and seperating it from all intermixtures. If I had Eyes and Nerves,

I would go through both Testaments and mark all that I understand. To examine the Mishna Gemara Cabbala Jezirah, Sohar Cosri and Talmud of the Hebrews [85] would require the life of Methuselah, and after all, his 969 Years would be wasted to very little purpose. The Dæmon of Hierarchical despotism has been at Work, both with the Mishna and Gemara. In 1238 a French Jew, made a discovery to the Pope (Gregory 9th) of the heresies of the Talmud.[86] The Pope sent 35 Articles of Error, to the Archbishops of France, requiring them to seize the books of the Jews, and burn all that contained any Errors. He wrote in the same terms to the Kings of France, England Arragon, Castile Leon, Navarre and Portugal. In consequence of this Order 20 Cartloads of Hebrew Books were burnt in France: and how many times 20 Cartloads were destroyed in the other Kingdoms? The Talmud of Babylon and that of Jerusalem were composed from 120 to 500 Years after the destruction of Jerusalem. If Lightfoot derived Light from what escaped from Gregorys fury in explaining many passages in the New Testament by comparing the Expressions of the Mishna, with those of the Apostles and Evangelists, how many proofs of the Corruptions of Christianity might We find in the Passages burnt?

JOHN ADAMS

Adams to Jefferson

Quincy November 15.13

DEAR SIR

I cannot appease my melancholly commiseration for our Armies in this furious snow storm in any way so well as by studying your Letter of Oct. 28.

We are now explicitly agreed, in one important point, vizt. That "there is a natural Aristocracy among men; the grounds of which are Virtue and Talents."

You very justly indulge a little merriment upon this solemn subject of Aristocracy. I often laugh at it too, for there is nothing in this laughable world more ridiculous than the management of it by almost all the nations of the Earth. But while We smile, Mankind have reason to say to Us, as the froggs said to the Boys, What is Sport to you is Wounds and death

85. The principal literary expressions of the Hebrew religion. The Talmud as the main teaching of Judaism was under attack by the Catholic Church from the thirteenth century on and at times copies by the cartload were burned; hence manuscripts of the Talmud are extremely rare.
86. These burnings were ordered under Pope Innocent IV, not Gregory IX.

to Us. When I consider the weakness, the folly, the Pride, the Vanity, the Selfishness, the Artifice, the low craft and meaning cunning, the want of Principle, the Avarice the unbounded Ambition, the unfeeling Cruelty of a majority of those (in all Nations) who are allowed an aristocratical influence; and on the other hand, the Stupidity with which the more numerous multitude, not only become their Dupes, but even love to be Taken in by their Tricks: I feel a stronger disposition to weep at their destiny, than to laugh at their Folly.

But tho' We have agreed in one point, in Words, it is not yet certain that We are perfectly agreed in Sense. Fashion has introduced an indeterminate Use of the Word "Talents." Education, Wealth, Strength, Beauty, Stature, Birth, Marriage, graceful Attitudes and Motions, Gait, Air, Complexion, Physiognomy, are Talents, as well as Genius and Science and learning. Any one of these Talents, that in fact commands or influences true Votes in Society, gives to the Man who possesses it, the Character of an Aristocrat, in my Sense of the Word.

Pick up, the first 100 men you meet, and make a Republick. Every Man will have an equal Vote. But when deliberations and discussions are opened it will be found that 25, by their Talents, Virtues being equal, will be able to carry 50 Votes. Every one of these 25, is an Aristocrat, in my Sense of the Word; whether he obtains his one Vote in Addition to his own, by his Birth Fortune, Figure, Eloquence, Science, learning, Craft Cunning, or even his Character for good fellowship and a bon vivant.

What gave Sir William Wallace his amazing Aristocratical Superiority? His Strength. What gave Mrs. Clark, her Aristocratical Influence to create Generals Admirals and Bishops? her Beauty. What gave Pompadour and Du Barry the Power of making Cardinals and Popes? their Beauty. You have seen the Palaces of Pompadour and Du Barry: and I have lived for years in the Hotel de Velentinois, with Franklin who had as many Virtues as any of them. In the investigation of the meaning of the Word "Talents" I could write 630 Pages, as pertinent as John Taylors of Hazelwood. But I will select a single Example: for female Aristocrats are nearly as formidable in Society as male.

A daughter of a green Grocer, walks the Streets in London dayly with a baskett of Cabbage, Sprouts, Dandlions and Spinage on her head. She is observed by the Painters to have a beautiful Face, an elegant figure, a graceful Step and a debonair. They hire her to Sitt. She complies, and is painted by forty Artists in a Circle around her. The scientific Sir William Hamilton outbids the Painters, sends her to Schools for a genteel Education and Marries her. This Lady not only causes the Tryumphs of the Nile of Copinhagen and Trafalgar, but seperates Naples from France and finally banishes the King and Queen from Sicilly. Such is the Aristocracy of the natural Talent of Beauty. Millions of Examples might be quoted from History sacred and profane, from Eve, Hannah, Deborah Susanna Abigail, Judith, Ruth, down to Hellen Madame de Maintenon and Mrs. Fitcherbert. For mercy's sake do not compell me to look to our chaste States and Territories, to find Women, one of whom lett go, would, in the Words of Holopherne's Guards "deceive the whole Earth."

The Proverbs of Theognis, like those of Solomon, are Observations on human nature, ordinary life, and civil Society, with moral reflections on the facts. I quoted him as a Witness of the Fact, that there was as much difference in the races of Men as in the breeds of Sheep; and as a sharp reprover and censurer of the sordid mercenary practice of disgracing Birth by preferring gold to it. Surely no authority can be more expressly in point to prove the existence of Inequalities, not of rights, but of moral intellectual and physical inqualities in Families, descents and Generations. If a descent from, pious, virtuous, wealthy litterary or scientific Ancestors is a letter of recommendation, or introduction in a Mans his favour, and enables him to influence only one vote in Addition to his own, he is an Aristocrat, for a democrat can have but one Vote. Aaron Burr had 100,000 Votes from the single Circumstance of his descent from President Burr and President Edwards.

Your commentary on the Proverbs of Theognis reminded me of two solemn Charactors, the one resembling John Bunyan, the other Scarron. The one John Torrey: the other Ben. Franklin. Torrey a Poet, an Enthusiast, a superstitious Bigot, once very gravely asked my Brother Cranch, "whether it would not be better for Mankind, if Children were always begotten from religious motives only"? Would not religion, in this sad case, have as little efficacy in encouraging procreation, as it has now in discouraging it? I should apprehend a decrease of population even in our Country where it increases so rapidly. In 1775 Franklin made a morning Visit, at Mrs. Yards to Sam. Adams and John. He was unusually loquacious. "Man, a rational Creature"! said Franklin. "Come, Let Us suppose a rational Man. Strip him of all his Appetites, especially of his hunger and thirst. He is in his Chamber, engaged in making Experiments, or in pursuing some Problem. He is highly entertained. At this moment a Servant Knocks, "Sir dinner is on Table." "Dinner! Pox! Pough! But what have you for dinner?" Ham and Chickens. "Ham"! "And must I break the chain of my thoughts, to go down and knaw a morsel of a damn'd Hogs Arse"? "Put aside your Ham." "I will dine tomorrow."

Take away Appetite and the present generation would not live a month and no future generation would ever exist. Thus the exalted dignity of human Nature would be annihilated and lost. And in my opinion, the whole loss would be of no more importance, than putting out a Candle, quenching a Torch, or crushing a Firefly, *if in this world only We have hope.*

Your distinction between natural and artificial Aristocracy does not appear to me well founded. Birth and Wealth are conferred on some Men, as imperiously by Nature, as Genius, Strength or Beauty. The Heir is honours and Riches, and power has often no more merit in procuring these Advantages, than he has in obtaining an handsome face or an elegant figure. When Aristocracies, are established by human Laws and honour Wealth and Power are made hereditary by municipal Laws and political Institutions, then I acknowledge artificial Aristocracy to commence: but this never commences, till Corruption in Elections becomes dominant and uncontroulable. But this artificial Aristocracy can never last. The everlasting Envys, Jealousies, Rivalries and quarrells among them, their cruel rapacities upon the poor ignorant People their followers, compell these to sett up Caesar, a Demagogue to be a Monarch and Master, pour mettre chacun a sa place ["to put each one in his place"]. Here you have the origin of all artificial Aristocracy, which is the origin of all Monarchy. And both artificial Aristocracy, and Monarchy, and civil, military, political and hierarchical Despotism, have all grown out of the natural Aristocracy of "Virtues and Talents." We, to be sure, are far remote from this. Many hundred years must roll away before We shall be corrupted. Our pure, virtuous, public spirited federative Republick will last for ever, govern the Globe and introduce the perfection of Man, his perfectability being already proved by Price Priestly, Condorcet Rousseau Diderot and Godwin.

"Mischief has been done by the Senate of U.S." I have known and felt more of this mischief, than Washington, Jefferson and Madison altoge[the]r. But this has been all caused by the constitutional Power of the Senate in Executive Business, which ought to be immediately, totally and eternally abolished.

Your distinction between the aristoi and pseudo aristoi, will not help the matter. I would trust one as soon as the other with unlimited Power. The Law wisely refuses an Oath as a witness in his own cause to the Saint as well as to the Sinner.

No Romance would be more amusing, than the History of your Virginian and our new England Aristocratical Families. Yet even in Rhode Island, where there has been no Clergy, no Church, and I had almost said, no State, and some People say no religion, there has been a constant respect for certain old Families. 57 or 58 years ago, in company with Col. Counsellor, Judge, John Chandler, whom I have quoted before, a Newspaper was brought in. The old Sage asked me to look for the News from Rhode Island and see how the Elections had gone there. I read the List of

Wantons, Watsons, Greens, Whipples, Malbones etc. "I expected as much" said the aged Gentleman, "for I have always been of Opinion, that in the most popular Governments, the Elections will generally go in favour of the most ancient families." To this day when any of these Tribes and We may Add Ellerys, Channings Champlins etc are pleased to fall in with the popular current, they are sure to carry all before them.

You suppose a difference of Opinion between You and me, on the Subject of Aristocracy. I can find none. I dislike and detest hereditary honours, Offices Emoluments established by Law. So do you. I am for ex[c]luding legal hereditary distinctions from the U.S. as long as possible. So are you. I only say that Mankind have not yet discovered any remedy against irresistable Corruption in Elections to Offices of great Power and Profit, but making them hereditary.

But will you say our Elections are pure? Be it so; upon the whole. But do you recollect in history, a more Corrupt Election than that of Aaron Burr to be President, or that of De Witt Clinton last year. By corruption, here I mean a sacrifice of every national Interest and honour, to private and party Objects.

I see the same Spirit in Virginia, that you and I see in Rhode Island and the rest of New England. In New York it is a struggle of Family Feuds. A fewdal Aristocracy. Pensylvania is a contest between German, Irish and old English Families. When Germans and Irish Unite, they give 30,000 majorities. There is virtually a White Rose and a Red Rose a Caesar and a Pompey in every State in this Union and Contests and dissentions will be as lasting. The Rivalry of Bourbons and Noailleses produced the French Revolution, and a similar Competition for Consideration and Influence, exists and prevails in every Village in the World.

Where will terminate the Rabies Agri ["madness for land"]? The Continent will be scattered over with Manors, much larger than Livingstons, Van Ranselaers or Phillips's. Even our Deacon Strong will have a Principality among you Southern Folk. What Inequality of Talents will be produced by these Land Jobbers?

Where tends the Mania for Banks? At my Table in Philadelphia, I once proposed to you to unite in endeavours to obtain an Amendment of the Constitution, prohibiting to the separate States the Power of creating Banks; but giving Congress Authority to establish one Bank, with a branch in each State; the whole limited to Ten Millions of dollars. Whether this Project was wise or unwise, I know not, for I had deliberated little on it then and have never thought it worth thinking much of since. But you spurned the Proposition from you with disdain.

This System of Banks begotten, hatched and brooded by Duer, Robert and Governeur Morris, Hamilton and Washington, I have always considered as a System of national Injustice. A Sacrifice of public and private Interest to a few Aristocratical Friends and Favourites. My scheme could have had no such Effect.

Verres plundered Temples and robbed a few rich Men; but he never made such ravages among private property in general, nor swindled so much out of the pocketts of the poor and the middle Class of People as these Banks have done. No people but this would have borne the Imposition so long. The People of Ireland would not bear Woods half pence. What Inequalities of Talent, have been introduced into this Country by these Aristocratical Banks!

Our Winthrops, Winslows, Bradfords, Saltonstalls, Quincys, Chandlers, Leonards Hutchinsons Olivers, Sewalls etc are precisely in the Situation of your Randolphs, Carters and Burwells, and Harrisons. Some of them unpopular for the part they took in the late revolution, but all respected for their names and connections and whenever they fall in with the popular Sentiments, are preferred, cetoris paribus to all others. When I was young, the Summum Bonum in Massachusetts, was to be worth ten thousand pounds Sterling, ride in a Chariot, be Colonel of a Regiment of Militia and hold a seat in his Majesty's Council. No Mans Imagination aspired to any thing higher beneath the Skies. But these Plumbs, Chariots, Colonelships and counsellorships are recorded and will never be forgotten. No great Accumulations of Land were made by our early Settlers. Mr. Bausoin a French Refugee, made the first great Purchases and your General Dearborne, born under a fortunate Starr is now enjoying a large Portion of the Aristocratical sweets of them.

As I have no Amanuenses but females, and there is so much about generation in this letter that I dare not ask any one of them to copy it, and I cannot copy it myself I must beg of you to return it to me, your old Friend

JOHN ADAMS

Adams to Jefferson

Quincy Decr. 3. 13

DEAR SIR

The Proverbs of the old greek Poets, are as short and pithy as any of Solomon or Franklin. Hesiod has several. His

Αθανατως μεν πρωτα θωες νομω ως διακειται τιμα.

Honour the Gods established by Law. I know not how We can escape Martyrdom, without a discreet Attention to this præcept. You have suffered, and I have suffered more than You, for want of a strict if not a due Observance of this Rule.

There is another Oracle of this Hesiod, which requires a kind of dance upon a tight rope, and a slack rope too, in Philosophy and Theology.

πιστεις δ'ἄρα ὁμῶς κ' απιστιας ὤλεσαν ανδρας.[87]

If believing too little or too much, is so fatal to Mankind what will become of Us all?

In studying the Perfectability of human Nature and its progress towards perfection, in this World, on this Earth, (remember that) I have met many curious things, and interesting Characters.

About three hundred Years ago, There appeared a number of Men of Letters, who appeared to endeavour to believe neither too little, nor too much. They laboured to imitate the Hebrew Archers who could shoot to an hairs breadth. The Pope and his Church believed too much: Luther and his Church believed too little. This little band was headed by three great Scholars, Erasmus, Vives, and Budeus. This Triumvirate is said to have been at the head of the Republick of Letters, in that Age. Had Condorcet been Master of his Subject, I fancy he would have taken more Notice in his History of the progress of Mind, of these Characters. Have you their Writings? I wish I had. I shall confine myself at present to Vives. He wrote Commentaries on the City of God of St. Augustine, some parts of which were censured by the Doctors of the Louvain as too bold and too free. I know not, whether the following passage of the learned Spaniard was among the Sentiments condemned, or not.

"I have been much afflicted," says Vives, "when I have seriously considered, how diligently, and with what exact care, the Actions of Alexander, Hannibal, Scipio Pompey, Caesar and other Commanders: and the Lives of Socrates Plato Aristotle, and other Phylosophers, have been written and fixed in an everlasting Remembrance, so that there is not the least danger they can ever be lost: but then the Acts of the Apostles and Martyrs and Saints of our religion and of the Affairs of the rising and established Church, being involved in much darkness, are almost totally unknown, though they are of so much greater Advantage, than the Lives of the Phylosophers, or great Generals, both as to the improvement of our knowledge and Practice. For, what is written of these holy men, except a very few things is very much corrupted and defaced, with the mixture of many fables; while the Writer, indulging his own humour, doth not tell Us what the Saint did, but what the Historian would have had him done:

87. "Ah, faith and likewise faithlessness have destroyed men."

and the fancy of the Writer dictates the Life and not the truth of things."
And again, Vives says

"There have been men, who have thought it a great piece of Piety, to invent Lies for the sake of religion."

The great Cardinal Barronius too, confesses "There is nothing, which seems so much neglected to this day, as a true and certain Account of the Affairs of the Church, collected with an exact diligence. And that I may speak of the more Ancient, it is very difficult to find any of them, who have published Commentaries on this Subject which have hit the truth in all points."

Canus, too another Spanish Prelate of great name says "I speak it with grief, and not by way of reproach, Laertius has written the lives of the Philosophers, with more care and industry, than the Christians have those of the Saints; Suetonius has represented the Lives of the Caesars with much more truth and sincerity, than the Catholicks have the Affairs, I will not say of the Emperors, but even those of the Martyrs, holy Virgins and Confessors. For they have not concealed the Vices nor the very Suspicions of Vice, in good and commendable Philosophers or Princes, and in the worst of them, they discover the very colours or Appearances of Virtue. But the greatest part of our Writers, either follow the Conduct of their Affections, or industriously fain many things; so that I, for my part am very often both weary and ashamed of them; because I know they have thereby brought nothing of Advantage to the Church of Christ, but very much inconvenience."

Vives and Canus are Moderns, but Arnobius the Converter of Lactantius was ancient. He says "But neither could all that was done be written or arrive at the knowledge of all men. Many of our great Actions being done by obscure Men, and those who had no knowledge of Letters: and if some of them are committed to Letters and Writings; yet even here, by the malice of the Devils, and of men like them, whose great design and Study it is to intercept and ruin this truth, by interpolating, or adding some things to them, or by changing or taking out Words, Syllables, or Letters, they have put a Stop to the Faith of wise Men, and corrupted the truth of things."

Indeed, Mr. Jefferson, what could be invented to debase the ancient Christianism, which Greeks Romans, Hebrews, and Christian Factions, above all the Catholicks, have not fraudulently imposed upon the Publick? Miracles after Miracles have rolled down in Torrents, Wave succeeding Wave, in the Catholic Church from the Council of Nice, and long before, to this day. Aristotle, no doubt, thought his οὔτε πᾶσα πιστευοντες, οὔτε πασιν ἀπιστοῦντες [88] very wise and very profound: but what is its Worth? What Man, Woman or Child, ever believed, every Thing, or nothing?

Oh! that Priestley could live again! and have leisure and means. An Enquirer after Truth, who had neither time nor means might request him to search and research for answers to a few Questions.

1. Have We more than two Witnesses of the Life of Jesus? Mathew and John?
2. Have We one Witness to the Existence of Mathews Gospel in the first Century?
3. Have We one Witness of the Existence of Johns Gospell in the first Century?
4. Have We one Witness of the Existence of Marks Gospell in the first Century?
5. Have We one Witness of the Existence of Lukes Gospell in the first Century?
6. Have We any Witness of the existence of St. Thomas's Gospell, that is the Gospell of the Infancy in the first Century?
7. Have We any Evidence of the Existence of the Acts of the Apostles in the first Century?
8. Have We any Evidence of the Existence of the Supplement to the Acts of the Apostles, Peter and Paul, or Paul and Tecle, in the first Century?

Here I was interrupted, by a new book, Chataubriands Travels in Greece Palestine and Egypt [89] and by a Lung Fever, with which the amiable Companion [of] My Life has been violently And dangerously attacked.

December   13. I have fifty more questions to put to Priestley: but must adjourn them to a future Opportunity.

I have read Chateaubriand, with as much delight, as I ever read Bunyan['s] Pilgrims Progress, Robinson Crusoes Travels or Gullivers; or Whitefields; or Westleys Life; or the Life of St. Francis, St. Anthony or St. Ignatius Loyaula. A Work of infinite Learning, perfectly well written, a Magazine of Information: but an enthusiastic, biggotted, superstitious Roman Catholic throughout. If I were to indulge in jealous criticism and Conjecture, I should suspect, that there had been an Œcuemenical Counsel of Pope Cardinals and Bishops, and that this Traveller has been employed at their expence, to make this tour, to lay a foundation for the resurrection of the Catholic Hierarchy in Europe.

88. "Neither trusting all things nor distrusting all."
89. *Itineraire de Paris à Jerusalem et de Jerusalem à Paris; en allant par la Grèce et revenant par l'Egypte, la Barbarie et l'Espagne*, 3 vols. (Paris, 1811).

Have you read La Harpes Course de Litterature, in 15. Volumes? have you read St. Pierres Studies of Nature?

I am now reading the Controversy between Voltaire and Nonotte.[90]

Our Friend Rush has given Us for his last Legacy, an Analysis of some of the diseases of the Mind. Johnson said We are all more or less mad; and who is or has been more mad than Johnson?

I know of no Philosopher, or Theologian, or Moralist ancient or modern more profound; more infallible than Whitefield, if the Anecdote that I have heard be true.

He began; "Father Abraham"! with his hands and Eyes gracefully directed to the Heavens as I have more than once seen him; "Father Abraham," "who have you there with you"? ["]have you Catholicks?" No. "Have you Protestants". No. "Have you Churchmen". No. "Have you Dissenters". No. "Have you Presbyterians"? No. "Quakers?" No. ["]Anabaptists"? No. "Who have you then?" "Are you alone"? No.

"My Brethren,! You have the Answer to all these questions in the Words of my Text, "He who feareth God and worketh Righteousness, shall be accepted of him."

Allegiance to the Creator and Governor of the Milky Way and the Nebulae, and Benevolence to all his Creatures, is my Religion. Si quid novisti rectius estis [i.e., istis], Candidus imperti.[91] I am as ever

JOHN ADAMS

Adams to Jefferson

Quincy December 19. 1813

DEAR SIR

Ridendo dicere Verum, quid vetat.[92] I must make you and myself merry or melancholly by a little more Phylosophical Speculation about the formidable Subject of Aristocracy.

Not long after General Dearborn's return to Boston from the Army, a violent Alarm was excited and spread in Boston and through the country, by a report at first only secretly whispered in private circles that an Affair of Love was commencing between the General and Madam Bowdoin, the

90. Voltaire's *L'Essai sur les moeurs* (1754-58) versus Nonnette's *Erreurs de Voltaire* (1762), and Voltaire's rebuttal: *Eclaircissements historiques* (1763).
91. "If you know anything better than these maxims, candidly share them." Horace, *Epistulae*, 1. 6. 67.
92. "What forbids a man to speak the truth by joking?" Horace, *Sermones*, 1. 1. 24.

virtuous and amiable relict of my Friend and your Ambassador, James Bowdoin. The Surprise, the astonishment, were universal and the indignation very general. The exclamations were in every mouth. "Impossible!" "It cannot be!" "It is a false report." "It is too bad!" "It is a scandalous fiction!" "It is a malicious Calumny against Mrs. Bowdoin!" "Would that Lady disgrace her Husband?" She was herself a Bowdoin: "Would she degrade her own and her Husbands Name and Blood?" "Would she disgrace the illustrious Name of Bowdoin which has been so long famous in France?" "Would she disgrace her Husband who has been an Ambassador? And her Father in Law, who was her Uncle, and had been Governor?"

This is no exaggeration. I have heard all these exclamations. Have you read Cecilia,[93] or the Scottish Chiefs? [94] Is there any thing in the Character of the Delville Family, or in any of the Scotch Thanes, more outrageously Aristocratical, than these popular Sentiments in this our Democratical Country?

I undertook like a genuine Knight Errant to be the Champion of the Lady: and said some things very shocking to some Companies. To some very grave Ladies I said "Why, Madam, if Mrs. Bowdoins Object is Love and domestic comfort, the General is an healthy, robust and personable Man, which her former Husband was not. If her Object is Ambition, She will advance her Degree and condition by this Alliance; for neither Governors nor Ambassadors nor Earls hold so high a Rank as a Secretary at War and Commander in Chief, of all the Armies of a great Nation. Her Object cannot be Wealth, for She has enough; but if it was, Collectorships and other Offices must have given the General a Competency."

Till very lately the French descent of the Bowdoins has been known to very few and never boasted by any body. But it has been published and proclaimed by Mr. William Jenks, Secretary to the Board of Trustees of Bowdoin Colledge in his Eulogy on Mr. Bowdoin. This Eulogy Mrs. Bowdoin, I presume has sent to You as well as to me. If not, I will send you an extract.

The Race of Baudouins it is true has long been notable in France. The Name I believe is to be found among the Crusaders to Jerusalem, when, no doubt, they were Orthodox Catholicks: but afterwards, in the Crusades against the Albigenses, they were suspected on both Sides. In all the Seiges and in all the battles, there were many Nobles and Cavaliers among the Sectaries. The Counts De Foix, De Comminges, De Besiers, De Bearn, and almost all the Lords who inhabited towards the Pyrennes, were of the Sect, or at least favoured and protected it. The Count de Thoulouse, without de-

93. Fanny Burney, *Cecilia, or Memoirs of an Heiress,* 5 vols. (London, 1782).
94. Jane Porter, *The Scottish Chiefs,* 5 vols. (N. Y., 1810).

claring himself a Manichean (so they called the Albigenses as well as the Waldenses) had for the Sect and for their Preachers a respect which bordered on extravagance, and laid the foundation of all the misfortunes of his princely house. Baudouin, Brother of the Count de Thoulouse, was hanged on a Tree by the Hereticks, notwithstanding the Tenderness of the Family for them, and though he begged for time to confess and receive the Communion.

The Count de Thoulouse (Baudouin) acted a mysterious part. Though he protested his orthodox faith, yet he obstinately protected the Hereticks. He made Promisses, but could not determine to fullfill them. The Pope innocent the third, interrested himself in his favour, and arrested, for some time, the Proceedings of the Legates against him. But he knew not how to take Advantage of these dispositions. Without Firmness, without Wisdom, without Prudence, he could not conquer the secret Inclination he had for Heresy; nor foresee that he was commencing the misfortunes of his Family; nor that the Ambition of the neighbouring Potentate, would soon compleat its destruction. A Miracle, it seems, was wrought for the destruction of this Family. Simon de Monfort with only Eight hundred Men, and One Thousand Fantassins, attacked the Army of the King of Arragon and the Count de Thoulouse, which was of one hundred thousand men, and totally defeated them.

This I learn from Nonotte, the Scourge of Voltaire, whom Voltaire scourges in his turn with a long Catalog of "Sottises." This is however but a ray of the historical Glory of the name. Baudoin the eighth Count of Flanders was Emperor of Constantinople in 1204. Baudouin the 2d. was the last latin Emperor of Constantinople in 1228. A Baudouin was King of Jerusalem in the 12th. Century and Saladin or Noraddin his Enemy said he had not left his equal. The name has been distinguished in Lettres as well as in War and Politicks. A Baudouin was solicited by Henry 3, then Duke of Anjou, to write in Justification of the Massacre of St. Bartholemy. But he was too honest a man. Another Baudouin, who died in 1650 translated all the Classicks and wrote many other Things.

All these litterary, civil, political, millitary, religious, noble, royal and imperial honours are now to be devolved on the Bowdoin Family of Massachusetts. But the name is extinct in the male line. To repair this breach a law of the State has been procured to alter the Name of a Sisters Son from Temple to Bowdoin, and to him the Family Estate is given. Sir John Temple, too, the Father of that Son, has poured a Stream of English noble blood into the mighty river of Bawdoin. A splendid Funeral Sermon of Mr. Gardner has been printed: "On the Death of Elizabeth Lady Temple." The name of Bowdoin is immortalized, by a flourishing University founded by the Family. You have immortalized the Name by making an Ambassador of it, and by making a Cousin another Ambassador.

Do you call this natural or artificial Aristocracy? Aristocracy it is most certainly, for the Name of Bowdoin in this State has more influence than the name of Russell or Howard has in England. So have the names of Livingston and Clinton in New York. We had a General Sterling, but that Title would not satisfy. He must be called Lord Sterling, and his Daughter "Lady Kitty Duer." Our Russell Family wear the Arms, and claim Relation to the Dukes of Bedford. Our Quincys are descended from Saer de Quincy, Marquis of Winchester, who extorted Magna Charta from King John, and whose Signature to that Instrument, "Sayer de Winton," you have seen in the British Musæum and in Blacstones Copy. General Talmadge of Connecticutt is by Law a Member of the British House of Peers. And who knows but We may have Lord and Ladies Yrujo's from Spain and Lord and Ladies Mansfields from Great Britain? Aristocracy, like Waterfowl, dives for Ages and then rises with brighter Plumage. It is a subtle Venom that diffuses itself unseen, over Oceans and Continents, and tryumphs over time. If I could prevent its deleterious influence I would put it all into "The Hole" of Calcutta: [95] but as this is impossible, as it is a Phœnix that rises again out of its own Ashes, I know no better Way than to chain it in a "Hole by itself," and place a Watchfull Centinel on each Side of it.

An hundred other foreign Aristocracies have sown and are sowing their Seeds in this Country: and We have an Abundance of them springing up in this Country not from Virtues and Talents so much as from Banks and Land Jobbing. I am as ever Yours

JOHN ADAMS

Adams to Jefferson

Quincy Decr. 25th. 1813

DEAR SIR

Answer my Letters at Your Leisure. Give yourself no concern. I write as for a refuge and protection against Ennui.

The fundamental Principle of all Phylosophy and all Christianity is "REJOICE ALWAYS IN ALL THINGS. Be thankfull at all times for all good and all that We call evil." Will it not follow, that I ought to rejoice and be

95. The narrow prison into which the Nawab of Bengal threw his European prisoners in July 1756. Most of them perished by suffocation.

thankful that Priestley has lived? Aye! that Voltaire has lived? [96] That Gibbon has lived? That Hume has lived, though a conceited Scotchman? That Bolingbroke has lived, tho' a haughty arrogant supercilious Dogmatist? that Burke and Johnson have lived, though superstitious Slaves or Self deceiving Hypocrites both. Is it not laughable to hear Burke call Bolingbroke a superficial Writer? To hear him ask "Who ever read him through?" Had I been present I would have answered him "I, I, myself, I have read him through, more than fifty Years ago, and more than five times in my Life, and once within five Years past. And in my Opinion the epithat "Superficial" belongs to you and your Friend Johnson more than to him. I might say much more. But I believe Burke and Johnson to have been as political Christians, as Leo 10th.

I return to Priestley, though I have great Complaints against him for personal Injuries and Persecution, at the same time that I forgive it all, and hope and pray that he may be pardoned for it all, above. Dr. Broklesby an intimate Friend and convivial Companion of Johnson told me, that Johnson died in Agonies of Horror of Annihilation, and all the Accounts We have of his death corroborate this Account of Broklesby. Dread of Annihilation! Dread of Nothing? A dread of Nothing I should think would be no dread at all. Can there be any real substantial rational fear of nothing? Were you on your deathbed, and in your last moments informed by demonstration or Revelation that you would cease to think and to feel at your dissolution, should you be terrified? You might be ashamed of yourself for having lived so long, to bear the proud Mans Contumely. You might be ashamed of your Maker, and compare him to a little Girl amusing herself her Brothers and Sisters by blowing Bubbles in Soap Sudds. You might compare him to Boys sporting with Crakers and Rocketts: or to Men employed in making more artificial Fire Works; or to Men and Women at Farces and Operas, or Sadlers Wells Exploits; or to Politicians in their Intrigues; or to Heroes in their Butcheries; or to Popes in their Devilisms. But what should you fear? Nothing. Emori nolo Sed me mortuum esse nihil estimo. [97]

To return to Priestley. You could make a more luminous Book, than his upon "the Doctrines of Heathen Phylosophers compared with those of Revelation." Why has he not given Us a more satisfactory Account of the Pythagorean Phylosophy and Theology? He barely names Ocellus, who lived long before Plato. His Treatise of Kings and Monarchy has been destroyed, I conjecture by Platonic Phylosophers, Platonic Jews or Chris-

96. JA's marginal note: "I should have given my Reason for rejoicing in Voltaire etc. It is because I believe they have done more than Even Luther or Calvin, to lower the Tone of that proud Hierarchy that shot itself up above the Clouds, and more to propagate religious Liberty than Calvin or Luther, or even lock [i.e., Locke]."
97. "I have no wish to die, but that I be dead and considered as nothing."

tians, or by fraudulent Republicans or Despots. His Treatise of "The Universe["] has been preserved. He labours to prove the Eternity of the World. The Marquiss D'Argens translated it, in all its noble Simplicity. The Abby Batteux has since given another translation. D'Argens not only explains the Text, but sheds more light upon the antient Systems. His remarks are so many Treatisses, which devellop the concatenation of antient Opinions. The most essential Ideas of the Theology, of the Physics and of the Morality of the antients are clearly explained: and their different Doctrines, compared with one another, and with the modern discoveries. I wish I owned this Book and 100,000 more that I want every day, now when I am almost incapable of making any Use of them. No doubt he informs Us that Pythagoras was a great Traveller.

Priestley barely mentions Timaeus: but it does not appear that he had read him. Why has he not given Us an Account of him and his Book? He was before Plato and gave him the Idea of his Timæus, and much more of his Phylosophy. After his Master he maintained the existence of Matter: that Matter was capable of receiving all sorts of forms: that a moving Power agitatated all the Parts of it: and that an Intelligence directed the moving Power; that this Intelligence produced a regular and harmonious World. This Intelligence had seen a Plan, an *Idea* (Logos) in conformity to which, it wrought, and without which it would not have known what it was about, nor what it wanted to do. This Plan was the *Idea*, Image or Model, which had represented, to the Supream Intelligence, the World before it existed, which had directed it, in its Action upon the moving Power, and which it contemplated in forming the Elements the Bodies and the World. This Model was distinguished from The Intelligence which produced the World as the Architect is from his plans. He divided, The productive Cause of the World into a Spirit, which directed the moving Force, and into an Image, which determined it in the choice of the directions which it gave to the moving Force, and the forms which it gave to matter.

I wonder that Priestley has overlooked this because it is the same Phylosophy with Plato's and would have shewn that the Pythagorean as well as the Platonic Phylosophers probably concurred in the fabrication of the Christian Trinity. Priestley mentions the name of Archytas, but does not appear to have read him; tho he was a Sucessor of Pythagoras, and a great Mathematician, a great Statesman and a great General. John Gram a learned and honourable Dane has given a handsome Edition of his Works with a latin translation, and an ample Account of his Life and Writings. Saleucus The Legislator of Locris and Charondas of Sybaris were Disciples of Pythagoras, and both celebrated to immortality for the Wisdom of their Laws, 500 Years before Christ. Why are those Laws lost?

I say *the Spirit of Party* has destroyed them, civil, political and ecclesiastical Bigotry. Despotical, monarchical Aristocratical and democratical Fury,
have all been employed in this Work of destruction of every Thing that
could give Us true light and a clear insight of Antiquity. For every One
of these Parties, when possessed of Power, or when they have been Under-
most and Struggling to get Uppermost, has been equally prone to every
Species of fraud and Violence, and Usurpation.

Why has not Priestley mentioned these Legislators? The Preamble to
the Laws of Zaleucus, which is all that remains, is as orthodox Christian
Theology as Priestleys: and Christian Benevolence and forgiveness of
Injuries almost as clearly expressed.

Priestley ought to have done impartial Justice to Philosophy and
Phylosophers, Phylosophy which is the result of Reason, is the first, the
original Revelation of The Creator to his Creature, Man. When this
Revelation is clear and certain, by Intuition or necesary Induction, no
subsequent Revelation supported by Prophecies or Miracles can supercede
it. Philosophy is not only the love of Wisdom, but the Science of the
Universe and its Cause. There is, there was and there will be but one
Master of Philosophy in the Universe. Portions of it, in different degrees
are revealed to Creatures. Phylosophy looks with an impartial Eye on all
terrestrial religions. I have examined all, as well as my narrow Sphere, my
streightened means and my busy Life would allow me; and the result is,
that the Bible is the best book in the World. It contains more of my little
Phylosophy than all the Libraries I have seen: and such Parts of it as I
cannot reconcile to my little Phylosophy I postpone for future Investigation.

Priestley ought to have given Us a Sketch of the Religion and Morals
of Zoroaster of Sanchoniathon of Confucius, and all the Founders of Religions before Christ, whose superiority, would from such a comparison
have appeared the more transcendant.

Priestley ought to have told us, that Pythagoras passed twenty Years, in
his Travels in India, in Egypt, in Chaldea, perhaps in Sodom and Gomor-
rah, Tyre and Sydon. He ought to have told Us that in India he conversed with the Brahmans and read the Shast[r]a,[98] 5000 Years old, written
in the Language of the sacred Sanscrists with the elegance and Sentiments
of Plato. Where is to be found Theology more orthodox or Phylosophy
more profound than in the Introduction to the Shast[r]a? "God is one,
creator of all, Universal Sphere, without beginning, without End. God
governs all the Creation by a general Providence, resulting from his eternal
designs. ——— Search not the Essence and the nature of the Eternal, who

98. The shastra, or sastra (treatise), especially that explaining the Vedas, the most
ancient sacred literature of the Hindus.

is one; Your research will be vain and presumptuous. It is enough that, day by day, and night by night, You adore his Power, his Wisdom and his Goodness, in his Works." ["]The Eternal willed, in the fullness of time, to communicate of his Essence and of his Splendor, to Beings capable of perceiving it. They as yet existed not. The Eternal Willed, and they were. He created Birma, Vitsnow, and Sib." These Doctrines, sublime if ever there were any sublime, Pythagoras learned in India and taught them to Zaleucus and his other disciples. He there learned also his Metempsychosis, but this never was popular, never made much progress in Greece or Italy, or any other Country besides India and Tartary, the Region of the Grand immortal Lama: And how does this differ, from the Possessions of Demons in Greece and Rome, from the Demon of Socrates from the Worship of Cows and Crocodiles in Egypt and elsewhere. After migrating throw various Animals from Elephants to Serpents according to their behaviour, Souls that at last behaved well became Men and Women, and then if they were good, they went to Heaven. All ended in Heaven if they became virtuous. Who can wonder at the Widow of Malabar. Where is the Lady, who, if he[r] faith were without doubt, that she should go to Heaven with her Husband on the one, or migrate into a Toad or a Waspe on the other, would not lay down on The Pile and set fire to the Fuel? Modifications and disguises of the Metempsichosis had crept into Egypt and Greece and Rome and other Countries. Have you read Farmer on the Dæmons and Possessions of the New Testament?

According to the Shast[r]a, Moisazor, with his Companions rebelled against the Eternal, and were precipitated, down to Ondero, the region of Darkness. Do you know any thing of the Prophecy of Enoch? [99] Can you give me a Comment on the 6th. the 9th. the 14th verses of the Epistle of Jude? [100]

If I am not weary of writing, I am sure you must be of reading such inchoherent rattle. I will not persecute you so severely in future, if I can help it. So farewell

JOHN ADAMS

99. The Book(s) of Enoch, written *ca.* 170 B.C. to 64 B.C., constitutes an important piece of apocalyptic literature. The Christian Church began to discredit it *ca.* 300 and it was lost from the ninth century until 1773, when two manuscripts were discovered. They were translated frequently and critical inquiries made into their contents.

100. The Epistle of Jude, verse "6. And the angels which kept not their first estate, but left their own habitation, he hath reserved in everlasting chains, under darkness, unto the judgment of the great day.

"9. Yet Michael the archangel, when contending with the devil, he disputed about the body of Moses, durst not bring against him a railing accusation, but said, The Lord rebuke thee.

"14. And Enoch also, the seventh from Adam, prophesied of these, saying Behold, the Lord cometh with ten thousand of his saints,

"15. To execute judgment upon all. . . ."

11

"The Eighteenth Century...
most honourable to human Nature"

❋ JANUARY 1814 – MAY 1816 ❋

A S PHILOSOPHICAL CITIZENS of the eighteenth century, Adams and
Jefferson witnessed the rude shaking and shattering of their
world by the Napoleonic Wars. With Europe in turmoil and reactionary forces in the ascendant during the opening decades of the new
century, the two American statesmen weighed their own era and
found the balance in its favor. In spite of errors and vices, declared
Adams, it was "the most honourable to human Nature.... Arts, Sciences useful to Men, ameliorating their condition, were improved,
more than in any former equal Period." [1] Jefferson agreed. "I think
too we may add, to the great honor of science and the arts, that their
natural effect is, by illuminating public opinion, to erect it into a
Censor, before which the most exalted tremble for their future, as well
as present fame.... You must have observed while in Europe, as I
thought I did, that those who administered the governments of the
greater powers at least, had a respect to faith, and considered the
dignity of their governments as involved in it's integrity." [2]

The American Revolution had become a factor in this civilizing and
liberating process, nourishing the revolutionary movement in France
which, Jefferson admitted, turned out to be far more bloody than he
had expected in 1789. "That same light from our West seems to have
spread and illuminated the very engines employed to extinguish it....
The idea of representative government has taken root and growth

1. JA to TJ, Nov. 13, 1815, below, 456.
2. TJ to JA, Jan. 11, 1816, below, 458-59.

among them.... Opinion is power, and that opinion will come." [3] Although the science of government had never been much studied, Adams took hope from experiments in constitution-making in America and Europe since 1776 and from the advancement in civil and religious liberties, recalling, no doubt, his own contribution to this great achievement. Realist that he was, however, he could not overlook the low "Morality of Patriotism" that prevailed among nations. All contemporary sovereigns "have acted on the same Principle 'All things were made for my Use.'" Adams scoffed at philosophers and priests in all ages who, expressing belief in the perfectability of human nature, had no respect for Truth. [4]

If Adams and Jefferson agreed that the eighteenth century was an age of progress in science and the arts, including republican government, how did they assess the status of the individual in this class-ridden society? Amid concern over the universal rights of man in the abstract, how well had men in the flesh fared in their pursuit of life, liberty, and happiness? Adams, desiring to get down to specific examples, soon provoked a reply from Jefferson concerning the reliving of his seventy years. "I think with you," Jefferson affirmed, "that it is a good world on the whole, that it has been framed on a principle of benevolence, and more pleasure than pain dealt out to us.... How much pain have cost us the evils which have never happened? My temperament is sanguine. I steer my bark with Hope in the head, leaving Fear astern." [5] In contributing toward the good life of his fellow men this philosopher relied on science (accumulated knowledge) to serve practical ends for the benefit of all.

Adams carried the concept a step farther. He was willing to sail in Jefferson's bark because "Hope is all that endures"—the hope of a future and better state. "The Maker of the Universe, the Cause of all Things, whether we call it, *Fate* or *Chance* or *God*, has inspired this Hope. If it is a *Fraud*, We shall never know it." But if death were revealed as eternal extinction, "What would Men say to their Maker? ... They would reproach him; they would curse him to his Face." [6] To end up with such a conclusion was impossible for Adams. "Why then should We abhor the Word God, and fall in Love with the Word

3. *Ibid.*
4. JA to TJ, July 16, 1814, Feb. 2, 1816, below, 436, 462.
5. JA to TJ, March 2, 1816, and TJ to JA, April 8, 1816, below, 464, 467.
6. JA to TJ, May 3, 1816, below, 471.

Fate?" Such negation was atheism in which Liberty and Spirit and the Universe could have no meaning.[7] Adams rejected this philosophy, which he attributed to Diderot and Voltaire, but found these philosophers no less "restless vain extravagant Animals" than Robespierre and Bonaparte.

As ambassadors who had served in Europe before the storm broke, Adams and Jefferson were intensely interested in Napoleon's meteoric career. During the days of the *ancien régime* they had sought to maintain American neutrality as the cornerstone of foreign policy. While in office President Adams and President Jefferson adhered to this same policy. Personal sympathies aside, they regarded both belligerents as inimical to the United States and they watched for any advantage that the turn of events offered. But their country could not escape the world-wide repercussions of Bonaparte's conquest of the Continent. It precipitated the War of 1812, which brought in its train the threat of disunion by New England's commercial interests, reminding Adams of the Virginia and Kentucky Resolutions of 1798-99. "The Northern States are now retaliating," he exclaimed. "It is a mortification to me, to see how servile Mimicks they are." [8]

How much closer the war seemed to Massachusetts and to Adams than to Virginia and to Jefferson, George Ticknor, a youthful Bostonian of twenty-two, had an unusual opportunity to observe. Seeking a letter of introduction from Adams to Jefferson, he approached Adams through a mutual friend, George Cabot, merchant-banker in the inner circles of New England business interests. At Quincy, in the Adams's parlor, with Mrs. Adams knitting and the awe-struck Ticknor listening, the conversation became a soliloquy by Mr. Adams. He expatiated on the serious condition of the country made worse by the Hartford Convention of malcontents, presided over by Cabot, who, fearful of secession, was providing a moderating influence. Adams was dressed in a tightly buttoned single-breasted coat into which he tried to thrust his hand as his voice became more and more animated. When the buttons did not yield readily, he forced his hand in, exclaiming, "Thank God, thank God! George Cabot's close-buttoned ambition has broke out at last: he wants to be President of New England, sir!" [9]

7. JA to TJ, March 2, 1816, below, 465.
8. JA to TJ, July [3], 1813, above, 350.
9. G. S. Hillard, ed., *Life, Letters, and Journals of George Ticknor* (Boston, 1877), I, 13; JA to TJ, Dec. 11 and 20, 1814, below, 440, 441.

About six weeks later Ticknor was Jefferson's guest at Monticello, along with a fellow Bostonian, Francis C. Gray, and Daniel Webster. In the serene atmosphere of the mountain top they browsed among the seven thousand books which Mr. Jefferson had just sold to the United States—volumes to become the nucleus of a new Library of Congress after the rebuilding of the Capitol which the British had burned. Delighted with his young guests, Jefferson considered Ticknor "the best bibliograph I have met with," [10] and their conversation ranged over many subjects, ancient and modern. Jefferson captivated the young men as he talked freely about the public debt and the expediency of separation of powers in government. And Ticknor recalled an amusing incident concerning the "old philosopher." Late one night Jefferson's grandson brought the newspaper from Charlottesville reporting the defeat of the British by General Jackson in the Battle of New Orleans, but Jefferson, who had gone to bed, was content to wait until morning to read the account.[11]

While the last chapter of the Napoleonic regime was being recorded during the Hundred Days, March to June 1815, Jefferson and Adams from their long-range vantage point expressed mixed feelings about the denouement of the protracted drama. Jefferson had referred to Bonaparte, banished to the island of Elba in 1814, as "the Attila of the age dethroned," a usurper in civil life and no statesman; and Adams castigated him for his vanity, swollen by conquest. Yet these Americans could not forget their long-time foe: was Bonaparte the greater tyrant, they asked, or John Bull, who had never ceased to domineer in the play of power politics? [12]

When Napoleon escaped from Elba and was welcomed back by the French people as deliverer of the nation, Jefferson could rationalize the outcome by saying that the Emperor in his new role was preferable to a Bourbon king. "At least he is defending the cause of his nation," wrote Jefferson, "and that of all mankind, the rights of every people to independance and self-government. . . . We had better take the chance of his word for doing right, than the certainty of the wrong which his adversaries are doing and avowing." Before Jefferson mailed

10. TJ to JA, June 10, 1815, below, 443.
11. Hillard, ed., *Life of Ticknor*, I, 34-38; Francis Calley Gray, *Thomas Jefferson in 1814; being an Account of a Visit to Monticello, Virginia*, ed. by Henry S. Rowe and T. Jefferson Coolidge, Jr. (Boston, 1924), 67-74; Fletcher Webster, ed., *The Private Correspondence of Daniel Webster* (Boston, 1857), I, 304-66.
12. TJ to JA, July 5, 1814, and JA to TJ, July 16, 1814, below, 431, 436.

this letter, he received news of Bonaparte's second abdication. He then added a postscript: "Very well. . . . [The French] have taken the allies at their word, that they had no object in the war but his removal. The nation is now free to give itself a good government, either with or without a Bourbon." [13] Adams hoped that Liberty, Equality, and Fraternity would never again blindly surrender to Ambition, but such was not the prevailing spirit at the Congress of Vienna where reactionary leaders established the peace of 1815. "When," asked Adams, "will the Rights of Mankind, the Liberties and Independence of Nations be respected?" [14]

In passing judgment on the Age of the Enlightenment and the recent cataclysm of Europe, Adams and Jefferson discoursed not only from their own experience but also from a knowledge of history which provided perspective on the near past. They realized that to the younger generation of the early nineteenth century the American Revolution was history in a somewhat different sense from what they as participants regarded it and that the "external facts" which were the sole concern of many of their inquirers fell far short of telling the whole story. These founding fathers were anxious that the American people should profit by a thorough knowledge of the Revolution. An understanding of the origin of the United States would be useful in making them appreciative of republican government. "Who shall write the history of the American revolution? Who can write it?" asked Adams as he found leisure to reflect upon those momentous times.[15] Not John Marshall, whose dull biography of Washington, a "party diatribe," never penetrated the externals. Not the Italian Carlos Botta, who copied too much from other writers, including Marshall. Jefferson had a higher regard for Botta's precision and candor and his "just sense of right in opposition to usurpation"; [16] strangely he overlooked David Ramsay's well-tempered *History of the American Revolution* (1789), although the author had sent him a copy soon after publication.[17] It was disturbing to the reminiscent patriots that young Americans regarded the Revolution and the War for Independence as

13. TJ to JA, Aug. 10[-11], 1815, and TJ to AA, Jan. 11, 1817, below, 454, 503.
14. JA to TJ, Aug. 24, 1815, May 26, 1817, below, 455-56, 517.
15. JA to TJ, July 30, 1815, below, 451.
16. TJ to JA, Aug. 10, 1815, May 5, 1817, below, 452-53, 513 and nn.
17. TJ had read Ramsay's *History of the Revolution of South-Carolina* (Trenton, 1785) and assisted in getting a French translation printed in France. Sowerby, *Catalogue of the Library of Thomas Jefferson*, I, 229-35.

identical. When Adams declared that "the Revolution was in the Minds of the People," he gave the whole problem new perspective.[18] Jefferson thought that it was difficult, if not impossible, to date the beginning of the Revolution,[19] and neither he nor Adams speculated on its termination, perhaps because they still saw evidence of its effects in their declining years.

Emphasis on the philosophical and interpretive aspects of history should not obscure Jefferson's persistent queries concerning authenticity of the sources. He rescued and preserved numerous manuscripts pertaining to colonial and revolutionary Virginia. He saved some unique records of the Continental Congress and he appreciated the basic importance of Madison's Journal of the Federal Convention, although it was inaccessible during Jefferson's lifetime. Adams, too, in his study of the state constitutions pointed out that he was personally acquainted with most of the gentlemen who "had the principal share in the first draughts of these documents," [20] and of course he had access to the texts.

It is understandable, in the light of Jefferson's attention to historical sources, that he reacted vigorously to the news about the purported Mecklenburg Declaration of Independence of 1775, which was belatedly published in 1819. This was both a challenge to the priority of his own great document and a mustering of inconclusive, misdirected evidence to contradict history. His clear-cut refutation won the support of Adams, who at first had been inclined to accept the North Carolina claim; but this was only the beginning of a prolonged controversy that has been revived from time to time for more than a century.[21] In the same spirit of historical criticism Adams reviewed the historiography of the *Acta Sanctorum*, compiled and preserved by the Jesuit Bollandists before their suppression by the papacy and after the restoration of the order in 1813. Adams could not accept as authentic historical research their attempt to discriminate among true, false, and dubious miracles. He could only conclude that the *Lives of the Saints* as ecclesiastical history, when exposed to rational criticism

18. JA to TJ, Aug. 24, 1815, below, 455.
19. TJ to JA, May 17, 1818, and JA to TJ, May 29, 1818, below, 524, 525.
20. "Defence of the Constitutions," *Works*, IV, 293.
21. JA to TJ, June 22, 1819; TJ to JA, July 9, 1819; and JA to TJ, July 21 and 28, 1819, below, 542-46; William H. Hoyt, *The Mecklenburg Declaration of Independence; a Study of Evidence* ... (N. Y. and London, 1907).

and interpretation, was an "enormous Mass of Lies Frauds, Hypocracy and Imposture," and Jefferson agreed.[22]

Close students of history themselves, Adams and Jefferson recognized the significance of the revolutionary age through which they had lived and anticipated its usefulness as history to posterity. They regarded history as a humanistic study through which the recorded deeds of men were assessed in relation to the advancement of society; and they believed that the discoverable truth, when applied by reasonable men, would benefit their contemporaries and offer assurance for the future. As history could scarcely be divorced from philosophy, so its didactic quality strengthened its usefulness. It was likely to be "whig" or "tory," reinforcing the author's prejudices and point of view. Nevertheless, history was a product of reason, not revelation; but impartiality, that chimera of the twentieth-century historian, had not yet joined forces with scientific objectivity.

In the spirit of the Enlightenment, philosophers put the facts to useful purposes for the amelioration of society. In America the prospects of accomplishment seemed best and the Revolution had confirmed that hope through the establishment of republican government. The indoctrination of the heirs of the Enlightenment in the United States is suggested by the advice of Mrs. Adams to her son John Quincy in his early teens, when he was in Holland with his father in 1781:

I would recommend it to you to become acquainted with the history of that country, as in many respects it is similar to the Revolution of your own. Tyranny and oppression were the original causes of the revolt of both countries. It is from a wide and extensive view of mankind that a just and true estimate can be formed of the powers of human nature.[23]

Man and nature, history and philosophy, collaborated in an Age of Reason and Progress.

22. JA to TJ, June 22, 1815, and TJ to JA, Aug. 10, 1815, below, 450, 452. JA also cited the *Acta Sanctorum* as evidence against reactionary theologians by branding it "the most complete History of the Corruptions of Christianity." JA to TJ, Aug. 24, 1815, below, 454-55.

23. AA to J. Q. Adams, May 26, 1781, Charles Francis Adams, ed., *Familiar Letters of John Adams and His Wife Abigail Adams, during the Revolution* (N.Y. and Cambridge, 1876), 395.

Jefferson to Adams

Monticello Jan. 24. 14.

DEAR SIR

I have great need of the indulgence so kindly extended to me in your favor of Dec. 25. of permitting me to answer your friendly letters at my leisure. My frequent and long absences from home are a first cause of tardiness in my correspondence, and a 2d. the accumulation of business during my absence, some of which imperiously commands first attentions. I am now in arrear to you for your letters of Nov. 12. 14. 16. Dec. 3. 19. 25.

I have made some enquiry about Taylor's book,[24] and I learn from a neighbor of his that it has been understood for some time that he was writing a political work. We had not heard of it's publication, nor has it been announced in any of our papers. But this must be the book of 630. pages which you have recieved; and certainly neither the style nor the stuff of the author of Arator can ever be mistaken. In the latter work, as you observe, there are some good things, but so involved in quaint, in far-fetched, affected, mystical conciepts, and flimsy theories, that who can take the trouble of getting at them?

You ask me if I have ever seen the work of J. W. Goethens Schristen? Never. Nor did the question ever occur to me before Where get we the ten commandments? The book indeed gives them to us verbatim. But where did it get them? For itself tells us they were written by the finger of god on tables of stone, which were destroyed by Moses: it specifies those on the 2d. set of tables in different form and substance, but still without saying how the others were recovered. But the whole history of these books is so defective and doubtful that it seems vain to attempt minute enquiry into it: and such tricks have been plaid with their text, and with the texts of other books relating to them, that we have a right, from that cause, to entertain much doubt what parts of them are genuine. In the New testament there is internal evidence that parts of it have proceeded from an extraordinary man; and that other parts are of the fabric of very inferior minds. It is as easy to separate those parts, as to pick out diamonds from dunghills. The matter of the first was such as would be preserved in the memory of the hearers, and handed on by tradition for a long time; the latter such stuff as might be gathered up, for imbedding it, any where, and at any time.

24. Taylor, *An Inquiry into the Government of the United States.*

I have nothing of Vives, or Budaeus, and little of Erasmus. If the familiar histories of the saints, the want of which they regret, would have given us the histories of those tricks which these writers acknolege to have been practised, and of the lies they agree have been invented for the sake of religion, I join them in their regrets. These would be the only parts of their histories worth reading. It is not only the sacred volumes they have thus interpolated, gutted, and falsified, but the works of others relating to them, and even the laws of the land. We have a curious instance of one of these pious frauds in the Laws of Alfred. He composed, you know, from the laws of the Heptarchy, a Digest for the government of the United kingdom, and in his preface to that work he tells us expressly the sources from which he drew it, to wit, the laws of Ina, of Offa and Aethelbert, (not naming the Pentateuch.) But his pious Interpolator, very awkwardly, *premises* to his work four chapters of Exodus (from the 20th. to the 23d.) as a part of the laws of the land; so that Alfred's *preface* is made to stand in the body of the work. Our judges too have lent a ready hand to further these frauds, and have been willing to lay the yoke of their own opinions on the necks of others; to extend the coercions of municipal law to the dogmas of their religion, by declaring that these make a part of the law of the land. In the Year Book 34. H. 6, fo. 38. in Quare impedit,[25] where the question was how far the Common law takes notice of the Ecclesiastical law, Prisot, Chief Justice, in the course of his argument says 'a tiels leis que ils de Seint eglise ont en *ancien scripture,* covient a nous a donner credence; car ces Common ley sur quels touts manners leis sont fondes: et auxy, Sir, nous sumus obliges de conustre lour ley de saint eglise Etc.' [26] Finch begins the business of falsification by mistranslating and mistating the words of Prisot thus 'to such laws of the church as have warrant in *holy scripture* our law giveth credence,' citing the above case and the words of Prisot in the margin, Finch's law. B. 1. c. 3. Here then we find *ancien scripture,* antient writing, translated 'holy scripture.' This, Wingate in 1658. erects into a Maxim of law, in the very words of Finch, but citing Prisot, and not Finch. And Sheppard tit. Religion, in 1675 laying it down in the same words of Finch, quotes the Year Book, Finch and Wingate. Then comes Sr. Matthew Hale, in the case of the King v. Taylor 1 Ventr. 293. 3 Keb. 607. and declares that 'Christianity is parcel of the laws of England.' Citing nobody, and resting it, with his judgment against the

25. Reports of cases in the *Year Book* cover the period from Edward I (1292) to Henry VIII (1536). The reference is to a law of the thirty-fourth year of Henry VI's reign, folio 38. Cases in Quare impedit are actions in English law brought only in the Court of Common Pleas to recover the right of a patron over a church or benefice.

26. "To such laws of the church as have warrant in ancient writing our law giveth credence; for it is the common law on which all laws are based; and also, Sir, we are obliged to recognize the law of the church, etc."

witches,[27] on his own authority, which indeed was sound and good in all cases into which no superstition or bigotry could enter. Thus strengthened, the court in 1728 in the King v. Woolston, would not suffer it to be questioned whether to write against Christianity was punishable at Common law, saying it had been so settled by Hale in Taylor's case. 2 Stra. 834. Wood therefore, 409. without scruple, lays down as a principle that all blasphemy and profaneness are offences at the Common law, and cites Strange. Blackstone, in 1763. repeats in the words of Sr. Matthew Hale that 'Christianity is part of the laws of England,' citing Ventris and Strange ubi supra. And Ld. Mansfield in the case of the Chamberlain of London v. Evans, in 1767. qualifying somewhat the position, says that 'the essential principles of revealed religion are part of the Common law.' [28] Thus we find this string of authorities all hanging by one another on a single hook, a mistranslation by Finch of the words of Prisot, or on nothing. For all quote Prisot, or one another, or nobody. Thus Finch misquotes Prisot; Wingate also, but using Finch's words; Sheppard quotes Prisot, Finch and Wingate; Hale cites nobody; the court in Woolston's case cite Hale; Wood cites Woolston's case; Blackstone that and Hale; and Ld. Mansfield volunteers his own ipse dixit. And who now can question but that the whole Bible and Testament are a part of the Common law? And that Connecticut, in her blue laws, laying it down as a principle that the laws of god should be the laws of their land, except where their own contradicted them, did anything more than express, with a salvo, what the English judges had less cautiously declared without any restriction? And what I dare say our cunning Chief Justice [Marshall] would swear to, and find as many sophisms to twist it out of the general terms of our Declarations of rights, and even the stricter text of the Virginia 'act for the freedom of religion' as he did to twist Burr's neck out of the halter of treason.[29] May we not say then with him who was all candor and benevolence 'Woe unto you, ye lawyers, for ye lade men with burdens grievous to bear.'

27. In King v. Taylor, 1661-62, at the Bury St. Edmonds Assizes two women were tried for witchcraft. In directing the jury Hale stated there was no doubt of the existence of witches as proved by the Bible, the general consent, and acts of Parliament.

28. In this case Mansfield spoke in favor of a Dissenter's not accepting official appointment which required that he take communion in the Anglican Church and excused him from payment of a fine.

29. Aaron Burr was indicted for treason in 1807 in connection with his "conspiracy" in the West and was brought to trial in the United States Circuit Court at Richmond, Va., before Chief Justice John Marshall sitting as circuit judge. The interpretation Marshall gave to the treason clause in the Constitution so restricted the meaning that Burr was acquitted. The trial had its political overtones in the friction between President Jefferson and the Chief Justice. Thomas P. Abernethy, *The Burr Conspiracy* (N.Y., 1954), 227-49.

I think with you that Priestley, in his comparison of the doctrines of Philosophy and of revelation, did not do justice to the undertaking, but he felt himself pressed by the hand of death. Enfield has given us a more distinct account of the ethics of the antient philosophers; but the great work, of which Enfield's is an abridgment, Brucker's history of Philosophy, is the treasure which I would wish to possess, as a book of reference or of special research only, for who could read 6. vol. 4to. [quarto] of 1000 pages each, closely printed, of modern Latin? Your account of D'Argens' Ocellus makes me wish for him also. Ocellus furnishes a fruitful text for a sensible and learned commentator. The Abbé Batteaux', which I have, is a meagre thing.

You surprise me with the account you give of the strength of family distinction still existing in your state. With us it is so totally extinguished that not a spark of it is to be found but lurking in the hearts of some of our old tories. But all bigotries hang to one another; and this in the Eastern states hangs, as I suspect, to that of the priesthood. Here youth, beauty, mind and manners are more valued than a pedigree.

I do not remember the conversation between us which you mention in yours of Nov. 15. on your proposition to vest in Congress the exclusive power of establishing banks. My opposition to it must have been grounded, not on taking the power from the states, but on leaving any vestige of it in existence, even in the hands of Congress; because it would only have been a change of the organ of abuse. I have ever been the enemy of banks; not of those discounting for cash; but of those foisting their own paper into circulation, and thus banishing our cash. My zeal against those institutions was so warm and open at the establishment of the bank of the U.S. that I was derided as a Maniac by the tribe of bank-mongers, who were seeking to filch from the public their swindling, and barren gains. But the errors of that day cannot be recalled. The evils they have engendered are now upon us, and the question is how we are to get out of them? [30] Shall we build an altar to the old paper money of the revolution, which ruined individuals but saved the republic, and burn on that all the bank charters present and future, and their notes with them? For these are to ruin both republic and individuals. This cannot be done. The Mania is too strong. It has siesed by it's delusions and corruptions all the members of our governments, general, special, and individual. Our circulating paper of the last year was estimated at 200. millions of dollars. The new

30. From 1811, when the first Bank of the United States expired, until 1817, when the second Bank of the United States went into operation, all such business was conducted by state banks. Land speculation and the expanding economy during the War of 1812 brought about tremendous inflation, suspension of specie payments by many banks, and the need for a central financial institution. Bray Hammond, *Banks and Politics in America from the Revolution to the Civil War* (Princeton, 1957), 225-50.

banks now petitioned for, to the several legislatures, are for about 60. millions additional capital, and of course 180. millions of additional circulation, nearly doubling that of the last year; and raising the whole mass to near 400. millions, or 40. for 1. of the wholesome amount of circulation for a population of 8. millions circumstanced as we are: and you remember how rapidly our money went down after our 40. for 1. establishment in the revolution. I doubt if the present trash can hold as long. I think the 380. millions must blow all up in the course of the present year; or certainly it will be consummated by the reduplication to take place of course at the legislative meetings of the next winter. Should not prudent men, who possess stock in any monied institution, either draw and hoard the cash, now while they can, or exchange it for canal stock, or such other as being bottomed on immoveable property, will remain unhurt by the crush? I have been endeavoring to persuade a friend in our legislature to try and save this state from the general ruin by timely interference. I propose to him 1. to prohibit instantly all foreign paper. 2. to give our banks 6. months to call in all their 5. Dollar bills (the lowest we allow) another 6. months to call in their 10. D. notes, and 6. months more to call in all below 50. Dollars. This would produce so gradual a diminution of medium as not to shock contracts already made; would leave finally bills of such size as would be called for only in transactions between merchant and merchant, and ensure a metallic circulation for those of the mass of citizens. But it will not be done. You might as well, with the sailors, whistle to the wind, as suggest precautions against having too much money. We must scud then before the gale, and try to hold fast, ourselves, by some plank of the wreck. God send us all a safe deliverance, and to yourself every other species and degree of happiness.

TH: JEFFERSON

P.S. I return your letter of Nov. 15. as it requests: and supposing that the late publication of the life of our good and really great Rittenhouse [31] may not have reached you, I send a copy for your acceptance. Even it's episodes and digressions may add to the amusement it will furnish you. But if the history of the world were written on the same scale, the whole world would not hold it. Rittenhouse, as an astronomer, would stand on a line with any of his time, and as a mechanician he certainly has not been equalled. In this view he was truly great; but, placed along side of Newton, every human character must appear diminutive, and none would have shrunk more feelingly from the painful parallel than the modest and amiable Rittenhouse, whose genius and merit are not the less for this exaggerated comparison of his over zealous biographer.

31. William Barton, *Memoirs of the Life of David Rittenhouse* ... (Philadelphia. 1813).

Adams to Jefferson

Quincy Feb[–March 3] 1814.

DEAR SIR

I was nibbing my pen and brushing my Faculties, to write a polite Letter of Thanks to Mr. Counsellor Barton for his valuable Memoirs of Dr. Rittenhouse though I could not account for his sending it to me, when I received your favour of Jan. 24th. I now most cordially indorse my Thanks over to you. The Book is in the modern American style, an able imitation of Marshalls Washington, though far more entertaining and instructive; a Washington Mausolæum; an Egyptian Pyramid, I shall never read it, any more than Taylors Aristocracy. Mrs. Adams reads it, with great delight, and reads to me, what she finds interresting, and that is indeed the whole Book. I have not time to hear it all.

Writtenhouse was a virtuous and amiable Man; an exquisite Mechanician; Master of the Astronomy known in his time; an expert Mathematician, a patient calculator of Numbers. But We have had a Winthrop an Andrew Oliver a Willard a Webber, his equals and We have a Bowditch his Superior in all these particulars, except the Mechanism. But you know, Phyladelphia is the Heart, the Censorium, the Pineal Gland of U. S. In Politicks, Writtenhouse was a good, simple ignorant well meaning Franklinian Democrat, totally ignorant of the World, as an Anachorite, an honest Dupe of the French Revolution; a mere Instrument of Jonathan Dickinson Sargent, Dr. Hutchinson, Genet and Mifflin. I give him all the Credit of his Planetarium. The Improvement of the Orrery [32] to the Planetarium was an easy, natural thought and nothing was wanting but caculations of Orbits Distrances, and Periods of Revolutions all of which were made to his hands, long before he existed. Patience, Perseverance and Slight of hand is his undoubted Merit and Praise.

I had heard Taylor in Senate, till his Style was so familiar to me that I had not read 3 pages before I suspected the Author. I wrote a Letter to him and he candidly acknowledged that the 650 Pages were sent me, with his consent. [33] I wait with impatience for the Publication and Annunciation of the Work. Arator ought not to have been adulterated with Politicks: but his precept "Gather up the Fragments that nothing be lost" is

32. The Rittenhouse orrery, long lost to view or misplaced, was rediscovered at Princeton University in 1948 and is on display in the library. Howard C. Rice, *The Rittenhouse Orrery; Princeton's Eighteenth-Century Planetarium, 1767-1954* (Princeton, 1954), 62-63.

33. Taylor, *An Inquiry into the Government of the United States.*

of inestimable Value in Agriculture and Horticulture. Every Weed Cob, Husk Stalk ought to be saved for manure.

Your research in the Laws of England, establishing Christianity as the Law of the Land and part of the common Law, are curious and very important. Questions without number will arise in this Country. Religious Controversies, and Ecclesiastical Contests are as common and will be as Sharp as any in civil Politicks foreign, or domestick? In what sense and to what extent the Bible is Law, may give rise to as many doubts and quarrells as any of our civil political military or maritime Laws and will intermix with them all to irritate Factions of every sort. I dare not look beyond my Nose into futurity. Our Money, our Commerce, our Religion, our National and State Constitutions, even our Arts and Sciences, are so many seed Plotts of Division, Faction, Sedition and Rebellion. Every thing is transmuted into an Instrument of Electioneering. Election is the grand Brama, the immortal Lama, I had almost said, the Jaggernaught, for Wives are almost ready to burn upon the Pile and Children to be thrown under the Wheel.

You will perceive, by these figures that I have been looking into Oriental History and Hindoo religion. I have read Voyages and travels and every thing I could collect, and the last is Priestleys "Comparison of the Institutions of Moses, with those of the Hindoos and other ancient Nations," a Work of great labour, and not less haste. I thank him for the labour, and forgive, though I lament the hurry. You would be fatigued to read, and I, just recruiting a little from a longer confinement and indisposition than I have had for 30 Years, have not strength to write many Observations. But I have been disappointed in the principal Points of my Curiosity.

1. I am disappointed, by finding that no just Comparison can be made, because the original Shast[r]a, and the original Vedams are not obtained, or if obtained not yet translated into any European Language.

2. In not finding such Morsells of the Sacred Books as have been translated and published which are more honourable to the original Hindo[o] Religion than any thing he has quoted.

3. In not finding a full devellopement of the History of the Doctrine of the Metempsichosis which orig[i]nated

4. In the History of the Rebellion of innumerable Hosts of Angells in Heaven against the Supream Being, who after some thousands of Years of War conquered them and hurled them down to the Region of total darkness, where they suffered a part of the Punishment of their Crime, and then were mercifully released from Prison permitted to ascend to Earth and migrate into all sorts of Animals, reptiles, Birds Beasts and Men according to their Rank and Chara[c]ter, and even into Vegetables and Minerals, there to serve on probation. If they passed without reproach

their Several gradations they were permitted to become Cows and Men. If as Men they behaved well, i. e. to the satisfaction of the Priests, they were restored to their Original rank and Bliss in Heaven.

5 In not finding the Trinity of Pythagoras and Plato, their contempt of Matter, flesh and blood, their almost Adoration of Fire and Water, their Metempsicosis, and even the prohibition of Beans so evidently derived from India.

6. In not finding the Prophecy of Enoch deduced from India in which the fallen Angels make such a figure.

But you are weary. Priestly has proved the superiority of the Hebrews to the Hindoos, as they Appear in the Gentoo Laws and Institutes of Menu: but the comparison remains to be made with the Shast[r]a.

In his remarks on Mr. Dupuis, p. 342. Priestley says, "The History of the fallen Angels is another Circumstance, on which Mr. Dupuis lays much Stress.["] "According to the Christians," he says, Vol. 1. p. 336, "there was from the beginning, a division among the Angels; some remaining faithful to the light, and others taking the part of Darkness" etc. But this supposed history is not found in the Scriptures. It has only been inferred, from a wrong interpretation of one passage in the 2d. Epistle of Peter, and a corresponding One in that of Jude, as has been shewn by judicious Writers. That there is such a Person as The Devil is no part of my Faith, nor that of many other Christians; nor am I sure that it was the belief of any of the christian Writers. Neither do I believe the doctrine of demoniacal possessions, whether it was believed by the sacred Writers or not; and yet my unbelief in these Articles does not affect my faith in the great facts of which the Evangelists were eye and ear Witnesses. They might not be competent Judges, in the one case, tho perfectly so, with respect to the other."

I will ask Priestley, when I see him, Do you believe those Passages in Peter and Jude to be interpolations? If so, by whom made? and when? and where? and for what End? Was it to support, or found the doctrine of The Fall of Man, Original Sin, the universal Corruption depravation and guilt of human nature and mankind; and the subsequent Incarnation of God to make Attonement and Redemption?   Or do you think that Peter and Jude believed the Book of Enoch to have been written, by the 7th. from Adam, and one of the sacred cannonical Books of the Hebrew Prophets? Peter, 2. Ep. c. 2. v. 4, says "For if God spared not the Angels that sinned, but cast them down to HELL and delivered them into chains of DARKNESS, to be reserved unto Judgment." Jude v. 6th. says "And the Angels which kept not their first Estate, but left their own habitations, he hath reserved in everlasting Chains under darkness, unto the Judgment of the great day. v. 14th.["] "And Enoch also, the 7th. from Adam, prophesied of these Saying, behold the Lord cometh with ten thousands of his Saints, to execute Judgment upon all etc" Priestley says "a wrong Interpretation" has been given to these Texts. I wish he had favoured Us with his right interpretation of them.

In another place. p. 326. Priestley says "There is no Circumstance of which Mr. Dupuis avails himself so much, or repeats so often, both with respect to the Jewish and Christian religions, as the history of *the Fall of Man*, in the beginning of the Book of Genesis. I believe with him, and have maintained in my Writings, that this history is either an Allegory, or founded on uncertain Tradition: that it is an hypothesis to account for the origin of evil, adopted by Moses, which by no means Accounts for the Facts."

March 3d. So far, was written almost a month ago: but Sickness has prevented Progress. I had much more to say about this Work. I shall never be a Disciple of Priestley. He is as absurd inconsistent, credulous and incomprehensible as Athanasius. Read his Letter to The Jews in this Volume. Could a rational Creature write it? Aye! such rational Creatures as Rochefaucault and Condorsett and John Taylor in Politicks, and Towers's, Juricus [Jurieu?] and French Prophets in Theology.

Priestleys Account of the Philosophy and Religion of India appears to me to be much such a Work, as a Man of busy research would produce, who should undertake to describe Christianity from the sixth to the twelfth Century, when a deluge of Wonders overflowed the World; when Miracles were performed and proclaimed from every Convent and Monastry, Hospital, Church Yard, Mountain Valley Cave and Cupola.

There is a Work, which I wish I possessed. It has never crossed the Atlantic. It is entitled Acta Sanctorum, in forty seven Volumes in Folio. It contains the Lives of the Saints. It was compiled in the beginning of the 16th. Century by Bollandus, Henschenius and Papebrock. What would I give to possess in one immense Mass, One Stupendous draught all the Legends, true doubtful and false. These Bollandists dared to discuss some of the Facts and to hint that some of them were doubtful, E. G. Papebrock doubted The Antiquity of the Carmellites from Elias; and whether the Face of J. C. was painted on the Handkerchief of St. Veronique; and whether the Prepuce of the Saviour of the World, which was shewn in the Church at Antwerp, could be proved to be genuine? For these bold Scepticisms he was libelled in Pamphlets and denounced to the Pope and the Inquisition in Spain. The Inquisition condemned him: but the Pope not daring to acquit or condemn him, prohi[bi]ted all Writings, Pro and Con. But as the Physicians cure one disease by exciting Another, as a Fever by a Salivation, this Bull was produced by a new Claim. The Brothers of the

Order of Charity asserted a Descent from Abraham 900 Years anterior to the Carmelites.

A Phylosopher who should write a description of Christianism from the Bollandistic Saints of the sixth or the tenth Century would probably produce a Work tolerably parrallel to Priestleys upon the Hindoos.

JOHN ADAMS

Jefferson to Adams

Monticello May 18.14.

MY DEAR SIR

This will be handed you by Mr. Rives a young gentleman of this state and my neighborhood. He is an eleve of mine in law, of uncommon abilities, learning and worth. When you and I shall be at rest with our friends of 1776, he will be in the zenith of his fame and usefulness. Before entering on his public career he wishes to visit our sister states, and would not conceive he had seen any thing of Massachusets were he not to see the venerable patriot of Braintree. I therefore request your indulgence of his wishes to be presented to you, a favor to which his high esteem for your character will give double value. But his wishes would be but partly gratified were he not presented to Mrs. Adams also. May I then ask this additional favor of you which I shall value the more as it will give him the opportunity which I hope of bringing back to me a favorable report of both your healths. Accept as heretofore the assurances of my affectionate esteem and respect.

TH: JEFFERSON

Jefferson to Adams

Monticello July 5. 14.

DEAR SIR

Since mine of Jan. 24. yours of Mar. 14. was recieved. It was not acknoleged in the short one of May 18. by Mr. Rives, the only object of that having been to enable one of our most promising young men to have the advantage of making his bow to you. I learned with great regret the serious illness mentioned in your letter: and I hope Mr. Rives will be able to tell me you are entirely restored. But our machines have now been running for 70. or 80. years, and we must expect that, worn as they are, here a pivot, there a wheel, now a pinion, next a spring, will be giving way: and however we may tinker them up for awhile, all will at length surcease motion. Our watches, with works of brass and steel, wear out within that period. Shall you and I last to see the course the seven-fold wonders of the times will take? The Attila of the age dethroned, the ruthless destroyer of 10. millions of the human race, whose thirst for blood appeared unquenchable, the great oppressor of the rights and liberties of the world, shut up within the circuit of a little island of the Mediterranean,[34] and dwindled to the condition of an humble and degraded pensioner on the bounty of those he had most injured. How miserably, how meanly, has he closed his inflated career! What a sample of the Bathos will his history present! He should have perished on the swords of his enemies, under the walls of Paris.

'Leon piagato a morte Cosi fra l'ire estrema
Sente mancar la vita, rugge, minaccia, e freme,
Guarda la sua ferita, Che fa tremar morendo
Ne s'avilisce ancor. Tal volta il cacciator.' [35]
        Metast Adriano.

But Bonaparte was a lion in the field only. In civil life a cold-blooded, calculating unprincipled Ursurper, without a virtue, no statesman, knowing nothing of commerce, political economy, or civil government, and supplying ignorance by bold presumption. I had supposed him a great man until his entrance into the Assembly des cinq cens, 18. Brumaire (an. 8.) [36] From that date however I set him down as a great scoundrel only. To the wonders of his rise and fall, we may add that of a Czar of Muscovy dictating, *in Paris*, laws and limits to all the successors of the Caesars,[37] and holding even the balance in which the fortunes of this new world are suspended. I own that, while I rejoice, for the good of mankind, in the deliverance of Europe from the havoc which would have never ceased while Bonaparte should have lived in power, I see with anxiety the tyrant of the ocean remaining in vigor, and even participating in the merit

34. Napoleon was banished to the island of Elba in 1814. He escaped on March 1, 1815, to lead the French armies during the Hundred Days until his final defeat at Waterloo, June 18.

35. "The lion stricken to death Then with his final wrath
realizes that he is dying, he roars, threatens, and screams,
and looks at his wounds from which which makes the hunter
he grows ever weaker and weaker. tremble at him dying."

36. The coup d'état of Nov. 9, 1799, in which Bonaparte drove the legislative Council of 500 of the French Republic (the Directory) from its meeting place and proclaimed the Consulate (headed by three consuls) with himself as First Consul.

37. The "constitutional charter," issued in 1814 by Louis XVIII of the restored Bourbon dynasty, partly at the insistence of Tsar Alexander I.

of crushing his brother tyrant. While the world is thus turned up side down, on which side of it are we? All the strong reasons indeed place us on the side of peace; the interests of the continent, their friendly dispositions, and even the interests of England. Her passions alone are opposed to it. Peace would seem now to be an easy work, the causes of the war being removed. Her orders of council will no doubt be taken care of by the allied powers, and, war ceasing, her impressment of our seamen ceases of course. But I fear there is foundation for the design intimated in the public papers, of demanding a cession of our right in the fisheries.[38] What will Massachusets say to this? I mean her majority, which must be considered as speaking, thro' the organs it has appointed itself, as the Index of it's will. She chose to sacrifice the liberty of our seafaring citizens, in which we were all interested, and with them her obligations to the Co-states; rather than war with England. Will she now sacrifice the fisheries to the same partialities? This question is interesting to her alone: for to the middle, the Southern and Western States they are of no direct concern; of no more than the culture of tobacco, rice and cotton to Massachusets. I am really at a loss to conjecture what our refractory sister will say on this occasion. I know what, as a citizen of the Union, I would say to her. 'Take this question ad referendum. It concerns you alone. If you would rather give up the fisheries than war with England, we give them up. If you had rather fight for them, we will defend your interests to the last drop of our blood, chusing rather to set a good example than follow a bad one.' And I hope she will determine to fight for them. With this however you and I shall have nothing to do; ours being truly the case wherein 'non tali auxilio, nec defensoribus istis Tempus eget.'[39] Quitting this subject therefore I will turn over another leaf.

I am just returned from one of my long absences, having been at my other home for five weeks past. Having more leisure there than here for reading, I amused myself with reading seriously Plato's republic. I am wrong however in calling it amusement, for it was the heaviest task-work I ever went through. I had occasionally before taken up some of his other works, but scarcely ever had patience to go through a whole dialogue. While wading thro' the whimsies, the puerilities, and unintelligible jargon of this work, I laid it down often to ask myself how it could have been that the world should have so long consented to give reputation to such nonsense as this? How the soi-disant Christian world indeed should have

38. No agreement was reached on the Anglo-American fisheries at the peace conference at Ghent in 1814, but the Convention of 1818 allowed Americans to fish off the northern coast of North America and to dry and cure fish on the unsettled shores of Labrador and southern Newfoundland. Bemis, *Diplomatic History of U.S.*, 174-75.

39. "We do not, at this time, want such aid as that, nor such defenders." Virgil, *Aen.*, II, 521.

ABIGAIL ADAMS

Preliminary study by Gilbert Stuart, *ca.* 1812
(See p. vii)

THOMAS JEFFERSON

Bronze casting from the life mask by John Henri Isaac Browere, 1825
(See p. vii)

done it, is a piece of historical curiosity. But how could the Roman good sense do it? And particularly how could Cicero bestow such eulogies on Plato? Altho' Cicero did not wield the dense logic of Demosthenes, yet he was able, learned, laborious, practised in the business of the world, and honest. He could not be the dupe of mere style, of which he was himself the first master in the world. With the Moderns, I think, it is rather a matter of fashion and authority. Education is chiefly in the hands of persons who, from their profession, have an interest in the reputation and the dreams of Plato. They give the tone while at school, and few, in their after-years, have occasion to revise their college opinions. But fashion and authority apart, and bringing Plato to the test of reason, take from him his sophisms, futilities, and incomprehensibilities, and what remains? In truth, he is one of the race of genuine Sophists, who has escaped the oblivion of his brethren, first by the elegance of his diction, but chiefly by the adoption and incorporation of his whimsies into the body of arti-ficial Christianity. His foggy mind, is forever presenting the semblances of objects which, half seen thro' a mist, can be defined neither in form or dimension. Yet this which should have consigned him to early oblivion really procured him immortality of fame and reverence. The Christian priesthood, finding the doctrines of Christ levelled to every understanding, and too plain to need explanation, saw, in the mysticisms of Plato, ma-terials with which they might build up an artificial system which might, from it's indistinctness, admit everlasting controversy, give employment for their order, and introduce it to profit, power and pre-eminence. The doctrines which flowed from the lips of Jesus himself are within the comprehension of a child; but thousands of volumes have not yet explained the Platonisms engrafted on them: and for this obvious reason that non-sense can never be explained. Their purposes however are answered. Plato is canonized; and it is now deemed as impious to question his merits as those of an Apostle of Jesus. He is peculiarly appealed to as an advocate of the immortality of the soul; and yet I will venture to say that were there no better arguments than his in proof of it, not a man in the world would believe it. It is fortunate for us that Platonic republicanism has not obtained the same favor as Platonic Christianity; or we should now have been all living, men, women and children, pell mell together, like beasts of the field or forest. Yet 'Plato is a great Philosopher,' said La Fontaine. But says Fontenelle 'do you find his ideas very clear'? 'Oh no! he is of an obscurity impenetrable.' 'Do you not find him full of contradictions?' 'Certainly,' replied La Fontaine, 'he is but a Sophist.' Yet immediately after, he exclaims again, 'Oh Plato was a great Philosopher.' Socrates had reason indeed to complain of the misrepresentations of Plato; for in truth his dialogues are libels on Socrates.

But why am I dosing you with these Ante-diluvian topics? Because I am glad to have some one to whom they are familiar, and who will not recieve them as if dropped from the moon. Our post-revolutionary youth are born under happier stars than you and I were. They acquire all learning in their mothers' womb, and bring it into the world ready-made. The information of books is no longer necessary; and all knolege which is not innate, is in contempt, or neglect at least. Every folly must run it's round; and so, I suppose, must that of self-learning, and self sufficiency; of rejecting the knolege acquired in past ages, and starting on the new ground of intuition. When sobered by experience I hope our successors will turn their attention to the advantages of education. I mean of education on the broad scale, and not that of the petty *academies*, as they call themselves, which are starting up in every neighborhood, and where one or two men, possessing Latin, and sometimes Greek, a knolege of the globes, and the first six books of Euclid, imagine and communicate this as the sum of science. They commit their pupils to the theatre of the world with just taste enough of learning to be alienated from industrious pursuits, and not enough to do service in the ranks of science. We have some exceptions indeed. I presented one to you lately, and we have some others. But the terms I use are general truths. I hope the necessity will at length be seen of establishing institutions, here as in Europe, where every branch of science, useful at this day, may be taught in it's highest degrees. Have you ever turned your thoughts to the plan of such an institution? I mean to a specification of the particular sciences of real use in human affairs, and how they might be so grouped as to require so many professors only as might bring them within the views of a just but enlightened economy? I should be happy in a communication of your ideas on this problem, either loose or digested. But to avoid my being run away with by another subject, and adding to the length and ennui of the present letter, I will here present to Mrs. Adams and yourself the assurance of my constant and sincere friendship and respect.

TH: JEFFERSON

Adams to Jefferson

Quincy July 16. 1814

DEAR SIR

I recd. this morning your favour of the 5th. and as I can never let a Sheet of your's rest I sit down immediately to acknowledge it.

Whenever Mr. Rives, of whom I have heard nothing, shall arrive he shall receive all the cordial Civilities in my power.

I am sometimes afraid that my "Machine" will not "surcease motion" soon enough; for I dread nothing so much as "dying at top" and expiring like Dean Swift "a driveller and a Show" or like Sam. Adams, a Grief and distress to his Family, a weeping helpless Object of Compassion for Years.

I am bold to say that neither you nor I, will live to see the Course which "the Wonders of the Times" will take. Many Years, and perhaps Centuries must pass, before the current will acquire a settled direction. If the Christian Religion as I understand it, or as you understand it, should maintain its Ground as I believe it will; Yet Platonick Pythagoric, Hindoo, and cabballistical Christianity which is Catholic Christianity, and which has prevailed for 1500 Years, has recd. a mortal Wound of which the Monster must finally die; Yet so strong is his constitution that he may endure for Centuries before he expires. Government has never been much studied by Mankind. But their Attention has been drawn to it, in the latter part of the last Century and the begining of this, more than at any former Period: and the vast Variety of experiments that have been made of Constitutions, in America in France, in Holland, in Geneva in Switzerland, and even in Spain and South America, can never be forgotten. They will be studied, and their immediate and remote Effects, and final Catastrophys noted. The result in time will be Improvements. And I have no doubt that the horrors We have experienced for the last forty Years, will ultimately, terminate in the Advancement of civil and religious Liberty, and Ameliorations, in the condition of Mankind. For I am a Believer, in the probable improvability and Improvement, the Ameliorabi[li]ty and Amelioration in human Affairs: though I never could understand the Doctrine of the Perfectability of the human Mind. This has always appeared to me, like the Phylosophy or Theology of the Gentoos, viz. "that a Brachman by certain Studies for a certain time pursued, and by certain Ceremonies a certain number of times repeated, becomes Omniscient and Almighty."

Our hopes however of sudden tranquility ought not to be too sanguine. Fanaticism and Superstition will still be selfish, subtle, intriguing, and at times furious. Despotism will still struggle for domination; Monarchy will still study to rival nobility in popularity; Aristocracy will continue to envy all above it, and despize and oppress all below it; Democracy will envy all, contend with all, endeavour to pull down all; and when by chance it happens to get the Upper hand for a short time, it will be revengefull bloody and cruel. These and other Elements of Fanaticism and Anarchy will yet for a long time continue a Fermentation, which will excite alarms and require Vigilance.

Napoleon is a Military Fanatic like Achilles, Alexander, Caesar, Mahomet, Zingis Kouli, Charles 12th. etc. The Maxim and Principle of all of them was the same "Jura negat sibi cata [i.e., nata], nihil non arrogat Armis." [40]

But is it strict, to call him An Usurper? Was not his Elevation to the Empire of France as legitimate and authentic a national Act as that of William 3d. or the House of Hanover to the throne of the 3 Kingdoms or as the Election of Washington to the command of our Army or to the Chair of the States.

Human Nature, in no form of it, ever could bear Prosperity. That peculiar tribe of Men, called Conquerors, more remarkably than any other have been swelled with Vanity by any Series of Victories. Napoleon won so many mighty Battles in such quick succession and for so long a time, that it was no Wonder his brain became compleatly intoxicated and his enterprises, rash, extravagant and mad.

Though France is humbled, Britain is not. Though Bona is banished a greater Tyrant and wider Usurper still domineers. John Bull is quite as unfeeling, as unprincipled, more powerful, has shed more blood, than Bona. John by his money his Intrigues and Arms, by exciting Coalition after coalition against him made him what he was, and at last, what he is. How shall the Tyrant of Tyrants, be brought low? Aye! there's the rub. I still think Bona great, at least as any of the Conquerors. "The Wonders of his rise and fall," may be seen in the Life of King Theodore, or Pascall Paoli or Rienzi, or Dyonisius or Mazzionelli, or Jack Cade or Wat Tyler. The only difference is that between miniatures and full length pictures. The Schoolmaster at Corinth, was a greater Man, than the Tyrant of Syracuse; upon the Principle, that he who conquers himself is greater than he who takes a City. Tho' the ferocious Roar of the wounded Lion, may terrify the Hunter with the possibility of another dangerous leap; Bona was shot dead at once, by France. He could no longer roar or struggle growl or paw, he could only gasp the grin of death. I wish that France may not still regret him. But these are Speculations in the Clouds. I agree with you that the Milk of human kindness in the Bourbons is safer for Mankind than the fierce Ambition of Napoleon.

The Autocrator, appears in an imposing Light. Fifty Years ago English Writers, held up terrible Consequences from "thawing out the monstrous northern Snake." If Cossacks and Tartars, and Goths and Vandalls and Hunns and Ripuarians, should get a taste of European Sweets, what may happen? Could Wellingtons or Bonapartes, resist them? The greatest trait of Sagacity, that Alexander has yet exhibited to the World is his Courtship of the United States. But whether this is a mature well digested Policy or

40. "He denies that laws were made for him; he arrogates everything to himself by force of arms." Horace, *Ars Poetica*, 122.

only a transient gleam of thought, still remains to be explained and proved by time.

The "refractory Sister" [Massachusetts] will not give up the Fisheries. Not a Man here dares to hint at so base a thought.

I am very glad you have seriously read Plato: and still more rejoiced to find that your reflections upon him so perfectly harmonize with mine. Some thirty Years ago I took upon me the severe task of going through all his Works. With the help of two Latin Translations, and one English and one French Translation and comparing some of the most remarkable passages with the Greek, I laboured through the tedious toil. My disappointment was very great, my Astonishment was greater and my disgust was shocking. Two Things only did I learn from him. 1. that Franklins Ideas of exempting Husbandmen and Mariners etc. from the depredations of War were borrowed from him. 2. that Sneezing is a cure for the Hickups. Accordingly I have cured myself and all my Friends of that provoking disorder, for thirty Years with a Pinch of Snuff.

Some Parts of some of his Dialogues are entertaining, like the Writings of Rousseau: but his Laws and his Republick from which I expected most, disappointed me most. I could scarcely exclude the suspicion that he intended the latter as a bitter Satyre upon all Republican Government, as Xenophon undoubtedly designed by his Essay on Democracy, to ridicule that Species of Republick. In a late letter to the learned and ingenious Mr. Taylor of Hazelwood, I suggested to him the Project of writing a Novel, in which The Hero should be sent upon his travels through Plato's Republick, and all his Adventures, with his Observations on the principles and Opinions, the Arts and Sciences, the manners Customs and habits of the Citizens should be recorded. Nothing can be conceived more destructive of human happiness; more infallibly contrived to transform Men and Women into Brutes, Yahoos, or Dæmons than a Community of Wives and Property. Yet, in what, are the Writings of Rousseau and Helvetius wiser than those of Plato? "The Man who first fenced a Tobacco Yard, and said this is mine ought instantly to have been put to death" says Rousseau. "The Man who first pronounced the barbarous Word "Dieu," ought to have been immediately destroyed," says Diderot. In short Philosophers antient and modern appear to me as Mad as Hindoos, Mahomitans and Christians. No doubt they would all think me mad; and for any thing I know this globe may be, the bedlam, Le Bicatre [i.e., Bicêtre] of the Universe.

After all; as long as Property exists, it will accumulate in Individuals and Families. As long as Marriage exists, Knowledge, Property and Influence will accumulate in Families. Your and our equal Partition of intestate Estates, instead of preventing will in time augment the Evil, if it is one.

The French Revolutionists saw this, and were so far consistent. When they burned Pedigrees and genealogical Trees, they anni[hi]lated, as far as they could, Marriages, knowing that Marriage, among a thousand other things was an infallible Source of Aristocracy. I repeat it, so sure as the Idea and the existence of PROPERTY is admitted and established in Society, Accumulations of it will be made, the Snow ball will grow as it rolls.

Cicero was educated in the Groves of Academus where the Name and Memory of Plato, were idolized to such a degree, that if he had wholly renounced the Prejudices of his Education his Reputation would have been lessened, if not injured and ruined. In his two Volumes of Discourses on Government We may presume, that he fully examined Plato's Laws and Republick as well as Aristotles Writings on Government. But these have been carefully destroyed; not improbably, with the general Consent of Philosophers, Politicians and Priests. The Loss is as much to be regretted as that of any Production of Antiquity.

Nothing seizes the Attention, of the stareing Animal, so surely, as Paradox, Riddle, Mystery, Invention, discovery, Mystery, Wonder, Temerity.

Plato and his Disciples, from the fourth Century Christians, to Rousseau and Tom Paine, have been fully sensible of this Weakness in Mankind, and have too successfully grounded upon it their Pretensions to Fame. I might indeed, have mentioned Bolingbroke, Hume, Gibbon Voltaire Turgot Helvetius Diderot, Condorcet, Buffon De La Lande and fifty others; all a little cracked! Be to their faults a little blind; to their Virtues ever kind.

Education! Oh Education! The greatest Grief of my heart, and the greatest Affliction of my Life! To my mortification I must confess, that I have never closely thought, or very deliberately reflected upon the Subject, which never occurs to me now, without producing a deep Sigh, an heavy groan and sometimes Tears. My cruel Destiny seperated me from my Children, allmost continually from their Birth to their Manhood. I was compelled to leave them to the ordinary routine of reading writing and Latin School, Accademy and Colledge. John alone was much with me, and he, but occasionally. If I venture to give you any thoughts at all, they must be very crude. I have turned over Locke, Milton, Condilac Rousseau and even Miss. Edgeworth as a bird flies through the Air. The Præcepter,[41] I have thought a good Book. Grammar, Rhetorick, Logic, Ethicks mathematicks, cannot be neglected; Classicks, in spight of our Friend Rush,[42] I must think indispensable. Natural History, Mechanicks,

41. [Robert Dodsley], *The Preceptor: Containing a General Course of Education* ...2 vols. (5th edn.; London, 1764). Listed in *Catalogue of the John Adams Library in the Public Library of the City of Boston* (Boston, 1917).

42. Benjamin Rush advocated dropping Greek and Latin from the school curriculum, except for the few students who would go to college. The vast majority ought to

and experimental Philosophy, Chymistry etc att least their Rudiments, can not be forgotten. Geography Ast[ron]omy, and even History and Chronology, tho' I am myself afflicted with a kind of Pyrrhonism in the two latter, I presume cannot be omitted. Theology I would leave to Ray, Derham, Nicuenteyt and Payley, rather than to Luther Zinzindorph, Sweedenborg Westley, or Whitefield, or Thomas Aquinas or Wollebius.[43] Metaphysics I would leave in the Clouds with the Materialists and Spiritualists, with Leibnits, Berkley Priestley and Edwards, and I might add Hume and Reed, or if permitted to be read, it should be with Romances and Novels. What shall I say of Musick, drawing, fencing, dancing and Gymnastic Exercises? What of Languages Oriental or Occidental? of French Italian German or Russian? of Sanscrit or Chinese?

The Task you have prescribed to me of Grouping these Sciences, or Arts, under Professors, within the Views of an inlightened Economy, is far beyond my forces. Loose indeed and indigested must be all the hints, I can note. Might Gramar, Rhetoric, Logick and Ethicks be under One Professor? Might Mathematicks, Mechanicks, Natural Phylosophy, be under another? Geography and Astro[no]my under a third. Laws and Gover[n]ment, History and Chronology under a fourth. Classicks might require a fifth.

Condelacs course of Study has excellent Parts. Among many Systems of Mathematicks English, French and American, there is none preferable to Besouts Course La Harps Course of Litterature is very valuable.[44]

But I am ashamed to add any thing more to the broken innuendos except Assurances of the continued Friendship of

JOHN ADAMS

Adams to Jefferson

Quincy Oct 28 1814

DEAR SIR

I have great pleasure in giving this Letter to the Gentleman who requests it. The Revd Edward Everett, the successor of Mr. Buckminster

take practical subjects; but he did "not reject modern languages as a part of academical education." Butterfield, ed., *Letters of Rush*, I, 524, 531, 605-7.

43. In other words, JA would leave theology to the naturalists rather than to the revealed religionists.

44. See JA to TJ, July 18, Dec. 3, 1813, above, 362, 406.

and Thatcher and Cooper in the politest Congregation in Boston,[45] and probably the first litterary Character of his Age and State, is very desirous of seeing Mr. Jefferson. I hope he will arrive before your Library is translated to Washington.[46]

By the Way I envy you that immortal honour: but I cannot enter into competition with you for my books are not half the number of yours: and moreover, I have Shaftesbury, Bolingbroke, Hume Gibbon and Raynal, as well as Voltaire.

Mr. Everett is respectable in every View; in Family fortune Station Genius Learning and Character. What more ought to be said to Thomas Jefferson by

JOHN ADAMS

Adams to Jefferson

Quincy December 11. 1814

DEAR SIR

The Bearer of this Letter, after an Education at our Cambridge, travelled with J. Q. A. to Russia, spent two Years in looking at parts of Europe, returned to Boston, read Law with one of our first Professors in Boston, is admitted to the Bar, and now Wishes to have the honour of seeing Montecello and paying his respects to President Jefferson. His Name is Francis C. Gray, a Son of our Lt. Governor Gray.

If he can explain to you the incomprehensible Politicks of New England, he can do more than I shall or can pretend to do.

Paine, Lovel and Gerry are gone and I am left alone. Gerry is happy in his Death; for what horrors of Calumny has he not escaped in the Electioneering Campaigne of next Summer? But what is to be the destiny of an amiable Widow and nine Children all as amiable as they are destitute?

JOHN ADAMS

45. The Brattle Street Church.
46. TJ sold his library to the United States in 1815 to form the nucleus of the second Library of Congress after the burning of the Capitol by the British in 1814. Congress paid TJ $23,950, or an average of $3.50 per volume; the titles of the books, arranged under his scheme of classification, were printed in *The Catalogue of the Library of the United States* (Washington, 1815). Randolph G. Adams, *Three Americanists*... (Philadelphia, 1939), 84-94.

Adams to Jefferson

Quincy December 20. 1814

Dear Sir

The most exalted of our young Genius's in Boston have an Ambition to see Montecello, its Library and its Sage. I lately gave a Line of Introduction to Mr. Everett, our most celebrated Youth: But his Calls at home, forced him back from Washington.

George Ticknor Esquire who will have the Honour to present this to you, has a reputation here, equal to the Character given him in the enclosed Letter from my Nephew, our Athenæum Man,[47] whom you know.

As you are all Heluones Librorum ["gluttons for books"], I think you ought to have a Sympathy for each other.

I gave a Letter to Francis Gray, a Son of our great Merchant and Patriot, which I hope he will have the Honor to present in due time.

The Gentleman recommended to me, to my great regret has not arrived. I hope no Misfortune has befallen him.

Paine, Lovell and Gerry are gone and left alone

John Adams

Jefferson to Adams

Monticello June 10. 15.

Dear Sir

It is long since we have exchanged a letter, and yet what volumes might have been written on the occurrences even of the last three months. In the first place, Peace, God bless it! has returned to put us all again into a course of lawful and laudable pursuits: a new trial of the Bourbons has proved to the world their incompetence to the functions of the station they have occupied: and the recall of the Usurper has clothed him with

47. William Smith Shaw ("Athenaeum Shaw"), whose mother was a sister of Abigail Adams, helped found the Anthology Society in 1805, out of which grew the Boston Athenaeum in 1807. His sobriquet resulted from the enthusiastic support he gave the Athenaeum as librarian to 1822 and secretary to 1823. Josiah Quincy, *The History of the Boston Athenaeum* ... (Cambridge, Mass., 1851), Chaps. I-III, 90-92; biographical section, 22-44.

the semblance of a legitimate Autocrat.[48] If adversity should have taught him wisdom, of which I have little confidence, he may yet render some service to mankind by teaching the antient dynasties that they can be changed for misrule, and by wearing down the maritime power of England to limitable and safe dimensions. But it is not possible he should love us, and of that our commerce had sufficient proofs during his power. Our military atchievements indeed, which he is capable of estimating, may in some degree moderate the effect of his aversions; and he may perhaps fancy that we are to become the natural enemies of England, as England herself has so steadily endeavored to make us and as some of our own overzealous patriots would be willing to proclaim. And in this view he may admit a cold toleration of some intercourse and commerce between the two nations. He has certainly had time to see the folly of turning the industry of France from the cultures for which nature has so highly endowed her to those of sugar, cotton, tobacco and others which the same creative power has given to other climates: and on the whole, if he can conquer the passions of his tyrannical soul, if he has understanding enough to pursue, from motives of interest, what no moral motives lead him to, the tranquil happiness and prosperity of his country, rather than a ravenous thirst for human blood, his return may become of more advantage than injury to us. And if again some great man could arise in England, who could see and correct the follies of his nation in their conduct as to us, and by exercising justice and comity towards ours bring both into a state of temperate and useful friendship, it is possible we may thus attain the place we ought to occupy between these two nations without being degraded to the condition of mere partisans of either.

A little time will now inform us whether France, within it's proper limits, is big enough for it's ruler, on the one hand, and whether, on the other, the allied powers are either wicked or foolish enough to attempt the forcing on the French a ruler and government which they refuse? Whether they will risk their own thrones to reestablish that of the Bourbons? If this is attempted, and the European world again committed to war, will the jealousy of England at the commerce which neutrality will give us, induce her again to add us to the number of her enemies, rather than see us prosper in the pursuits of peace and industry? And have our commercial citizens merited from their country it's encountering another war to protect their gambling enterprises? That the persons of our citizens shall be safe in freely traversing the ocean, that the transportation of our

48. The Treaty of Ghent ending the war between the United States and Great Britain had been signed on Dec. 24, 1814; Bonaparte's return from Elba to become emperor of the French again had forced the abdication of Louis XVIII. TJ was writing eight days before the Battle of Waterloo where Bonaparte met his final defeat; Louis XVIII then regained the Bourbon throne.

own produce, in our own vessels, to the markets of our choice, and the return to us of the articles we want for our own use shall be unmolested I hold to be fundamental, and that the gauntlet must be for ever hurled at him who questions it. But whether we shall engage in every war of Europe to protect the mere agency of our merchants and shipowners in carrying on the commerce of other nations, even were those merchants and ship owners to take the side of their country in the contest, instead of that of the enemy, is a question of deep and serious consideration, with which however you and I shall have nothing to do; so we will leave it to those whom it will concern.

I thank you for making known to me Mr. Ticknor and Mr. Gray. They are fine young men indeed, and if Massachusets can raise a few more such, it is probable she would be better counselled as to social rights and social duties. Mr. Ticknor is particularly the best bibliograph I have met with, and very kindly and opportunely offered me the means of reprocuring some part of the literary treasures which I have ceded to Congress to replace the devastations of British Vandalism at Washington.[49] I cannot live without books: but fewer will suffice where amusement, and not use, is the only future object. I am about sending him a catalogue to which less than his critical knolege of books would hardly be adequate. Present my high respects to Mrs. Adams, and accept yourself the assurance of my affectionate attachment.

Th: Jefferson

Adams to Jefferson

Quincy June 19. 1815

Dear Sir

Education, which you brought into View in one of your Letters, is a Subject so vast, and the Systems of Writers are so various and so contradictory: that human Life is too short to examine it; and a Man must die before he can learn to bring up his Children. The Phylosophers, Divines, Politicians and Pædagogues, who have published their Theories and Practices in this department, are without number.

49. Ticknor and Gray spent three days at Monticello early in Feb. 1815. TJ was especially impressed with Ticknor, whom he commissioned to buy in Europe certain editions of the classics. After Ticknor's return to America, TJ offered him a professorship at the University of Virginia, but commitments at Harvard necessitated his refusal. Orie W. Long, *Thomas Jefferson and George Ticknor* (Williamstown, Mass., 1933), 11-34.

Your present Inquiries, I presume, are not confined to early Education, perhaps do not comprehend it. The Constitution of a University is your Object, as I understand you. Here also the Subject is infinite. The Science has so long laboured with a Dropsy, that it is a wonder the Patient has not long since expired. Sciences of all kinds have need of Reform, as much as Religion and Government.

I never know what to write to you, because I consider it as sending Coal to Newcastle.

Tallerand Perigord, soon after his Arrival at Philadelphia, presented to me his "Rapport sur l'instruction publique." [50] I presume he presented the same Work to you. This production has some fame and may suggest some Ideas to you.

The Universities in Protestant Germany have at present the Vogue and the Ton in their favour. There is in Print a "Coup-D'Œil sur les Universités, et le mode D'Instruction Publique de L'Allemagne Protestante; en particulier Du Royaume de Westphalie, Par Charles Villers," Correspondant de l'Institut national de France, de la Societé Royale des Sciences de Gœttingue, etc.[51]

There is also in print, "Recueil de recherches sur l'education; memoire qui a concouru, en l'an XI a la Société des Sciences et Arts de Grenoble, sur cette question, Quells sont les moyens de perfectioner l'Education physique et morale des enfans?" ["]Par. J. J. Droüin, employé au ministere des relations exterieures." [52]

If I had not reason to presume that you possess these Pamp[h]lets, I would attempt to give you some Account of them. They will convince you that you have a task difficult and perplexed enough.

The War of the Reformation still continues. The Struggle between different and opposite Systems of Religion and Government has lasted from Huss and Wickliff to Lindsey and Priestly. How many powder Plotts, Bartholomews days, Irish Massacres, Paris Guillotines, how many Charles's and Maurices, Louis's and Williams, Georges and Napoleons, have intervened. And the Philosophers, if We believe Condorcet, have been as arrant Hypocrites as any of them. I am, as ever,

JOHN ADAMS.

50. This "Report on Public Instruction" was made to the National Assembly by the Committee on the Constitution in 1791.

51. "A Look at the Universities, and the Method of Public Instruction of the German Protestant; in Particular of the Kingdom of Westphalia" (Cassel, 1808).

52. "Collection of Researches on Education; a Memoir in the year XI to the Society of Sciences and Arts of Grenoble which has contributed to this Question, What are the Means of perfecting the Physical and Moral Education of Children?" (Paris, An XII [1804]).

Adams to Jefferson

Quincy June 20. 1815

DEAR SIR

The fit of recollection came upon both of Us, so nearly at the same time that I may, sometime or other, begin to think there is some thing in Priestleys and Hartleys vibrations.[53] The day before Yesterday I sent to the Post office a letter to you, and last night I received your kind favour of the 10th.

The question before the human race is, Whether the God of nature shall govern the World by his own laws, or Whether Priests and Kings shall rule it by fictitious Miracles? Or, in other Words, whether Authority is originally in the People? or whether it has descended for 1800 Years in a succession of Popes and Bishops, or brought down from Heaven by the holy Ghost in the form of a Dove, in a Phyal of holy Oil?

Who shall take the side of God and Nature? Brachmans,? Mandarins? Druids? Or Tecumseh and his Brother the Prophet? Or shall We become Disciples of the Phylosophers? And who are the Phylosophers? Frederick? Voltaire? Rousseau? Buffon? Diderot? or Condorcet? These Phylosophers have shewn them selves as incapable of governing mankind, as the Bou[r]bons or the Guelphs.

Condorcet has let the Cat out of the Bag. He has made precious confessions. I regret that I have only an English Translation of his "Outlines of an historical View of the progress of the human Mind." But in pages 247. 248 and 249 you will find it frankly acknowledged that the Phylosophers of the 18th Century, adopted all the Maxims and practiced all the Arts of the Pharisees, the ancient Priests of all Countries, the Jesuits, the Machiavillians etc etc to overthrow the Institutions that such Arts had established. This new Phylosophy, was by his own Account, as insideous, fraudulent hypocritical and cruel, as the old Policy of Priests, Nobles and Kings. When and where were ever found or will be found, Sincerity, Honesty or Veracity in any Sect or Party in Religion Government or Phylosophy? Johnson and Burke were more of Catholicks than Protestants at Heart and Gibbon became an Advocate for the Inquisition. There is no Act of

53. David Hartley, founder of the associationist school of psychology, presented two theories, the doctrine of vibrations (sensation is the result of vibration of particles of nerves) and the doctrine of associations. He pointed out the close relationship between the physiological and the psychical. Under Hartley's influence Priestley modified his traditional Calvinism to "necessarianism." David Hartley, *Observations on Man, His Frame, His Duty, and His Expectations* (London, 1749; reprinted 1801).

Uniformity in the Church or State phylosophick. As many Sects and Systems among them as among Quakers and Baptists.

Bona will not revive Inquisitions Jesuits or Slave Trade for which hebetudes, Bourbons have been driven again into Exile.

We shall get along, with or without War.

I have at last procured the Marquis D'Argens's Ocellus Timaeus [54] and Julian. Three such Volumes I never read. They are a most perfect exemplification of Condorcetts precious Confessions. It is astonishing they have not made more Noise in the World.

Our Athanasians have printed in a Pamphlet in Boston Your Letters and Priestleys from Belshams Lindsey.[55] It will do you no harm. Our Correspondence shall not again be so long interrupted. Affectionately,

JOHN ADAMS

Mrs. Adams thanks Mr. Jefferson for his friendly remembrance of her, and reciprocates to him, a thousand good wishes.[56]
P. S. Tickner and Gray were highly delighted with their Visit; charmed with the whole Family.

Have you read Carnot? Is it not afflicting to see a Man of such large Views so many noble Sentiments and such exalted integrity, groping in the dark for a Remedy? a ballance or a mediator between Independence and Despotism? How shall his "Love of Country," his "Honor" and his "national Spirit" be produced.

I cannot write a hundreth part of what I wish to say to you.

J. A.

Adams to Jefferson

Quincy June 22d. 15

DR. SIR

Can you give me any Information, concerning A. G. Camus? Is he a Chateaubriand? or a Marquis D'Argens? Does he mean to abolish Christianity? or to restore the Inquisition, the Jesuits, the Pope and the Devil?

Within a few days, I have received a thing as unexpected to me as an

54. See JA to TJ, Dec. 25, 1813, above, 411.
55. *American Unitarianism* . . . Compiled, . . . by Rev. Thomas Belsham . . . (Boston, 1815).
56. This sentence is in AA's hand.

Apparition from the dead; "Rapport a L'Institut National, Par A. G. Camus, imprime par Ordre de L'Institut, Pluviose An XI["] [1803].

In page 55 of this report he says

"Certain Pieces which I found in the Chamber of Accounts in Brussells gave me useful indications, concerning the grand Collection of the Bollandists; and conducted me, to make researches into the State of that Work, unfortunately interrupted at this day. It would add to the Institut to propose to Government the means of compleating it; as it has done with Success, for the collection of the historians of France, of diplomas and Ordinances." Permit me, to dwell a few minutes on this important Work. Note. "The Committee of the Institut for proposing and superintending the litterary labours, in the month of Frimaire an XI. wrote to the Minister of the interiour, requesting him to give orders, to the Prefect of the Dyle, and to the Prefect of the two Nethes, to summon the Citizens, Debue, Fonson, Heyten and all others, who had taken any part, in the Sequel of the Work of the Bollandists; to confer with these persons, as well concerning the continuation of this Work, as concerning the cession of the materials destined for the continuation of it; to promise to the Continuators of the Bollandists the support of the french Government, and to render an Account of their Conferences." End of the Note.

"Almost all the History of Europe, and a part of that of the East, from the seventh Century, to the thirteenth, is in the Lives of Personages, to whom have been given the title of *Saints*. Every one may have remarked, that in reading history, there is no event of any importance, in civil order, in which, some Bishop, some Abby, some Monk, or some Saint, did not take a part. It is therefore, a great Service, rendered by the Jesuits, known under the name of the Bollandists, to those who would write History, to have formed the immense Collection, extended to Fifty two Volumes in folio, known under the title of The Acts of the Saints.[57] The Service they have rendered to Litterature, is considerably augmented, by the insertion in their Acts of the Saints, a great number of Diplomas and dissertations, the greatest part of which, are Models of Criticism. There is no man, among the learned, who does not interest himself, in this great collection. My intension is not to recall to your recollection the original Authors or their first labours. We may easily know them, by turning over the leaves

57. After the Bollandists' library was dispersed by the French government in 1794, many of the volumes were lost. When the persecution abated, some of the books were salvaged and restored to the abbey of Tougerloo until 1825. Since there seemed to be no hope of resuming the work, a public sale of the volumes was held and the remainder deposited in the Royal Library of The Hague; the manuscripts were placed in the Library of Bourgogne, Brussels. The Institute of France tried in 1802 without success to induce the former Bollandists to resume the task; but it was re-established in 1836. In addition to the present letter, quoting from Camus, see JA to TJ, Feb. [–March 3], 1814, above, 429-30.

of the Collection, or if We would find the result already written, it is in the historical library of Meusel, T. 1. part 1. p. 306. or in the Manuel of litterary history by Bouginé. T. 2. p. 641. I shall date what I have to say to you, only from the Epoch of the Suppression of the Society of which the Bollandists were Members.

"At that time, three Jesuits were employed in the collection of the Acts of the Saints; to Witt; the Fathers, De Bie, De Bue, and Hubens. The Father Gesquière who had also laboured at the Acts of the Saints, reduced a particular collection intitled Select fragments from belgical Writers, and extracts or Refferences to matters contained in a collection intitled Musæum of Bellarmine. These four Monks inhabited the House of the Jesuits at Antwerp. Independently of the Use of the Library of the Convent, the Bollandists had their particular Library, the most important portion of which was a State of the Lives of the Saints for every day of the Month, with indi[c]ations of the Books in which were found those which were already printed, and the original Manuscripts, or the copies of Manuscripts, which were not yet printed. They frequently quote this particular Collection in their general Collection. The greatest part of the Copies they had assembled were the fruit of a Journey of the Fathers Papebroch and Henshen made to Rome in 1660; They remained there 'till 1662. Papebroch and his Associate brought from Rome, Copies of seven hundred Lives of Saints in greek or in latin. The Citizen La Serna, has in his Library a Copy taken by himself, from the Originals, of the relation of the Journey of Papebroch to Rome, and of the Correspondence of Henshen with his Colleagues. The Relation and the Correspondence are in latin. See Catalogue de La Serna.[58] T. 3. No. 3903.

"After the suppression of the Jesuits, The Commissione[r]s apposed their Seals upon the Library of the Bollandists, as well as on that of the Jesuits of Antwerp. But Mr. Girard, then Secretary of the Accademy of Brussells, who is still living, and who furnished me a part of the documents I use; charged with the Inventory and Sale of the Books, withdrew those of the Bollandists and transported them to Brussells.

"The Academy of Brussells, proposed to continue the Acts of the Saints under its own Name, and for this purpose to admit the four Jesuits into the number of its members. The Father Gesquiere alone consented to this Arrangement. The Other Jesuits obtained of Government, through the intervention of the Bishop of Neustadt, the Assurance, that they might continue their Collection. In Effect, the Empress Maria Theresa approved,

58. Carlos Antonio de La Serna Santander, *Catalogue des livres de la bibliotheque de M. C. de La Serna Santander* ... corrected and enlarged, 4 vols. [Brussels, 1803]. La Serna had first published a catalogue of his uncle's library (1792), the richest collection in the Low Countries.

by a decree of the 19th. of June 1778 a plan which was presented to her, for the continuation of the Works, both of the Bollandists and of Gesquiere. This plan is in ample detail. It contains twenty Articles, and would be Useful to consult, if any Persons should resume the Acts of the Saints. The establishment of the Jesuits was fixed in the Abby of Cauden-berg at Brussells; the library of the Bollandists was transported to that place; One of the Monks of the Abby, was associated with them; and the Father Hubens being dead, was replaced by Father Berthod, a Benedictin, who died in 1789.

"The Abby of Caudenberg, having been suppressed, the Government Assigned to the Bollandists a place in the ancient Colledge of the Jesuits at Brussells. They there placed their Library and went there to live. There they published the Fifty first Volume of their collection in 1786. the fifth tome of the month of October, printed at Brussells, at the Printing Press, Imperial and Royal, in Types Imperial and Royal (in Typis Caesario regiis). They had then two Associates, and they flattered themselves that the Emperor would continue to furnish the expence of their labours. Nevertheless, in 1788, the establishment of the Bollandists was suppressed, and they even proposed to sell the Stock of the printed Volumes; But, by an Instruction (Avis) of the 6th. December 1788, the Ecclesiastical Commission superceded the Sale, till the result could be known of a Negotiation which the Father De Bie, had commenced with the Abby of Saint Blaise to establish the Authors and transport the Stock of the Work, as well as the materials for its continuation at Saint-Blaise.

"In the meantime, the Abby of Tongerloo, offered the Government, to purchase the Library and the Stock of the Bollandists, and to cause the Work to be continued by the ancient Bollandists with the Monks of Tongerloo associated with them. These propositions were accepted: the Fathers De Bie, De Bue, and Gesquiere removed to Tongerloo; the Monks of Caudenberg refused to follow them, though they had been associated with them. On the Entry of the French Troops into Belgium, the Monks of Tongerloo quitted their Abbay: the Fathers de Bie and Gesquiere retired into Germany where they died; the Father De Bue, retired to the City of Hall, hereto fore Province of Hainault, his native Country. He lives, but is very aged. One of the Monks of Tongerloo, who had been associated with them is the Father Heylen: they were not able to inform me of the place of his residence. Another Monk, associated with the Bollandists of 1780 is the Father Fonson, who resides at Brussells.

"In the midst of these troubles, the Bollandists have caused to be printed the fifty second Volume of the Acts of the Saints, the sixth Volume of the Month of October. The fifty first volume is not common in commerce; because the sale of it, has been interrupted, by the continual Changes of the residence of the Bollandists. The fifty second Volume, or the Sixth of the same month of October, is much more rare. Few Persons know its Existence.

"The Citizen Serna has given me the 296 first pages of the Volume which he believes were printed at Tongerloo. He is persuaded that the Rest of the Volume exists; and he thinks it was at Rome that it was finished. (terminé).

"The Citizen D'Herbouville, Préfect of the department of the two Neths at Antwerp, has made, for about 18 months, Attempts, with the Ancient Bollandists, to engage them, to resume their labours. They have not had Success. Perhaps the present moment, would be the most critical. (opportune), especially if the Government should consent to give to the Bollandists Assurance of their Safety.

"The essential point would be to make sure of the Existence of the Manuscripts which I have indicated; and which by the relation of the Citizen *La Serna*, filled a Body of a Library of about three Toises in Length, and two in breadth. If these Manuscripts still exist, it is easy to terminate, the Acts of the Saints; because We shall have all the necessary Materials. If these Manuscripts are lost, We must despair to see this Collection compleated.

"I have enlarged, a little, in this digression, on the Acts of the Saints, because it is a Work of great importance; and because these documents, which cannot be obtained with any Exactitude but upon the Spots; seem to me to be among the principal Objects, which your Travellers, have to collect, and of which they ought to give you an Account."

Now, my Friend Jefferson! I await your observations on this Morcell. You may think I waste my time and yours. I do not think so. If you will look into the "Nouveau Dictionaire Historique," under the Words Bollandus, Heinshemius and Papebrock you will find more particulars of the Rise and progress of this great Work "The Acts of the Saints."

I shall make only an Observation or two.

1. The Pope never suppressed the Work, and Maria Theresia established it. It therefore, must be Catholick.

2. Notwithstanding the Professions of the Bollandists, to discriminate the true from the false Miracles and the dubious from both; I suspect that the false, will be found the fewest, the dubious the next, and the true the most numerous of all.

3. From all that I have read, of the Legends, of the Lives and Writings of the Saints and even of the Fathers, and of Ecclesiastical History in general: I have no doubt that the Acta Sanctorum is the most enormous Mass of Lies Frauds, Hypocracy and Imposture, that ever was heaped together upon this Globe. If it were impartially consulted it would do

more to open the Eyes of Man kind, than all the Phylosophers of the 18th. Century, who were as great Hypocrites as any of the Phylosophers or Theologians of Antiquity.

JOHN ADAMS

Adams to Jefferson and Thomas McKean

Quincy July 30th 1815

DEAR SIR

Who shall write the history of the American revolution? Who can write it? Who will ever be able to write it?

The most essential documents, the debates and deliberations in Congress from 1774 to 1783 were all in secret, and are now lost forever. Mr. Dickinson printed a speech, which he said he made in Congress against the Declaration of Independence; [59] but it appeared to me very different from that, which you, and I heard. Dr. Witherspoon has published speeches [60] which he wrote beforehand, and delivered Memoriter, as he did his Sermons. But these I believe are the only speeches ever committed to writing. The Orators, while I was in Congress from 1774 to 1778 appeared to me very universally extemporaneous, and I have never heard of any committed to writing before or after delivery.

These questions have been suggested to me, by a review, in the Analectic Magazine, for May 1815, published in Philadelphia, page 385 of the Chevalier Botta's "Storia della Guerra Americana." The Reviewers inform us, that it is the best history of the revolution that ever has been written. This Italian Classick has followed the example, of the Greek and Roman Historians, by composing speeches for his Generals and Orators. The Reviewers have translated, one of Mr R H Lee in favour of the declaration of Independence. A splendid morcell of oratory it is; how faithful, you can judge.

I wish to know your sentiments, and opinions of this publication. Some future Miss Porter, may hereafter, make as shining a romance, of what passed in Congress, while in Conclave, as her Scottish Chiefs. Your friend durante Vitæ.

JOHN ADAMS [61]

59. First published in Carlo Guiseppo Guglielmo Botta, Storia della guerra Americana (Paris, 1809); French transl. (Paris, 1812-13).

60. No such speeches were published by Witherspoon, according to Varnum L. Collins, President Witherspoon (Princeton, 1925), I, 219-21.

61. McKean replied that Botta "appears to me a vain and presuming character to have attempted such a history" and suggested that perhaps poverty "impelled him." McKean to JA, Nov. 20, 1815, Works, X, 177.

Jefferson to Adams

Monticello Aug. 10.[-11] 15.

DEAR SIR

The simultaneous movements in our correspondence have been really remarkable on several occasions. It would seem as if the state of the air, or state of the times, or some other unknown cause produced a sympathetic effect on our mutual recollections. I had sat down to answer your letters of June 19. 20. 22. with pen, ink, and paper before me, when I recieved from our mail that of July 30.

You ask information on the subject of Camus. All I recollect of him is that he was one of the deputies sent to arrest Dumourier at the head of his army, who were however themselves arrested by Dumourier, and long detained as prisoners. I presume therefore he was a Jacobin. You will find his character in the most excellent revolutionary history of Toulongeon: I believe also he may be the same person who has given us a translation of Aristotle's natural history from the Greek into French. Of his report to the National Institute on the subject of the Bollandists your letter gives me the first information. I had supposed them defunct with the society of Jesuits, of which they were: and that their works, altho' above ground, were, from their bulk and insignificance, as effectually entombed on their shelves, as if in the graves of their authors. Fifty two volumes in folio of the Acta Sanctorum, in dog-Latin, would be a formidable enterprize to the most laborious German. I expect, with you, they are the most enormous mass of lies, frauds, hypocrisy and imposture that ever was heaped together on this globe. By what chemical process M. Camus supposed that an Extract of truth could be obtained from such a farrago of falsehood, I must leave to the Chemists and Moralists of the age to divine.

On the subject of the history of the American revolution, you ask Who shall write it? Who can write it? And who ever will be able to write it? Nobody; except merely it's external facts. All it's councils, designs and discussions, having been conducted by Congress with closed doors, and no member, as far as I know, having even made notes of them, these, which are the life and soul of history must for ever be unknown. Botta, as you observe, has put his own speculations and reasonings into the mouths of persons whom he names, but who, you and I know, never made such speeches. In this he has followed the example of the antients, who made their great men deliver long speeches, all of them in the same style, and in that of the author himself. The work is nevertheless a good one, more judicious, more chaste, more classical, and more true than the party diatribe of Marshall. It's greatest fault is in having taken too much from him. I possessed the work, and often recurred to considerable portions of it, altho' I never read it through. But a very judicious and well informed neighbor of mine went thro' it with great attention, and spoke very highly of it. I have said that no member of the old Congress, as far as I knew, made notes of the discussions. I did not know of the speeches you mention of Dickinson and Witherspoon. But on the questions of Independance, and on the two articles of Confederation respecting taxes and voting, I took minutes of the heads of the arguments. On the first I threw all into one mass, without ascribing to the speakers their respective arguments; pretty much in the manner of Hume's summary digests of the reasonings in parliament for and against a measure. On the last, I stated the heads of arguments used by each speaker. But the whole of my notes on the question of independance does not occupy more than 5. pages, such as of this letter: and on the other questions two such sheets. They have never been communicated to any one.[62]

Do you know that there exists in MS. the ablest work of this kind ever yet executed, of the debates of the Constitutional convention of Philadelphia in 1788 [i.e., 1787]? The whole of everything said and done there was taken down by Mr. Madison, with a labor and exactness beyond comprehension.[63]

I presume that our correspondence has been observed at the post offices, and thus has attracted notice. Would you believe that a printer has had the effrontery to propose to me the letting him publish it? These people think they have a right to everything however secret or sacred. I had not before heard of the Boston pamphlet with Priestly's letters and mine.

At length Bonaparte has got on the right side of a question. From the time of his entering the legislative hall to his retreat to Elba, no man has execrated him more than myself. I will not except even the members of the Essex junto; altho' for very different reasons; I, because he was warring against the liberty of his own country, and independance of others; they, because he was the enemy of England, the Pope, and the Inquisition. But at length, and as far as we can judge, he seems to have become the choice

---

62. "Notes of Proceedings in the Continental Congress" [June 7 to Aug. 1, 1776], Boyd, I, 309-27. Boyd regards TJ's graphic account as "perhaps the best single source of information concerning the movement toward independence and the formation of the Articles of Confederation, not even excepting the similar notes made by John Adams"; *ibid.*, 299. The "Notes" were inserted in TJ's Autobiography some time between 1822 and 1825; *ibid.*, 299-301. TJ had sent a copy to Madison on June 1, 1783; *ibid.*, 327n.

63. First published in Madison's *Papers ... being His Correspondence and Reports of Debates*, ed. by Henry D. Gilpin, 3 vols. (Washington, 1840). The best edition is Farrand, ed., *Records of the Federal Convention of 1787*.

of his nation. At least he is defending the cause of his nation, and that of all mankind, the rights of every people to independance and self-government. He and the allies have now changed sides. They are parcelling out among themselves Poland, Belgium, Saxony, Italy, dictating a ruler and government to France, and looking askance at our republic, the splendid libel on their governments: and he is fighting for the principle of national independance, of which his whole life hitherto has been a continued violation. He has promised a free government to his own country, and to respect the rights of others: and altho' his former conduct inspires little confidence in his promises yet we had better take the chance of his word for doing right, than the certainty of the wrong which his adversaries are doing and avowing. If they succeed, ours is only the boon of the Cyclops to Ulysses, of being the last devoured. Present me affectionately and respectfully to Mrs. Adams, and heaven give you both as much more of life as you wish, and bless it with health and happiness.

TH: JEFFERSON

Aug. 11. P.S. I had finished my letter yesterday, and this morning recieve the news of Bonaparte's second abdication. Very well. For him personally I have no feeling but of reprobation. The representatives of the nation have deposed him. They have taken the allies at their word, that they had no object in the war but his removal. The nation is now free to give itself a good government, either with or without a Bourbon; and France unsubdued will still be a bridle on the enterprises of the combined powers, and a bulwark to others.

Adams to Jefferson

Quincy Aug. 24. 15

DEAR SIR

If I am neither deceived by the little Information I have, or by my Wishes for its truth, I should say that France is the most *Protestant* Country of Europe At this time, though I cannot think it the most *reformed*. In consequence of these Reveries I have imagined that Camus and the Institute, meant, by the revival and continuance of the Acta Sanctorum, to destroy the Pope and the Catholic Church and Hierarchy, de fonde en comble ["from top to bottom"], or in the language of Frederick, Voltaire, D'Alembert etc "ecraser le miserable," "crush the Wretch." This great Work must contain the most complete History of the corruptions of Christianity, that has ever appeared; Priestleys not excepted. And his History of ancient Opinions not excepted.

As to the history of the Revolution, my Ideas may be peculiar, perhaps singular. What do We Mean by the Revolution? The War? That was no part of the Revolution. It was only an Effect and Consequence of it. The Revolution was in the Minds of the People, and this was effected, from 1760 to 1775, in the course of fifteen Years before a drop of blood was drawn at Lexington. The Records of thirteen Legislatures, the Pamp[h]-lets, Newspapers in all the Colonies ought [to] be consulted, during that Period, to ascertain the Steps by which the public Opinion was enlightened and informed concerning the Authority of Parliament over the Colonies. The Congress of 1774, resembled in some respects, tho' I hope not in many, the Counsell of Nice in Ecclesiastical History.[64] It assembled the Priests from the East and the West the North and the South, who compared Notes, engaged in discussions and debates and formed Results by one Vote and by two Votes, which went out to the World as unanimous.

Mr. Madisons Notes of the Convention of 1787 or 1788 are consistent with his indefatigable Character. I shall never see them; but I hope Posterity will.

That our correspondence has been observed is no Wonder; for your hand is more universally known than your face. No Printer has asked me for copies: but it is no Surprize that you have been requested. These Gentry will print whatever will sell: and our Correspondence is thought such an Oddity by both Parties, that the Printers imagine an Edition would soon go off and yeild them a Profit. There has however been no tampering with Your Letters to me. They have all arrived in good Order.

Poor Bonaparte! Poor Devil! What has and what will become of him? Going the Way of King Theodore, Alexander Cæsar, Charles 12th Cro[m]well, Wat Tyler and Jack Cade; i.e. to a bad End. And what will become of Wellington? Envied, hated despized by all the Barons, Earls, Viscounts, Marquis's as an Upstart a Parvenue elevated Over their heads. For these People have no Idea of any Merit, but Birth. Wellington must pass the rest of his days buffetted ridiculed, scorned and insulted by Factions as Marlborough and his Dutchess did. Military Glory dazzles the Eyes of Mankind, and for a time eclipses all Wisdom all Virtue, all Laws humane and divine; and after this it would be Bathos to desend to Services merely civil or political.

Napoleon has imposed Kings Upon Spain Holland Sweeden Westphalia Saxony Naples etc. The combined Emperors and Kings are about to retaliate Upon France, by imposing a King upon her. These are all abominable Examples, detestable Precedents. When will the Rights of Mankind

64. See above, Chap. 9, n. 43.

the Liberties and Independence of Nations be respected? When the Perfectibility of the human Mind shall arrive at Perfection. When the Progress of Manillius's *Ratio* shall have not only

Eripuit Cælo fulmen, Jovisque fulgoves [i.e., fulgores],[65] but made Mankind rational Creatures

It remains to be seen whether The Allies were honest in their Declaration that they were at War only with Napoleon.

Can the French ever be cordially reconciled to the Bourbons again? If not, who can they find for a head? The Infant or one of the Generals? Innumerable difficulties will embarrass either Project. I am as ever

JOHN ADAMS

Adams to Jefferson

Quincy Nov. 13 1815

DEAR SIR

The fund[a]mental Article of my political Creed is, that Despotism, or unlimited Sovereignty, or absolute Power is the same in a Majority of a popular Assembly, an Aristocratical Counsel, an Oligarchical Junto and a single Emperor. Equally arbitrary cruel bloody and in every respect diabolical.

Accordingly arbitrary Power, wherever it has resided, has never failed to destroy all the records Memorials and Histories of former times which it did not like and to corrupt and interpolate such as it was cunning enough to preserve or to tolerate. We cannot therefore say with much confidence, what Knowledge or what Virtues may have prevailed in some former Ages in some quarters of the World.

Nevertheless, according to the few lights that remain to Us, We may say that the Eighteenth Century, notwithstanding all its Errors and Vices has been, of all that are past, the most honourable to human Nature. Knowledge and Virtues were increased and diffused, Arts, Sciences useful to Men, ameliorating their condition, were improved, more than in any former equal Period.

But, what are We to say now? Is the Nineteenth Century to be a Contrast to the Eighteenth? Is it to extinguish all the Lights of its Predecessor? Are the Sorbonne, the Inquisition, the Index expurgatorius, and the Knights Errant of St Ignatius Loyola to be revived and restored to all their salutary Powers of supporting and propagating the mild Spirit of

65. "He snatched the thunderbolt from the sky, and the lightning of Jove."

Christianity? The Proceedings of the Allies and their Congress at Vienna, the Accounts from Spain France etc the Chateaubriands and the Genlis, indicate which Way the Wind blows. The Priests are at their Old Work again. The Protestants are denounced and another St Bartholomew's day, threatened.

This however, will probably, 25 Years hence, be honoured with the Character of "*The effusions of a splenetic mind, rather than as the sober reflections of an unbiassed Understanding.*" I have recd. "Memoirs of the Life of Dr. Price["] by William Morgan F.R.S.[66] In pages 157 and 155 [i.e., 158] Mr. Morgan says. "So well assured was Dr. Price of the establishment of a free Constitution in France, and of the subsequent Overthrow of Despotism throughout Europe as the consequence of it, that he never failed to express his Gratitude to Heaven for having extended his life to the present happy Period in which After sharing the Benefits of one Revolution, he had been spared to be a Witness to two others Revolutions both glorious." But some of his Correspondents were not quite so sanguine in their expectations from the last of these Revolutions; and among these, the late American Ambassador, Mr. John Adams. In a long letter which he wrote to Dr. Price at this time,[67] so far from congratulating him, on the Occasion, he expresses himself in terms of contempt, in regard to the French revolution; and after asking rather too severely what good was to be expected from a Nation of Athei[s]ts, he concludes with foretelling the destru[c]tion of a million of human Beings as the probable consequence of it. These harsh censures and gloomy Predictions were particularly ungratefull to Dr. Price; nor can it be denied that they must have then appeared as *the effusions of a splenetic mind, rather than as the sober reflections of an unbiassed Understanding.*"

I know not what a candid Public will think of this practice of Mr. Morgan after the Example of Mr. Belsham, who finding private Letters in the Cabinet of a great and good Man after his decease, written in the Utmost fre[e]dom and confidence of intimate friendship, by Persons still living, though after the lapse of a quarter of a Century, produces them before the World.[68] Dr. Disney had different Feelings, and a different Judgment. Finding some cursory Letters among the Papers of Mr. Hollis he would not publish them without my consent.[69] In Answer to his request

66. William Morgan, *Memoirs of the Life of the Rev. Richard Price* (London, 1815). In view of Morgan's statement about JA's letter (below), it is ironical that in his preface (p. vi) Morgan said he had used Price's private correspondence sparingly, since he should not "under any circumstances, have thought myself justified in gratifying an idle curiosity by the indiscriminate publication of letters...written in the confidence of private friendship."

67. JA to Price, April 19, 1790, *Works*, IX, 563-65.

68. See JA to TJ, May 29, June 10, 11, 14, and 25, 1813, above, 325-30, 333-34.

69. John Disney, *Memoirs of T. Brand-Hollis* (London, 1808).

I submitted them to his discretion and might have done the same to Mr. Morgan. Indeed had Mr. Morgan published my Letter entire I should not have given him nor myself any concern about it. But as in his Summary he has not done this Letter Justice, I shall give it with all its faults.

Mr. Morgan has been more discrete and complaisant to you than to me. He has mentioned respectfully Your Letters from Paris to Dr. Price, but has given Us none of them.[70] As I would give more for those Letters that [i.e., than] for all the rest of [the] book, I am more angry with him for disappointing me; than for all he says of me and my Letter which, scambling as it is, contains nothing but the sure Words of Prophecy. I am as usual Yours

JOHN ADAMS

Jefferson to Adams

Monticello Jan. 11. 16.

DEAR SIR

Of the last five months I have past four at my other domicil, for such it is in a considerable degree. No letters are forwarded to me there, because the cross post to that place is circuitous and uncertain. During my absence therefore they are accumulating here, and awaiting acknolegments. This has been the fate of your favor of Nov. 13.

I agree with you in all it's eulogies on the 18th. century. It certainly witnessed the sciences and arts, manners and morals, advanced to a higher degree than the world had ever before seen. And might we not go back to the aera of the Borgias, by which time the barbarous ages had reduced national morality to it's lowest point of depravity, and observe that the arts and sciences, rising from that point, advanced gradually thro' all the 16th. 17th. and 18th. centuries, softening and correcting the manners and morals of man? I think too we may add, to the great honor of science and the arts, that their natural effect is, by illuminating public opinion, to erect it into a Censor, before which the most exalted tremble for their future, as well as present fame. With some exceptions only, through the 17th. and 18th. centuries morality occupied an honorable chapter in the political code of nations. You must have observed while in Europe, as I thought I did, that those who administered the governments of the greater

70. Morgan explained that he did not quote TJ because events had either sustained or falsified his predictions about the French Revolution. Morgan, *Memoirs of Price*, 151.

powers at least, had a respect to faith, and considered the dignity of their government as involved in it's integrity. A wound indeed was inflicted on this character of honor in the 18th. century by the partition of Poland.[71] But this was the atrocity of a barbarous government chiefly, in conjunction with a smaller one still scrambling to become great, while one only of those already great, and having character to lose, descended to the baseness of an accomplice in the crime. France, England, Spain shared in it only inasmuch as they stood aloof and permitted it's perpetration. How then has it happened that these nations, France especially and England, so great, so dignified, so distinguished by science and the arts, plunged at once into all the depths of human enormity, threw off suddenly and openly all the restraints of morality, all sensation to character, and unblushingly avowed and acted on the principle that power was right? Can this sudden apostacy from national rectitude be accounted for? The treaty of Pilnitz [72] seems to have begun it, suggested perhaps by the baneful precedent of Poland. Was it from the terror of monarchs, alarmed at the light returning on them from the West, and kindling a Volcano under their thrones? Was it a combination to extinguish that light, and to bring back, as their best auxiliaries, those enumerated by you, the Sorbonne, the Inquisition, the Index expurgatorius, and the knights of Loyola? Whatever it was, the close of the century saw the moral world thrown back again to the age of the Borgias, to the point from which it had departed 300. years before. France, after crushing and punishing the conspiracy of Pilnitz, went herself deeper and deeper into the crimes she had been chastising. I say France, and not Bonaparte; for altho' he was the head and mouth, the nation furnished the hands which executed his enormities. England, altho' in opposition, kept full pace with France, not indeed by the manly force of her own arms, but by oppressing the weak, and bribing the strong. At length the whole choir joined and divided the weaker nations among them. Your prophecies to Dr. Price proved truer than mine; and yet fell short of the fact, for instead of a million, the destruction of 8. or 10. millions of human beings has probably been the effect of these convulsions. I did not, in 89. believe they would have lasted so long, nor have cost so much blood. But altho' your prophecy has proved true so far, I hope it does not preclude a better final result. That same light from our West seems to have spread and illuminated the very engines employed to extinguish it. It has given them a glimmering of their rights and their power. The idea of representative government has taken root and growth among

71. By Austria, Russia, and Prussia in 1773, 1793, and 1795.
72. In Aug. 1791 the Emperor Leopold and Frederick William II of Prussia agreed to take common action against any attack by the French and thus formed the basis for the first coalition against France.

them. Their masters feel it, and are saving themselves by timely offers of this modification of their own powers. Belgium, Prussia, Poland, Lombardy etc. are now offered a representative organization: illusive probably at first, but it will grow into power in the end. Opinion is power, and that opinion will come. Even France will yet attain representative government. You observe it makes the basis of every constitution which has been demanded or offered: of that demanded by their Senate; of that offered by Bonaparte; and of that granted by Louis XVIII. The idea then is rooted, and will be established, altho' rivers of blood may yet flow between them and their object. The allied armies now couching upon them are first to be destroyed, and destroyed they will surely be. A nation united can never be conquered. We have seen what the ignorant bigotted and unarmed Spaniards could do against the disciplined veterans of their invaders. What then may we not expect from the power and character of the French nation? The oppressors may cut off heads after heads, but like those of the Hydra, they multiply at every stroke. The recruits within a nation's own limits are prompt and without number; while those of their invaders from a distance are slow, limited, and must come to an end. I think too we percieve that all these allies do not see the same interest in the annihilation of the power of France. There are certainly some symptoms of foresight in Alexander that France might produce a salutary diversion of force were Austria and Prussia to become her enemies. France too is the natural ally of the Turk, as having no interfering interests, and might be useful in neutralizing and perhaps turning that power on Austria. That a re-acting jealousy too exists with Austria and Prussia I think their late strict alliance indicates; and I should not wonder if Spain should discover a sympathy with them. Italy is so divided as to be nothing. Here then we see new coalitions in embrio which after France shall in turn have suffered a just punishment for her crimes, will not only raise her from the earth on which she is prostrate, but give her an opportunity to establish a government of as much liberty as she can bear, enough to ensure her happiness and prosperity. When insurrection begins, be it where it will, all the partitioned countries will rush to arms, and Europe again become an Arena of gladiators. And what is the definite object they will propose? A restoration certainly of the status quo prius, of the state of possession of 89. I see no other principle on which Europe can ever again settle down in lasting peace. I hope your prophecies will go thus far, as my wishes do, and that they, like the former, will prove to have been the sober dictates of a superior understanding, and a sound calculation of effects from causes well understood. Some future Morgan will then have an opportunity of doing you justice, and of counterbalancing the breach of confidence of which you so justly complain, and in which no one has had more frequent occasion of fellow-feeling than myself. Permit me to place here my affectionate respects to Mrs. Adams, and to add for yourself the assurances of cordial friendship and esteem.

TH: JEFFERSON

Adams to Jefferson

Quincy Feb. 2. 1816

DEAR SIR

I know not what to say of your Letter of the 11th. of Jan. but that it is one of the most consolatory, I ever received.

To trace the Commencement of the Reformation I suspect We must go farther back than Borgia, or even than Huss or Wickliff, and I want the Acta Sanctorum to assist me in this Research. That stupendous Monument of human Hypocricy and Fanaticism the Church of St. Peter at Rome, which was a Century and an Half in Building; excited the Ambition of Leo the tenth, who believed no more of the Christian Religion than Diderot, to finish it: and finding St. Peters Pence insufficient, he deluged all Europe with Indulgences for Sale, and excited Luther to contravert his Authority to grant them. Luther and his Associates and Followers, went less than half way in detecting the Corruptions of Christianity; but they acquired Reverence and Authority among their Followers almost as absolute as that of the Popes had been. To enter into details would be endless. But I agree with you, that the natural Effect of Science and Arts is to erect public opinion into a Censor, which must in some degree be respected by all.

There is no difference of Opinion or Feeling between Us, concerning the Partition of Poland, the intended Partitions of Pilnitz or the more daring Partitions of Vienna.[73]

Your Question "How the Apostacy from National Rectitude can be Accounted for" is too deep and wide for my Capacity to answer. I leave Fisher Ames to dogmatize up[on] the Affairs of Europe and Mankind. I have done too much in this Way. A burned Child dreads the Fire. I can only say at present, that it should seem that human Reason and human Conscience, though I believe there are such things, are not a Match, for human Passions, human Imaginations and human Enthusiasm. You however I believe have hit one Mark, "the Fires the Governments of Europe

73. At the Congress of Vienna, 1814-15.

felt kindling under their Seats": and I will hazard a shot at another, The Priests of all Nations imagined they felt Approaching such Flames as they had so often kindled about the Bodies of honest Men. Priests and Politicians, never before, so suddenly and so unanimously concurred in re-establishing Darkness and Ignorance Superstition and Despotism.

The Morality of Tacitus, is the Morality of Patriotism, and Britain and France have adopted his Creed; i.e. that all things were made for Rome. Jura negat sibi Cata [i.e., nata], nihil non arrogat Armis,[74] said Achilles. Laws were not made for me, said the Regent of France and his Cardinal Minister Du Bois. The Universe was made for me, says Man. Jesus despized and condemned this Patr[i]otism: But what Nation or What Christian has adopted his System? He was, as you say "the most benevolent Being, that ever appeard on Earth." France and England, Bourbons and Bonaparte, and all the Sovereigns at Vienna, have acted on the same Principle "All things were made for my Use." "Lo! Man for mine, replies a Pampered Goose".[75] The Philosophers of the 18th. Century have acted on the same Principle. ["]When it is to combat Evil, 'tis lawful to employ the Devil." [76] Bonus Populus Vult decipi; decipiatur.[77] They have employed the same Fals[e]h[o]od the same deceit, which Philosophers and Priests of all Ages have employed for their own selfish Purposes. We now know how their Efforts have succeeded. The old Deceivers have tryumphed over the New. Truth, must be more respected than it ever has been, before, any great Improvement can be expected in the Condition of Mankind. As Rochfaucault his Maxims drew, from history and from Practice, "I believe them true." From the whole Nature of Man, Moral intellectual and physical he did not draw them. We must come to the Principles of Jesus. But, when will all Men and all Nations do as they would be done by? Forgive all Injuries and love their Enemies as themselves? I leave those profound Phylosophers whose Sagacity perceives the Perfectibility of Humane Nature, and those illuminated Theologians who expect the Apocalyptic Reign, to enjoy their transporting hopes; provided always that they will not engage Us in Crusades and French Revolutions, nor burn Us for doubting. My Spirit of Prophecy reaches no farther than, *New England* GUESSES.

You ask, how it has happened that all Europe, has acted on the Principle "that Power was Right." I know not what Answer to give you, but this,

74. "He denies that laws were made for him; he arrogates everything to himself by force of arms."

75. See Maynard Mack, ed., *Alexander Pope, An Essay on Man* (London and New Haven, 1950 and 1951), 96.

76. Matthew Prior, "Hans Carvel," *Works* (London, 1779), 124, lines 69-70.

77. "The people wish to be deceived; then let them be deceived," Jacques-Auguste de Thou.

that Power always sincerely, conscientiously, de tres bon Foi, believes itself Right. Power always thinks it has a great Soul, and vast Views, beyond the Comprehension of the Weak; and that it is doing God Service, when it is violating all his Laws. Our Passions, Ambition, Avarice, Love, Resentment etc possess so much metaphysi[c]al Subtilty and so much overpowering Eloquence, that they insinuate themselves into the Understanding and the Conscience and convert both to their Party. And I may be deceived as much as any of them, when I say, that Power must never be trusted without a Check.

Morgan has misrepresented my Guess.[78] There is not a Word in my Letter about "a Million of human Beings." Civil Wars, of an hundred Years, throughout Europe, were guest at, and this is broad enough for your Ideas; for Eighteen or twenty Million would be a moderate Computation for a Century of civil Wars throug[h]out Europe. I still pray that a Century of civil Wars, may not desolute Europe and America too South, and North.

Your Speculations into Futurity in Europe are so probable that I can suggest no doubts to their disadvantage. All will depend on the Progress of Knowledge. But how shall Knowledge Advance? Independant of Temporal and Spiritual Power, the Course of Science and Litterature is obstructed and discouraged by so many Causes that it is to be feared, their motions will be slow. I have just finished reading four Volumes of D'Israeli, two on the Calamities and two on the Quarrels of Authors. These would be sufficient to shew that, slow rises Genius by Poverty and Envy oppressed. Even Newton and Lock and Grotius could not escape. France could furnish four other Volumes of the Woes and Wars of Authors.

My Compliments to Mrs Randolph, her Daughter Ellen and all her other Children, and believe me, as ever,

JOHN ADAMS

To which Mrs Adams adds her affectionate regards, and a wish that distance did not seperate Souls congenial.[79]

78. See JA to TJ, Nov. 13, 1815, above, 457.
79. This sentence is in AA's hand.

Adams to Jefferson

Quincy March 2. 16

DEAR SIR

I cannot be serious! I am about to write You, the most frivolous letter, you ever read.

Would you go back to your Cradle and live over again Your 70 Years? I believe You would return me a New England Answer, by asking me another question "Would you live your 80 Years over again?"

If I am prepared to give you an explicit Answer, the question involves so many considerations of Metaphysicks and Physicks, of Theology and Ethicks of Phylosophy and History, of Experience and Romance, of Tragedy Comedy and Farce; that I would not give my Opinion without writing a Volume to justify it.

I have lately lived over again, in part, from 1753, when I was junior Sophister at Colledge till 1769 when I was digging in the Mines, as a Barrister at Law, for Silver and gold, in the Town of Boston; and got as much of the shining dross for my labour as my Utmost Avarice at that time craved.

At the hazard of all the little Vision that is left me, I have read the History of that Period of 16 Years, in the six first Volumes of the Baron de Grimm. In a late Letter to you, I expressed a Wish to see an History of Quarrels and Calamities of Authors in France, like that of D'Israeli in England. I did not expect it so soon: but now I have it in a manner more masterly than I ever hoped to see it. It is not only a Narration of the incessant great Wars between the Ecclesiasticks and the Phylosophers, but of the little Skirmishes and Squabbles of Poets, Musicians, Sculptors Painters Architects Tragedians, Comediens, Opera Singers and Dancers, Chansons, Vaudevilles Epigrams, Madrigals Epitaphs, Anagrams Sonnets etc.

No man is more Sensible than I am, of the Service to Science and Letters, Humanity, Fraternity, and Liberty, that would have been rendered by the Encyclopedists and Œconomists, By Voltaire, Dalembert, Buffon Diderot, Rouseau La Lande, Frederick and Catharine, if they had possessed Common Sense. But they were all totally destitute of it. They all seemed to think that all Christendom was convinced as they were, that all Religion was "Visions Judaicques" and that their effulgent Lights had illuminated all the World. They seemed to believe, that whole Nations and Continents had been changed in their Principles Opinions Habits and Feelings by the Sovereign Grace of their Almighty Philosophy, almost as suddenly as

JOHN ADAMS

Bronze casting from the life mask by John Henri Isaac Browere, 1825
(See p. viii)

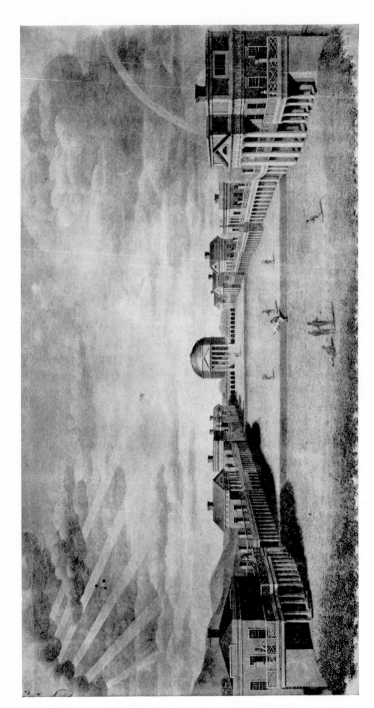

UNIVERSITY OF VIRGINIA Drawing by Mr. Williams, 1824
(See p. viii)

Catholicks and Calving[is]ts believe in instantaneous Conversion. They had not considered the force of early Education on the Millions of Minds who had never heared of their Philosophy.

And what was their Phylosophy? Atheism; pure unadulterated Atheism. Diderot, D'Alembert, Frederick, De Lalande and Grimm were indubitable Atheists. The Univer[s]e was Matter only and eternal; Spirit was a Word Without a meaning; Liberty was a Word Without a Meaning. There was no Liberty in the Universe; Liberty was a Word void of Sense. Every thought Word Passion Sentiment Feeling, all Motion and Action was necessary. All Beings and Attributes were of eternal Necessity. Conscience, Morality were all nothing but Fate.

This was their Creed and this was to perfect human Nature and convert the Earth into a Paradise of Pleasure. Who, and what is this Fate? He must be a sensible Fellow. He must be a Master of Science. He must be Master of spherical Trigonometry and Great Circle sailing. He must calculate Eclipses in his head by Intuition. He must be Master of the Science of Infinitesimal "Le Science des infiniment petits." He must involve and extract all the Roots by Intuition and be familiar with all possible or imaginable Sections of the Cone. He must be a Master of Arts Mechanical and imitative. He must have more Eloquence than Demosthenes, more Wit than Swift or Volltaire, more humour than Butler or Trumbull. And what is more comfortable than all the rest, he must be good natured, for this is upon the whole a good World. There is ten times as much pleasure as pain in it.

Why then should We abhor the Word God, and fall in Love with the Word Fate? We know there exists Energy and Intellect enough to produce such a World as this, which is a sublime and beautiful one, and a very benevolent one, notwithstanding all our snarling, and a happy one, if it is not made otherwise by our own fault.

Ask a Mite, in the Center of your Mammoth Cheese,[80] what he thinks of the "το παν." [81]

I should prefer the Philosophy of Tymæus of Locris, before that of Grimm and Diderot, Frederick and D'Alembert. I should even prefer the Shast[r]a of Indostan, or the Chaldean Egyptian, Indian, Greek, Christian Mahometan Tubonic or Celtic Theology.

---

80. "The Mammoth Cheese," made by the citizens of Cheshire, Mass., in honor of TJ and his Republicanism, was presented to him at the executive mansion in Washington on Jan. 1, 1802, by the Reverend John Leland, Baptist elder, former citizen of Virginia. He had lent valuable support toward Virginia's ratification of the Constitution in 1788 and the passage of the Bill of Rights by Congress in 1791. L. H. Butterfield, "Elder John Leland, Jeffersonian Itinerant," American Antiquarian Society, *Proceedings*, 62, pt. 2 (Oct. 1952), 214-29.

81. "The all," i.e., "totality.

Timæus and Ocellus taught that three Principles were eternal, God, Matter and Form. God was good, and had Ideas. Matter was Necessity, Fate, dead, without Ideas, without form without Feeling, perverse, untractible, capable however of being cutt into Forms of Spheres Circles, Triangles, Squares cubes Cones etc. The Ideas of the good God laboured upon matter to bring it into Form: but Matter was Fate Necessity, Dulness Obstinacy and would not always conform to the Ideas of the good God who desired to make the best of all possible Worlds but Matter, Fate Necessity resisted and would not let him compleat his Idea. Hence all the Evil and disorder, Paine Misery and Imperfection of the Universe.

We all curse Robespierre and Bonaparte; but were they not both such restless vain extravagant Animals as Diderot and Voltaire? Voltaire was the greatest Litterary Character and Bona the greatest Millitary Character of the 18 Century. There is all the difference between them. Both equally Heros and equally Cowards.

When You asked my Opinion of a University, it would have been easy to Advise Mathematicks Experimental Phylosophy, Natural History Chemistry and Astronomy Geography and the Fine Arts, to the Exclusion of Ontology Metaphysicks and Theology. But knowing the eager Impatience of the human Mind to search into Eternity and Infinity, the first Cause and last End of all Things I thought best to leave it, its Liberty to inquire till it is convinced as I have been these 50 Years that there is but one Being in the Universe, who comprehends it; and our last Resource is Resignation.

This Grimm must have been in Paris when You was there. Did You know him or hear of him?

I have this moment recd. two Volumes more, but these are from 1777 to 1782, leaving the Chaine broken from 1769 to 1777. I hope hereafter to get the two intervening Volumes. I am your old Friend

JOHN ADAMS

Jefferson to Adams

Monticello Apr. 8. 16.

DEAR SIR

I have to acknolege your two favors of Feb. 16. and Mar. 2. and to join sincerely in the sentiment of Mrs. Adams, and regret that distance separates us so widely. An hour of conversation would be worth a volume of letters. But we must take things as they come.

You ask if I would agree to live my 70. or rather 73. years over again? To which I say Yea. I think with you that it is a good world on the whole, that it has been framed on a principle of benevolence, and more pleasure than pain dealt out to us. There are indeed (who might say Nay) gloomy and hypocondriac minds, inhabitants of diseased bodies, disgusted with the present, and despairing of the future; always counting that the worst will happen, because it may happen. To these I say How much pain have cost us the evils which have never happened? My temperament is sanguine. I steer my bark with Hope in the head, leaving Fear astern. My hopes indeed sometimes fail; but not oftener than the forebodings of the gloomy. There are, I acknolege, even in the happiest life, some terrible convulsions, heavy set-offs against the opposite page of the account. I have often wondered for what good end the sensations of Grief could be intended. All our other passions, within proper bounds, have an useful object. And the perfection of the moral character is, not in a Stoical apathy, so hypocritically vaunted, and so untruly too, because impossible, but in a just equilibrium of all the passions. I wish the pathologists then would tell us what is the use of grief in the economy, and of what good it is the cause, proximate or remote.

Did I know Baron Grimm while at Paris? Yes, most intimately. He was the pleasantest, and most conversible member of the diplomatic corps while I was there: a man of good fancy, acuteness, irony, cunning, and egoism: no heart, not much of any science, yet enough of every one to speak it's language. His fort was Belles-lettres, painting and sculpture. In these he was the oracle of the society, and as such was the empress Catharine's private correspondent and factor in all things not diplomatic. It was thro' him I got her permission for poor Ledyard to go to Kamschatka, and cross over thence to the Western coast of America, in order to penetrate across our continent in the opposite direction to that afterwards adopted for Lewis and Clarke: which permission she withdrew after he had got within 200. miles of Kamschatska, had him siesed, brought back and set down in Poland. Altho' I never heard Grimm express the opinion, directly, yet I always supposed him to be of the school of Diderot, D'Alembert, D'Holbach, the first of whom committed their system of atheism to writing in 'Le bon sens,' and the last in his 'Systeme de la Nature.' It was a numerous school in the Catholic countries, while the infidelity of the Protestant took generally the form of Theism. The former always insisted that it was a mere question of definition between them, the hypostasis of which on both sides was 'Nature' or 'the Universe:' that both agreed in the order of the existing system, but the one supposed it from eternity, the other as having begun in time. And when the atheist descanted on the unceasing motion and circulation of matter thro' the animal vegetable and mineral kingdoms, never resting, never annihilated, always changing form, and under all forms gifted with the power of reproduction; the Theist pointing 'to the heavens above, and to the earth beneath, and to the waters under the earth,' asked if these did not proclaim a first cause, possessing intelligence and power; power in the production, and intelligence in the design and constant preservation of the system; urged the palpable existence of final causes, that the eye was made to see, and the ear to hear, and not that we see because we have eyes, and hear because we have ears; an answer obvious to the senses, as that of walking across the room was to the philosopher demonstrating the non-existence of motion. It was in D'Holbach's conventicles that Rousseau imagined all the machinations against him were contrived; and he left, in his Confessions the most biting anecdotes of Grimm. These appeared after I left France; but I have heard that poor Grimm was so much afflicted by them, that he kept his bed several weeks. I have never seen these Memoirs of Grimm. Their volume has kept them out of our market.

I have been lately amusing myself with Levi's book in answer to Dr. Priestley. It is a curious and tough work. His style is inelegant and incorrect, harsh and petulent to his adversary, and his reasoning flimsey enough. Some of his doctrines were new to me, particularly that of his two resurrections: the first a particular one of all the dead, in body as well as soul, who are to live over again, the Jews in a state of perfect obedience to god, the other nations in a state of corporeal punishment for the sufferings they have inflicted on the Jews. And he explains this resurrection of bodies to be only of the original stamen of Leibnitz, or the homunculus in semine masculino, considering that as a mathematical point, insusceptible of separation, or division. The second resurrection a general one of souls and bodies, eternally to enjoy divine glory in the presence of the supreme being. He alledges that the Jews alone preserve the doctrine of the unity of god. Yet their god would be deemed a very indifferent man with us: and it was to correct their Anamorphosis of the deity that Jesus preached, as well as to establish the doctrine of a future state. However Levi insists that that was taught in the old testament, and even by Moses himself and the prophets. He agrees that an anointed prince was prophecied and promised: but denies that the character and history of Jesus has any analogy with that of the person promised. He must be fearfully embarrassing to the Hierophants of fabricated Christianity; because it is their own armour in which he clothes himself for the attack. For example, he takes passages of Scripture from their context (which would give them a very different meaning) strings them together, and makes them point towards

what object he pleases; he interprets them figuratively, typically, ana-
logically, hyperbolically; he calls in the aid of emendation, transposition,
ellipsis, metonymy, and every other figure of rhetoric; the name of one
man is taken for another, one place for another, days and weeks for
months and years; and finally avails himself of all his advantage over his
adversaries by his superior knolege of the Hebrew, speaking in the very
language of the divine communication, while they can only fumble on
with conflicting and disputed translations. Such is this war of giants. And
how can such pigmies as you and I decide between them? For myself I
confess that my head is not formed tantas componere lites.[82] And as you
began your Mar. 2. with a declaration that you were about to write me the
most frivolous letter I had ever read, so I will close mine by saying I have
written you a full match for it, and by adding my affectionate respects to
Mrs. Adams, and the assurance of my constant attachment and consideration for yourself.

TH: JEFFERSON

Adams to Jefferson

Quincy May 3. 1816

DEAR SIR.
    Yours Ap. 8 has long since been recd.
J. "Would you agree to live your 80 Years over again?"
A. ["]Aye! And sanse Phrases."
J. "Would You agree to live Your Eighty Years over again forever?"
A. I once heard our Acquaintance, Chew, of Philadelphia say, "He should
like to go back to 25, to all Eternity": but I own my Soul would start and
shrink back on itself, at the Prospect of an endless Succession of Boules de
Savon ["balls of soap"], almost as much as at the Certainty of Annihilation. For what is human Life? I can speak only for one. I have had more
comfort than distress, more pleasure than paine, ten to one, nay if you
please an hundred to one. A pretty large Dose however of Distress and
Paine. But after all, What is human Life? A Vapour, a Fog, a Dew, a
Clould, a Blossom a flower, a Rose a blade of Grass, a glass Bubble, a Tale
told by an Idiot, a Boule de Savon, Vanity of Vanities, an eternal succession of which would terrify me, almost as much as Annihilation.

82. "It is not for me to settle for you such great arguments." Virgil, *Eclogues*, III,
108.

J. "Would you prefer to live over again rather than Accept the Offer of a better Life in a future state?" A. Certainly not. J. "Would you live again, rather than chang[e] for the worse in a future State, for the sake of trying something new?" Certainly Yes.

J. "Would you live over again once or forever, rather than run the risque of Annihilation, or of a better or a worse State at or affter death"? A. Most certainly I would not.

J. "How valiant you are!" A. Aye, at this moment, and at all other moments of my Life that I can recollect: but who can tell what will become of his Bravery when his Flesh and his heart shall fail him?

Bolin[g]broke said "his Philosophy was not sufficient to support him in his last hours." D'Alembert said "Happy are they who have Courage, but I have none." Voltaire the greatest Genius of them all, behaved like the greatest Coward of them all, at his death as he had like the wisest fool of them all in his Lifetime. Hume aukwardly Affect[ed] to sport away all sober thoughts. Who can answer for his last Feelings and Reflections? especially as the Priests are in possession of the Custom of making them the great Engines of their Craft. [Procul o,] Procul este Prophani ["Back, ye unhallowed"]!

J. "How shall We, how can We, estimate the real Value of human Life?" A. "I know not. I cannot weigh Sensations and Reflections, Pleasures and Pains, Hopes and Fears in Money Scales. But I can tell you how I have heard it estimated by some Phylosophers. One of my old Friends and Clients, a Mandamus Counseller against his Will, a Man of Letters and Virtues without one Vice, that I ever knew or suspected, except Garrulity, William Vassall, asserted to me, and strenuously maintained that "*pleasure is no Compensation for Pain.*" "An 100 Years of the keenest delights of human Life could not atone for one hour of Billious Cholic, that he had felt." The sublimity of this Philosophy my dull Genius could not reach. I was willing to state a fair Account between Pleasure and Pain, and give Credit for the Ballance, which I found very great in my favour. Another Philosopher, who as We say, believed nothing, ridiculed the Notion of a future State. One of the Company asked "Why are you an Ennemy to a future State?" ["]Are you weary of Life?" "Do you detest existence?" "Weary of Life!—Detest Existence!["] said the Philosopher, No, "I love Life so well, and am so attached to Existence, that to be sure of Immortality I would consent, to be pitched about with forks by the Devils among flames of fire and Brimstone to all Eternity."

I find no Resources in my Courage, for this exalted Philosophy. I had rather be blotted out.

Il faut trancher Cet Mot ["One must speak out"]! What is there in Life to attach Us, to it; but the hope of a future and a better? It is a Cra[c]ker, a Rocquett a Firework, at best.

I admire your Navigation and should like to sail with you, either in your Bark or in my own, along side of yours; Hope with her gay Ensigns displayed at the Prow; fear with her Hobgoblins behind the Stern. Hope springs eternal; and Hope is all that endures. Take away hope and What remains? What pleasure? I mean. Take away Fear, and what Pain remains? 99/100ths of the Pleasures and Pains of Life are nothing but Hopes and Fears.

All Nations, known in History or in Travels have hoped, believed, an[d] expected a future and a better State. The Maker of the Universe, the Cause of all Things, whether We call it, *Fate* or *Chance* or God has inspired this Hope. If it is a *Fraud*, We shall never know it. We shall never resen[t] the Imposition, be grateful for the Illusion, nor grieve for the disappointment. We shall be no more. Credat Grim, Diderot, Buffon, La Lande, Condorcet, D'Holbach, Frederick Catherine; Non Ego. Arrogant as it may be, I shall take the Liberty to pronounce them all, *Idiologians*. Yet I would not persecute a hair of their Heads. The World is wide enough for them and me.

Supose, the Cause of the Universe, should reveal to all Man kind, at once a *Certainty* that they must all die within a Century, and that death is an eternal Extinction of all living Powers, of all Sensation and Reflection. What would be the Effect? Would there be one Man Woman or Child existing on this Globe, twenty Years hence? Would not every human Being be, a Madame Deffand, Voltaires "Aveugle clairvoiante ["blind clairvoyant"]," all her Lifetime regretting her Existance, be wailing that She had ever been born; grieving that She had ever been dragged without her Consent, into being. Who would bear the Gout the Stone the Cholick, for the sake of a Boule de Savon when a Pistol a Cord, a Pond, or a Phyal of Laudanum was at hand? What would Men say to their Maker? would they thank him? No They would reproach him; they would curse him to his Face.

Voila! a sillier Letter than my last! For a Wonder, I have filled a Sheet. And a greater Wonder, I have read fifteen Volumes of Grim. Digito comesce Labellum.[83] I hope to write you more upon this and other Topicks of your Letter. I have read also a History of the Jesuits in four Volumes.[84] Can you tell me the Author or any Thing of this Work?

John Adams

83. "Hold your tongue." Juvenal, *Satires,* I, 160.
84. See JA to TJ, Aug. 9, Nov. 4, 1816, below, 486, 494.

Adams to Jefferson

Quincy May 6 1816

DEAR SIR

Neither Eyes Fingers or Paper held out, to dispatch all the Trifles I wished to write in my last Letter.

In your favour of April 8th, You "wonder for what good End the Sensations of Grief could be intended"? You ["]wish the Pathologists would tell Us, what the Use of Grief, in Our Œconomy, and of what good it is the Cause proximate or remote." When I approach such questions as this, I consider myself, like one of those little Eels in Vinaigre, or one of those Animalcules in black or red Peper or in the Horse radish Root, that bite our Tongues so cruelly, reasoning upon the το παν ["totality"]. Of what Use is this Sting upon the Tongue? Why might We not have the Benefit of these Stimulants, without the Sting? Why might We not have the fragrance and Beauty of the Rose without the Thorn?

In the first place, however, We know not the Connections between pleasure and Pain. They seem to be mechanical and inseperable. How can We conceive a strong Passion, a Sanguine Hope suddenly disappointed without producing Pain? or Grief? Swift at 70, recollected the Fish he had angled out of Water when a Boy, which broke loose from his hoock, and said I feel the disappointment at this Moment. A Merchant plans all his fortune and all his Credit, in a single India or China Ship. She Arrives at the Viniard with a Cargo worth a Million, in Order. Sailing round the Cape for Boston a sudden Storm wrecks her, Ship Cargo and Crew all lost. Is it possible that the Merchant ruined, bankrupt sent to Prison by his Creditors, his Wife and Children starving, should not grieve? Suppose a young Couple, with every Advant[a]ge of Persons, fortunes and Connection on the Point of an indissoluble Union. A flash of Lightening or any one of those millions of Accidents which are alloted to Humanity prove fatal to one of the Lovers. Is it possible that the other, and all the Friends of both should not grieve? It should seem that Grief, as a mere Passion must necesarily be in Proportion to Sensibility.

Did you ever see a Portrait or a Statue of a great Man, without perceiving strong Traits of Paine and Anxiety? These Furrows were all ploughed in the Countenance, by Grief. Our juvenile Oracle, Sir Edward Coke, thought that none were fit for Legislators and Magistrates, but "Sad Men." And Who were these sad Men? They were aged Men, who had been tossed and buffeted in the Vicissitudes of Life, forced upon profound Reflection by Grief and disappointments and taught to command their Passions and Prejudices.

But, All this, You will say, is nothing to the purpose. It is only repeating and exemplifying a Fact, which my question supposed to be well known, viz the Existence of Grief; and is no Answer to my Question, "What Are the Uses of Grief." This is very true, and you are very right: but may not the Uses of Grief be inferred, or at least suggested by such Exemplifications of known facts? Grief Compels the India Merchant to think; to reflect upon the plan of his Voyage. "Have I not been rash, to trust my Fortune, my Family, my Liberty, to the Caprices of Winds and Waves in a single Ship? I will never again give a loose to my Imagination and Avarice." ["]It had been wiser and more honest to have traded on a smaller Scale upon my own Capital." The dessolated Lover and disappointed Connections, are compelled by their Grief to reflect on the Vanity of human Wishes and Expectations; to learn the essential Lesson of Resignation; to review their own Conduct towards the deceased; to correct any Errors or faults in their future Conduct towards their remaining friends and towards all Men; to recollect the Virtues of the lost Friend and resolve to imitate them; his Follies and Vices if he had any and resolve to avoid them. Grief drives Men into habits of serious Reflection sharpens the Understanding and softens the heart; it compells them to arrouse their Reason, to assert its Empire over their Passions Propensities and Prejudices; to elevate them to a Superiority over all human Events; to give them the Felicis Annimi immotan tranquilitatem ["the imperturbable tranquillity of a happy heart"]; in short to make them Stoicks and Christians.

After all, as Grief is a Pain, it stands in the Predicament of all other Evil and the great question Occurs what is the Origin and what the final cause of Evil. This perhaps is known only to Omnicience. We poor Mortals have nothing to do with it, but to fabricate all the good We can out of all inevitable Evils, and to avoid all that are avoidable, and many such there are, among which are our own unnecessary Apprehensions and imaginary Fears. Though Stoical Apathy is impossible, Yet Patience and Resignation and tranquility may be acquired by Consideration in a great degree, very much for the hapiness of Life.

I have read Grim, in fifteen Volumes of more than five hundred pages each. I will not say, like Uncle Tobey "You shall not die till you have read him." But you ought to read him, if possible. It is the most entertaining Work I ever read. He appears exactly as you represent him. What is most of all remarkable, is his Impartiality. He spares no Characters, but Necker and Diderot. Voltaire, Buffon, D'Alembert, Helvetius Rousseau, Marmontel, Condorcet, La Harpe, Beaumarchais and all others are lashed without Ceremony. Their Portraits as faithfully drawn as possible. It is a compleat Review of French Litterature and fine Arts from 1753 to 1790. No Politicks. Criticisms very just. Anecdotes with out number, and very merry. One ineffably ridiculous I wish I could send you, but it is immeasurably long. D'Argens, a little out of health and shivering with the cold in Berlin asked leave of the King to take a ride to Gascony his Native Province. He was absent so long that Frederick concluded the Air of the South of France was like to detain his Friend and as he wanted his Society and Services he contrived a Trick to bring him back. He fabricated a Mandement in the Name of the Archbishop of Aix, commanding all the Faithful to seize The Marquis D'Argens, Author of Ocellus, Timæus and Julian, Works Atheistical, Deistical, Heretical and impious in the highest degree. This Mandement composed in a Style of Ecclesiastical Eloquence that never was exceeded by Pope, Jesuite, Inquisitor, or Sorbonite he sent in Print by a courier to D'Argens, who frightened out of his Witts fled by cross roads out of France and back to Berlin, to the greater Joy of the Philosophical Court for the laugh of Europe which they had raised at the Expence of the learned Marquis.

I do not like the late Resurrection of the Jesuits.[85] They have a General, now in Russia, in correspondence with the Jesuits in the U. S. who are more numerous than every body knows. Shall We not have Swarms of them here? In as many shapes and disguises as ever a King of the Gypsies, Bamfie[l]d More Carew himself, assumed? In the shape of Printers, Editors, Writers School masters etc. I have lately read Pascalls Letters over again, and four Volumes of the History of the Jesuits. If ever any Congregation of Men could merit, eternal Perdition on Earth and in Hell, According to these Historians though like Pascal true Catholicks, it is this Company of Loiola. Our System however of Religious Liberty must afford them an Assylum. But if they do not put the Purity of our Elections to a severe Tryal, it will be a Wonder.

J. ADAMS

85. During the 1760's the Jesuits, distasteful to monarchs and civil officials of the Enlightenment, were expelled from most Catholic countries, and in 1773 the Pope dissolved the Society of Jesus. It was not reconstituted until 1814.

12

"The advantages of education...
on the broad scale"

✳ AUGUST 1816 – DECEMBER 1819 ✳

URING THE EARLY YEARS of reconciliation between Adams and Jefferson, the latter's correspondence with Mrs. Adams was resumed, but it was sparse and restrained and without any regularity. She had terminated their exchange of 1804 and it was proper that she make the first gesture for renewal of their friendship. At the urging of her husband, she added a halfhearted postscript to his letter to Jefferson in May 1812, and a year later, by the same device, she sent "the regards of an old Friend, which are still cherished and preserved through all the changes and vi[ci]ssitudes which have taken place since we first became acquainted." [1] Jefferson acknowledged Mrs. Adams's greeting politely to ask "how you do, how you have done?" but his heart warmed as he told her that he had "$10\frac{1}{2}$ grandchildren, and $2\frac{3}{4}$ great-grand-children; and these fractions will ere long become units." [2] A few days afterward he received from Adams the sad news of the death of their daughter Abigail on August 15 and a month later Mrs. Adams wrote him at length about her bereavement. Jefferson's letter had encouraged her to write, she explained. "But altho, time has changed the outward form, and political 'Back wounding calumny' for a period interrupted the Friendly intercourse and harmony which subsisted, it is again renewed, purified from the dross." [3] Jefferson directed his sincere, though brief, expression of condolence to Adams. [4]

1. JA to TJ, May 3, 1812, July 15, 1813, above, 304, 358.
2. TJ to AA, Aug. 22, 1813, above, 367.
3. JA to TJ, Aug. [14?], 1813, and AA to TJ, Sept. 20, 1813, above, 366, 378.
4. TJ to JA, Oct. 12, 1813, above, 386.

No further word passed between Mrs. Adams and Jefferson until February 1816, when she penned another postscript to a letter from her husband; and during the last two years of her life she and Jefferson wrote each other twice. In his dreams of the future he always fancied the Adamses by his side, while she recalled the pleasure of "the continued Friendship of the phylosopher of Monticello."[5] Their last letters were cordial enough, concerning favors asked and granted and regrets that they could not enjoy a visit in Quincy or at Monticello.[6] Mrs. Adams died of typhoid fever on October 28, 1818, at the age of seventy-three, leaving her aged husband to an increasingly lonely existence during his last eight years. The news of Mrs. Adams's death moved Jefferson to write his old friend a tender note of sympathy, but even then his reticent nature dictated that "for ills so immeasurable, time and silence are the only medecines."[7]

Although Adams and Jefferson were often engrossed in philosophical questions, they were very much aware of the post-war world after the Peace of 1815. They followed closely the news of depression and social turbulence in England, as they reconsidered the common interests of Great Britain and the United States, seldom utilized as yet by both nations for their mutual gain. Jefferson, still resentful of past insults to his country and unsympathetic toward Britain's internal difficulties, anticipated dire consequences to her world position; but Adams better understood the flexibility of the British and expected them to "stick with their Constitution." Nevertheless, Adams, remembering his rebuffs as American minister in London, thought that "Britain will never be our Friend, till we are her Master."[8] But can we "preserve our Union?" he asked. If not, independence would be precarious. And the menace of the slavery controversy, exhibited in the Missouri question, compromised in 1820, made both statesmen fearful of the future.[9]

Conditions in the new South American republics also attracted the attention of the two elder statesmen. Adams was more confident than

5. JA to TJ, Feb. 2, 1816, above, 463; TJ to JA, Aug. 1, 1816; and AA to TJ, Dec. 15, 1816, below, 485, 500.
6. TJ to AA, Jan. 11, May 15, 1817, and AA to TJ, April 29, 1817, below, 503-4, 514, 511.
7. Whitney, *Abigail Adams*, 326; JA to TJ, Oct. 20, 1818, and TJ to JA, Nov. 13, 1818, below, 529.
8. TJ to JA, Oct. 14, Nov. 25, and JA to TJ, Dec. 16, 1816, below, 492, 496-99, 501-2.
9. JA to TJ, Dec. 16, 1816, Nov. 23, Dec. 21, 1819, and TJ to JA, Dec. 10, 1819, below, 502, 548, 551, 549.

Jefferson that the Latin American revolutions made independence secure, but both felt that ignorance and superstition, fostered by the Roman Catholic Church, cast a dark shadow on free government.[10] If the Latin Americans were not ready for republican government, however, they would grow up to it, freed from their colonial status. And "what a colossus shall we be when the Southern continent comes up to our mark!" exclaimed Jefferson. "What a stand will it secure as a ralliance for the reason and freedom of the globe! I like the dreams of the future better than the history of the past."[11]

One of Jefferson's favorite "dreams of the future" was educational reform. The epitaph which he composed—a memorial of his founding of the University of Virginia as well as his authorship of the Declaration of Independence and the Virginia Statute for Religious Freedom —does not suggest the years of frustration ending in only partial fulfillment of his hopes for free public education. He was thirty-five when he drafted the Bill for the More General Diffusion of Knowledge in 1778, which was never enacted. He was seventy-five when the act establishing the University was passed in 1819, and he had almost reached the age of eighty-two before the first academic session, of 1825-26, began.

Adams's and Jefferson's discussion of natural and artificial aristocracy led the latter into reflections on education. Good government and public education had long been inseparably associated in his mind. Inevitably he harked back to his Bill No. 79, for the More General Diffusion of Knowledge, which declared that laws wisely formed and honestly administered assure the greatest happiness and in turn the best laws, "whence it becomes expedient for promoting the publick happiness that those persons, whom nature hath endowed with genius and virtue, should be rendered by liberal education worthy to receive, and able to guard the sacred deposit of the rights and liberties of their fellow citizens, and that they should be called to that charge without regard to wealth, birth or other accidental condition or circumstance."[12]

The bill provided for three levels of education: elementary or ward schools for all children; district schools for the cream of the crop deserving of higher education; and the university for the élite of the

10. JA to TJ, Jan. 28, 1818, Feb. 3, 1821, Sept. 18, 1823, and TJ to JA, May 17, 1818, Jan. 22, 1821, Sept. 4, 1823, below, 523, 571, 599, 524, 570, 596.
11. TJ to JA, Aug. 1, 1816, below, 485.
12. Boyd, II, 527.

natural aristocracy. To Adams, Jefferson emphasized that he had proposed the ward, rather than the existing county, as the unit of local government, because he conceived it to be a "little republic," well governed by well-informed citizens. Having abolished primogeniture and entail and guaranteed religious freedom by legislative act, Jefferson hoped that the bill "on Education would have raised the mass of the people to the high ground of moral responsibility necessary to their own safety, and to orderly government." [13] He had stated the case in his *Notes on Virginia* a few years afterward. But even with Madison's support in the legislature, the bill, labeled by Jefferson as "the most important bill in our whole code," failed of passage.[14] He had to take cold comfort in the act of 1796, which provided for elementary schools for poor children but only on an optional basis.[15] In spite of prolonged inaction and half-measures, Jefferson wrote Adams in 1813 of his "great hope that some patriotic spirit will, at a favorable moment, call it [the original bill] up, and make it the key-stone of the arch of our government." [16]

In 1817 Jefferson drafted the Bill for Establishing a System of Public Education, his last attempt in a campaign begun almost forty years earlier. It might be said that he was giving the legislature a final opportunity to do right by the people of Virginia, but from past experience he reluctantly reached the conclusion that the members "do not generally possess information enough to perceive the important truths, that knolege is power, that knolege is safety, and that knolege is happiness." Again Jefferson's comprehensive plan met with defeat, but the real loss was suffered by the Commonwealth, which set up no bona fide public school system until the 1870's. As an alternative to his broad plan for public education, Jefferson was prepared to proceed with private funds to establish "a college of general science" near Charlottesville, on the same site where he was still hoping to locate the state university.[17]

13. TJ to JA, Oct. 28, 1813, above, 390; TJ to Governor Wilson C. Nicholas, April 2, 1816, Andrew A. Lipscomb and Albert Ellery Bergh, eds., *The Writings of Thomas Jefferson* (Washington, D.C., 1903-4), XIV, 454.

14. *Notes on Virginia*, ed. by Peden, 148-49; Boyd, II, 535*n.;* also TJ to George Wythe, Aug. 13, 1786, *ibid.*, X, 244.

15. Roy J. Honeywell, *The Educational Work of Thomas Jefferson* (Cambridge, Mass., 1931), 14.

16. TJ to JA, Oct. 28, 1813, above, 390.

17. Honeywell, *Educational Work of Jefferson*, 233-43; TJ to George Ticknor, Nov. 25, 1817, Ford, X, 95-96.

To Jefferson, who kept abreast of the rapid advancement of knowledge during the Age of the Enlightenment and responded to the spirit of scientific investigation, the higher education of youth seemed antiquated in many respects. He complained to Adams that "education is chiefly in the hands of persons who, from their profession, have an interest in the reputation and the dreams of Plato"; but the mysticism of Plato could not stand the test of reason, and Jefferson had no more respect for Platonic republicanism than he did for Platonic Christianity. "Our post-revolutionary youth," he observed sarcastically, "are born under happier stars than you and I were. They acquire all learning in their mothers' womb, and bring it into the world ready-made. The information of books is no longer necessary; and all knolege which is not innate, is in contempt, or neglect at least." Jefferson was advocating "education on the broad scale, not that of the petty *academies* ... starting up in every neighborhood," where the sum-total of knowledge consisted of some Latin and Greek, a measure of geography, and the first six books of Euclid. These pedagogues, he feared, "commit their pupils to the theatre of the world with just enough taste of learning to be alienated from industrious pursuits, and not enough to do service in the ranks of science." [18]

The real hope for reform and modernization seemed to be at the university level. During the Revolution, Jefferson had drafted Bill No. 80 for Amending the Constitution of the College of William and Mary, a companion piece to Bill No. 79. As one of the College's visitors during his governorship, Jefferson had succeeded in abolishing the professorships of divinity and oriental languages as well as the grammar school; but the legislature rejected the opportunity to convert the College into the state university.[19] By 1800 Jefferson concluded that the condition of the College, his alma mater, was hopeless and therefore outlined his ideas for a new institution, centrally located, "on a plan so broad and liberal and *modern*, as to be worth patronizing with the public support, and to be a temptation to the youth of other states." [20]

In July 1814, he requested Adams's advice on such an institution of higher learning and asked him to specify "the particular sciences of real use in human affairs" and "bring them within the views of a just

18. TJ to JA, July 5, 1814, above, 434.
19. Boyd, II, 535-42 and *nn*.
20. TJ to Joseph Priestley, Jan. 18, 1800, Ford, VII, 407-9.

but enlightened economy." [21] "Education! Oh Education!" replied Adams, who confessed he had never deliberately reflected on the subject. He would omit theology and metaphysics, but grouping the arts and sciences was beyond his capacity. What he jotted down, however, belied this statement and compared favorably with Jefferson's more studied effort.[22] For Adams had long believed that "the whole people must take upon themselves the education of the whole people, and must be willing to bear the expenses of it." [23] Massachusetts had won an enviable reputation in its early development of public education at the town level (which Jefferson had vainly hoped to emulate) and Harvard College provided society with its natural aristocracy; [24] indeed, Adams had never faced a glaring lack of education or public apathy such as Jefferson was combatting in Virginia.

But slow progress did not make the aging Jefferson apathetic. In 1814 he was elected a trustee of Albemarle Academy, a paper organization which had sought for a decade the means to become a reality. There was mutual advantage in this association, for Jefferson agreed to prepare a plan which, from his standpoint, could provide another opportunity to publicize the need for a system of public education and do so under specific auspices. Out of his letter of September 7, addressed to President Peter Carr of the Academy and first published in the Richmond *Enquirer*, developed a train of events leading to the establishment of the University of Virginia by legislative act of 1819. In accordance with his basic philosophy that every citizen should receive some education at public expense, depending upon his occupation and condition of life, Jefferson divided the population into two classes, "the laboring and the learned." Elementary schools would prepare the former for their pursuits in life, the latter for higher learning in "general schools" (college) and professional schools (the university). All branches of "useful science" ought to be taught in the general schools, arranged in three departments: (1) language: ancient and modern languages and history, history being associated with languages "on a principle of economy, because both may be attained by the same course of reading"; (2) mathematics, including the nat-

21. TJ to JA, July 5, 1814, above, 434.
22. JA to TJ, July 16, 1814, June 19, 1815, March 2, 1816, above, 438-39, 443-44, 466.
23. JA to John Jebb, Sept. 10, 1785, *Works*, IX, 540.
24. JA to John Taylor, [Dec. 26, 1814], *ibid.*, VI, 494-95.

ural sciences and the theory of medicine; (3) philosophy, including the law of nature and nations, government, and political economy.[25]

The professional schools, in which "each science is to be taught in the highest degree it has yet attained," were outlined as (1) fine arts, including civil architecture; (2) military and naval architecture; agriculture and veterinary; medicine, pharmacy, and surgery; (3) theology and ecclesiastical history, municipal and foreign law. To assure a continuing high caliber of the faculty Jefferson advised that the "sciences" "must be subdivided from time to time, as our means increase, until each professor shall have no more under his care than he can attend to with advantage to his pupils and ease to himself"—a utopian vision of the light "teaching load," still an ideal rather than an actuality in most institutions of higher learning. He hoped to begin with four professors: (1) language and history; (2) mathematics, physics, and medicine; (3) chemistry, zoology, botany, and mineralogy; and (4) philosophy.[26] The grouping of subjects suggests a professorial versatility that was taken for granted.

In 1816 the trustees of Albemarle Academy secured legislation to establish Central College, as a tactical move toward a university. The Board of Visitors of the new College included the President of the United States and two former Presidents—Monroe, Madison, and Jefferson—who were conferring at Monticello when Jefferson informed Adams of the new institution. Although Adams was in a pessimistic mood, he felt that "from such a noble Tryumvirate, the World will expect something very great and very new," but it would "not always have three such colossal reputations to support it." [27]

Jefferson proceeded to develop plans for a community of pavilions, rather than a single large building, on a tract of two hundred acres just west of Charlottesville. Anticipating their need for public funds in the near future, the Visitors petitioned the legislature in January 1818 and suggested tactfully that, if a state university were to be established, their College would provide the ideal site.[28] On February 21 the legislature authorized the founding of a university "in some

25. [Nathaniel F. Cabell, ed.], *Early History of the University of Virginia as contained in the Letters of Thomas Jefferson and Joseph C. Cabell* ... (Richmond, 1856), 384-86.

26. *Ibid.*, 387-89.

27. *Ibid.*, 391-93; TJ to JA, May 5, 1817, and JA to TJ, May 18 and 26, 1817, below, 513, 516, 518.

28. Cabell, *Early History of University of Va.*, 400-4; TJ to JA, Sept. 8, 1817, below, 519.

convenient and proper part of the State, ... wherein all the branches of useful science shall be taught." Commissioners appointed by the governor met at Rockfish Gap Tavern in the Blue Ridge on August 1 and selected Charlottesville for the location of the University of Virginia.[29] Jefferson's presence on the commission and the recent development of Central College undoubtedly strengthened their case.

The *Report of the Commissioners to fix the Scite of the University of Virginia* is a Jeffersonian document in its statement of educational principles, and it reiterates and expands his ideas on the curriculum and professorships.[30] The site, the plan of buildings, the program of education—all were Jefferson's. The act of January 25, 1819, confirmed the establishment of the University of Virginia on the site of Central College. This assurance was a relief to Jefferson, for, as he wrote in transmitting a copy of the *Report* to Adams, "Being a good piece of a century behind the age they [the legislators] live in, we are not without fear as to their conclusions." [31] Later he was pleased with the critical review of the *Report* in the *North American Review*. Although the reviewer regarded the omission of a professorship of divinity as a "hazardous experiment," he saw fit to quote at length the principle of religious freedom upon which the omission was based.[32]

Appointed to the University's Board of Visitors, Jefferson was chosen by them as rector in 1819. He thought himself fortunate to be "mounted on a Hobby, ... whose easy amble is still sufficient to give exercise and amusement to an Octogenary rider." [33] But the pace was often more strenuous than an "easy amble." Six years intervened before the University opened its doors to the first students in February 1825. During that period he directed its architecture—he boasted that "it's plan is unique." [34] Jefferson searched for a faculty and helped raise funds. The University's curriculum was broadly conceived to provide a liberal education in the "useful sciences" as well as in the humanities, in modern languages as well as the classics, and to offer training for the professions. Unfettered by medieval tradition, the University of Virginia would set an example to be emulated haltingly

29. Cabell, *Early History of University of Va.*, 430-32.
30. *Ibid.*, 430-47.
31. *Ibid.*, 447-50; TJ to JA, Jan. 19, 1819, below, 532.
32. TJ to JA, Aug. 15, 1820, below, 565-66. *North American Review*, 10 (Jan. 1820), 130-31.
33. TJ to JA, Oct. 12, 1823, below, 599.
34. Cabell, *Early History of University of Va.*, 452; TJ to JA, Aug. 15, 1820, below, 565.

by its elder sister institutions. Following Jefferson's advice that the ablest scholars would be found abroad, the Board of Visitors sent Francis Walker Gilmer to Europe to engage professors and to buy books for the University library. In 1824 the Visitors, faced with a shortage of funds, courageously instituted eight professorships and gave priority to salaries while wrestling with financial problems.[35]

In December of that year Jefferson took his guests, Mr. and Mrs. George Ticknor and Daniel Webster, on a tour of the University buildings then nearing completion. Ticknor concluded prophetically, "Mr. Jefferson is entirely absorbed in it, and its success would make a *beau finale* indeed to his life." [36]

Jefferson to Adams

Monticello Aug. 1. 16.

DEAR SIR

Your two philosophical letters of May 4. and 6. have been too long in my carton of 'Letters to be answered.' To the question indeed on the utility of Grief, no answer remains to be given. You have exhausted the subject. I see that, with the other evils of life, it is destined to temper the cup we are to drink.

> Two urns by Jove's high throne have ever stood,
> The source of evil one, and one of good;
> From thence the cup of mortal man he fills,
> Blessings to these, to those distributes ills;
> To most he mingles both.[37]

Putting to myself your question, Would I agree to live my 73. years over again for ever? I hesitate to say. With Chew's limitations from 25. to 60., I would say Yes; and might go further back, but not come lower down. For, at the latter period, with most of us, the powers of life are sensibly on the wane, sight becomes dim, hearing dull, memory constantly enlarging it's frightful blank and parting with all we have ever seen or

35. Cabell, *Early History of University of Va.*, 222, 453, 455, 481-83; Richard Beale Davis, ed., *Correspondence of Thomas Jefferson and Francis Walker Gilmer, 1814-1826* (Columbia, S.C., 1946), 80-82.

36. Ticknor to William H. Prescott, Dec. 16, 1824, Hillard, ed., *Life of Ticknor*, I, 348; TJ to JA, Sept. 8, 1817, below, 519-20.

37. Pope's translation of the *Iliad*, XXIV, 663-67.

known, spirits evaporate, bodily debility creeps on palsying every limb, and so faculty after faculty quits us, and where then is life? If, in it's full vigor, of good as well as evil, your friend Vassall could doubt it's value, it must be purely a negative quantity when it's evils alone remain. Yet I do not go into his opinion entirely. I do not agree that an age of pleasure is no compensation for a moment of pain. I think, with you, that life is a fair matter of account, and the balance often, nay generally in it's favor. It is not indeed easy, by calculation of intensity and time, to apply a common measure, or to fix the par between pleasure and pain: yet it exists, and is measurable. On the question, for example, whether to be cut for the stone? the young, with a longer prospect of years, think these overbalance the pain of the operation. Dr. Franklin, at the age of 80., thought his residuum of life, not worth that price. I should have thought with him, even taking the stone out of the scale. There is a ripeness of time for death, regarding others as well as ourselves, when it is reasonable we should drop off, and make room for another growth. When we have lived our generation out, we should not wish to encroach on another. I enjoy good health; I am happy in what is around me. Yet I assure you I am ripe for leaving all, this year, this day, this hour. If it could be doubted whether we would go back to 25. how can it be, whether we would go forward from 73? Bodily decay is gloomy in prospect; but of all human contemplations the most abhorrent is body without mind. Perhaps however I might accept of time to read Grimm before I go. 15. volumes of anecdotes and incidents, within the compass of my own time and cognisance, written by a man of genius, of taste, of point, an acquaintance, the measure and traverses of whose mind I knew, could not fail to turn the scale in favor of life during their perusal. I must write to Ticknor to add it to my catalogue, and hold on till it comes.

There is a Mr. Vanderkemp of N.Y. a correspondent I believe of yours, with whom I have exchanged some letters, without knowing who he is. Will you tell me?

I know nothing of the history of the Jesuits you mention in 4. vols. Is it a good one? I dislike, with you, their restoration; because it marks a retrograde step from light towards darkness. We shall have our follies without doubt. Some one or more of them will always be afloat. But ours will be the follies of enthusiasm, not of bigotry, not of Jesuitism. Bigotry is the disease of ignorance, of morbid minds; enthusiasm of the free and buoyant. Education and free discussion are the antidotes of both. We are destined to be a barrier against the returns of ignorance and barbarism. Old Europe will have to lean on our shoulders, and to hobble along by our side, under the monkish trammels of priests and kings, as she can. What a Colossus shall we be when the Southern continent comes up to our mark!

What a stand will it secure as a ralliance for the reason and freedom of the globe. I like the dreams of the future better than the history of the past. So good night. I will dream on, always fancying that Mrs Adams and yourself are by my side marking the progress and the obliquities of ages and countries.

TH: JEFFERSON

Adams to Jefferson

Quincy August 9. 1816

DEAR SIR

The Biography of Mr. Vander Kemp would require a Volume which I could not write if a Milion were offered me as a Reward for the Work. After a learned and scientific Education he entered the Army in Holland and served as a Captain, with Reputation: but loving Books more than Arms he resigned his Commission and became a Preacher. My Acquaintance with him commenced at Leyden in 1780. He was then Minister of the Menonist Congregation the richest in Europe; in that City where he was celebrated as the most elegant Writer in the Dutch Langu[a]ge. He was the intimate Friend of Luzac and De Gyselaar. In 1788 when the King of Prussia threatened Holland with Invasion, his Party insisted on his taking a Command in the Army of defence and he was appointed to the Command of the most exposed and most important Post in the Seven Provinces. He was soon surrounded by the Prussian Forces. But he defended his Fortress with a Prudence Fortitude Patience and Perseverance, which were admired by all Europe, Till, abandoned by his Nation, destitute of Provisions and Amunition, still refusing to surrender, he was offered the most honourable Capitulation. He accepted it. Was offered very Advantageous Proposals, but despairing of the Liberties of his Country, he retired to Antwerp determined to emigrate to New York; wrote to me in London requesting Letters of Introduction. I sent him Letters to Governor Clinton and several others of our little great Men. His History in this Country is equally curious and affecting. He left Property in Holland, which the Revolutions there, have annihilated and I fear is now pinched with Poverty. His head is deeply learned and his heart is pure. I scarcely know a more amiable Character. A Gentleman here asked my Opinion of him. My Answer was, he is a *Mountain of Salt* of the Earth. He has written to me, occasionally and I have answered his Letters in great haste. You may well suppose that such a Man has not always been able to

Understand our American Politicks. Nor have I. Had he been as great a Master of our Langu[a]ge as he was of his own he would have been at this day one of the most conspicuous Characters in the U. S.

So much for Vanderkemp: now for your Letter of Aug. 1. Your Poet, the Ionian I suppose, ought to have told Us, whether Jove in the distribution of good and Evil from his two Urns, observes any Rule of Equity or not. Whether he thunders out flames of eternal Fire on the Many, and Power Glory and Felicity on the Few, without any consideration of Justice?

Let Us state a few Questions, sub rosâ.

1. Would you accept a Life, if offered You, of equal pleasure and Paine? E.G. one million of moments of Pleasure and one Million of Moments of Pain? 1,000,000 Pleasure = 1,000,000 Paine. Suppose the Pleasure as exquisite as any in Life and the Paine as exquisite as any. E.G. Stone, Gravel, Gout, Head Ache, Ear Ache, Tooth Ache, Cholick. etc. I would not. I would rather be blotted out.

2. Would you accept a Life of one Year of incessant Gout, Head Ache etc for Seventy two Years of such Life as you have injoyed? I would not.

1 Year of Cholic = 72. of Boule de Savon. pretty but unsubstantial. I had rather be extinguished. You may vary these Algebraical Equations at pleasure and without End. All this Ratiocination Calculation, call it what you will, is founded on the Supposition of no future State. Promise me eternal Life free from Pain, tho' in all other respects no better than our present terrestrial Existence, I know not how many thousand Years of Smithfield fires I would not endure to obtain it.

In fine, without the Supposition of a future State, Mankind and this Globe appear to me the most sublime and beautifull Bubble and Bauble that Imagination can conceive.

Let Us then wish for Immortality at all hazards and trust the Ruler with his Skies. I do: and earnestly wish for his Commands which to the Utmost of my Power shall be implicitly and piously obeyed.

It is worth while to live to read Grimm, whom I have read, And La Harpe and Mademoiselle D'Espinasse the fair Friend of D'Allembert both of whom Grimm Characterises very distinctly are I am told in Print. I have not seen them but hope soon to have them.

My History of the Jesuits is not elegantly written but is supported by unquesti[on]able Authorities, is very particular and very horrible. Their Restoration is indeed "a Step towards Darkness" Cruelty Perfidy Despotism Death and ———! I wish We were out of "danger of Bigotry and Jesuitism!" May We be "a Barrier against the Returns of Ignorance and Barbarism!" "What a Colossus shall We be?" But will it not be of Brass

Iron and Clay? Your Taste is judicious in likeing better the dreams of the Future, than the History of the Past. Upon this Principle I prophecy that you and I shall soon meet and be better Friends than ever. So wishes

JOHN ADAMS

Adams to Jefferson

Quincy Septr. 03. 1816

DEAR SIR

Dr. James Freeman, is a learned, ingenious, honest and benevolent Man, who wishes to see President Jefferson, and requests me to introduce him. If you would introduce some of Your Friends to me, I could with more confidence introduce mine to You. He is a Christian, but not a Pythagorian a Platonick or a Philonick Christian. You will ken him and he will ken You: but you may depend, he will never betray, deceive or injure You.

Without hinting to him, any Thing which had passed between You and me, I asked him, your Question *"What are the Uses of Grief?"* He stared. Said "the question was new to him." All he could say at present was that he had known in his own Parish, more than one Instance of Ladies, who had been thoughtless, modish, extravagant in a high degree; who upon the death of a Child, had become thoughtfull, modest, humble, as prudent amiable Women as any he had known. Upon this I read to him Your Letters and mine, upon this Subject of Grief, with which he seemed to be pleased. You see I was not afraid to trust him: and you need not be.

Since I am, accidentally, invited to write to You, I may add a few Words Upon Pleasures and Pains of Life. Vassall thought, an hundred Years, nay an eternity of Pleasure was no Compensation for one hour of billious Cholic. Read again Mollieres Spsyke [i.e., Psyche]. Act. 2. Scene 1st. On the Subject of Grief. And read in another place "On est payé de mille Maux Par un heureux moment." [38] Thus differently do Men speak of Pleasures and Pains.

Now, Sir, I will tease you with another Question. What have been the *Abuses* of Grief?

In Answer to this question, I doubt not, you might write an hundred volumes. A few hints may convince You that the Subject is ample.

1. The Death of Socrates excited a general Sensibility of Grief in Athens, in Attica and in all Greece. Plato and Xenophon two of his Disciples took

---

38. "One happy moment compensates for a thousand ills."

Advantage of that general Sentiment, by employing their enchanting Style to represent their Master to be greater and better than he probably was. And What have been the Effects of Socratic, Platonick which were Pythagorean, which was Indian Philosophy, in the World?

2. The Death of Caesar, Tyrant as he was, spread a general Compassion which always includes Grief, among the Romans. The Scoundrel, M. Anthony availed himself of this momentary Grief to destroy the Republick, to establish the Empire, and to proscribe Cicero.

3. But to skip over all Ages and Nations for the present, and descend to our own Times. The Death of Washington, diffused a general Grief. The Old Tories, the Hyperfederalists, the Speculators, sett up a general Howl. Orations Prayers Sermons Mock Funerals, were all employed, not that they loved Washington, but to keep in Countenance the Funding and Banking Systems; And to cast into the Background and the Shade all others who had been concerned in the Service of their Country in the Revolution.

4. The Death of Hamilton, under all its circumstances, produced a General Grief. His most determined Ennemies did not like to get rid of him, in that Way. They pitied too his Widow and Children. His Party seized the moment of publick Feeling to come forward with Funeral Orations and Printed Panegyricks reinforced with mock Funerals and solemn Grimaces, and all this by People who have buried Otis, Sam. Adams Handcock and Gerry in Comparitive Obscurity. And Why? Merely to disgrace the old Whiggs, and keep the Funds and Banks in Countenance.

5. The Death of Mr. Ames excited a General Regret. His long Consumption his amiable Character and respectable Talents had attracted a general Interest, and his Death a general Mourning. His Party made the most of it, by Processions Orations, and a Mock Funeral. And Why? To glorify the Torys, to abash the Whiggs, and maintain the Reputation of Funds, Banks and Speculation. And all this was done in honour of that insignificant Boy, by People who have let a Dana a Gerry and a Dexter go to their Graves without Notice.

6. I almost shudder at the thought of alluding to the most fatal Example of the Abuses of Grief, which the History of Man kind has preserved. The Cross. Consider what Calamities that Engine of Grief has produced! With the rational Respect that is due to it, knavish Priests have added Prostitutions of it, that fill or might fill the blackest and bloodiest Pages of human History. I am with ancient friendly Sentiments

JOHN ADAMS

Adams to Jefferson

Quincy Sept. 30. 16

PRESIDENT JEFFERSON.

DEAR SIR

The Seconds of Life, that remain to me, are so few and so short; (and they seem to me shorter and shorter every minute) that I cannot stand upon Epistolary Ettiquette: and though I have written two Letters, yet unnoticed I must write a third. Because I am not acquainted with any Man on this side of Montecello, who can give me any Information upon Subjects that I am now *analysing* and *investigating;* if I may be permitted to Use the pompous Words now in fashion.

When I read Dr. Priestleys Remarks upon *"Du Puis,"* I felt a Curiosity to know more about him. I wrote to Europe and engaged another to write. I had no Idea of more than one or two Volumes in 8° [octavo] or 12mo [duodecimo].

But Lo! I am overwhelmed with 8 or ten Volumes and another of Planches!

Sixteen Years of Research the Author acknowledges, and as he quotes his Authorities I would not undertake to verify them in 16 Years, If I had all his Books which surely are not to be found in America.

If you know any Thing of this "Monsieur Du Puis["] or his *"Origine de tous les Cultes";* Candidus imperti ["candidly impart it"].

I have read only the first Volume. It is learned and curious. The whole Work will afford me Business, Study and Amusement for the Winter.

Dr. Priestley pronounced him an Atheist, and his Work "The Ne Plus ultra of Infidelity." Priestley agrees with him, that the History of the Fall of Adam and Eve, is "an Alegory," a Fable, an Arabian Tale, and so does Dr. Middleton, to account for the Origin of Evil; which however it does not.

Priestly says that the Apocalypes, according to Dupuis is the most learned Work that ever was written.

With these brief Fletrissures, Priestly seems to have expected to anni[hi]late the Influence of Dupuis Labours; as Swift destroyed Blackmore with his

"Did off Creation with a Jerk
And of Redemption made damn'd Work." And as he disgraced Men as good at least as himself by his

"Wicked Will Whiston
And Good Master Ditton." [39]

But Dupuis is not to be so easily destroyed. The Controversy between Spiritualism and Materialism between Spiritualists and Materialists, will not be settled by Scurrilous Epigrams of Swift, nor by dogmatical Censures of Priestly.

You and I have as much Authority to settle these Disputes as Swift Priestley or Dupuis, or The Pope.

And if you will agree with me, We will issue our Bulls, and enjoin upon all these Gentlemen to be Silent, till they can tell Us, What Matter is and What Spirit is! And in the mean time to observe the Commandments and the Sermon on the Mount.

J. ADAMS

Jefferson to Adams

Monticello Oct. 14. 16.

Your letter, dear Sir, of May 6. had already well explained the Uses of grief, that of Sep. 3. with equal truth adduces instances of it's abuse; and when we put into the same scale these abuses, with the afflictions of soul which even the Uses of grief cost us, we may consider it's value in the economy of the human being, as equivocal at least. Those afflictions cloud too great a portion of life to find a counterpoise in any benefits derived from it's uses. For setting aside it's paroxysms on the occasions of special bereavements, all the latter years of aged men are overshadowed with it's gloom. Whither, for instance, can you and I look without seeing the graves of those we have known? And whom can we call up, of our early companions, who has not left us to regret his loss? This indeed may be one of the salutary effects of grief; inasmuch as it prepares us to lose ourselves also without repugnance. Dr. Freeman's instances of female levity cured by grief are certainly to the point, and constitute an item of credit in the account we examine.

I was much mortified by the loss of the Doctor's visit by my absence from home. To have shewn how much I feel indebted to you for making good people known to me would have been one pleasure; and to have

39. *The Works of the Rev. Jonathan Swift, D.D.*, arranged by Thomas Sheridan, A.M.... corrected and revised by John Nichols (London, 1803), XXIV, 39, 73. In the first ditty the first line should read: "Undid Creation with a Jerk."

enjoyed that of his conversation, and the benefits of his information so favorably reported by my family, would have been another. I returned home on the third day after his departure. The loss of such visits is among the sacrifices which my divided residence costs me.

Your undertaking the 12. volumes of Dupuis is a degree of heroism to which I could not have aspired even in my younger days. I have been contented with the humble atchievement of reading the Analysis of his work by Destutt-Tracy in 200 pages 8vo [octavo]. I believe I should have ventured on his own abridgment of the work in one 8vo. volume, had it ever come to my hands; but the marrow of it in Tracy has satisfied my appetite: and, even in that, the preliminary discourse of the Analyser himself, and his Conclusion, are worth more in my eye than the body of the work. For the object of that seems to be to smother all history under the mantle of allegory. If histories so unlike as those of Hercules and Jesus, can, by a fertile imagination, and Allegorical interpretations, be brought to the same tally, no line of distinction remains between fact and fancy. As this pithy morsel will not overburthen the mail in passing and repassing between Quincy and Monticello, I send it for your perusal. Perhaps it will satisfy you, as it has me; and may save you the labor of reading 24 times it's volume. I have said to you that it was written by Tracy; and I had so entered it on the title-page, as I usually do on Anonymous works whose authors are known to me. But Tracy had requested me not to betray his anonyme, for reasons which may not yet perhaps have ceased to weigh. I am bound then to make the same reserve with you. Destutt-Tracy is, in my judgment, the ablest writer living on intellectual subjects, or the operations of the understanding. His three 8vo. volumes on Ideology,[40] which constitute the foundation of what he has since written, I have not entirely read; because I am not fond of reading what is merely abstract, and unapplied immediately to some useful science. Bonaparte, with his repeated derisions of Ideologists (squinting at this author) has by this time felt that true wisdom does not lie in mere practice without principle. The next work Tracy wrote was the Commentary on Montesquieu, never published in the original, because not safe; but translated and published in Philadelphia [1811], yet without the author's name. He has since permitted his name to be mentioned. Although called a Commentary, it is in truth an elementary work on the principles of government, comprised in about 300. pages 8vo. He has lately published a third work on Political economy, comprising the whole subject within about the same compass; in which all it's principles are demonstrated with the severity of Euclid, and, like him, without ever using a superfluous word. I have procured this to be translated, and have been 4 years endeavoring to get it printed.

40. *Elements d'ideology*..., 5 pts. (Paris, 1803-15).

But, as yet, without success.[41] In the mean time the author has published the original in France, which he thought unsafe while Bonaparte was in power. No printed copy, I believe, has yet reached this country. He has his 4th. and last work now in the press at Paris, closing, as he concieves, the circle of metaphysical sciences. This work which is on Ethics, I have not seen, but suspect I shall differ from it in it's foundation, altho not in it's deductions. I gather from his other works that he adopts the principle of Hobbes, that justice is founded in contract solely, and does not result from the construction of man. I believe, on the contrary, that it is instinct, and innate, that the moral sense is as much a part of our constitution as that of feeling, seeing, or hearing; as a wise creator must have seen to be necessary in an animal destined to live in society: that every human mind feels pleasure in doing good to another; that the non-existence of justice is not to be inferred from the fact that the same act is deemed virtuous and right in one society, which is held vicious and wrong in another; because as the circumstances and opinions of different societies vary, so the acts which may do them right or wrong must vary also: for virtue does not consist in the act we do, but in the end it is to effect. If it is to effect the happiness of him to whom it is directed, it is virtuous, while in a society under different circumstances and opinions the same act might produce pain, and would be vicious. The essence of virtue is in doing good to others, while what is good may be one thing in one society, and it's contrary in another. Yet, however we may differ as to the foundation of morals, (and as many foundations have been assumed as there are writers on the subject nearly) so correct a thinker as Tracy will give us a sound system of morals. And indeed it is remarkable that so many writers, setting out from so many different premises, yet meet, all, in the same conclusions. This looks as if they were guided, unconsciously, by the unerring hand of instinct.

Your history of the Jesuits, by what name of the Author, or other description is it to be enquired for?

What do you think of the present situation of England? Is not this the great and fatal crush of their funding system, which, like death, has been foreseen by all, but it's hour, like that of death, hidden from mortal prescience? It appears to me that all the circumstances now exist which render recovery desperate. The interest of the national debt is now equal to such a portion of the profits of all the land and the labor of the island, as not to leave enough for the subsistence of those who labor. Hence the owners of the land abandon it and retire to other countries, and the

41. *A Treatise on Political Economy* ... By the Count Destutt de Tracy ... Translated from the unpublished French original (Georgetown, D.C., 1817). The original was not published until five years later (Paris, 1822). See below, JA's and TJ's comments on this work, 493, 495-96.

laborer has not enough of his earnings left to him to cover his back, and to fill his belly. The local insurrections, now almost general,[42] are of the hungry and the naked, who cannot be quieted but by food and raiment. But where are the means of feeding and clothing them? The landholder has nothing of his own to give, he is but the fiduciary of those who have lent him money: the lender is so taxed in his meat, drink, and clothing, that he has but a bare subsistence left. The landholder then, must give up his land, or the lender his debt, or they must compromise by giving up each one half. But will either consent *peaceably* to such an abandonment of property? Or must it not be settled by civil conflict? If peaceably compromised, will they agree to risk another ruin under the same government unreformed? I think not; but I would rather know what you think; because you have lived with John Bull, and know, better than I do the character of his herd. I salute Mrs Adams and yourself with every sentiment of affectionate cordiality and respect.

TH: JEFFERSON

Adams to Jefferson

Quincy Nov. 4 1816

DR. SIR

Your Letter of Oct. 14 has greatly obliged me. Tracys Analysis, I have read once; and wish to read it a second time. It shall be returned to you. But I wish to be informed whether this Gentleman is of that Family of Tracys with which the Marquis La Fayette is connected by intermarriages?

I have read, not only the Analysis, but Eight Volumes out of 12 of The Origine de tous les Cultes, and if Life lasts will read the other four.

But, my dear Sir, I have been often obliged to stop; and talk to myself like the Reverend, Alegorical, Hierogriphical and Apocaliptical Mr. John Bunyan; and say "Sobrius esto John ["John, be sober"]!" Be not carried away by sudden blasts of Wind, by unexpected flashes of Lightening, nor terrified by the sharpest Crashes of Thunder!"

We have now, it seems a National Bible Society,[43] to propagate King

42. They resulted from the new Corn Law of 1815, raising the import duties on grains to the point of excluding them unless prices were very high. Wage earners suffered not only from exorbitant food prices but also from the post-war depression in industry, bringing low wages and unemployment.

43. The American Bible Society was organized in New York in 1816 at a convention of delegates from 31 local societies. Henry O. Dwight, *The Centennial History of the American Bible Society* (N.Y., 1916), 18-30.

James's Bible, through all Nations. Would it not be better, to apply these pious Subscriptions, to purify Christendom from the Corruptions of Christianity; than to propagate those Corruptions in Europe Asia, Africa and America!

Suppose, We should project a Society to translate Dupuis into all Languages and offer a Reward in Medals and Diamonds to any Man or Body of Men who would produce the best answer to it.

Enthusiams, Crusades, French Revolutions are Epidemical or Endemial Distempers, to which Man kind are liable. They are not tertian or Quartan Agues. Ages and Centuries are sometimes required to cure them.

It is more worth your while to live to read Dupuis than Grim. Of all the Romanc[e]s, and true Histories I ever read, it is the most entertain[in]g And instructive, though Priestley calls it "*dull*."

Conclude not from all this, that I have renounced the Christian Religion, or that I agree with Dupuis in all his Sentiments. Far from it. I see in every Page, Something to recommend Christianity in its Purity, and Something to discredit its Corruptions.

If I had Strength, I would give you my Opinion of it in a Fable of the Bees.[44]

The Ten Commandments and The Sermon on the Mount contain my Religion.

I agree perfectly with you, that "The Moral Sense is as much a part of our Constitution as that of Feeling," and in all that You say, upon this Subject.

My History of the Jesuits, is in 4. Vol. in twelves, under the Title of "Histoire Generale de la naissance et des progres, de la Compagnie de Jesus, et l'analyse de ses Constitutions et ses Privileges.["] Printed at Amsterdam in 1761. The Work is anonymous;[45] because, as I suppose, the Author was afraid as all the Monarks of Europe were at that time, of Jesuitical Assassination. The Author however supports his Facts by authentic Records and known Authorities which the Publick may consult.

This Society has been a greater Calamity to Mankind than the French Revolution or Napoleons Despotism or Idiology. It has obstructed the Progres of Reformation and the Improvement of the human Mind in Society much longer and more fatally.

44. Bernard Mandeville, *The Fable of the Bees: or, Private Vices, Public Benefits* (London, 1714; Oxford, 1924): "As to Religion, the most knowing and polite Part of a Nation have every where the least of it; ... Vice in general is no where more predominant than where Arts and Sciences flourish.... It is certain that we shall find Innocence and Honesty no where more general than among the most illiterate, the poor silly Country People"; 1924 edn., I, 269.
45. The *Histoire* was written by Christophe Coudrette, the *Analyse* by Louis-Adrien Le Paige.

The Situation of England may be learned from the enclosed Letter,[46] which I pray you to return to me.

Little reason as I have to love the old Lady, I cannot but dread that she is going after France, into a Revolution which will end like that of England in 1660 and like that of France in 1816. In all Events, our Country must rise. England cannot.

We have been long afflicted with a Report that your Books and Harvard Colledge Books, and John Q. Adams's Ouranologia were lost at Sea.[47] But lo! The Astronomy has arrived in one Ship and Colledge Books in another. We hope your Books are equally safe: but should be glad to know.

It seems that Father and Son have been employed in contemplating The Heavens. I should like to sitt down with him and compare Du Puis with his Uranologia.

I have been disappointed in the Review of Sir John Malcoms History of Persia.[48] Those cunning Edinburgh men break off, at the Point of the only Subject that excited my Curiosity the ancient modern Religion and Government of Persia. I should admire to read an Edinburg or a Quarterly Review of Du Puis 12. Volumes. They have reviewed Grim who is not of half the importance to Mankind. I suspect the Reviewers evaded the Religion of Persia for fear they should be compelled to compare it with Du Puis.

A Scrap of an English Paper in which you are honorably mentioned and I am not much abused must close this Letter from your Friend

JOHN ADAMS

Jefferson to Adams

Poplar Forest. Nov. 25. 16.

I recieve here, dear Sir, your favor of the 4th. just as I am preparing my return to Monticello for winter quarters; and I hasten to answer to some of your enquiries. The Tracy I mentioned to you is the one con-

46. See TJ to JA, Nov. 25, 1816, below, 496-99. The enclosure was probably from John Quincy Adams, American minister to Great Britain at this time.
47. All of these books, bought by George Ticknor in Europe, were shipped to Boston in care of his father; TJ's were then to be forwarded to Monticello. Elisha Ticknor to TJ, Oct. 22, 1818, "The Jefferson Papers," Mass. Hist. Soc., *Collections,* 7th ser., 1 (1900), 263-65.
48. In the *Edinburgh Review,* 26 (1816), 282-304.

nected by marriage with La Fayette's family. The mail which brought your letter brought one also from him. He writes me that he is become blind and so infirm that he is no longer able to compose any thing. So that we are to consider his works as now closed. They are 3. vols. of Ideology. 1. on political economy. 1. on Ethics, and 1. containing his Commentary on Montesquieu, and a little tract on education. Altho' his Commentary explains his principles of government, he had intended to have substituted for it an elementary and regular treatise on the subject: but he is prevented by his infirmities. His Analyse de Dupuys he does not avow.

My books are all arrived, some at New York, some at Boston; and I am glad to hear that those for Harvard are safe also; and the Uranologia you mention, without telling me what it is. It is something good, I am sure, from the name connected with it, and if you would add to it your Fable of the bees, we should recieve valuable instruction as to the Uranologia both of the father and son; more valuable than the Chinese will from our bible-societies. These Incendiaries, finding that the days of fire and faggot are over in the Atlantic hemisphere, are now preparing to put the torch to the Asiatic regions. What would they say were the Pope to send annually to this country colonies of Jesuit priests with cargoes of their Missal and translations of their Vulgate, to be put gratis into the hands of every one who would accept them? and to act thus nationally on us as a nation?

I proceed to the letter you were so good as to inclose to me. It is an able letter, speaks volumes in few words, presents a profound view of awful truths, and lets us see truths more awful, which are still to follow. George the IIId. then, and his minister Pitt, and successors, have spent the fee-simple of the kingdom, under pretence of governing it. Their sinecures, salaries, pensions, priests, prelates, princes and eternal wars have mortgaged to it's full value the last foot of their soil. They are reduced to the dilemma of a bankrupt spendthrift who, having run thro' his whole fortune, now asks himself what he is to do? It is in vain he dismisses his coaches and horses, his grooms, liveries, cooks and butlers. This done, he still finds he has nothing to eat. What was his property, is now that of his creditors. If still in his hands, it is only as their trustee. To them it belongs, and to them every farthing of it's profits must go. The reformation of extravagancies comes too late. All is gone. Nothing left for retrenchment or frugality to go on. The debts of England however, being due from the whole nation, to one half of it, being as much the debt of the creditor as debtor, if it could be referred to a court of Equity, principles might be devised to adjust it peaceably. Dismiss their parasites, ship off their paupers to this country, let the landholders give half their lands to the money-lenders, and these last relinquish one half of their debts. They would still have a fertile island, a sound and effective population to labor it, and would hold that station among political powers, to which their natural resources and faculties entitle them. They would no longer indeed be the lords of the ocean, and paymasters of all the princes of the earth. They would no longer enjoy the luxuries of pyrating and plundering every thing by sea, and of bribing and corrupting every thing by land; but they might enjoy the more safe and lasting luxury of living on terms of equality, justice and good neighborhood with all nations. As it is, their first efforts will probably be to quiet things awhile by the palliatives of reformation; to nibble a little at pensions and sinecures; to bite off a bit here, and a bite there to amuse the people; and to keep the government agoing by encroachments on the interest of the public debt, 1. per cent. of which, for instance, withheld, gives them a spare revenue of 10 millions for present subsistence, and spunges in fact 200. millions of the debt. This remedy they may endeavor to administer in broken doses of a small pill at a time. The first may not occasion more than a strong Nausea in the moneylenders; but the 2d. will probably produce a revulsion of the stomach, borborisms, and spasmodic calls for fair settlement and compromise. But it is not in the character of man to come to any peaceable compromise of such a state of things. The princes and priests will hold to the flesh-pots, the empty bellies will seize on them, and these being the multitude, the issue is obvious, civil war, massacre, exile as in France, until the stage is cleared of everything but the multitude, and the lands get into their hands by such processes as the revolution will engender. They will then want peace and a government, and what will it be? certainly not a renewal of that which has already ruined them. Their habits of law and order, their ideas almost innate of the vital elements of free government, of trial by jury, habeas corpus, freedom of the press, freedom of opinion, and representative government, make them, I think, capable of bearing a considerable portion of liberty. They will probably turn their eyes to us, and be disposed to tread in our footsteps, seeing how safely these have led us into port. There is no part of our model to which they seem unequal, unless perhaps the elective presidency; and even that might possibly be rescued from the tumult of elections, by subdividing the electoral assemblages into very small parts, such as of wards or townships, and making them simultaneous. But you know them so much better than I do, that it is presumption to offer my conjectures to you.

While it is much our interest to see this power reduced from it's towering and borrowed height, to within the limits of it's natural resources, it is by no means our interest that she should be brought below that, or lose her competent place among the nations of Europe. The present exhausted state of the continent will, I hope, permit them to go through their struggle without foreign interference, and to settle their new government according to their own will. I think it will be friendly to us, as the nation itself would be were it not artfully wrought up by the hatred their government bears us. And were they once under a government which should treat us with justice and equality I should myself feel with great strength the ties which bind us together, or origin, language, laws and manners: and I am persuaded the two people would become in future, as it was with the antient Greeks, among whom it was reproachful for Greek to be found fighting against Greek in a foreign army. The individuals of the nation I have ever honored and esteemed, the basis of their character being essentially worthy: but I consider their government as the most flagitious which has existed since the days of Philip of Macedon, whom they make their model. It is not only founded in corruption itself, but insinuates the same poison into the bowels of every other, corrupts it's councils, nourishes factions, stirs up revolutions, and places it's own happiness in fomenting commotions and civil wars among others, thus rendering itself truly the hostis humani generis.[49] The effect is now coming home to itself. It's first operation will fall on the individuals who have been the chief instruments in it's corruptions, and will eradicate the families which have, from generation to generation been fattening on the blood of their brethren: and this scoria once thrown off, I am in hopes a purer nation will result, and a purer government be instituted, one which, instead of endeavoring to make us their natural enemies, will see in us, what we really are, their natural friends and brethren, and more interested in a fraternal connection with them than with any other nation on earth. I look therefore to their revolution with great interest. I wish it to be as moderate and bloodless, as will effect the desired object of an honest government, one which will permit the world to live in peace, and under the bonds of friendship and good neighborhood.

In this tremendous tempest, the distinctions of whig and tory will disappear like chaff on a troubled ocean. Indeed they have been disappearing from the day Hume first began to publish his history. This single book has done more to sap the free principles of the English constitution than the largest standing army of which their patriots have been so jealous. It is like the portraits of our countryman Wright, whose eye was so unhappy as to sieze all the ugly features of his subject, and to present them faithfully; while it was entirely insensible to every lineament of beauty. So Hume has consecrated, in his fascinating style, all the arbitrary proceedings of the English kings, as true evidences of the constitution, and glided over it's whig principles as the unfounded pretensions of factious dema-

49. I.e., Hostem generis humani, "an enemy of the human race." Pliny the Elder, *Natural History*, VII, 6.

gogues. He even boasts, in his life written by himself, that of the numerous alterations suggested by the readers of his work, he had never adopted one proposed by a whig.

But what, in this same tempest, will become of their colonies and their fleets? Will the former assume independance, and the latter resort to pyracy for subsistence, taking possession of some island as a point d'appui? A pursuit of these would add too much to the speculations on the situation and prospects of England, into which I have been led by the pithy text of the letter you so kindly sent me, and which I now return. It is worthy the pen of Tacitus. I add therefore only my affectionate and respectful souvenirs to Mrs Adams and yourself.

Th: Jefferson

Adams to Jefferson

Quincy Decr. 12 1816

Dear Sir

I return the Analysis of Dupuis with my thanks for the loan of it. It is but a feignt Miniature of the original.

I have read that original in twelve Volumes, besides a 13th. of plates.

I have been a Lover and a Reader of Romances all my Life. From Don Quixotte and Gill Blas to the Scottish Chiefs and an hundred others.

For the last Year or two I have devoted my self to this kind of Study: and have read 15 Volumes of Grim, Seven Volumes of Tuckers Neddy Search and 12 Volumes of Dupuis besides a 13th of plates and Traceys Analysis, and 4. Volumes of Jesuitical History! Romances all! I have learned nothing of importance to me, for they have made no Change in my moral or religious Creed, which has for 50 or 60 Years been contained in four short Words "*Be just and good.*" In this result they all agree with me.

I must acknowledge however, that I have found in Dupuis more Ideas that were new to me, than in all the others.

My Conclusion from all of them is Universal Tolleration.

Is there any Work extant so well calculated to discredit Corruptions and Impostures in Religion as Dupuis.

I am Sir, with Friendship, as of old

John Adams

Abigail Adams to Jefferson

Quincy December 15th 1816

DEAR SIR

My good Husband has called upon me for some Letters, written to me by my son, when he was last in paris, in 1815 in which he gives me a particular account of the Family of Count deTracy and of the circumstances which introduced him to their acquaintance.

Beleiving that it will give you pleasure to become acquainted with this happy domestic circle, I readily embrace this opportunity of transmitting them to you, with two or three other Letters which follow in succession, and are interesting, as they describe the novel and important events, to which Mr. Adams was an Eye witness.[50]

I rely upon your known care and punctuality to return them to me. I need not add, how valuable they are to me. They may also afford some entertainment to your Grandaughter Miss Ellen Randolph, whose praises are in the mouths, of all our northern Travellers, who have been so happy as to become acquainted with her. They bring us also: such delightfull accounts of Monticello and its inhabitants that I am tempted to wish myself twenty years younger, that [I might] visit them, but I am so far down Hill, that I must only think of those pleasures which are past. Amongst which, and not the least is my early acquaintance with, and the continued Friendship of the phylosopher of Monticello, to whom are offerd the respectfull attachment of Dear Sir your Friend

ABIGAIL ADAMS

Adams to Jefferson

Quincy Decr.16th. 1816

Your Letter dear Sir of Nov. 15 from Poplar Forrest, was sent to me from the Post Office the next day after I had sent "The Analysis" with my Thanks to you.

"3 Vols. of Idiology!" Pray explain to me this Neological Title! What

50. John Quincy Adams was in Paris during most of the Hundred Days of Bonaparte's return to power.

does it mean? When Bonaparte used it, I was delig[h]ted with it, upon
the Common Principle of delight in every Thing We cannot understand.
Does it mean Idiotism? The Science of Non compos Menticism. The
Science of Lunacy? The Theory of Delerium? Or does it mean the Science
of Self Love? of Amour propre? or the Elements of Vanity?

Were I in France, at this time, I could profess Blindness and Infirmity
and prove it too. I suppose he does not avow the Analysis, as Hume did
not avow his Essay on human Nature. That Analysis however does not
show a Man of excessive Mediocrity. Had I known any of these Things
two Years ago I would have written him a Letter. Of all Things, I wish to
see his Idiology upon Montesquieu. If you, with all Your Influence have
not been able to get your own translation of it with your own Notes upon
it, published in four Years, where and What is the Freedom of The
American Press.? Mr. Taylor of Hazel Wood Port Royal can have his
voluminous and luminous Works published with Ease and dispatch.

The Uranologia, as I am told, is a Collection of Plates, Stamps Charts
of the Heavens Upon a large Scale representing all the Constellations. The
Work of some Professor in Sweeden. It is said to be the most perfect that
ever has appeard. I have not seen it. Why should I ride 15 miles to see it
When I can see the original every clear Evening; and esp[e]cially as
Dupuis has almost made me afraid to enquire after any Thing more of it
than I can see with my naked Eye in a Star light night?

That the Pope will send Jesuits to this Cou[n]try I doubt not; and the
Church of England, Missionaries too. And the Methodists, and the Quakers
and the Moravians, and the Sweedenburgers and the Menonists, and the
Scottish Kirkers, and the Jacobites and the Jacobins and the Democrats
and the Aristocrats and the Monarkists and the Despotists of all Denominations And every Emissary of every one of these Sects will find a Party
here already formed, to give him a cordial R[e]ception; No Power or
Intelligence less than Raphaels Moderator can reduce this Chaos to order.

I am charmed with the fluency and rapidity of your Reasoning on the
State of Great Britain. I can deny none of your Premisses: but I doubt
your Conclusion. After all the Convulsions that you forsee, they will return to that Constitution which You say has ruined them, and I say has
been the Source of all their Power and Importance. They have as you
say too much Sense and Knowledge of Liberty, ever to submit to simple
Monarchy or absolute despotism on the one hand; And too much of the
Devil in them ever to be governed by popular Elections of Presidents,
Senators and Representatives in Congress. Instead of "turning their Eyes
to Us," their innate Feelings will turn them from Us. They have been
taught from their Cradles to despize scorn, insult and abuse Us. They
hate Us more Vigorously, than they do the French. They would sooner

adopt the simple Monarchy of France than our republican Institutions. You compliment me, with more knowledge of them than I can assume or pretend. If I should write you a Volume of Observations I made in England You would pronounce it, a Satyre. Suppose, the "Refrein" as the french call it, or the Burthen of the Song as the English express it; should be, the Religion, the Governmen[t] the Commerce the Manufactures, the Army and Navy of G. B. are all reduced to the Science of Pounds Shillings and Pence. Elections appeared to me a mere commercial Traffick; mere bargain and Sale. I have been told by sober steady Freeholders, that "they never had been and never would go to the Poll, without being paid for their Time, Travel and Expences." Now suppose an Election for a President of the British Empire. There must be a Nomination of Candidates by a National Convention, Congres, or Caucus, in which would be two Parties, Whigs and Tories. Of course two Candidates at least would be nominated. The Empire is instantly divided into two Parties at least. Every Man must be paid for his Vote, by the Candidate or his Party. The only Question would be, Which Party has the deepest Purse. The same Reasoning will apply to Elections of Senators and Representatives too. A Revolution might destroy the Burroughs and the Inequalities of Representation and might produce more toleration, and these Acquisitions might be worth all they would cost. But I dread the Experiment.

Britain will never be our Friend, till We are her Master. This will happen in less time than you and I have been struggling with her Power—provided We remain United. Aye! there's the rub! I fear there will be greater difficulties to preserve our Union, than You and I, our Fathers Brothers Friends Disciples and Sons have had to form it.

Towards G. B. I would adopt their own Maxim. An English Jocky says "If I have a wild horse to brake I begin by convincing him that I am his Master. And then I will convince him that I am his Friend." I am well assured that nothing will restrain G. B. from injuring Us, but fear.

You think that "in a revolution the distinction of Whig and Tory would disappear." I cannot believe this. That distinction arises from nature and Society; is now and ever will be time without End among Negroes Indians and Tartars as well as Federalists and Republicans. Instead of "disappearing since Hume published his History," that History has only increased the Tories and diminished the Whigs. That History has been the Bane of G. B. It has destroyed many of the best Effects of the Revolution of 1688. Style has governed the Empire. Swift, Pope and Hume have disgraced all the honest Historians. Rapin and Burnet Oldmixen and Coke, contain more honest Truth than Hume and Clarendon and all their disciples and Imitators. But Who reads any of them at this day? Every one of the fine Arts from the earliest times has been inlisted in the service of Superstition and Despotism. The whole World at this day Gazes with Astonishment at the grossest Fictions because they have been immortalized by the most exquisite Artists, Homer and Milton Phidias and Raphael. The Rabble of the Classic Skies and the Hosts of Roman Catholic Saints and Angells are still adored in Paint and Marble, and verse.

Raphael has sketched the Actors and Scenes in all Apuleus's Amours of Psyche and Cupid. Nothing is too offensive to morals delicacy or decency, for this Painter.

Raphael has painted in one of the most ostentati[o]us Churches in Italy, the Creation. And with what Genius? God Almighty is represented, as leaping into Chaos and boxing it about with his Fists and kicking it about With his feet, till he tumbles it into Order! ! ! Nothing is too impious or profane for this great Master who has painted so many inimitable Virgins and Childs.

To help me on in my career of improvement I have now read four Volumes of La Harps Correspondence with Paul and a Russian Minister.

Phylosophers! Never again think of annuling Superstition per Saltum ["by a leap"]. Festine lente ["Hasten slowly"].

JOHN ADAMS

Jefferson to Abigail Adams

Monticello Jan. 11. 17.

I owe you, dear Madam, a thousand thanks for the letters communicated in your favor of Dec. 15. and now returned. They give me more information than I possessed before of the family of Mr. Tracy, but what is infinitely interesting is the scene of the exchange of Louis XVIII for Bonaparte. What lessons of wisdom Mr. Adams must have read in that short space of time! more than fall to the lot of others in the course of a long life. Man, and the Man of Paris, under those circumstances, must have been a subject of profound speculation! It would be a singular addition to that spectacle to see the same beast in the cage of St. Helena, like a lion in the tower. That is probably the closing verse of the chapter of his crimes. But not so with Louis. He has other vicissitudes to go through.

I communicated the letters, according to your permission, to my grandaughter Ellen Randolph, who read them with pleasure and edification. She is justly sensible of, and flattered by your kind notice of her; and additionally so by the favorable recollections of our Northern visiting friends. If Monticello has anything which has merited their remembrance, it gives it a value the more in our estimation: and could I, in the spirit of your wish, count backwards a score of years, it would not be long before Ellen and myself would pay our homage personally to Quincy. But those 20. years, alas! where are they? With those beyond the flood. Our next meeting must then be in the country to which they have flown, a country, for us, not now very distant. For this journey we shall need neither gold nor silver in our purse, nor scrip, nor coats, nor staves. Nor is the provision for it more easy than the preparation has been kind. Nothing proves more than this that the being who presides over the world is essentially benevolent, stealing from us, one by one, the faculties of enjoyment, searing our sensibilities, leading us, like the horse in his mill, round and round the same beaten circle.

> to see what we have seen,
> To taste the tasted, and at each return,
> Less tasteful; o'er our palates to decant
> Another vintage.

Until satiated and fatigued with this leaden iteration, we ask our own Congé. I heard once a very old friend, who had troubled himself with neither poets nor philosophers, say the same thing in plain prose, that he was tired of pulling off his shoes and stockings at night, and putting them on again in the morning. The wish to stay here is thus gradually extinguished: but not so easily that of returning once in a while to see how things have gone on. Perhaps however one of the elements of future felicity is to be a constant and unimpassioned view of what is passing here. If so, this may well supply the wish of occasional visits. Mercier has given us a vision of the year 2440, but prophecy is one thing, history another. On the whole however, perhaps it is wise and well to be contented with the good things which the master of the feast places before us, and to be thankful for what we have, rather than thoughtful about what we have not. You and I, dear Madam, have already had more than an ordinary portion of life, and more too of health than the general measure. On this score I owe boundless thankfulness. Your health was, some time ago, not so good as it had been; and I perceive, in the letters communicated, some complaints still. I hope it is restored; and that life and health may be continued to you as many years as yourself shall wish is the sincere prayer of your affectionate and respectful friend

TH: JEFFERSON

Jefferson to Adams

Monticello Jan. 11. 17.

Forty three volumes read in one year, and 12. of them quartos! Dear Sir, how I envy you! Half a dozen 8vos. [octavos] in that space of time are as much as I am allowed. I can read by candlelight only, and stealing long hours from my rest; nor would that time be indulged to me, could I, by that light, see to write. From sun-rise to one or two aclock, and often from dinner to dark, I am drudging at the writing table. And all this to answer letters into which neither interest nor inclination on my part enters; and often for persons whose names I have never before heard. Yet, writing civilly, it is hard to refuse them civil answers. This is the burthen of my life, a very grievous one indeed, and one which I must get rid of. Delaplaine lately requested me to give him a line on the subject of his book; [51] meaning, as I well knew, to publish it. This I constantly refuse; but in this instance yielded, that, in saying a word for him, I might say two for myself. I expressed in it freely my sufferings from this source; hoping it would have the effect of an indirect appeal to the discretion of those, strangers and others, who, in the most friendly dispositions, oppress me with their concerns, their pursuits, their projects, inventions and speculations, political, moral, religious, mechanical, mathematical, historical etc. etc. etc. I hope the appeal will bring me relief, and that I shall be left to exercise and enjoy correspondence with the friends I love, and on subjects which they, or my own inclinations present. In that case your letters should not be so long on my files unanswered, as sometimes they have been to my great mortification.

To advert now to the subjects of those of Dec. 12. and 16. Tracy's Commentaries on Montesquieu have never been published in the original. Duane printed a translation from the original MS. a few years ago. It sold I believe readily, and whether a copy can now be had, I doubt. If it can, you will recieve it from my bookseller in Philadelphia, to whom I now write for that purpose. Tracy comprehends, under the word 'Ideology,' all the subjects which the French term *Morale*, as the correlative to *Physique*. His works on Logic, government, political economy, and morality, he considers as making up the circle of ideological subjects, or

51. Joseph Delaplaine's *Repository of the Lives and Portraits of Distinguished American Characters* (Philadelphia, 1815-16). Delaplaine had asked TJ for a sketch of Peyton Randolph, which TJ sent with his reply of July 26, 1816. Ford, X, 55-56 and *n.*, 56-60.

of those which are within the scope of the understanding, and not of the senses. His logic occupies exactly the ground of Locke's work on the understanding. The translation of that on Political economy is now printing; but it is no translation of mine. I have only had the correction of it; which was indeed very Laborious. Le premier jet having been by some one who understood neither French nor English, it was impossible to make it more than faithful. But it is a valuable work.

The result of your 50. or 60. years of religious reading in the four words 'be just and good' is that in which all our enquiries must end; as the riddles of all the priesthoods end in four more 'ubi panis, ibi deus ["where there is bread, there is God"].' What all agree in is probably right; what no two agree in most probably wrong. One of our fan-colouring biographers, who paints small men as very great, enquired of me lately, with real affection too, whether he might consider as authentic, the change in my religion much spoken of in some circles. Now this supposed that they knew what had been my religion before, taking for it the word of their priests, whom I certainly never made the confidants of my creed. My answer was 'say nothing of my religion. It is known to my god and myself alone. It's evidence before the world is to be sought in my life. If that has been *honest and dutiful to society*, the religion which has regulated it cannot be a bad one.' Affectionately Adieu.

TH: JEFFERSON

Adams to Jefferson

Quincy Feb. 2d. 1817

DEAR SIR

In our good old English language of Gratitude, I owe you and give you a thousand thanks for Tracy's Review of Montesquieu, which Mr. Dufief has sent me by your Order. I have read an hu[n]dred pages, and will read the rest. He is a sensible Man and is easily understood. He is not an abstruse, misterious, incomprehensi[ble] Condorcet. Though I have banished the Subject from my thoughts for many Years, yet if Tracy and I were thirty Years Younger I would ask him an hundred or two of questions. His book was written when the French Experiment was glowing in the furnace not yet blown out. He all along supposes that Men are rational and consciencious Creatures. I say so too: but I say at the same time that their passions and Interests generally prevail over their Reason and their consciences: and if Society does not contrive some means of controuling and restrain[in]g the former the World will go on as it has done.

I was tollerably well informed, fifty years ago, how it had gone on, and formed some plausible conjectures how it would go on. Grim, Dupuis and Eustace have confirmed all my former Notions and made immense Additions to them. Eustace is a Suppliment to Dupuis; and both together contain a compleat draught of the Superstition, Credulity and Despotism of our terrestrial Universe. They show how Science, Litteratur, Mechanic Arts, and those fine Arts of Architecture, Painting, Statuary, Poetry, Musick and Eloquence: which you love so well and taste so exquisitely, have been subservient to Priests and Kings Nobles and commons Monarchies and Republicks. For they have all Used them when they could, but as the rich had them oftener than the poor, in their power, the latter have always gone to the Wall.

Eustace is inestimable to a young Schollar, and a Classic Traveller: but he is a plausible, insidious Roman Catholick Priest and I doubt not Jesuit. He should have read Dupuis before he comenced his Travels. Very little, of the Religions of Nations more antient than the Greeks and Romans, appears to have been known to him.

I am glad to see, that De la plane has published a part of your Letter, and I hope it will procure You some relief. I have suffered in the same manner, though not probably in the same degree. Necessity has compelled me to resort to two expedients to avoid or escape excessive importunity. One has been, by totally neglecting to answer Letter, after Letter. But this Method has cost me very dear in the loss of many Correspondances that had been and would have been instructive and profitable to me, as well as honourable and entertain[in]g. The other has been by giving gruff, short, unintelligible, misterious, enigmatical, or pedantical Answers. This resource is out of your power, because it is not in your nature to avail Yourself of it.

The practice, however, of publishing private Letters without leave, though even as rude ones as mine, is an Abuse and must be reformed.

Theodore Lyman Esqr., Junior, will I hope, deliver you this. He is an Educated and travelled Son of one of our Richest Merchants. His Hea[l]th has been, and is precarious. I have been indebted to him for the perusal of the Baron de Grim. I find that all our Young Gentlemen who have any *Nous*, and can afford to travel, have an ardent Curiosity to visit, what shall I say? the Man of the Mountain? The Sage of Monticello? Or the celebrated Philosopher and Statesman of Virginia? They all apply to me for Introduction. In hopes of softening asperities and promoting Union, I have refused none whom I thought Men of Sense.

I forgot one thing that I intended to say. I pitty our good Brother

Madison. You and I have had Children and Grand Children and great grand Children. Though they have cost us Grief, Anxiety, often Vexation, and some times humiliation; Yet it has been cheering to have them hovering about Us; and I verily believe they have contributed largely to keep Us alive. Books cannot always expell Ennui. I therefore pitty Brother Madison and especially his Lady. I pitty him the more, because, notwithstand[ing] a thousand Faults and blunders, his Administration has acquired more glory, and established more Union, than all his three Predecessors, Washington Adams and Jefferson, put together. I am, as ever

JOHN ADAMS

Adams to Jefferson

Quincy April 19 1817

DEAR SIR

My loving and beloved Friend, Pickering, has been pleased to inform the World that I have "few Friends." I wanted to whip the rogue, and I had it in my Power, if it had been in my Will to do it, till the blood come. But all my real Friends as I thought them, with Dexter and Grey at their Head insisted "that I should not say a Word." "That nothing that such a Person could write would do me the least Injury. That it would betray the Constitution and the Government, if a President out or in should enter into a Newspaper controversy, with one of his Ministers whom he had removed from his Office, in Justification of himself for that removal or any thing else." And they talked a great deal about "*The Dignity*" of the Office of President, which I do not find that any other Persons, public or private regard very much.

Nevertheless, I fear that Mr. Pickerings Information is too true. It is impossible that any Man should run such a Gauntlet as I have been driven through, and have many Friends at last. This "all who know me know" though I cannot say "who love me tell."

I have, however, either Friends who wish to amuse and solace my old age; or Ennemies who mean to heap coals of fire on my head and kill me with kindness: for they overwhelm me with Books from all quarters, enough to offuscate all Eyes, and smother and stifle all human Understanding. Chateaubriand, Grim, Tucker, Dupuis, La Harpe, Sismondi, Eustace A new Translation of Herodotus by Belloe with more Notes than Text. What should I do, with all this lumber? I make my "Woman kind" as the

Antiquary expresses it, read to me, all the English: but as they will not read the French, I am obliged to excruciate my Eyes to read it myself. And all to what purpose? I verily believe I was as wise and good, seventy Years ago, as I am now.

At that Period Lemuel Bryant was my Parish Priest; and Joseph Cleverly my Latin School Master. Lemuel was a jolly jocular and liberal Schollar and Divine. Joseph a Scollar and Gentleman; but a biggoted episcopalian of the School of Bishop Saunders and Dr. Hicks, a down right conscientious passive Obedience Man in Church and State. The Parson and the Pedagogue lived much together, but were eternally disputing about Government and Religion. One day, when the Schoolmaster had been more than commonly fanatical, and declared "if he were a Monark, *He would have but one Religion in his Dominions*" The Parson coolly replied "Cleverly! You would be the best Man in the World, if You had no Religion."

Twenty times, in the course of my late Reading, have I been upon the point of breaking out, "This would be the best of all possible Worlds, if there were no Religion in it." ! ! ! But in this exclamati[on] I should have been as fanatical as Bryant or Cleverly. Without Religion this World would be Something not fit to be mentioned in polite Company, I mean Hell. So far from believing in the total and universal depravity of human Nature; I believe there is no Individual totally depraved. The most abandoned Scoundrel that ever existed, never Yet Wholly extinguished his Conscience, and while Conscience remains there is some Religion. Popes, Jesuits and Sorbonists and Inquisitors have some Conscience and some Religion. So had Marius and Sylla, Caesar Cataline and Anthony, and Augustus had not much more, let Virgil and Horace say what they will.

What shall We think of Virgil and Horace, Sallust Quintillian, Pliny and even Tacitus? and even Cicero, Brutus and Seneca? Pompey I leave out of the question, as a mere politician and Soldier. Every One of these great Creatures has left indelible marks of Conscience and consequently of Religion, tho' every one of them has left abundant proofs of profligate violations of their Consciences by their little and great Passions and paltry Interests.

The vast prospect of Mankind, which these Books have passed in Review before me, from the most ancient records, histories, traditions and Fables that remain to Us, to the present day, has sickened my very Soul; and almost reconciled me to Swifts Travels among The Yahoo's. Yet I never can be a Misanthrope. Homo Sum ["I am a man"]. I must hate myself before I can hate my Fellow Men: and that I cannot and will not do. No! I will not hate any of them, base, brutal and devilish as some of them have been to me.

From the bottom of my Soul, I pitty my Fellow Men. Fears and Terrors appear to have produced an univer[s]al Credulity. Fears of Calamities in Life and punishments after death, seem to have possessed the Souls of all Men. But fear of Pain and death, here, do not seem to have been so unconquerable as fear of what is to come hereafter. Priests, Hierophants, Popes, Despots Emperors, Kings, Princes Nobles, have been as credulous as Shoeblacks, Boots, and Kitchen Scullions. The former seem to have believed in their divine Rights as sincerely as the latter. Auto de fee's in Spain and Portugal have been celebrated with as good Faith as Excommunications have been practiced in Connecticutt or as Baptisms have been refused in Phyladelphia.

How it is possible than [i.e., that] Mankind should submit to be governed as they have been is to me an inscrutable Mystery. How they could bear to be taxed to build the Temple of Diana at Ephesus, the Pyramyds of Egypt, Saint Peters at Rome, Notre Dame at Paris, St. Pauls in London, with a million Etceteras; when my Navy Yards, and my quasi Army made such a popular Clamour, I know not. Yet all my Peccadillos, never excited such a rage as the late Compensation Law! ! ! [52]

I congratulate you, on the late Election in Connecticutt.[53] It is a kind of Epocha. Several causes have conspired. One which you would not suspect. Some one, no doubt instigated by the Devil, has taken it into his head to print a new Edition of "The independent Whig" even in Connecticut, and has scattered the Volumes through the State. These Volumes it is said, have produced a Burst of Indignation against Priestcraft Bigotry and Intollerance, and in conjunction with other causes have produced the late Election. When writing to you I never know when to Subscribe

JOHN ADAMS

52. In 1816 and 1817 Congress passed several invalid-pension bills for veterans of the War of 1812. Adams apparently refers to the bill enacted on March 3, 1817; *U. S. Stat. at L.*, III, 394. Also see William H. Glasson, *Federal Military Pensions in the United States* (N. Y., 1918), 108-9.

53. The campaign issue in the spring election of 1817 was "whether freemen shall be tolerated in the free exercise of their religious and political rights." Oliver Wolcott, father of the Constitution of 1818 (Connecticut's first), was elected governor. George L. Clark, *A History of Connecticut, Its People and Institutions* (N.Y., [1914]), 349.

Abigail Adams to Jefferson

Quincy, April 29th 1817

DEAR SIR

What right have I to be one of your tormentors? And amongst the numerous applicants for introductory letters?

Why I will plead, old acquaintance, old Friendship and your well known benevolence. But to the subject of my present address. Mr. Theodore Lyman, who possesses an ardent thirst for Literature, and whose Father, is one of our most respectable Characters for probity, honour, and wealth, this young Gentleman has been much out of health, occasioned by too close application to his studies. He is now going abroad with the hopes of regaining it. He is desirious of getting an introduction to some Gentlemen of Letters in France—my good Husband has furnished him, with one to the Marquis La Fayette, one to Mr. Marbois, and one to Mr. Gallatin. But as your acquaintance with men of Letters in France is of a more recent date, I thought it probable that you might give him a Letter or two, which might be of much service to him, from the weight and respectability of your Character. He understands the French language, and is a young Gentleman of most estimable Character, and acquirements, whom I am not ashamed to recommend. He is a nephew of Mr. Williams, late consul of the U S in England. He has been once in England and in France before, and knows full well that to Men of Letters he cannot be easily admitted, without honorable introduction. He has been so attentive in supplying us with such rare and valuable Books that I feel indebted to him for his kindness. And as I am not able myself to repay his civility, like other debtors, I am drawing upon my Friend's. Any Letter you may think proper to forward, you will please to send under cover to my Husband, and they will be gratefully acknowledged by your old and steady Friend

ABIGAIL ADAMS

Jefferson to Adams

Monticello. May 5. 17.

DEAR SIR

Absences and avocations had prevented my acknoleging your favor of Feb. 2. when that of Apr. 19. arrived. I had not the pleasure of recieving the former by the hands of Mr. Lyman. His business probably carried him in another direction; for I am far inland, and distant from the great line of communication between the trading cities. Your recommendations are always welcome, for indeed the subjects of them always merit that welcome, and some of them in an extraordinary degree. They make us acquainted with what there is of excellent in our ancient sister state of Massachusets, once venerated and beloved, and still hanging on our hopes, for what need we despair of after the resurrection of Connecticut to light and liberality.[54] I had believed that, the last retreat of Monkish darkness, bigotry, and abhorrence of those advances of the mind which had carried the other states a century ahead of them. They seemed still to be exactly where their forefathers were when they schismatised from the Covenant of works, and to consider, as dangerous heresies, all innovations good or bad. I join you therefore in sincere congratulations that this den of the priesthood is at length broken up, and that a protestant popedom is no longer to disgrace the American history and character. If, by *religion*, we are to understand *Sectarian dogmas*, in which no two of them agree, then your exclamation on that hypothesis is just, 'that this would be the best of all possible worlds, if there were no religion in it.' But if the moral precepts, innate in man, and made a part of his physical constitution, as necessary for a social being, if the sublime doctrines of philanthropism, and deism taught us by Jesus of Nazareth in which all agree, constitute true religion, then, without it, this would be, as you again say, 'something not fit to be named, even indeed a Hell.'

You certainly acted wisely in taking no notice of what the malice of Pickering could say of you. Were such things to be answered, our lives would be wasted in the filth of fendings and provings, instead of being employed in promoting the happiness and prosperity of our fellow citizens. The tenor of your life is the proper and sufficient answer. It is

54. Massachusetts continued the state-supported church until 1833, but in Connecticut the election of the liberal Oliver Wolcott as governor in 1817 brought about the Constitutional Convention of 1818. Article VII of the new Constitution provided for religious freedom. Clark, *History of Conn.*, 350-52.

fortunate for those in public trust that posterity will judge them by their works, and not by the malignant vituperations and invectives of the Pickerings and Gardeniers of their age. After all, men of energy of character must have enemies: because there are two sides to every question, and taking one with decision, and acting on it with effect, those who take the other will of course be hostile in proportion as they feel that effect. Thus in the revolution, Hancock and the Adamses were the rawhead and bloody bones of tories and traitors; who yet knew nothing of you personally but what was good.

I do not entertain your apprehensions for the happiness of our brother Madison in a state of retirement. Such a mind as his, fraught with information, and with matter for reflection, can never know ennui. Besides, there will always be work enough cut out for him to continue his active usefulness to his country. For example, he and Monroe (the president) are now here on the work of a collegiate institution to be established in our neighborhood, of which they and myself are three of six Visitors. This, if it succeeds, will raise up children for Mr. Madison to employ his attentions thro' life. I say, if it succeeds; for we have two very essential wants in our way 1. means to compass our views and 2dly. men qualified to fulfill them. And these you will agree are essential wants indeed.

I am glad to find you have a copy of Sismondi, because his is a field familiar to you, and on which you can judge him. His work is highly praised, but I have not yet read it. I have been occupied and delighted with reading another work, the title of which did not promise much useful information or amusement, 'l'Italia avanti il dominio dei Romani dal Micali.' It has often you know been a subject of regret that Carthage had no writer to give her side of her own history, while her wealth, power, and splendor prove she must have had a very distinguished policy and government. Micali has given the counterpart of the Roman history for the nations over which they extended their domination. For this he has gleaned up matter from every quarter, and furnished materials for reflection and digestion to those who, thinking as they read have percieved there was a great deal of matter behind the curtain, could that be fully withdrawn. He certainly gives new views of a nation whose splendor has masked and palliated their barbarous ambition.

I am now reading Botta's history of our own revolution. Bating the antient practice, which he has adopted, of putting speeches into mouths which never made them, and fancying motives of action which we never felt, he has given that history with more detail, precision and candor, than any writer I have yet met with. It is to be sure compiled from those writers; but it is a good secretion of their matter, the pure from the impure, and presented in a just sense of right in opposition to usurpation.

Accept assurances for Mrs. Adams and yourself of my affectionate esteem and respect.

TH: JEFFERSON

Jefferson to Abigail Adams

Monticello May 15. 17.

Your letters, dear Madam, are always welcome, and your requests are commands to me. I only regret that I can do so little towards obeying them. But eight and twenty years since I left France would, in the ordinary course of mortality, have swept off seven eighths of my acquaintances, and when to this lapse of time are added the knife of the Guillotine and scythe of constant and sanguinary wars, I am left without a single personal acquaintance there of the literary family; for Dupont, the only one of that day still living, is in the US. A correspondence however has since taken place with some literati not known to me personally, nor their habits of society or situations in life. Among these I have chosen M. destutt-Tracy and Say; the former great in the moral sciences, the latter particularly in that of Political economy. Mr. Tracy's connection too with M. de la Fayette will facilitate Mr. Lyman's acquaintance with him. I have selected these two the rather because, in the course of our correspondence, I owe a letter to each, and am glad to avail myself of the opportunity by Mr. Lyman of paying the debt, adding to my letters the recommendations of him which your information authorises. Should therefore any circumstance prevent Mr. Lyman's visit to France direct, I will pray him to forward the letters by the first entirely safe conveyance, under cover to Mr. Gallatin. In the letter to M. de la Fayette I have associated my sollicitations with those of Mr. Adams for the courtesies to Mr. Lyman, which he so willingly extends to all Americans. Wishing a pleasant voyage and tour to him, and to yourself and Mr. Adams long years of health and happiness, I tender you the homage of my constant respect and attachment.

TH: JEFFERSON

Adams to Jefferson

Quincy May 18. 1817

DEAR SIR

Lyman was mortified that he could not visit Montecello. He is gone to Europe a second time. I regret that he did not see you, He would have executed any commision for you in the litterary line, at any pain or any expence. I have many Apprehensions for his health, which is very delicate and precarious. But he is seized with the Mania of all our young etherial Spirits, for foreign travel. I fear they will loose more than they will acquire. They will loose that unadulterated Enthusiam for their native Country which has produced the greatest Characters among Us.

Oh! Lord! Do you think that a Protestant Popedom is annihilated in America? Do you recollect, or have you ever attended to the ecclesiastical Strifes in Maryland Pensilvania, New York, and every part of New England? What a mercy it is that these People cannot whip and crop, and pillory and roast, *as yet* in the U. S.! If they could they would.

Do you know that The General of the Jesuits and consequently all his Host have their Eyes on this Country? Do you know that the Church of England is employing more means and more Art, to propagate their demipopery among Us, than ever? Quakers, Anabaptists Moravians Swedenborgians, Methodists, Unitarians, Nothingarians in all Europe are employing understrand [underhand?] means to propagate their sectarian Systems in these States.

The multitude and diversity of them, You will say, is our Security against them all. God grant it. But if We consider that the Presbyterians and Methodists are far the most numerous and the most likely to unite; let a George Whitefield arise, with a military cast, like Mahomet, or Loyola, and what will become of all the other Sects who can never unite?

My Friends or Enemies continue to overwhelm me with Books. Whatever may be their intension, charitable or otherwise, they certainly contribute, to continue me to vegetate, much as I have done for the sixteen Years last past.

Sir John Malcoms History of Persia, and Sir William Jones's Works are now poured out upon me and a little cargo is coming from Europe. What can I do with all this learned lumber? Is it necessary to Salvation to investigate all these Cosmogonies and Mythologies? Is Bryant Gebelin, Dupuis, or Sir William Jones, right?

What a frown upon Mankind, was the premature death of Sir William

Jones? Why could not Jones and Dupuis have conversed or corresponded with each other? Had Jones read Dupuis, or Dupuis Jones, the Works of both would be immensely improved though each would probably have adhered to his System.

I should admire to see a Counsel, composed of Gebelin, Bryant Jones and Dupuis. Let them live together and compare Notes. The human race ought to contribute to furnish them with all the Books in the Universe, and the means of Subsistence.

I am not expert enough in Italian to read Botta, and I know not that he has been translated. Indeed I have been so little satisfied with Histories of the American Revolution, that I have long since, ceased to read them. The Truth is lost, in adulatory Panegyricks, and in vituperary Insolence.

I wish You, Mr. Madison and Mr. Monroe Success, in Your Collegiate institution. And I wish that Superstition in Religion exciting Superstition in Politicks, and both united in directing military Force, alias glory may never blow up all your benevolent and phylanthropic Lucubrations. But the History of all Ages is against you. It is said, that no Effort in favour of Virtue, is ever lost. I doubt whether it was ever true; whether it is now true; but hope it will be true. In the moral Government of the World, no doubt it was, is, and ever will be true: but it has not Yet appeared to be true on this Earth. I am Sir, Sincerely your friend

JOHN ADAMS

P. S. Have You seen [Buchanan's] the Phylosophy of human Nature, and [McAfee's] the History of the War, in the Western States, from Kentucky? How vigorously Science and Litterature spring up, as well as Patriotism and Heroism in transalleganian Regions? Have you seen Wilkensons History? etc. etc. etc.

J. A.

Adams to Jefferson

Quincy May 26. 1817

DEAR SIR

Mr. Leslie Combs of Kentucky has sent me "a History of the late War, in the Western Country, by Mr. Robert B. McAffee" And "The Phylosophy of Human Nature by Joseph Buchanan."

["]The History," I am glad to see: because it will preserve facts, to the honour, and immortal Glory of the Western people. Indeed I am not sorry that "the Phylosophy" has been published, because it has been a maxim with me for Sixty Years at least, Never to be afraid of a Book.

Nevertheless I cannot foresee much Utility in reviving, in this Country, the controversy between the Spiritualistes and the Materialists. Why should time be wasted in disputing about two Substances when both parties agree that neither knows any thing about either. If Spirit is an abstraction, a conjecture, a Chimera: Matter is an abstraction, a conjecture, a Chimera; for We know as much, or rather as little of one as of the other. We may read Cudworth Clerk Leibnitz, Berkley Hume Bolin[g]broke and Priestley and a million other Volumes in all Ages, and be obliged at last to confess that We have learned nothing. Spirit and matter still remain Riddles. Define the terms however, and the controversy is soon settled. If Spirit is an active Something and matter an inactive Something, it is certain that one is not the other. We can no more conceive that Extension or Solidity can think or feel, or see, or hear, or taste or smell: than We can conceive that Perception Memory Imagination or Reason can remove a mountain or blow a rock. This Enigma has puzzled Mankind from the beginning, and probably will to the End. Œconomy of time requires that We should waste no more in so idle an Amusement. In the 11th. discourse of Sir William Jones before The Asiatic Society Vol. 3. p. 229. of his Works, We find that Materialists and Immaterialists existed in India and that they accused each other of Atheism, before Berkly or Priestley, or Dupuis, or Plato, or Pythagoras were born. Indeed Neuton himself, appears to have discovered nothing that was not known to the Antient Indians. He has only furnished more ample demonstrations of the doctrines they taught. Sir John Malcomb agrees with Jones and Dupuis in the Astrological origin of Heathen mithologies.

Vain Man! Mind Your own Business! Do no Wrong! Do all the good You can! Eat Your Canvas back ducks, drink Your burgundy, sleep Your S[i]esta, when necessary, And *Trust in God.!*

What a mighty bubble! What a tremendous Waterspout has Napolion been according to his Life, written by himself? He says he was the Creature of the Principles and manners of the Age. By which no doubt he means the Age of Reason; the progress of Manilius's Ratio; of Plato's Logos etc. I believe him. A Whirlwind raised him and a Whirlwind blowed him a Way to St. Helena. He is very confident that the Age of Reason is not past; and so am I; but I hope that Reason will never again rashly and hastily create such Creatures as him. Liberty, Equality, Fraternity, and Humanity will never again, I hope blindly surrender themselves to an unbounded Ambition for national Conquests, nor implicitly commit themselves to the custody and Guardianship of Arms and Heroes. If they do, they will again end in St. Helena, Inquisitions Jesuits and Sacre Ligues ["holy leagues"].

Poor Laureate Southey, is writhing in Torments under the Laugh of the three kingdoms all Europe and America, upon the publication of his Wat Tyler.[55] I wonder whether he, or Bona suffers most.

I congratulate You and Madison and Monroe, on your noble Employment in founding a University. From such a noble Tryumvirate, the World will expect something very great and very new. But if it contains any thing quite original, and very excellent, I fear the prejudices are too deeply rooted to suffer it to last long, though it may be accepted at first. It will not always have three such colossal reputations to support it.

The Pernambuco Ambassador, his Secretary of Legation and private Secretary, respectable People, have made me a Visit. Having been some Year or two in a similar Situation I could not but sympathize with him. As Bona says the Age of Reason is not ended. Nothing can tottally extinguish or eclipse the Light which has been shed abroad by the press. I am, Sir, with hearty wishes for Your health and hapiness Your Friend and humble Servant

JOHN ADAMS

Adams to Jefferson

Quincy July 15. 1817

DEAR SIR

I am impatient to see your Plan of a University and new System of Education. To assist You in your contemplations, I send you a Pamp[h]let, "The Politicks of Connecticut." By a federal Republican in the name of Hamilton. Was there ever such a combination? Two Copies were sent me from the Post on Saturday last: I know not from whence nor by whom.

Now Sir! please to hear a modest Proposal. Let me go back to twenty. Give me a million of Revenue, a Library of a Million of Volumes, and as many more as I should want. I would devote my Life to such an Œ[u]vrage as Condorcet tells us, that Turgot had in contemplation, all

55. Robert Southey's poem, *Wat Tyler*, written in 1794, expressed strongly republican sentiments which he had later renounced. In 1817, when the poem was surreptitiously published, he was poet laureate and suffered criticism for being a traitor to his early liberalism.

his Lifetime. I would digest Bryant, Gebelin, Dupuis, Sir William Jones and above all the Acta Sanctorum of the Bolandists.

I know where the investigation would end. In Montesquieus 12 duodecimo Pages.

Is the Biography of Democratus and Heraclitus a Fable, or History? I cannot contemplate human Affairs, without laughing or crying. I choose to laugh. When People talk of the Freedom of Writing Speaking or thinking, I cannot choose but laugh. No such thing ever existed. No such thing now exists: but I hope it will exist. But it must be hundreds of years after you and I shall write and speak no more.

JOHN ADAMS

Jefferson to Adams

Poplar Forest, near Lynchburg. Sep. 8. 17.

DEAR SIR

A month's absence from Monticello has added to the delay of acknoleging your last letters; and indeed for a month before I left it our projected College gave me constant employment; for being the only Visitor in it's immediate neighborhood, all it's administrative business falls on me, and that, where building is going on, is not a little. In yours of July 15. you express a wish to see our plan. But the present visitors have sanctioned no plan as yet. Our predecessors, the first trustees, had desired me to propose one to them, and it was on that occasion I asked and recieved the benefit of your ideas on the subject. Digesting these with such other schemes as I had been able to collect, I made out a Prospectus, the looser and less satisfactory, from the uncertain amount of the funds to which it was to be adapted. This I addressed, in the form of a letter to their President Peter Carr; which going before the legislature, when a change in the constitution of the College was asked, got into the public papers, and, among others, I think you will find it in Niles's register, in the early part of 1815.[56] This, however, is to be considered but as a premiere ebauche, for the consideration and amendment of the present visitors, and to be accommodated to one of two conditions of things. If the institution is to depend on private donations alone, we shall be forced to

56. TJ to Peter Carr, Sept. 7, 1814, Lipscomb and Bergh, eds., *Writings*, XIX, 211; "Jefferson on Education," *Niles' Weekly Register*, 10, no. 3 (March 16, 1816), reprinted from the Richmond *Enquirer*.

accumulate on the shoulders of 4. professors a mass of sciences which, if the legislature adopts it, should be distributed among ten. We shall be ready for a professor of languages in April next; for two others the following year, and a 4th a year after. How happy should we be if we could have a Ticknor for our first. A critical classic is scarcely to be found in the US. To this professor, a fixed salary of 500. D. with liberal tuition fees from the pupils will probably give 2000. D. a year. We are now on the look-out for a professor, meaning to accept of none but of the very first order.

You ask if I have seen Buchanan's, McAfee's, or Wilkinson's books? I have seen none of them; but have lately read with great pleasure, Reid and Eaton's life of Jackson, if life may be called what is merely a history of his campaign of 1814. Reid's part is well written; Eaton's continuation is better for it's matter than style. The whole however is valuable.

I have lately recieved a pamphlet of extreme interest from France. It is De Pradt's historical recital of the first return of Louis XVIII to Paris. It is precious for the minutiae of the proceedings which it details, and for their authenticity, as from an eye witness. Being but a pamphlet, I enclose it for your perusal, assured, if you have not seen it, that it will give you pleasure. I will ask it's return, because I value it as a morsel of genuine history, a thing so rare as to be always valuable. I have recieved some information, from an eye witness also, of what passed on the occasion of the 2d. return of Louis XVIII. The Emperor Alexander it seems was solidly opposed to this. In the consultation of the allied sovereigns and their representatives, with the Executive council at Paris, he insisted that the Bourbons were too incapable and unworthy of being placed at the head of the nation, declared he would support any other choice, they should freely make, and continued to urge most strenuously that some other choice should be made. The debates ran high and warm, and broke off after midnight, every one retaining his own opinion. He lodged, as you know, at Talleyrand's. When they returned into council the next day, his host had overcome his firmness. Louis XVIII. was accepted, and thro' the management of Talleyrand, accepted without any capitulation, altho' the sovereigns would have consented that he should be first required to subscribe and swear to the constitution prepared, before permission to enter the kingdom. It would seem as if Talleyrand had been afraid to admit the smallest interval of time, lest a change of wind would bring back Bonaparte on them. But I observe that the friends of a limited monarchy there consider the popular representation as much improved by the late alteration, and confident it will in the end produce a fixed government in which an elective body, fairly representative of the people will be an efficient element.

I congratulate Mrs. Adams and yourself on the return of your excellent and distinguished son, and our country still more on such a minister of their foreign affairs, and I renew to both the assurance of my high and friendly respect and esteem.

TH: JEFFERSON

Adams to Jefferson

Quincy Oct. 10. 1817

DEAR SIR

I thank you for your kind congratulations on the return of my little family from Europe. To receive them all in fine health and good Spirits, after so long an absence, was a greater Blessing, than at my time of Life when they went away I had any right to hope or reason to expect. If the Secretary of State can give Satisfaction to his fellow Citizens in his new Office it will be a Source of consolation to me while I live: [57] though it is not probable that I shall long be a Witness of his good Success or ill Success. I shall soon be obliged to say to him and to you and to your Country and mine, God bless you all! Fare Ye Well. Indeed I need not wait a moment. I can say all that now with as good a Will and as clear a conscience as at any time past or future.

I thank you also for the loan of Depradts narration of the Intrigues at the second restoration of the Bourbons. In this as in many other Instances is seen the influence of a Single subtel mind and a trifling Accident in deciding the fate of Mankind for Ages. De Pradt and Talleyrand were well associated. I have ventured to send the Pamphlet to Washington with a charge to return it to you. The French have a King a Chamber of Peers and a Chamber of Deputies. Voila! Les Ossemen[t]s ["The Bones"] of a constitution of a limited monarchy; and of a good one, provided the bones are united by good joints and knitted together by strong tendons. But where does the Souvereignty reside? Are the three branches sufficiently defined? A fair representation of the body of the People by Elections sufficiently frequent is essential to a free Government: but if the commons cannot make themselves respected by the Peers and the King, they can do no good nor prevent any evil. Can any Organisation of

57. John Quincy Adams, American minister to the Court of St. James, 1815-17, had returned to the United States to become secretary of state under President Monroe. Bemis, *John Quincy Adams,* 246-49.

Government secure public and private liberty without a general or universal freedom without Licence or licentiousness of thinking speaking and writing. Have the French such Freedom? Will their Religion, or Policy allow it? When I think of Liberty and a Free Government, in an ancient opulent populous and commercial empire I fear I shall always recollect a Fable of Plato.

Love is a Son of the God of Riches and the Godess of Poverty. He inherits from his father, the intrepidity of his Courage, the Enthusiasm of his thoughts, his Generosity, his prodigality, his confidence in himself, the Opinion of his own merit, his impatience to have always the preference: but he derives from his mother that indigence which makes him always a begger, that importunity with which he demands every thing, that timidity which sometimes hinders him from daring to ask any thing, that disposition which he has to Servitude, and that dread of being despised which he can never overcome.

Such is Love according to Plato, who calls him a Demon, and such is Liberty in France and England and all other great rich old corrupted commercial Nations. The Opposite qualities of the father and mother are perpetually tearing to pieces himself and his friends as well as his Enemies.

Mr. Monroe has got the un[i]versal Character among all our Common People of "A very smart Man" And verily I am of the same Mind. I know not another who could have executed so great a plan so cleverly. I wish him the same happy Success through his whole Administration. I am, Sir with respect and Frien[d]ship Your

JOHN ADAMS

Adams to Jefferson

Quincy Jan. 28 1818

DEAR SIR

Permit me to introduce to you Mr. Horace Holley, who is on his Way to Kentucky where he has been invited to undertake the Superintendance of a University. This Gentleman was settled very young at Greenfield as Successor to Dr. Dwight; but having a Mind too inquisitive for Connecticut he removed to Boston, where he has been settled nine Years and where his fame has erected one of the loftyest Temples and assembled the most numerous Congregation of Auditors in Boston.

You will find him frank enough candid enough, social enough, learned enough and eloquent enough. He is indeed an important Character; and if Superstition Bigotry, Fanaticism and Intolerance will allow him to live in Kentucky, he will contribute Somewhat to the illumination of the darkest and most dismal Swamps in the Wilderness. I shall regret his Removal from Boston because that City ought always to have one Clergyman at least who will compell them to think and enquire: but if he can be supported in Kentucky I am convinced he will be more extensively usefull. If upon conversing with him Your Conscience will allow you to give him a Line to any of your Friends in Kentucky where all are your Friends, you will do him more Service and perhaps more Service to our Country and our kind than you or I may be aware. He is one of the few who give me delight.

I am anxious for South America. They will be independent of Spain. But can they have free Governments? Can the Roman Religion and a free Government exist together? I am, dear Sir with the old Friendship your

JOHN ADAMS

Jefferson to Adams

Monticello May 17. 18.

DEAR SIR

I was so unfortunate as not to recieve from Mr. Holly's own hand your favor of Jan. 28. being then at my other home. He dined only with my family, and left them with an impression which has filled me with regret that I did not partake of the pleasure his visit gave them. I am glad he is gone to Kentucky. Rational Christianity will thrive more rapidly there than here. They are freer from prejudices than we are, and bolder in grasping at truth. The time is not distant, tho' neither you nor I shall see it, when we shall be but a secondary people to them. Our greediness for wealth, and fantastical expense has degraded and will degrade the minds of our maritime citizens. These are the peculiar vices of commerce.

I had been long without hearing *from* you, but I had heard *of* you thro' a letter from Dr. Waterhouse. He wrote to reclaim against an expression of Mr. Wirt's, as to the commencement of motion in the revolutionary ball.[58] The lawyers say that words are always to be expounded secundum

58. In William Wirt's laudatory *Sketches of the Life and Character of Patrick Henry* (Philadelphia, 1818), especially secs. iv-vi.

subjectam materiem ["according to the subject matter"], which in Mr. Wirt's case was Virginia. It would moreover be as difficult to say at what moment the revolution began, and what incident set it in motion, as to fix the moment that the embryo becomes an animal, or the act which gives him a beginning.

But the most agreeable part of his letter was that which informed me of your health, your activity, and strength of memory; and the most wonderful that which assured me that you retained your industry and promptness in epistolary correspondence. Here you have entire advantage over me. My repugnance to the writing table becomes daily and hourly more deadly and insurmountable. In place of this has come on a canine appetite for reading. And I indulge it: because I see in it a relief against the taedium senectutis ["weariness of old age"]; a lamp to lighten my path thro' the dreary wilderness of time before me, whose bourne I see not. Losing daily all interest in the things around us, something else is necessary to fill the void. With me it is reading, which occupies the mind without the labor of producing ideas from my own stock.

I enter into all your doubts as to the event of the revolution of S. America. They will succeed against Spain. But the dangerous enemy is within their own breasts. Ignorance and superstition will chain their minds and bodies under religious and military despotism. I do believe it would be better for them to obtain freedom by degrees only; because that would by degrees bring on light and information, and qualify them to take charge of themselves understandingly; with more certainty if in the mean time under so much controul only as may keep them at peace with one another. Surely it is our duty to wish them independance and self-government, because they wish it themselves, and they have the right, and we none, to chuse for themselves: and I wish moreover that our ideas may be erroneous, and theirs prove well founded.

But these are speculations, my friend, which we may as well deliver over to those who are to see their developement. We shall only be lookers on, from the clouds above, as now we look down on the labors, the hurry, and bustle of the ants and bees. Perhaps in that super-mundane region we may be amused with seeing the fallacy of our own guesses, and even the nothingness of those labors which have filled and agitated our own time here. En attendant, with sincere affections to Mrs. Adams and yourself, I salute you both cordially.

TH: JEFFERSON

P.S. There is now here a Mr. Coffee, a sculptor and Englishman, who has just taken my bust, and is going on to take those of Madison and

Monroe.[59] He resides at New York and promises me he will ask permission to take yours and send me one. I hope you will permit him. He is a fine artist. He takes them about half the size of life in plaster.

Adams to Jefferson

Quincy May 29. 1818

DEAR SIR

As Holly is a Diamond of a Superiour Water, it would be crushed to pouder by mountainous oppression in any other Country. Even in this, he is a light shining in a dark place. His System is founded in the hopes of Mankind: but they delight more in their Fears. When will Men have juster Notions of the Universal eternal Cause? Then will rational Christianity prevail. I regret Hollys Misfortune in not finding you, on his Account to whom an Interview with you would have been a lasting Gratification.

Waterhouses Pen "Labitur et labetur ["overflows and will overflow"]." He has let it run on with too much fluency. I have not a tenth part of the Vivacity, Activity, Memory, or Promptitude and pun[c]tuality in Correspondence that he ascribes to me. I can answer but few of the Letters I receive, and those only with short Scratches of the Pen.

I agree with you that "it is difficult to say at what moment the Revolution began." In my Opinion it began as early as the first Plantation of the Country. Independence of Church and Parliament was a fixed Principle of our Predecessors in 1620 as it was of Sam. Adams and Chris. Gadsden in 1776. And Independence of Church and Parliament were always kept in View in this Part of the Country and I believe in most others. The Hierarchy and Parliamentary Authority were dreaded and detested even by a Majority of professed Episcopalians.

I congratulate you on your "Canine Appetite for reading." I have been equally voracious for several Years and it has kept me alive. It is policy in me to despize and abhor the "Writing Table" for it is a Bunch of Grapes out of reach. Had I Your Eyes and Fingers I should Scribble forever, such poor Stuff as you know I have been writting by fits and

59. William J. Coffee's bust of TJ has been lost, but those of other members of the family are extant. TJ commissioned Coffee to do the ornaments of cornices at the University of Virginia and at Poplar Forest. In 1822 Coffee returned to Monticello to restore the paintings in TJ's collection. Fiske Kimball, "The Life Portraits of Jefferson and Their Replicas," Amer. Philo. Soc., *Proceedings*, 88 (1944), 532.

starts for fifty or sixty Years without ever correcting or revising any thing.

Helluo ["Glutton"] as I am, I hunger and thirst after what I shall never see, Napolions Publication of the Report of his Institute of Cairo.[60] Denons Volumes have excited an inextinguishable Curiosity for an unattainable Object.

Mr. Coffee has been mentiond to me by my Son. He will be welcome. But though Robin is alive he is not alive like to be. Mr. Coffee must be very qui[c]k or Robbin may die in his hand.

Mr. Binon a French Artist from Lyons who has studied Eight Years in Italy has lately taken my Bust. He appears to be an Artist and a Man of Letters. I let them do what they please with my old head.

When We come to be cool in the future World, I think We cannot choose but smile at the gambols of Ambition Avarice Pleasure, Sport and Caprice here below. Perhaps We may laugh like the Angels in the French Fable. At a convivial repast of a Clubb of Choice Spirits of whom Gabriel and Michael were the most illustrious, after Nectar and Ambrosia had sett their hearts at Ease, they began to converse upon the Mechanique Cœleste. After discussing the Zodiack and the Constellations and the Solar System they condescended to this Speck of dirt the Earth, and remarked some of its Inhabitants, The Lyon the Elephant the Eagle and even the Fidelity Gratitude and Adroitness of the Dog. At last one of them recollected Man. What a fine Countenance! What an elegant figure! What Subtilty, Ingenuity, Versatillity Agility! And above all, *a rational Creature!* At this the whole board broke out into a broad Ha! Ha! Ha! that resounded through the Vault of Heaven: exclaiming *"Man a rational Creature!"* How could any rational Being even dream that Man was a rational Creature?

After all, I hope to meet my Wife and Friends, Ancestors and Posterity, Sages ancient and modern. I believe I could get over all my Objections to meeting Alec Hamilton and Tim Pick, if I could perceive a Symptom of sincere Penitence in either. My fatigued Eyes and Fingers command me very reluctantly to subscribe abruptly

JOHN ADAMS

60. *Memoirs relative to Egypt, Written in That Country during the Campaigns of General Bonaparte, in the Years 1798 and 1799, by the Learned and Scientific Men Who Accompanied the French Expedition*... (London, 1800). The Institut d'Egypte, 1798-1801, established by Napoleon, was modeled after the Institut de France.

Adams to Jefferson

Quincy July 18. 1818

DEAR SIR

Will you accept a curious Piece of New England Antiquities? [61] It was a tolerable Chatechism for The Education of a Boy of 14 Years of Age, who was destined in the future Course of his Life to dabble in so many Revolutions in America, in Holland and in France.

This Doctor Mayhew had two Sisters established in Families in this Village which he often visited and where I often saw him. He was intimate with my Parson Bryant and often exchanged with him, which gave me an Opportunity often to hear him in the Pulpit. This discourse was printed, a Year before I entered Harvard Colledge and I read it, till the Substance of it was incorporated into my Nature and indelibly engraved on my Memory.

It made a greater Sensation in New England than Mr. Henrys Philippick against the Parsons did in Virginia.[62] It made a Noise in Great Britain where it was reprinted and procured the Author a Diploma of Doctor in Divinity.

That your Health and voracious Appetite for reading may long continue is the Wish of your Old Friend and humble Servant

JOHN ADAMS

61. Jonathan Mayhew, *Discourse concerning Unlimited Submission and Non-Resistance to the Higher Powers* (Boston, 1750); reprinted in Richard Barron, ed., *The Pillars of Priestcraft and Orthodoxy Shaken* (London, 1752). Mayhew, almost a Unitarian, was a staunch upholder of civil liberty and defended popular disobedience in all cases where orders contrary to God's laws were given. The University of Aberdeen conferred on him the degree of D.D. in 1751. Alice M. Baldwin, *The New England Clergy and the American Revolution* (Durham, N. C., 1928), 44-45, 69-70; John W. Thornton, ed., *The Pulpit of the American Revolution* (Boston, 1860), 46.

62. In the "Parson's Cause" the Reverend James Maury brought suit in Hanover County Court, Va., 1763, to recover on his salary (17,200 lbs. of tobacco per year) the difference between the legal rate of two pence per pound (act of 1758) and the current market price. Patrick Henry defended the parish against the clergy and attacked the royal disallowance of provincial laws necessary for the public good (the King had disallowed the act and the Hanover Court had ruled it invalid from its passage). The jury awarded Maury one penny damages. Robert D. Meade, *Patrick Henry, Patriot in the Making* (Philadelphia and N. Y., 1957), 114-38.

Jefferson to Adams

Monticello Oct. 7. 18.

It is very long, my dear friend, since I have written to you. The fact is that I was scarcely at home at all from May to September,[63] and from that time I have been severely indisposed and not yet recovered so far as to sit up to write, but in pain. Having been subject to troublesome attacks of rheumatism for some winters past, and being called by other business into the neighborhood of our Warmsprings, I thought I would avail myself of them as a preventative of future pain. I was then in good health and it ought to have occurred to me that the medecine which makes the sick well, may make the well sick. Those powerful waters produced imposthume, general eruption, fever, colliquative sweats, and extreme debility, which aggravated by the torment of a return home over 100. miles of rocks and mountains reduced me to extremity. I am getting better slowly and, when I can do it with less pain shall always have a pleasure in giving assurances to Mrs. Adams and yourself of my constant and affectionate friendship and respect.

TH: JEFFERSON

Adams to Jefferson

Quincy Octr. 20. 1815 [i.e., 1818]

MY DEAR FRIEND

One trouble never comes alone! At our Ages We may expect more and more of them every day in groups, and every day less fortitude to bear them.

When I saw in Print that You was gone to the Springs, I anxiously suspected that all was not healthy at Monticello.

You may be surprised to hear that your favour of the 7th has given me hopes. "Imposthume, general Eruptions, colliquative Sweats," sometimes and I believe often indicate Strength of Constitution and returning

63. During Aug. 1 to 4 TJ had been at Rockfish Gap as a member of the commission to select the site of the University of Virginia. Philip Alexander Bruce, *History of the University of Virginia, 1819-1919* (N.Y., [1920-22]), I, 210-21.

Vigour. I hope and believe they have given you a new Lease for Years, many Years.

Your Letter which is written with your usual neatness and firmness confirms my hopes.

Now Sir, for my Griefs! The dear Partner of my Life for fifty four Years as a Wife and for many Years more as a Lover, now lyes in extremis, forbidden to speak or be spoken to.[64]

If human Life is a Bubble, no matter how soon it breaks. If it is as I firmly believe an immortal Existence We ought patiently to wait the Instructions of the great Teacher. I am, Sir, your deeply afflicted Friend

JOHN ADAMS

Jefferson to Adams

Monticello Nov. 13. 18.

The public papers, my dear friend, announce the fatal event of which your letter of Oct. 20. had given me ominous foreboding. Tried myself, in the school of affliction, by the loss of every form of connection which can rive the human heart, I know well, and feel what you have lost, what you have suffered, are suffering, and have yet to endure. The same trials have taught me that, for ills so immeasurable, time and silence are the only medecines. I will not therefore, by useless condolances, open afresh the sluices of your grief nor, altho' mingling sincerely my tears with yours, will I say a word more, where words are vain, but that it is of some comfort to us both that the term is not very distant at which we are to deposit, in the same cerement, our sorrows and suffering bodies, and to ascend in essence to an ecstatic meeting with the friends we have loved and lost and whom we shall still love and never lose again. God bless you and support you under your heavy affliction.

TH: JEFFERSON

64. Mrs. Adams died of typhoid fever on Oct. 28, 1818, at the age of nearly seventy-four. Whitney, *Abigail Adams*, 326.

Adams to Jefferson

Quincy Dec. 8. 18.

DEAR SIR

Your Letter of Nov. 13 gave me great delight not only by the divine Consolation it Afforded me under my great Affliction: but as it gave me full Proof of your restoration to Health.

While you live, I seem to have a Bank at Montecello on which I can draw for a Letter of Friendship and entertainment when I please.

I know not how to prove physically that We shall meet and know each other in a future State; Nor does Revelation, as I can find give Us any possitive Assurance of such a felicity. My reasons for believing, it, as I do, most undoubtingly, are all moral and divine.

I believe in God and in his Wisdom and Benevolence: and I cannot conceive that such a Being could make such a Species as the human merely to live and die on this Earth. If I did not believe a future State I should believe in no God. This Un[i]verse; this all; this το παν ["totality"]; would appear with all its swelling Pomp, a boyish Fire Work.

And if there be a future State Why should the Almighty dissolve forever all the tender Ties which Unite Us so delightfully in this World and forbid Us to see each other in the next?

Trumbull with a band of Associates drew me by the Cords of old Frien[d]ships to see his Picture [65] on Saturday where I got a great Cold. The Air of Ph[an]euil Hall is changed. I have not been Used to catch Cold there.

Sick or Well the frien[d]ship is the same of your old Acquaintance

JOHN ADAMS

65. In Feb. 1816 Congress commissioned the sixty-year-old John Trumbull to paint four scenes of the Revolution for the rotunda of the Capitol, as he had conceived them a quarter-century earlier. He painted the 12' x 18' canvases in New York and exhibited them commercially before they were installed in the Capitol in 1824. J. Q. Adams saw the "Declaration of Independence" on exhibit in Sept. 1818. It was shown in New York, Philadelphia, and Baltimore. Was this the picture JA went to Boston to see? Theodore Sizer, "Trumbull, John," *DAB*, XIX, 14.

Adams to Jefferson

Quincy Dec 30th. 1818

DEAR SIR

Late last night I received Your Report and your translation of Tracy,[66] for both of which, tho' I have read neither, I thank You. But the full proof of your returning health has given me more Pleasure than both. I envy your Eyes and hands and Horse. Mine are too dim, too tremulous and my head is too dizzy for the Sovereign Doctor.

All is now still and tranquil. There is nothing to try Mens Souls nor to excite Men's Souls but Agriculture. And I say, God speed the Plough, and prosper stone Wall.

Had I your Eyes and Fingers, and 100 Years to live, I would write an 100 Volumes in folio; but neither myself nor the World would be the wiser or the better for any thing that could be done by your assured Friend

JOHN ADAMS

Jefferson to Adams

Monticello Jan. 19. 19.

DEAR SIR

About a week before I recieved your favor of Dec. 30. the 22d. No. of the North American review had come to hand, without my knowing from what quarter. The letter of Mr. Channing to Mr. Shaw, which you have been so good as to inclose, founds a presumption that it was from Mr. Channing, and that he is the editor. I had never before seen the work; but have read this No. with attention and great satisfaction. It may stand boldly on the shelf by the side of the Edinburg Review; and, as I find that Mr. Channing has agents in George town and Richmond, where I can readily make the necessary payments, I shall write to one of them to enter me as a subscriber. I see with pride that as we are ahead of Europe in Political science, so on other subjects we are getting along side of them.

66. *Report of the Commissioners appointed to fix the Scite of the University of Virginia, Thomas Jefferson [and others]*, Aug. 4, 1818 [Richmond, 1818]. For Jefferson's discussion of Tracy's work, see above, 491-92 and n. 41.

I hope you have read our University Report with approbation, as I am sure you will the work of Tracy, if you trouble yourself with such subjects. We are all atiptoe here in the hourly expectation of hearing what our legislature decides on the Report.[67] Being a good piece of a century behind the age they live in, we are not without fear as to their conclusions. We have to contend with so many biasses, personal, local, fanatical, financial etc. that we cannot foresee in what their combinations will result.

God bless you, and preserve you in good health and spirits.

TH: JEFFERSON

Adams to Jefferson

Quincy January 29th. 1819

DEAR SIR

If I am not humble I ought to be, when I find myself under the necessity of borrowing a juvenile hand to acknowledge your kind favour of the 19th. I have read your university report throughout with great pleasure and hearty approbation; Of Tracy's report I have read as much as I could. The Translation appears to me an original written with all the purity, accuracy, and elegance of its author in his maturest age. If it can destroy the Parasite Institutions of our country it will merit immortal honor.

The Medici rose to the despotism of Europe, ecclesiastical and political, by the machinery of banks. Hundreds of mushrooms or Jonah's gourds have sprung up in one night in America by the strength of the same rotten manure. How has it happened that the Bank of Amsterdam has for so many years conducted all most all the commerce of Europe without making any profit to the proprietors? And how has it happened that religious liberty, fiscal science, coin and commerce, and every branch of political economy, should have been better understood and more honestly practised in that Frog land, than any other country in the world?

Your letter shall be communicated without loss of time to Mr. Shaw and consequently to Mr. Channing by your friend

JOHN ADAMS

67. The *Report* recommending Central College as the site for the University of Virginia was presented to the General Assembly in Dec. and a bill for this purpose was passed on Jan. 25. Joseph Carrington Cabell, ardent advocate of higher education in Virginia, wrote to TJ on Jan. 18, 1819: "Grateful, truly grateful, is it to my heart, to be able to announce to you the result of this day's proceedings in the House of Delegates." Cabell, *Early History of University of Va.*, 149, 152, 153, 447-50. The Senate also passed the bill on Jan. 25.

Adams to Jefferson

Quincy Feby. 13th. 1819.

DEAR SIR

As you was so well acquainted with the philosophers of France I presume the name and character of Mademoiselle De Lespinasse is not unknown to you.

I have almost put out my eyes by reading two volumes of her letters which as they were printed in 1809 I presume you have read long ago. I confess I have never read any thing with more ennui, disgust and loathing. The eternal repitition of mon dieu and mon ami—je vous aime; je vous aime eperdument; je vous aime a la follie; je suis au desespoir, je espere la mort; je suis morte; je premme l'opium etc. etc. etc.

She was constantly in love with other womens husbands, constantly violating her fidelity to her own keepers with other women's husbands constantly tormented with remords [i.e., remorse] and regrets constantly wishing for death and constantly threatning to put herself to death etc. etc. etc.

Yet this great lady was the confidential friend of Mr. Turgot the Duke De la Rochefaucault the Duchess D'anville, Mr. Condorcet; the only lady who was admitted to the dinners which Madame Geoffrim made for the litterati of France and the world and the intimate friend of Madame Boufflers and the open acknowledged mistress of the great D'allembert and much admired by Marmontel.

If these letters and the fifteen volumes of De Grimm are to give me an idea of the amelioration of society and government and manners in France I should think the age of reason has produced nothing much better than the Mahometans the Mamalukes or the Hindoos or the North American Indians have produced in different parts of the world.

Festine lente ["Hasten slowly"], my friend, in all your projects of reformation abolish polytheism however in every shape if you can, and unfrock every priest who teaches it, if you can. To compensate in some measure for this crazy letter I enclose to you Mr. Pickering's essay on the pronounciation of the Greek language [68] which very probably you have received from various quarters before now and with it I pray you to accept assurances of the unabated friendship of your humble servant

JOHN ADAMS

68. Published in the *Memoirs* of the American Academy of Arts and Sciences (Cambridge, Mass., 1818).

Adams to Jefferson

Quincy Feby. 19th. 1819

DEAR SIR

As you know I have often been ambitious of introducing to your acquaintance some of our literary characters. I now send you in the same spirit, some mathematical papers by our Mr. Bowditch, who has translated La Place's mechanique coeliste and has written commentaries upon it as voluminous as the book, which are thought by our scientific people to be one of the greatest astronomical productions of the present age: I hope the public will soon see it in print. I would write you news if I had any, but this is "the piping time of peace." I am as ever your friend and humble servant,

JOHN ADAMS

Adams to Jefferson

Quincy Feb'y. 24th. 1819

DEAR SIR

I am diligently and laboriously occupied, in reading and hearing your "political economy"—I call it yours because I do not believe that Tracys is more of an original in point of purity, perspicuity or precission. I have read as yet only to the 90th page. It is a connected chain of ideas and propositions, of which I know not which link to strike out. His philosophy appears to me to be precisely that of Dupuis—that is, the eternity, infinity, and mechanism of the universe. His philosophy appears to me to roll on in a continued stream untill it disembogues itself into the unfathomable gulph of liberty and necessity.

Is liberty a word void of sense? If it is, there [is] no merit or guilt, and there can be neither reward or punishment in the universe. His ethics appear to me in substance and essence to be those of Butlers sermons on human nature; and his preface to them of Hutchinsons writings throughout and of Tristram Shandy. At the bottom of the gulph of liberty and necessity for aught I know the key may lie which is to unlock the universe. But you know my opinion is that the key will never be found but by one being who will ever keep it in his own custody. Human understanding will never dive in this state of existence to such depths, and it is a vain and impertinent curiosity to think of it. Our duties are the charities of father, friend and brother. Fifty years ago I delighted more to see metaphysicians dance upon the point of their needles, than to see the exploits of dancers on the slack ropes or tight rope, but now my eyes are not keen enough to see the agility and capers of either. I am very glad however I have read so much and I intend to read the rest or hear it read. At present I will acknowledge one great obligation to it, that is the Chapter sixth, of money, page 21st: "When these denominations are admitted and employed in transactions, to diminish the quantity of metal to which they answer by an alteration of the real coins, is to steal. A theft of greater magnitude and still more ruinous is the making of paper. It is greater because in this money there is absolutely no real value. It is more ruinous because by its gradual depreciation during all the time of its existence it produces the effect which would be produced by an infinity of successive deteriorations of the coin." That is to say, an infinity of successive felonious larcenies. If this is true, as I believe it is, we Americans are the most thievish people that ever existed: we have been stealing from each other for an hundred and fifty years. If anything like health remains to me, you shall hear more upon this subject from your friend and humble servant,

JOHN ADAMS

Adams to Jefferson

Quincy March 2d. 1819

DEAR SIR

I have taxed my eyes with a very heavy impost to read the senator Tracy's Political Economy, and been amply rewarded for the expense. When I first saw the volume I thought it was impossible I should get through it, but when I had once made a beginning I found myself led on in so easy a train from proposition to proposition, every one of which appeared to me self evident, that I could not leave the book till I had finished. It is a condensation into a little globule not comparatively bigger than a nut shell of all the sound sense and solid knowledge of the grand master Quanay [i.e., Quesnay] and all the redoubtable knights his disciples and all their numerous huge volumes, and those of Sir James Stuart and Adam Smith, the Chevalier Pinto and the Enciclopedists, discarding all their mysteries, paradoxes and enigmas.

I have endeavoured and shall endeavour to draw the attention of all my acquaintances to this work. I would endeavour to get it reviewed but I should despair of success, for there is no man in this quarter who would dare to avow such sentiments; and no printer who would not think himself ruined by the publication of it for it is a magazine of gunpowder placed under the foundation of all our mercantile institutions. Yet every sensible man in the nation knows it to be founded in immutable truth though not one in a hundred would acknowledge it, and they only sub-rosa. I have never been so prudent. I have preached this doctrine thirty years in season and out of season and this heresy has been one of the principal causes of the immense unpopularity of Your old friend and humble servant

JOHN ADAMS

Jefferson to Adams

Monticello Mar. 21. 19.

DEAR SIR

I am indebted to you for Mr. Bowditch's very learned mathematical papers, the calculations of which are not for every reader, altho' their results are readily enough understood. One of these impairs the confidence I had reposed in La Place's demonstration that the excentricities of the planets of our system could oscillate only within narrow limits, and therefore could authorise no inference that the system must, by it's own laws, come one day to an end. This would have left the question of infinitude, at both ends of the line of time, clear of physical authority.

Mr. Pickering's pamphlet on the pronunciation of the Greek, for which I am indebted to you also, I have read with great pleasure. Early in life the idea occurred to me that the people now inhabiting the antient seats of the Greeks and Romans, altho' their languages in the intermediate ages had suffered great changes, and especially in the declensions of their nouns, and in the terminations of their words generally yet having preserved the body of the word radically the same, so they would preserve more of it's pronunciation. That at least it was probable that a pronunciation, handed down by tradition, would retain, as the words themselves do, more of the original than that of any other people whose language has no affinity to that original. For this reason I learnt, and have used the Italian pronunciation of the Latin. But that of the modern Greeks I had no opportunity of learning until I went to Paris. There I became acquainted with two learned Greeks, Count Carberri and Mr. Paradise, and with a lady, a native Greek, the daughter of Baron de Tott, who did not understand the ancient language. Carberri and Paradise spoke it. From these instructors I learnt the modern pronunciation, and in *general*, trusted to it's orthodoxy. I say, *in general*, because sound being more fugitive than the written letter, we must, after such a lapse of time, presume in it some degeneracies, as we see there are in the written words. We may not indeed be able to put our finger on them confidently, yet neither are they entirely beyond the reach of all indication. For example, in a language so remarkable for the euphony of it's sounds, if that euphony is preserved in particular combinations of it's letters, by an adherence to the powers ordinarily ascribed to them, and is destroyed by a change of these powers, and the sound of the word thereby rendered harsh, inharmonious and unidiomatical, here we may presume some degeneracy has taken place. While therefore I gave in to the modern pronunciation generally, I have presumed, as an instance of degeneracy, their ascribing the same sound to the six letters, or combinations of letters η, ι, υ, ει, οι, υι to all of which they give the sound of our double *e*, in the word *meet*. This useless equivalence of 3. vowels and 3. diphthongs did not probably exist among the antient Greeks; and the less probably as, while this single sound, *ee*, is overcharged by so many different representative characters, the sounds we usually give to these characters and combinations would be left witho[ut] any representative signs. This would imply either that they had not these sounds in their language, or no signs for their expression. Probability appears to me therefore against the practice of the modern Greeks of giving the same sound to all these different representatives, and to be in favor of that of foreign nations, who, adopting the Roman characters, have assimilated to them, in a considerable degree, the powers of the corresponding Greek letters. I have accordingly excepted this in my adoption of the modern pronunciation. I have been more doubtful in the use of the αυ, ευ, ηυ, ωυ, sounding the υ, upsilon, as our f. or v. because I find traces of that power of υ, or of u, in some modern languages. To go no further than our own, we have it in laugh, cough, trough, enough. The county of Louisa, adjacent to that in which I live, was, when I was a boy, universally pronounced Lovisa. That it is not the *gh* which gives the sound of f. or v. in these words is proved by the orthography of *plough, through, thought, fraught, caught*. The modern Greeks themselves too, giving to υ, upsilon, in ordinary the sound of our *ee* strengthen the presumption that its anomalous soun[d] of f or v. is a corruption. The same may be inferred from the cacophony of ηλαφνε (elavne) for ηλαυγε (elawne), Αχιλλεφς (Achillefs) for Αχιλλευς (Achilluse) ηφς (eves) for ηϋς (eeuse) οφκ (ovk) for ουκ (ouk) ωφτος (ovetos) for ωὖτος (o-u-tos) Ζεφς (zevs) for Ζευς (zuse) of which all nations have made their Jupiter; and the uselessness of the υ in ευφωνια, which would otherwise have been spelt εφωνια. I therefore except this also from what I consider as approvable pronunciation.

Against reading Greek by accent, instead of quantity, as Mr. Ciceitira proposes, I raise both my hands. What becomes of the sublime measure of Homer, the full sounding rythm of Demosthenes, if, abandoning quantity, you chop it up by accent? What ear can hesitate in it's choice between the two following rhythms?

Τὸν δ'απαμειβόμενος προσεφὴ πόδας ωκυς Αχιλλεύς, and
τόν δ'απαμείβομενός προσεφή ποδας ὠκυς Αχίλλευς.[69]

the latter noted according to prosody, the former by accent, and dislocating our teeth in it's utterance; every syllable of it, except the first and last, being pronounced against quantity. And what becomes of the art of prosody? [70] Is that perfect coincidence of it's rules with the structure of their verse merely accidental? or was it of design, and yet for no use.

On the whole I rejoice that this subject is taken up among us, and that it is in so able hands as those of Mr. Pickering. Should he ultimately establish the modern pronunciation of the letters without any exception I shall think it a great step gained, and giving up my exceptions shall willingly rally to him; and as he has promised us another paper on the question whether we shall read by quantity or by accent, I can confidently trust it to the correctness of his learning and judgment. Of the origin of accentuation I have never seen satisfactory proofs. But I have generally supposed the accents were intended to direct the inflexions and modulation of the voice; but not to affect the quantity of the syllables.

You did not expect, I am sure, to draw on yourself so long a disquisition on letters and sounds. Nor did I intend it. But the subject run before me, and yet I have dropped much of it by the way.

I am delighted with your high approbation of Tracy's book. The evils of this deluge of paper money are not to be removed until our citizens are generally and radically instructed in their cause and consequences, and silence by their authority the interested clamors and sophistry of speculat-

69. "And answering him, swift-footed Achilles said...." Homer, *Iliad*, I, 58, 64, *et passim.*

70. In an undated letter to Chastellux, apparently written after Jefferson returned from France in 1789, TJ sent his Thoughts on English Prosody, based upon a comparative study of Greek and Latin and English verse. Lipscomb and Bergh, eds., *Writings*, XVIII, 414-51. With his letter of Oct. 30, 1798, to Herbert Croft of London, who was preparing an etymological dictionary, TJ sent his Essay on the Anglo-Saxon Language, first printed by order of the Board of Trustees, University of Virginia (N.Y., 1851); also in Lipscomb and Bergh, eds., *Writings*, XVIII, 361-411.

ing, shaving and banking institutions. Till then we must be content to return, quoad hoc, to the savage state, to recur to barter in the exchange of our property, for want of a stable, common measure of value, that now in use being less fixed than the beads and wampum of the Indian, and to deliver up our citizens, their property and their labor passive victims to the swindling tricks of bankers and mountebankers. If I had your permission to put your letter into the hands of the editor (Milligan) with or without any verbal alterations you might chuse, it would ensure the general circulation, which my prospectus and prefatory letter will less effectually recommend. There is nothing in the book of mine but these two articles, and the note on taxation in page 202. I never knew who the translator was: but I thought him some one who understood neither French nor English: and probably a Caledonian, from the number of Scotticisms I found in his MS. The innumerable corrections of that cost me more labor than would a translation of the whole de novo; and made at last but an inelegant altho' faithful version of the sense of the author. Dios guarde á V.S. muchos años [May God preserve your health for many years].

TH: JEFFERSON

Adams to Jefferson

Quincy April 2d. 1819

DEAR SIR

Your Letter of March 21st. I will communicate to Mr. Bowditch, and Pickering.

You may put my Letters upon the Subject of Tracy's Book into any hands you please, with or without any verbal alterations, as you may think fitt—"what you would have them, make them." Or as James Otis used to say to Samuel Adams—here, take it and "Quicu Wuicu" it.

I am obliged to borrow the hand of a friend to write you this Letter.

There seems to be some evil communication between Monticello and Montezillo, for at the same moment when your complaint appears to be perfectly cured, I am teazed with something very much like it. I wish you could convey to me by some Subterranean Canal or Air-Balloon as clear Eyes, and as steady hands as yours. I am as ever yours

JOHN ADAMS

Jefferson to Adams

Monticello May 15. 19.

DEAR SIR

Your letter of Apr. 2. was recieved in due time, and I have used the permission it gave me of sending a copy of that of Mar. 2. to the editor of Tracy's Political economy.

Mr. S. A. Wells of Boston, grandson of our old friend Saml. Adams, and who proposes to write the life of his grandfather,[71] has made some enquiries of me relative to revolutionary antiquities which are within your knolege as well as mine. I therefore put my answer under your cover, and open for your perusal and animadversion to him if I have committed any error. I fear none where I have taken facts from written notes. In other parts there may be error. When [rea]d, will you have the goodness to insert a wafer and send the lette[r to] the post office? Ever and affectionately yours.

TH: JEFFERSON

Adams to Jefferson

Quincy May 21st. 1819.

DEAR SIR

All the Literary Gentlemen of this part of the Country have an Ambitious Curiosity to see the Philosopher and Statesman of Monticello—and they all apply to me for Introductions—and if I had ever received one introduction from you, I should have less scruple of Conscience in granting their requests. In the Stile of our New-England, the Reverend Mr. Greenwood, the successor of Mr. Thatcher and Dr. Kirkland in the Church of Summer Street, Boston, will deliver you this letter with my affectionate respects.

Tho I cannot write I still live and enjoy Life. The World is dead. There is nothing to Communicate in Religion, Morals, Philosophy, or Politicks. I hope your Health is perfectly restored. Mine is pritty much like that of

71. The biography was written by the great-grandson: William Vincent Wells, *Life and Public Services of Samuel Adams* (Boston, 1865).

Voltaire Frankline and Samuel Adams, at my Age. But I am still un-
alterably your Friend,

J. ADAMS

Adams to Jefferson

Quincy May 27th. 1819.

DEAR SIR

I have transmitted your letter to Samuel Adams Welles, Esqr. in Boston,
as you desire.

This gentleman is a singular character. He is, I beleive, the only surviving male [heir] of his Grandfather, the late gove[r]nor of Massachusetts,
Samuel Adams, who never had but two children, a son and a daughter; his
son who bore his name died early, a surgeon in the army of the Revolution,
without issue; his daughter married a Mr. Welles and her only son, as I
beleive, is your correspondent, Samuel Adams Welles. He is now vir-
tuously, amiably and laudably employed in collecting memorials of his
grandfather, in which I heartily wish him success. His grandfather's
character however will never be accurately known to posterity, as it never
was sufficiently known to its own age: his merit in the Revolution, if there
was any merit in it, was and is beyond all calculation. I know but one
superior to it and that was James Otis. As your correspondent is the only
representitive of him, I feel a strong interest in his favour; he was bred a
merchant, has talents, industry, a taste for letters, and a fair, unspotted and
irreproachable character. I wish you would speak a good word for him to
Mr. Munroe. I believe him well qualified to be a commissioner under the
Spanish treaty to adjust the American claims for spoliations on our commerce, and I believe the appointment would be more popular in Massachusetts than any other that could be named, except among the old tory
refugees and their rancorous disciples. I am dear Sir Your friend and
humble Servant

JOHN ADAMS

Adams to Jefferson

Quincy June 22d. 1819

MY DEAR SIR.

May I inclose you one of the greatest curiositys and one of the deepest Mysterys that ever occoured to me. It is in the Essex Register of June the 5th. 1819. It is entitled from the Raleigh Register Declaration of Independence.[72] How is it possible that this paper should have been concealed from me to this day had it been communicated to me in the time of it, I know, if you do not know, that it would have been printed in every Whig News-paper upon this Continent. You know if I had possessed it, I would have made the Hall of Congress Echo and re-echo, with it fifteen Months before your Declaration of Independence.

What a poor ignorant, Malicious, short-sighted, Crapulous Mass, is Tom Pains Common Sense; [73] in comparision with this paper. Had I known it I would have Commented upon it from the day you entered Congress till the fourth of July 1776.

The Genuine sense of America at that Moment was never so well expressed before nor since. Richard Caswell, William Hooper, and Joseph Hughs the then Representatives of North Carolina in Congress you knew as well as I do, and you know that the Unanimity of the States finally depended on the Vote of Joseph Hughes, and was finally determined by him, and yet History is to ascribe the American Revolution to Thomas Pain—Sat verbum sapient[i] ["a word to the wise is sufficient"]. I am my dear Sir your invariable friend

JOHN ADAMS

72. The Raleigh *Register and North Carolina Gazette*, April 30, 1819, first printed the Mecklenburg Declaration of Independence, purportedly the work of a meeting of citizens at Charlotte, N.C., on May 20, 1775. According to the account they declared that "a free and independent people, are and of right ought to be a sovereign and self-governing association under the control of no other power than that of our God and the General Government of Congress." The resolutions were dispatched a few days later to the North Carolina delegates in the Continental Congress, who commended the meeting but felt that action on behalf of independence was premature. The original record of the meeting on May 20 was reported burned in 1800. While JA gave countenance to the document, TJ denounced it as spurious (TJ to JA, July 9, 1819, below, 543-44.); but its authenticity was not seriously questioned until 1847. Hoyt, *Mecklenburg Declaration*, Chap. I.

73. Paine's *Common Sense*, first printed in Philadelphia in Jan. 1776, and widely circulated in a short time, was powerful propaganda on behalf of independence; but JA always regarded Paine's influence as vastly overrated.

Jefferson to Adams

Monticello July 9. 19.

DEAR SIR

I am in debt to you for your letters of May 21. 27. and June 22. The first delivered me by Mr. Greenwood gave me the gratification of his acquaintance; and a gratification it always is to be made acquainted with gentlemen of candor, worth and information, as I found Mr. Greenwood to be. That on the subject of Mr. Samuel Adams Wells shall not be forgotten in time and place, when it can be used to his advantage. But what has attracted my peculiar notice is the paper from Mecklenburg county of N. Carolina, published in the Essex Register which you were so kind as to inclose in your last of June 22. And you seem to think it genuine. I believe it spurious. I deem it to be a very unjustifiable quiz, like that of the Volcano, so minutely related to us as having broken out in N. Carolina, some half dozen years ago, in that part of the country, and perhaps in that very county of Mecklenburg, for I do not remember it's precise locality. If this paper be really taken from the Raleigh Register, as quoted, I wonder it should have escaped Ritchie, who culls what is good from every paper, as the bee from every flower; and the National Intelligencer too, which is edited by a North Carolinian [Joseph Gales, Jr.], and that the fire should blaze out all at once in Essex, 1000. miles from where the spark is said to have fallen. But if really taken from the Raleigh Register, who is the Narrator, and is the name subscribed real, or is it as fictitious as the paper itself? It appeals too to an original book, which is burnt, to Mr. Alexander who is dead, to a joint letter from Caswell, Hughes and Hooper, all dead, to a copy sent to the dead Caswell, and another sent to Doctr. Williamson, whose memory, now probably dead, did not recollect, in the history he has written of N. Carolina, this Gigantic step of it's county of Mecklenburg. Horry too is silent in his history of Marion, whose scene of action was the country bordering on Mecklenburg. Ramsay, Marshal, Jones, Girardin, Wirt, historians of the adjacent states, all silent. When Mr. Henry's resolutions, far short of independance, flew like lightning thro' every paper, and kindled both sides of the Atlantic,[74] this flaming declaration, of the same date, of the independance of Mecklenburg county of

---

74. Patrick Henry's resolutions, introduced in the Virginia Convention in Richmond on March 20, 1775, and passed on March 23, provided that "this Colony be immediately put into a posture of defence." It was in his speech urging the passage of the resolutions that Henry proclaimed, "Give me liberty, or give me death." Peter Force, ed., *American Archives . . .* (Washington, 1837-53), 4th ser., II, 168.

N. Carolina, absolving it from British allegiance, and abjuring all political connection with that nation, altho' sent to Congress too, is never heard of. It is not known even a twelve month after when a similar proposition is first made in that body. Armed with this bold example, would not you have addressed our timid brethren in peals of thunder, on their tardy fears? Would not every advocate of independance have rung the glories of Mecklenburg county in N. Carolina in the ears of the doubting Dickinson and others, who hung so heavily on us? Yet the example of independant Mecklenberg county in N. Carolina, was never once quoted. The paper speaks too of the continued exertions of their delegation, (Caswell, Hooper, Hughes) 'in the cause of liberty and independance.' [75] Now you remember as well as I do, that we had not a greater tory in Congress than Hooper, that Hughes was very wavering, sometimes firm, sometimes feeble, according as the day was clear or cloudy; that Caswell indeed was a good whig, and kept these gentlemen to the notch, while he was present; but that he left us soon, and their line of conduct became then uncertain until Penn came, who fixed Hughes and the vote of the State. I must not be understood as suggesting any doubtfulness in the state of North Carolina. No state was more fixed or forward. Nor do I affirm positively that this paper is a fabrication: because the proof of a negative can only be presumptive. But I shall believe it such until positive and solemn proof of it's authenticity shall be produced. And if the name of McKnitt be real, and not a part of the fabrication, it needs a vindication by the production of such proof. For the present I must be an unbeliever in this apocryphal gospel.

I am glad to learn that Mr. Tickner has safely returned to his friends. But should have been much gladder had he accepted the Professorship in our University, which we should have offered him in form. Mr. Bowditch too refuses us. So fascinating is the vinculum of the dulce natale solum ["the bond of the sweet natal soil"]. Our wish is to procure natives where they can be found, like these gentlemen, of the first order of acquirement in their respective lines; but, preferring foreigners of the 1st. order to natives of the 2d. we shall certainly have to go, for several of our Professors, to countries more advanced in science than we are.

I set out within 3. or 4. days for my other home, the distance of which and it's cross mails, are great impediments to epistolary communications. I shall remain there about 2. months; and there, here and every where, I am and shall always be affectionately and respectfully your's.

TH: JEFFERSON

75. TJ misinterpreted the statement in the *Essex Register*. The "delegation" referred to was that of Mecklenburg County, not the three members of the North Carolina delegation in Congress. Hoyt, *Mecklenburg Declaration*, 9.

Adams to Jefferson

Quincy July 21st. 1819.

DEAR SIR,

I am greatly obliged to you for your letter of the 9th. It has entirely convinced me that the Mecklengburg Resolutions are a fiction. When I first read them in the Essex Register, I was struct with astonishment. It appeared to me utterly incredible that they should be genuine; but there were so many circumstances calculated to impose on the public, that I thought it my duty to take measures for the detection of the imposture. For this purpose I instantly inclosed the Essex Register to you, knowing that if you had either seen, or heard of these resolutions, you would have informed me of it. As they are unknown to you, they must have been unknown to all Mankind. I have sent a Copy of your letter to Salem, not to be printed but to be used as decisive authority for the Editor to correct his error in the Essex Register.[76]

But who can be the Demon to invent such a machine after five and forty years, and what could be his motive? [77] Was it to bring a charge of Plagiarism against the Congress in 76, or against you, the undoubted, acknowledged draughtsman of the Declaration of Independence? Or could it be the mere vanity of producing a jeu d'esprit, to set the world a gasp and afford a topic of Conversation in this piping time of Peace?

Had such Resolutions appeared in June 75, they would have flown through the Universe like wildfire; they would have Elevated the heads of the inhabitants of Boston and of all New England above the Stars, and they would have rung a peal in Congress, to the utter Confusion of Toryism and timidity, for a full Year before they were discomforted.

76. In an article containing the substance of TJ's letter to JA of July 9, 1819, but mentioning no names, the Essex Register announced on July 24 that the Mecklenburg resolutions had not been universally credited and that more information about them was desired. In reply on Aug. 6 the Raleigh Register explained how the resolutions had been brought to light and published. The editor claimed he could secure testimony of several persons who had been present on the occasion. Statements to this effect and other information were printed in the Raleigh Register, Aug. 13, 1819, Feb. 11 and 18, May 26, 1820 (reprinted as a pamphlet, 1822). These statements stood unchallenged publicly until TJ's letter to JA appeared in the first edition of his works in 1829, Randolph, ed., Correspondence, IV, 314-16.

77. It was rather an expression of state patriotism on the part of certain North Carolinians who were making known nationally an idea which had existed in the state since 1777. Hoyt, Mecklenburg Declaration, 113ff.

I wish you a pleasant tour to your second home, and remain your friend and Humble Servant

JOHN ADAMS

Adams to Jefferson

Quincy July 28th. 1819.

DEAR SIR

I inclose you a National Register, to convince you that the Essex Register is not to blame for printing the Mecklingburg County Resolutions. On the contrary I think it to be commended, for if those Resolutions were genuine, they ought to be published in every Gazette in the World. If they are one of those tricks which our fashionable Men in England call hoax'es and boares, they ought to be printed in all American journals, exposed to public resentment, and the Author of them hunted to his dark Cavern. For altho you and I should as easily believe that a flaming Brand might be thrust into a Magazine of Powder without producing an Explosion, as that those Resolutions could have passed in 1775; [and] had not been known to any Member of Congress in 1776. And if they were not known to you, as I am very sure they were not, It is impossible they could have been known to any other Member. I am, Sir, whether at your first, or second home, always affecly. and Respectfully your Friend

JOHN ADAMS

Jefferson to Adams

Monticello Nov. 7. 19.

DEAR SIR

Three long and dangerous illnesses within the last 12. months must apologize for my long silence towards you.

The paper bubble is then burst. This is what you and I, and every reasoning man, seduced by no obliquity of mind or interest, have long foreseen. Yet it's disastrous effects are not the less for having been foreseen. We were laboring under a dropsical fulness of circulating medium.

Nearly all of it is now called in by the banks who have the regulation of the safety valves of our fortunes and who condense or explode them at their will. Lands in this state cannot now be sold for a year's rent: and unless our legislature have wisdom enough to effect a remedy by a gradual diminution only of the medium, there will be a general revolution of property in this state. Over our own paper and that of other states coming among us, they have competent powers. Over that of the bank of the US. there is doubt; not here, but elsewhere. That bank will probably conform voluntarily to such regulations as the legislature may prescribe for the others. If they do not we must shut their doors and join the other states which deny the right of Congress to establish banks, and sollicit them to agree to some mode of settling this constitutional question. They have themselves twice decided against their right, and twice for it. Many of the states have been uniform in denying it, and between such parties the constitution has provided no umpire.[78] I do not know particularly the extent of this distress in the other states, but Southwardly and Westwardly I believe all are involved in it. God bless you and preserve you many years.

TH: JEFFERSON

Adams to Jefferson

Montezillo Alias the little Hill [79]
November 23d. 1819

MY DEAR SIR

I congratulate you and myself on your recovery from the three Ill-nesses that have distressed you. The means that have been used to preserve you may, and I hope will have laid a foundation for good Health and many more years of an already long Life. My Health is astonishing to

78. Overexpansion of banking and credit after the War of 1812, of which the Bank of the United States as well as the state banks was guilty, precipitated the Panic of 1819. When certain state legislatures tried to tax branches of the Bank of the United States out of existence, the question was appealed to the United States Supreme Court in McCulloch v. Maryland (1819). When the Court upheld the bank as an instrument of the federal government, Kentucky found ways of circumventing the decision. Having seen the effects of the panic in Virginia, which had followed a more conservative fiscal program, TJ sympathized with the states. He felt the pinch in his personal fortunes too. Frederick J. Turner, *Rise of the New West, 1819-1829* (N.Y., [1906]), 59, Chap. IX; George T. Starnes, *Sixty Years of Branch Banking in Virginia* (N.Y., 1931), 63-67.

79. Here JA began his imitation of TJ's Monticello.

myself. I can say, like Deborah Queen Ann Dutchess of Marlbourgh, who in one of her letters, after innumerating a Multitude of her griefs and Misfortunes, says, I believe nothing but Distemper will kill me. Though I have not had three remarkable Illnesses, I have been afflicted with three times three Misfortunes, grievous enough to have shaken the philosophy of the most hardened Stoic. I ought however, to remember the saying of a Bishop with whom I dined once at Versailles who asked me many questions concerning Dr. Frankline, his Health, his Spirits, and his Mind. I answered, his Health is very robust, his Spirits very cheerful, and his Intellect as bright as ever. Monseignieur reply'd, "mais a son age il ne faut que tres peu de chose pour abbatre un colasse ["but at his age he should be careful not to grow angry"]."

What a Murrain there has been among the Governours within a few Months—Langdon, Strong, Snyder, Johnson, Lee, Raban. I hope there will not be such an other among the ex and in Presidents.

Congress are about to assemble and the Clouds look Black and thick, Assembling from all points, threatening thunder and Lightning. The Spanish Treaty, the Missouri Slavery, the encouragement of Manufactures by protecting duties or absolute prohibitions, the project of a Bankrupt Act, the plague of Banks, perhaps even the Monument for Washington, and above all the bustle of Caucuses for the approaching Election for President and Vice President, will probably produce an effervescence, though there is no doubt that the present President and Vice President will be re-elected by great Majority's,[80] as they ought to be, unless Tompkins should be chosen Governour of New York.

May God preserve you many years, Amen.

JOHN ADAMS

Jefferson to Adams

Monticello Dec. 10. 19.

DEAR SIR

I have to acknolege the reciept of your favor of Nov. 23. The banks, bankrupt law, manufactures, Spanish treaty are nothing. These are occurences which like waves in a storm will pass under the ship. But the

80. In the election of 1820 Monroe and Tompkins were re-elected president and vice-president following the Republican party caucus which made no recommendations for the nomination. John Bach McMaster, *A History of the People of the United States . . .* (N.Y., 1883-1913), IV, 515-18, 598-600.

Missouri question is a breaker on which we lose the Missouri country by revolt, and what more, God only knows.[81] From the battle of Bunker's hill to the treaty of Paris we never had so ominous a question. It even damps the joy with which I hear of your high health, and welcomes to me the consequences of my want of it. I thank god that I shall not live to witness it's issue. Sed haec hactenus ["But more of these things later"].

I have been amusing myself latterly with reading the voluminous letters of Cicero. They certainly breathe the purest effusions of an exalted patriot, while the parricide Caesar is left in odious contrast. When the enthusiasm however kindled by Cicero's pen and principles, subsides into cool reflection, I ask myself What was that government which the virtues of Cicero were so zealous to restore, and the ambition of Caesar to subvert? And if Caesar had been as virtuous as he was daring and sagacious, what could he, even in the plenitude of his usurped power have done to lead his fellow citizens into good government? I do not say to *restore it*, because they never had it, from the rape of the Sabines to the ravages of the Caesars. If their people indeed had been, like ours, enlightened, peaceable, and really free, the answer would be obvious. 'Restore independance to all your foreign conquests, relieve Italy from the government of the rabble of Rome, consult it as a nation entitled to self government, and do it's will.' But steeped in corruption vice and venality as the whole nation was, (and nobody had done more than Caesar to corrupt it) what could even Cicero, Cato, Brutus have done, had it been referred to them to establish a good government for their country? They had no ideas of government themselves but of their degenerate Senate, nor the people of liberty, but of the factious opposition of their tribunes. They had afterwards their Titusses, their Trajans and Antoninuses, who had the will to make them happy, and the power to mould their government into a good and permanent form. But it would seem as if they could not see their way clearly to do it. No government can continue good but under the controul of the people: and their people were so demoralised and depraved as to be incapable of exercising a wholsome controul. Their reformation then was to be taken up ab incunabulis ["from the beginning"]. Their minds were to be informed, by education, what is right and what wrong, to be encoraged in habits of virtue, and deterred from those of vice by the dread of punishments, proportioned indeed, but irremissible; in all cases, to follow

81. The question of admission of Missouri to the Union as a slave state raised the explosive issue of expansion of slavery into the territories and brought about the drawing of an artificial geographical line (36° 30′ N. Lat.) "which on an abstract principle is to become the line of separation of these States, and to render desperate the hope that man can ever enjoy the two blessings of peace and self-government. The question sleeps for the present, but is not dead." TJ to Hugh Nelson, March 12, 1820, Lipscomb and Bergh, eds., *Writings*, XV, 238.

truth as the only safe guide, and to eschew error which bewilders us in one false consequence after another in endless succession. These are the inculcations necessary to render the people a sure basis for the structure of order and good government. But this would have been an operation of a generation or two at least, within which period would have succeeded many Neros and Commoduses, who would have quashed the whole process. I confess then I can neither see what Cicero, Cato and Brutus, united and uncontrouled, could have devised to lead their people into good government, nor how this aenigma can be solved, nor how further shewn why it has been the fate of that delightful country never to have known to this day, and through a course of five and twenty hundred years, the history of which we possess one single day of free and rational government. Your intimacy with their history, antient, middle and modern, your familiarity with the improvements in the science of government at this time, will enable you, if any body, to go back with our principles and opinions to the times of Cicero, Cato, and Brutus, and tell us by what process these great and virtuous men could have led so unenlightened and vitiated a people into freedom and good government, et eris mihi magnus Apollo. Cura ut valeas, et tibi persuade carissimum te mihi esse ["and you will be great Apollo to me. Take care of your health and be assured that you are most dear to me"].

TH: JEFFERSON

Adams to Jefferson

Montezillo December 21st. 1819

DEAR SIR

I must answer your great question of the 10th. in the words of Dalembert to his Correspondent, who asked him what is Matter—"Je vous avoue que Je n'en scais rien ["I confess that I know nothing about it"]."

In some part of my Life I read a great Work of a Scotchman on the Court of Augustus, in which with much learning, hard Study, and fatiguing labour, he undertook to prove that had Brutus and Cassius been conqueror, they would have restored virtue and liberty to Rome.

Mais Je n'en crois rien ["But I don't believe it"]. Have you ever found in history one single example of a Nation th[o]roughly Corrupted, that was afterwards restored to Virtue, and without Virtue, there can be no political Liberty.

If I were a Calvinest, I might pray that God by a Miracle of Divine Grace would instantaneously convert a whole Contaminated Nation from turpitude to purity, but even in this I should be inconsistent, for the fatalism of Mahometnism Material[i]sts, Atheists, Pantheists and Calvinests, and Church of England Articles, appear to me to render all prayer futile and absurd. The French and the Dutch in our day have attempted reforms and Revolutions. We know the results, and I fear the English reformers will have no better success.

Will you tell me how to prevent riches from becoming the effects of temperance and industry? Will you tell me how to prevent riches from producing luxury? Will you tell me how to prevent luxury from producing effeminacy intoxication extravagance Vice and folly? When you will answer me these questions, I hope I may venture to answer yours. Yet all these ought not to discourage us from exertion, for with my friend Jeb, I believe no effort in favour of Virtue is lost, and all good Men ought to struggle both by their Council and Example.

The Missouri question I hope will follow the other Waves under the Ship and do no harm. I know it is high treason to express a doubt of the perpetual duration of our vast American Empire, and our free Institution[s], and I say as devoutly as Father Paul, estor [i.e., esto] perpetua ["be thou everlasting"], but I am sometimes Cassandra enough to dream that another Hamilton, another Burr might rend this mighty Fabric in twain, or perhaps into a leash, and a few more choice Spirits of the same Stamp, might produce as many Nations in North America as there are in Europe.

To return to the Romans, I never could discover that they possessed much Virtue, or real Liberty there. Patricians were in general griping Usurers and Tyrannical Creditors in all ages. Pride, Strength and Courage were all the Virtues that composed their National Characters. A few of their Nobles effecting simplicity frugality and Piety, perhaps really possessing them, acquired Popularity amongst the Plebeians and extended the power and Dominions of the Republic and advanced in Glory till Riches and Luxury come in, sat like an incubus on the Republic, victamque ulcissitur orbem.[82]

Our Winter setts in a fortnight earlier than usual, and is pretty severe. I hope you have fairer skyes and Milder Air. Wishing your health, may last as long as your Life, and your Life as long as you desire it, I am dear Sir   Respectfuly and affectionately

JOHN ADAMS

82. "And take vengeance on a conquered world."

13

"Calms succeeding the storm which our Argosy . . .
so stoutly weathered"

✳ JANUARY 1820 – APRIL 1826 ✳

A DAMS AND JEFFERSON grew old gracefully, exemplifying some of
the better qualities that Cicero commended in his essay on the
subject, *De Senectute*, familiar to a generation steeped in the classics.
At least three reasons may be suggested for the contentment reflected
in their letters. Retirement, which came in their sixties, resulted from
desire, not compulsion. Adams was eager to return to Quincy in 1801
after his stormy presidential administration. He conceded that "ennui,
when it rains on a man in large drops, is worse than one of our north-
east storms; but the labors of agriculture and amusement of letters will
shelter me." ¹ When Jefferson was welcomed home in 1809 by fellow
citizens of Albemarle County, he told them that the pomp and turmoil
of office during "a wonderful era . . . have drawn but deeper sighs for
the tranquil and irresponsible occupations of private life." ²

In the second place, as philosophers, Adams and Jefferson were
mentally active, whether in reflection on first principles and the order
of the universe or in judgment on contemporary problems. The
"amusement of letters" (i.e., of literature) which occupied much of
their time was well mixed with the writing of letters. Keeping up with
their correspondence and thus abreast of the outside world continually
refreshed and stimulated the confinements of old age.

The third element conducive to happiness late in life was sound
health. Except for brief illnesses, both enjoyed this good fortune until
1818, although by this time the chronic condition of palsy prevented

1. JA to Christopher Gadsden, April 16, 1801, *Works*, IX, 585.
2. TJ "to the Inhabitants of Albemarle County, in Virginia," Ford, IX, 250.

Adams from writing and Jefferson's injured wrist became stiffer with advancing age. The elder statesman fared better than the younger, for Adams's physical condition did not deteriorate seriously until he was almost ninety.[3] In the late summer and early fall of 1818 Jefferson at seventy-five suffered his first prolonged sickness, which was aggravated by the waters of Warm Springs; they proved to be enervating rather than remedial and brought on a chronic condition of discomfort.[4]

Each continued his customary exercise until sheer weakness interfered and prevailed. For Adams it was walking and riding, and, when he could no longer mount his horse, he was still able to "walk three miles over a rugged rockey Mountain" (which should be rendered "hill" for the environs of Quincy).[5] For Jefferson it was riding and walking; he was often on horseback three to four hours a day and at the age of seventy he rode ninety miles to his second home, Poplar Forest, in Bedford County. A decade later, although he could walk from the house only to the near-by garden "and that with sensible fatigue," he might be seen daily near Monticello, mounted on Eagle, who likewise had long since passed his prime.[6] From a broken left arm Jefferson recovered remarkably well at the age of seventy-eight, and his handwriting shows ample evidence of a firm right hand until the last months of his life, even though the wrist was incurably stiff and painful.[7] The two philosophers found some consolation in comparing notes on their afflictions, as octogenarians are wont to do, but these were, for the most part, passing comments by men whose mental vigor was only slightly handicapped by physical infirmities.

In characteristic fashion they harked back occasionally to the distant past of their careers—to the years of the Revolution which had made the most indelible impression on their minds. Who first favored an American navy? How soon did New York support the movement for independence? Was reconciliation with Great Britain still a possibility in 1776? The obituary of a contemporary, the historical background of a current issue, an inquiry concerning the founding of the

3. TJ to Dr. Benjamin Waterhouse, March 3, 1818, Jan. 8, 1825, Ford, X, 103, 336.
4. TJ to JA, May 17, Oct. 7, 1818, above, 524, 528; Dec. 18, 1825, below, 614.
5. JA to TJ, Feb. 3, 1812, above, 296; June 11, 1822, below, 579.
6. TJ to JA, Jan. 21, 1812, above, 292; Aug. 15, 1820, June 1, 1822, below, 565, 578; Randall, *Jefferson*, III, 538.
7. JA to TJ, Dec. 2, 1822, and TJ to JA, Feb. 25, Oct. 12, 1823, Jan. 8, 1825, below, 585-86, 589, 599, 605.

Republic—all put Adams and Jefferson in a reminiscent mood. They became increasingly the arbiters of their country's early history, not by design, but by reason of their venerable reputation and their personification of American patriotism. Although they were no longer guiding the affairs of the nation, they had retained that element of statesmanship which correlates the historical past with the present. They saw their revolution projected into the nineteenth century, not always successfully, in view of the Napoleonic regime and its aftermath, but hopefully nevertheless, as in the case of Greek independence. Despite the prevalence of reactionary governments in Europe, Jefferson maintained that "the flames kindled on the 4th. of July 1776. have spread over too much of the globe to be extinguished by the feeble engines of despotism." [8] As the fiftieth anniversary of the Declaration of Independence approached, these assertions by the last of the signers expressed not the outmoded sentiments of a forgotten generation but rather the spirit of the young Republic.

During the last ten years of his life Jefferson's chief outside concern was the planning and establishing of the University of Virginia. Adams had no comparable absorbing activity, but he never lost interest in political issues. Jefferson had eschewed politics, even restricting his newspaper reading to the Richmond *Enquirer*, edited by his good friend Thomas Ritchie.[9] To the Massachusetts Constitutional Convention of 1820, Adams lent considerable prestige as a delegate (he declined the presidency), although his amendment to the Commonwealth's Bill of Rights, guaranteeing complete religious freedom, failed of adoption. Because he had not engaged in public debate since the convention of 1779, he minimized his part in revising the old constitution: "I boggled and blundered more than a young fellow just rising to speak at the bar." [10] This was his last public appearance, but his interest in national politics continued as keen as ever, for a very good reason. Secretary of State John Quincy Adams was presidential timber and became one of the four candidates in the acrimonious election of 1824. The son was as independent and as much a man of principle as the father—an ex-Federalist, a neo-Jeffersonian, who could do best as a free lance during this period of political transition, who

8. TJ to JA, Sept. 12, 1821, June 1, 1822, and JA to TJ, Dec. 29, 1823, below, 575, 578-79; 602.
9. TJ to Macon, Jan. 12, 1819, Ford, X, 120; Hillard, ed., *Life of Ticknor*, I, 349.
10. JA to TJ, Feb. 3, 1821, Jan. 23, 1825, below, 571-72, 608; C. F. Adams, "Life of John Adams," *Works*, I, 627-28.

was too much the individualist to play well the game of party politics. Although the election had to be settled in the House of Representatives, the victory of the younger Adams must have seemed utterly appropriate and justified to his father, who wrote, "The multitude of my thoughts, and the intensity of my feelings are too much for a mind like mine, in its ninetieth year." [11] Death spared him disappointment over his son's defeat in 1828.

In that phase of history called "past politics" the friendship of Jefferson and Adams had faced its severest tests. As late as 1823 repercussions of political storms of an earlier period threatened, as Jefferson expressed it, "to draw a curtain of separation between you and myself"; [12] but he had not forgotten previous unhappy experiences in which both of them were the victims of malignancy perpetrated by others for political purposes. On a previous occasion Jefferson had been on the spot to explain his words.[13] This time the embarrassment was Adams's, but Jefferson dissolved it with kindness. When it had seemed likely that President Jefferson would be a candidate for re-election in 1804 and the Federalists were seeking every means of recovery from their disastrous defeat of 1800, William Cunningham, one of their henchmen, requested of Adams some statements concerning the President which might be used in the coming campaign. Adams, whose political wounds of 1798-1800 remained unhealed long afterward, obliged Cunningham with some harsh comments on Jefferson, with the understanding that they would not be published during the writer's lifetime. He wished the President no ill, but "I shudder at the calamities which I fear his conduct is preparing for his country: from a mean thirst of popularity, an inordinate ambition, and a want of sincerity." [14] It was a characteristic Adamsian blast with more heat than right reason, unworthy of his honest conviction and his inherent respect for Jefferson. In 1823, immediately after Cunningham's death, his son published Adams's statements to turn discredit onto Adams and refract it toward John Quincy Adams and his presidential ambitions. Jefferson, the original object of attack, would not allow his friendship with John Adams to be exposed to accusations and suspicion derived from an "outrage on private confidence" and the revival of issues long buried. The cool detachment of old age proved

11. JA to J. Q. Adams, Feb. 18, 1825, *Works*, X, 416.
12. TJ to JA, Oct. 12, 1823, below, 600; Randall, *Jefferson*, III, 493.
13. See above, Chap. 7.
14. Gilbert Chinard, *Honest John Adams* (Boston, 1933), 320-21.

to be a saving grace. "It would be strange indeed," observed the Sage of Monticello, "if, at our years, we were to go to an age back to hunt up imaginary, or forgotten facts, to disturb the repose of affections so sweetening to the evening of our lives." [15] This expression of reassurance brought great relief to Adams. In reply he praised it as noble and magnanimous. Although it called for no explanation, Adams made an ineffectual attempt, with a concluding salute of cordial esteem and affection. This letter of November 10 Jefferson endorsed as received ten days later, and he consigned it to oblivion in his files.[16]

Year after year the aging statesmen pursued the epistolary art, to the lasting benefit of posterity. Not that they thought of it as an art; it was a necessity, an integral part of their daily lives. Both complained about the heavy burden of letter writing, but they felt an obligation they could not shirk. Once, in desperation, Adams resorted to two expedients: neglecting to answer his mail and "giving gruff, short, unintelligible, misterious, enigmatical, or pedantical answers." But he could not recommend the first device to Jefferson because one could ill afford deliberately to sacrifice instructive and entertaining letters; as for the second expedient, "this resource is out of your power, because it is not in your nature to avail Yourself of it." [17] Adams was not indulging in flattery but rather bespeaking his understanding of Jefferson's habits and conscience. The latter confessed that he was "drudging at the writing table" from sunrise to one or two o'clock, often from dinner (in the late afternoon) until dark. He begrudged these long hours all the more because they reduced the time available for reading. Although he envied Adams's gratification of a voracious appetite for reading, Jefferson could not rest content with an accumulation of unanswered correspondence.[18]

In 1822, while in one of his moods for recording data, he computed his incoming letters at 1,267 for the year 1820 and many of them required "elaborate research" to answer.[19] These represented an average of twenty-four per week; his replies, often of considerable length, written in his careful, steady hand, confirm the hours of labor that had become habitual early in his career. Adams doubted that he received throughout the year the equivalent of Jefferson's mail in a month or

15. TJ to JA, Oct. 12, 1823, below, 601.
16. JA to TJ, Nov. 10, 1823, below, 601-2.
17. JA to TJ, Feb. 2, 1817, above, 507.
18. TJ to JA, Jan. 11, 1817, above, 505.
19. TJ to JA, June 27, 1822, below, 581.

that ever during his public life he had received one-fourth as many (probably an underestimate), but, he added, "there are reasons enough for the difference." [20] Among those reasons, which he did not enumerate, were the wider range of Jefferson's intellectual interests, his political connections as first head of the Republican party, and the rigid self-discipline he imposed on his time throughout most of a busy life. If this phenomenal production seems less impossible after he retired from public office, the time required for managing his plantations must not be overlooked. One can only wonder how he kept up private as well as public correspondence along with his other duties as governor, diplomat, secretary of state, vice-president, and president of the United States. When Adams reflected on the problem of retiring on a reduced income, he could only conclude that old public servants turned out, "either by legal suffrages or from complaisance to a vulgar opinion," ought to be compensated. No doubt he was thinking of himself as well as Jefferson, and deservedly so. His argument is still applicable today to our higher officials, "for by making them conspicuous, and multiplying their acquaintances, they expose them to expences heavier than when in office." [21]

Although Jefferson had ample justification for expressing hearty agreement with this opinion and for citing his own case to confirm it, his correspondence with Adams contains no mention, indeed no hint, of the indebtedness from which he found it impossible to extricate himself. Jefferson was in large part a victim of postwar inflation and depression in the Old Dominion, with credits on a long-time basis and cash usually a scarce item. His social habits were those of openhanded hospitality in the Virginia tradition. His generosity, embracing financial obligations of others, complemented his hospitality. Perhaps Adams read about the lottery authorized by the state in 1825 to salvage the homestead of Virginia's first citizen and how it was replaced by a less embarrassing private subscription on his behalf by his fellow countrymen in many states.[22] It seemed certain now that Monticello would be saved. This assumption, which proved to be erroneous, put Jefferson's mind at ease during the remaining months of his life, but the menace to his papers and other choice possessions loomed up

20. JA to TJ, July 12, 1822, below, 581-82.
21. *Ibid.* See also TJ to James Madison, May 25, 1788, Boyd, XIII, 201-3.
22. Randall, *Jefferson,* III, 535-37; TJ to Thomas Jefferson Randolph, Feb. 8, 1826, TJ to James Madison, Feb. 17, 1826, TJ to James Monroe, Feb. 22, 1826, Ford, X, 374-79.

ominously. By contrast, Adams faced no such critical circumstances. According to his grandson and biographer, he "lived free from pecuniary obligations of every kind to others, a fate which has not always attached to the incumbents of the highest executive posts in America." [23] And the Adams Papers passed safely from father to son through successive generations.

The Argonauts of the revolutionary era (to use one of Jefferson's last allusions) continued their correspondence to within three months of their deaths. It lapsed in the early spring of 1826 on a pleasant note. Jefferson's favorite grandson and namesake, Thomas Jefferson Randolph, was making a trip to Boston which he could not consider complete without meeting Mr. Adams.[24] The visit was arranged, and young Randolph, in his early thirties, of a stature that impressed the venerable patriot, delivered Jefferson's last letter. It "has been a cordial to me," wrote Adams in his last reply, especially since Randolph was accompanied by Joseph Coolidge, recently married to Jefferson's granddaughter Ellen Wayles Randolph.[25] Thus the two brothers-in-law provided a double tie between Monticello and Montezillo, as Adams several years before had renamed Peacefield, the old house in Quincy.

Adams and Jefferson in collaboration had "done for our country the good which has fallen in our way, so far as commensurate with the faculties given us." [26] They had differed politically, suffered estrangement, and derived fresh satisfaction from renewal of their friendship. More than ever before, their minds were free to express conflicting opinions and to give fair consideration to opposing points of view. They found much in common in their religious ideas but in an era which had achieved religious freedom only haltingly by law and halfheartedly in spirit, they exchanged opinions in private. It was characteristic that Adams, not Jefferson, should have expressed the valedictory: "We shall meet again, so wishes and so believes your friend, but if we are disappointed we shall never know it." [27] Too feeble to accept invitations to celebrations of the fiftieth anniversary of the Declaration of Independence, they anticipated the spirit of the forthcoming occasion, Jefferson in thanking the citizens of Washing-

23. C. F. Adams, "Life of John Adams," *Works*, I, 639.
24. TJ to JA, March 25, 1826, below, 613-14.
25. JA to TJ, April 17, 1826, below, 614.
26. TJ to JA, March 14, 1820, below, 562.
27. JA to TJ, Feb. 25, 1825, below, 610.

ton: "Let the annual return of this day forever refresh our recollections of these rights [of man], and an undiminished devotion to them";
Adams in providing the citizens of Quincy at their request with a
toast: "Independence forever!" [28] On the day of celebration, July 4,
1826, they died, Jefferson at noon, Adams a few hours later.[29]

Adams to Jefferson

Montezillo January 20th. 1820

Dear Sir

When Harris was returned a Member of Parliament a Friend introduced
him to Chesterfield whom he had never seen. So Mr. Harris said his Lord-
ship you are a Member of the House of Commons. You have written upon
Universal and scientifick Grammer! You have written upon Art, upon
Musick, Painting and Poetry! And what has the House of Commons to
do with Art, or Musick, or Painting, or Poetry, or Taste? Have not you
written upon Virtue and Happiness? I have my Lord indulged myself in
Speculations upon those subjects. And what the devil has the House of
Lords to do with either Happiness or Virtue? This Idle Tale which I had
from the mouth of Sir James Harris, now Lord Malmsbury, I repeat to
you for a Preface to another idle tale which I am about to relate to you.

Viz—Too much confined by the Cold Weather, I have for a few days
past whirled away the time in reading these pieces of Harris, and another
intitled Philosophical Arrangements. The Dialogue upon happiness is one
of the first pieces of Morals I ever read; the Hermes is acknowledged a
Master piece. The others under the appearance of immense learning and
much ingenuity contain little information, and few Ideas that are new. I
have read them with the fond delight of a Young Lady reading a Romance,
on account of the investigation of the Sentiments of Ancient Philosophers,
Poets and Orators, and the quotations from them in their own Words—
such by David Williams called the beautiful rags and tatters of Antiquity.
By Philosophical Arrangements he says he means Catigories or Predica-
ments, or general or Universal Truths, or the first Philosophy. But I have
been most amused with his endeavours to find the meaning of the Ancient

28. TJ to Roger C. Weightman, June 24, 1826, Ford, X, 390-92; C. F. Adams, "Life
of John Adams," *Works*, I, 634-35.
29. Lester J. Cappon, "A Postscript from Monticello, July 4, 1826," Albemarle
County Historical Society, *Papers*, 1 (1940-41), 30; C. F. Adams, "Life of John
Adams," *Works*, I, 636.

Philosophers concerning the first Principles, or Elements of Matter which they reduce down to particles, so nice and mince as to become geometrical points, and this seems to me, to be much more Orthodox Philosophy, and Mathematics too, than Buffons Molecules Organiques or Epicurrus's Atoms.[30] With such games at push pins have the Childish Philosophers of all Ages diverted and distracted themselves, not once considering that neither human sense nor imagination nor Intellect were ever formed to comprehend all things. Harris's Dialogue on Happiness is worth all the Metaphysical researches of Philosophers from the beginning of the World into the Nature of Matter and Spirit, of Energy, of Power of Activity of Motion, or any such thing. When we say God is Spirit, we know what we mean as well as we do when we say that the Pyramids of Egypt are Matter. Let us be content therefore to believe Him to be a Spirit, that is, an Essence that we know nothing of, in which Originally and necessarily reside all energy, all Power, all Capacity, all Activity, all Wisdom, all Goodness.

Behold the Creed and Confession of Faith of your ever affectionate Friend

JOHN ADAMS

Adams to Jefferson

Montezillo February 21st. 1820.

DEAR SIR,

Was you ever acquainted with Dugald Stuart? Before I left France I received a letter from Benjamin Vaughn, Esqre. in London, Introducing and recommending in strong terms two Gentlemen from Scotland, one by the name of Dugald Stuart and the other Lord— [31] whose name and title I forget—as young Gentlemen of great talents and attainments sufficient to diminish our American prejudices against Scotland. I received the Letter, but never saw the Gentlemen, from which I conjecture that they did not reach Paris till after I went away, and that you probably had the Satisfaction to enjoy their Company. I regret very much that I missed his Visit. Can you tell me anything of his present State? I am informed that he

30. Buffon's system of organic molecules has been refuted by modern scientists. The principal theory of Epicurus in the field of physics was that all that exists is corporeal: that space is filled with innumerable indivisible atoms in perpetual motion and constantly making new worlds.

31. TJ identifies him in the following letter as Lord Dare, but the Marquis of Lansdowne had only one son in 1787 old enough to travel, John Henry (d. 1809); the title Lord Dare did not exist in the British nobility.

is dying at top, like Sir Isaac Newton and Dr. Swift. I have a prejudice against what they call Metaphysicks because they pretend to fathom deeper than the human line extends. I know not very well what e'er the *to metaphusica* [32] of Aristotle means, but I can form some idea of Investigations into the human mind, and I think Dugald in his Elements of the Philosophy of the human Mind has searched deeper and reasoned more correctly than Aristotle, Des Cartes, Locke, Berkeley, Hume, Condillac and even Reid. I would therefore propose this problem or Theorem for your consideration: whether it would not be adviseable to institute in the Universities Professorships of the Philosophy of the human Understanding, whose object should be to ascertain the Limits of human knowledge already acquired. If I was worth as much money as some of the shop Boys I left in Boston, I would give fifty thousand dollars to establish such a professorship—though I suppose you will have doubts of the propriety of setting any limits, or thinking of any limits of human Power, or human Wisdom, and human Virtue.

I wish the Missouri question may not sett too narrow limits to the Power and Respectability of the United States. Yet I hope some good natureal way or other will be found out to untie this very intricate knot, and am, dear Sir, as ever your friend,

JOHN ADAMS

Jefferson to Adams

Monticello Mar. 14. 20.

DEAR SIR

A continuation of poor health makes me an irregular correspondent. I am therefore your debtor for the two letters of Jan. 20. and Feb. 21. It was after you left Europe that Dugald Stuart, concerning whom you enquire, and L[or]d Dare, second son of the Marquis of Lansdowne came to Paris. They brought me a letter from L[or]d Wycombe whom you knew. I became immediately intimate with Stuart, calling mutually on each other and almost daily, during their stay at Paris, which was of some months. Ld. Dare was a young man of imagination, with occasional flashes indicating deep penetration, but of much caprice, and little judgment. He has been long dead, and the family title is now, I believe, in the 3d son who has shewn in parliament talents of a superior order. Stuart is a great man,

32. These two words were added in JA's hand after his scribe had written the letter.

and among the most honest living. I have heard nothing of his dying at top, as you suppose. Mr. Ticknor however can give you the best information on that subject; as he must have heard particularly of him when in Edinburgh, altho' I believe he did not see him. I have understood he was then in London superintending the publication of a new work. I consider him and Tracy as the ablest Metaphysicians living; by which I mean Investigators of the thinking faculty of man. Stuart seems to have given it's natural history, from facts and observations; Tracy it's modes of action and deducation, which he calls Logic, and Ideology; and Cabanis, in his Physique et Morale de l'homme, has investigated anatomically, and most ingeniously, the particular organs in the human structure which may most probably exercise that faculty. And they ask Why may not the mode of action called thought, have been given to a material organ of peculiar structure? as that of magnetism is to the Needle, or of elasticity to the spring by a particular manipulation of to the steel. They observe that on ignition of the needle or spring, their magnetism and elasticity cease. So on dissolution of the material organ by death it's action of thought may cease also. And that nobody supposes that the magnetism or elasticity retire to hold a substantive and distinct existence. These were qualities only of particular conformations of matter: change the conformation, and it's qualities change also. Mr. Locke, you know, and other materialists have charged with blasphemy the Spiritualists who have denied to the Creator the power of endowing certain forms of matter with the faculty of thought. These however are speculations and subtleties in which, for my own part, I have little indulged myself. When I meet with a proposition beyond finite comprehension, I abandon it as I do a weight which human strength cannot lift: [33] and I think ignorance, in these cases, is truly the softest pillow on which I can lay my head. Were it necessary however to form an opinion, I confess I should, with Mr. Locke, prefer swallowing one incomprehensibility rather than two. It requires one effort only to admit the single incomprehensibility of matter endowed with thought: and two to believe, 1st. that of an existence called Spirit, of which we have neither evidence nor idea, and then 2dly. how that spirit which has neither extension nor solidity, can put material organs into motion. These are things which you and I may perhaps know ere long. We have so lived as to fear neither horn of the dilemma. We have, willingly, done injury to no man; and have done for our country the good which has fallen in our way, so far as commensurate with the faculties given us. That we have not done more than we could cannot be imputed to us as

33. Karl Lehmann, *Thomas Jefferson, American Humanist* (N. Y., 1947), 76, discusses Jefferson's skepticism about human speculation beyond the realm of the tangible.

a crime before any tribunal. I look therefore to that crisis, as I am sure you also do, as one 'qui summum nec metuit diem nec optat.' [34] In the mean time be our last as cordial as were our first affections.

TH: JEFFERSON

Adams to Jefferson

Montezillo May 12th. 1820.

DEAR SIR

I have received with great pleasure your favour of March 14th. Mr. Ticknor informes me that Dugald Stuart was not reduced to a state of Idiocy as I had been informed, but that he was in bad Health, and by the advice of his friends and Physicians to remove to Devenshire in England, in hopes by the change of air, tranquil repose and retirement from the irritations of society, he might recover his health. But he said there was something mysterious in the business and the Gentlemen in Scotland did not love to converse upon the subject, but chose to wave as well as they could, questions concerning it—That he had not been in London superin-tending any work.

This account leaves ample scope for all our conjectures, but in all events it is very melancholy that so profound a genius should be obliged to retire before he had exhausted all his Speculations for the Illumination of his Species; for, indeed, all his writings are melancholy; they are humili-ating; for they show us our ignorance, and the utmost limits to which the human understanding may hope to go in this Inferior World. They ought, however, to be consolatory, because they furnish us with abundance of your pillows of Ignorance—an expression that I very much admire—on which to repose our puzzeld heads.

The question between spirit and matter appears to me nugatory be-cause we have neither evidence nor idea of either. All that we certainly know is that some substance exists, which must be the cause of all the qualitys and Attributes which we perceive: Extension, Solidity, Percep-tion, memory, and Reason, for all these are Attributes, or adjectives, and not Essences or substantives.

Sixty years ago, at College, I read Berkley, and from that time to this I have been fully persuaded that we know nothing of Essences, that some Essence does exist, which causes our minds with all their ideas, and

34. "Who neither fears the final day nor hopes for it."

this visible World with all its wonders. I am certain that this Cause is wise, Benevolent and powerful, beyond all conception; I cannot doubt, but what it is, I cannot conjecture.

Suppose we dwell a little on this matter. The Infinite divisibility of it had long ago been demonstrated by Mathematicians—When the Marquis De L'Hospital arose and demonstrated that there were quantities and not infinitely little, but others infinitely less than those infinitely littles, and he might have gone on, for what I know, to all Eternity demonstrating that there are quantities infinitely less than the last infinitely littles; and the Phenomena of nature seemes to coincide with De L'Hospitals demonstrations. For example, Astronomers inform us that the Star draconis is distant from the Earth 38. 000, 000. 000. 000. miles. The Light that proceeds from that Star, therefore, must fill a Sphere of 78. 000, 000, 000, 000, miles in diameter, and every part of that Sphere equal to the size of the pupil of the human Eye. Light is Matter, and every ray, every pencil of that light is made up of particles very little indeed, if not infinitely little, or infinitely less than infinitely little. If this Matter is not fine enough and subtle enough to perceive, to feel and to think, it is too subtle for any human intellect or imagination to conceive, for I defy any human mind to form any idea of anything so small. However, after all, Matter is but Matter; if it is infinitely less than infinitely little, it is incapable of memory, judgement, or feeling, or pleasure or pain, as far as I can conceive. Yet for anything I know, it may be as capable of Sensation and reflection as Spirit, for I confess I know not how Spirit can think, feel or act, any more than Matter. In truth, I cannot conceive how either can move or think, so that I must repose upon your pillow of ignorance, which I find very soft and consoleing, for it absolves my conscience from all culpability in this respect. But I insist upon it that the Saint has as good a right to groan at the Philosopher for asserting that there is nothing but matter in the Universe, As the Philosopher has to laugh at the Saint for saying that there are both Matter and Spirit, Or as the Infidel has to despise Berckley for saying that we cannot prove that there is anything in the Universe but Spirit and Idea—for this indeed is all he asserted, for he never denied the Existence of Matter. After all, I agree that both the groan and the Smile is impertinent, for neither knows what he says, or what he affirms, and I will say of both, as Turgot says of Berkley in his Article of Existence in the Encyclopedia: it is easier *to despise* than to answer them.

Cabanis's Ignition can destroy nothing in the Magnet. But motion, magnetism, Electricity, Galvanism, Attraction, Repulsion, are nothing but motion, and have no more relation to, Analogy or resemblance to, memory, Perception, conception or Volition, than black has to white, or falshood to truth, or right to wrong. When two Billiard Balls meet and repell each other, we know nothing of the Cause, Contact or repulsion than we do of Spirit. We see nothing but motion in the Case, and what motion is, we know not.

Oh delightful Ignorance! When I arrive at a certainty that I am Ignorant, and that I always must be ignorant, while I live I am happy, for I know I can no longer be responsible.

We shall meet hereafter and laugh at our present botherations. So believes your old Friend,

JOHN ADAMS

Jefferson to Adams

Monticello. Aug. 15. 20.

I am a great defaulter, my dear Sir, in our correspondence, but prostrate health rarely permits me to write; and, when it does, matters of business imperiously press their claims. I am getting better however, slowly, swelled legs being now the only serious symptom, and these, I believe, proceed from extreme debility. I can walk but little; but I ride 6. or 8. miles a day without fatigue; and within a few days, I shall endeavor to visit my other home, after a twelve month's absence from it. Our University, 4. miles distant, gives me frequent exercise, and the oftener as I direct it's architecture. It's plan is unique, and it is becoming an object of curiosity for the traveller. I have lately had an opportunity of reading a critique on this institution in your North American Review of January last, having been not without anxiety to see what that able work would say of us: and I was relieved on finding in it much coincidence of opinion, and even, where criticisms were indulged, I found they would have been obviated had the developements of our plan been fuller. But these were restrained by the character of the paper reviewed, being merely a report of outlines, not a detailed treatise, and addressed to a legislative body, not to a learned academy.[35] E.g. as an inducement to introduce the Anglo-Saxon into our plan, it was said that it would reward amply the *few weeks* of attention which alone would be requisite for it's attainment; leaving both term and degree under an indefinite expression, because I know that not much time is necessary to attain it to an

35. *Proceedings and Report of the Commissioners for the University of Virginia, presented 8th of December 1818* (Richmond, 1818), reviewed in *North American Review*, 10 (Jan. 1820), 115-37.

useful degree, sufficient to give such instruction in the etymologies of our language as may satisfy ordinary students, while more time would be requisite for those who would propose to attain a critical knolege of it. In a letter which I had occasion to write to Mr. Crofts (who sent you, I believe, as well as myself, a copy of his treatise on the English and German languages, as preliminary to an Etymological dictionary he meditated) I went into explanations with him of an easy process for simplifying the study of the Anglo-Saxon, and lessening the terrors, and difficulties presented by it's rude Alphabet, and unformed orthography.[36] But this is a subject beyond the bounds of a letter, as it was beyond the bounds of a Report to the legislature. Mr. Crofts died, I believe, before any progress was made in the work he had projected.

The reviewer expresses doubt, rather than decision, on our placing Military and Naval architecture in the department of Pure Mathematics. Military architecture embraces fortification and field works, which with their bastions, curtains, hornworks, redoubts etc. are based on a technical combination of lines and angles. These are adapted to offence and defence, with and against the effects of bombs, balls, escalades etc. But lines and angles make the sum of elementary geometry, a branch of Pure Mathematics: and the direction of the bombs, balls, and other projectiles, the necessary appendages of military works, altho' no part of their architecture, belong to the conic sections, a branch of transcendental geometry. Diderot and Dalembert therefore, in their Arbor scientiae, have placed military architecture in the department of elementary geometry. Naval architecture teaches the best form and construction of vessels; for which best form it has recourse to the question of the Solid of least resistance, a problem of transcendental geometry. And it's appurtenant projectiles belong to the same branch, as in the preceding case. It is true that so far as respects the action of the water on the rudder and oars, and of the wind on the sails, it may be placed in the department of mechanics, as Diderot and Dalambert have done: but belonging quite as much to geometry, and allied in it's military character, to military architecture, it simplified our plan to place both under the same head. These views are so obvious that I am sure they would have required but a second thought to reconcile the reviewer to their *location* under the head of Pure Mathematics. For this word *Location*, see Bailey Johnson, Sheridan, Walker etc. But if Dictionaries are to be the Arbiters of language, in which of them shall we find *neologism*. No matter. It is a good word, well sounding, obvious, and expresses an idea which would otherwise require circumlocution. The Reviewer was justifiable therefore in using it; altho' he noted at the same time, as unauthoritative, *centrality, grade, sparse;*

36. See Chap. 12, n. 70.

all which have been long used in common speech and writing. I am a friend to *neology*. It is the only way to give to a language copiousness and euphony. Without it we should still be held to the vocabulary of Alfred or of Ulphilas; and held to their state of science also: for I am sure they had no words which could have conveyed the ideas of Oxigen, cotyledons, zoophytes, magnetism, electricity, hyaline, and thousands of others expressing ideas not then existing, nor of possible communication in the state of their language. What a language has the French become since the date of their revolution, by the free introduction of new words! The most copious and eloquent in the living world; and equal to the Greek, had not that been regularly modifiable almost ad infinitum. Their rule was that whenever their language furnished or adopted a root, all it's branches, in every part of speech were legitimated by giving them their appropriate terminations. αδελφος ["brother"]. αδελφη ["sister"]. αδελφιδιον ["little brother"], αδελφοτης ["brotherly affection"], αδελφιξις ["brotherhood"], αδελφιδους ["nephew"], αδελφικος ["brotherly," adj.], αδελφιζω ["to adopt as a brother"], αδελφικως ["brotherly," adv.]. And this should be the law of every language. Thus, having adopted the adjective *fraternal,* it is a root, which should legitimate fraternity, fraternation, fraternisation, fraternism, to fraternate, fraternise, fraternally. And give the word neologism to our language, as a root, and it should give us it's fellow substantives, neology, neologist, neologisation; it's adjectives neologous, neological, neologistical, it's verb neologise, and adverb neologically. Dictionaries are but the depositories of words already legitimated by usage. Society is the work-shop in which new ones are elaborated. When an individual uses a new word, if illformed it is rejected in society, if wellformed, adopted, and, after due time, laid up in the depository of dictionaries. And if, in this process of sound neologisation, our transatlantic brethren shall not choose to accompany us, we may furnish, after the Ionians, a second example of a colonial dialect improving on it's primitive.

But enough of criticism: let me turn to your puzzling letter of May 12. on matter, spirit, motion etc. It's croud of scepticisms kept me from sleep. I read it, and laid it down: read it, and laid it down, again and again: and to give rest to my mind, I was obliged to recur ultimately to my habitual anodyne, 'I feel: therefore I exist.' I feel bodies which are not myself: there are other existencies then. I call them *matter.* I feel them changing place. This gives me *motion.* Where there is an absence of matter, I call it *void,* or *nothing,* or *immaterial space.* On the basis of sensation, of matter and motion, we may erect the fabric of all the certainties we can have or need. I can concieve *thought* to be an action of a particular organisation of matter, formed for that purpose by it's creator, as well as that *attraction* is an action of matter, or *magnetism* of loadstone. When he who denies to the Creator the power of endowing matter with the mode of action called *thinking* shall shew how he could endow the Sun with the mode of action called *attraction,* which reins the planets in the tract of their orbits, or how an absence of matter can have a will, and, by that will, put matter into motion, then the materialist may be lawfully required to explain the process by which matter exercises the faculty of thinking. When once we quit the basis of sensation, all is in the wind. To talk of *immaterial* existences is to talk of *nothings.* To say that the human soul, angels, god, are immaterial, is to say they are *nothings,* or that there is no god, no angels, no soul. I cannot reason otherwise: but I believe I am supported in my creed of materialism by Locke, Tracy, and Stewart. At what age of the Christian church this heresy of *immaterialism,* this masked atheism, crept in, I do not know. But a heresy it certainly is. Jesus taught nothing of it. He told us indeed that 'God is a spirit,' but he has not defined what a spirit is, nor said that it is not *matter.* And the antient fathers generally, if not universally, held it to be matter: light and thin indeed, an etherial gas; but still matter. Origen says 'Deus reapse corporalis est; sed graviorum tantum corporum ratione, incorporeus.' Tertullian 'quid enim deus nisi corpus?' and again 'quis negabit deum esse corpus? Etsi deus spiritus, spiritus etiam corpus est, sui generis, in sua effigie.' St. Justin Martyr 'το Θειον φαμεν ειναι ασωματον· ουκ ότι ασωματον· —επειδη δε το μη κρατεισθαι ύπο τινος, του κρατεισθαι τιμιωτερον εστι, δια τουτο καλουμεν αυτον ασωματον.' And St. Macarius, speaking of angels says 'quamvis enim subtilia sint, tamen in substantiâ, formâ et figurâ, secundum tenuitatem naturae eorum, corpora sunt tenuia.' [37] And St. Austin, St. Basil, Lactantius, Tatian, Athenagoras and others, with whose writings I pretend not a familiarity, are said by those who are, to deliver the same doctrine. Turn to your Ocellus d'Argens 97. 105. and to his Timaeus 17. for these quotations. In England these Immaterialists might have been burnt until the 29. Car. 2. when the writ de haeretico comburendo was abolished: [38]

37. Origen says, "God is in very fact corporeal, but, by reason of so much heavier bodies, incorporeal." Tertullian, "for what is God except body?" and again, "Who will deny that God is body? Although God is spirit, yet spirit is body, of his own nature, in his own image." St. Justin Martyr says, "We say that the divinity is without body, not because it is bodyless, but since the state of not being bounded by anything is a more honorable one than that of being bounded, for this reason we call him bodyless." And St. Macarius, speaking of angels, says, "For although their bodies are of light texture, nevertheless in substance, form, and figure, their bodies are rare, according to the rarity of their nature."

38. On the system of philosophy of the early Church fathers and its origins, see William Enfield, *Of the Philosophy of the Ancient Christians* (London, 1837), Bk. VI. 29. Car. 2. refers to the twenty-ninth year of Charles II's reign, 1678. The writ de haeretico had been used when a heretic was convicted, had abjured, and relapsed into heresy.

and here until the revolution, that statute not having extended to us. All heresies being now done away with us, these schismatists are merely atheists, differing from the material Atheist only in their belief that 'nothing made something,' and from the material deist who believes that matter alone can operate on matter.

Rejecting all organs of information therefore but my senses, I rid myself of the Pyrrhonisms with which an indulgence in speculations hyperphysical and antiphysical so uselessly occupy and disquiet the mind. A single sense may indeed be sometimes decieved, but rarely: and never all our senses together, with their faculty of reasoning. They evidence realities; and there are enough of these for all the purposes of life, without plunging into the fathomless abyss of dreams and phantasms. I am satisfied, and sufficiently occupied with the things which are, without tormenting or troubling myself about those which may indeed be, but of which I have no evidence. I am sure that I really know many, many, things, and none more surely than that I love you with all my heart, and pray for the continuance of your life until you shall be tired of it yourself.

TH: JEFFERSON

Jefferson to Adams

Monticello Jan. 22. 21.

I was quite rejoiced, dear Sir, to see that you had health and spirits enough to take part in the late convention of your state for revising it's constitution, and to bear your share in it's debates and labors. The amendments of which we have as yet heard prove the advance of liberalism in the intervening period; [39] and encourage a hope that the human mind will some day get back to the freedom it enjoyed 2000 years ago. This country, which has given to the world the example of physical liberty, owes to it that of moral emancipation also. For, as yet, it is but nominal with us. The inquisition of public opinion overwhelms in practice the freedom asserted by the laws in theory.

Our anxieties in this quarter are all concentrated in the question What does the Holy alliance, in and out of Congress, mean to do with us on the Missouri question? And this, by the bye, is but the name of the case. It is

39. JA proposed in the convention that the third article of the Massachusetts Bill of Rights be amended to abolish recognition of religious sects by the state. Chinard, *John Adams*, 340-41.

only the John Doe or Richard Roe of the ejectment. The real question, as seen in the states afflicted with this unfortunate population, is Are our slaves to be presented with freedom and a dagger? For if Congress has a power to regulate the conditions of the inhabitants of the states, within the states, it will be but another exercise of that power to declare that all shall be free. Are we then to see again Athenian and Lacedemonian confederacies? To wage another Peloponnesian war to settle the ascendancy between them? Or is this the tocsin of merely a servile war? That remains to be seen: but not I hope by you or me. Surely they will parley awhile, and give us time to get out of the way. What a Bedlamite is man!

But let us turn from our own uneasinesses to the miseries of our Southern friends. Bolivar and Morillo it seems, have come to a parley with dispositions at length to stop the useless effusions of human blood in that quarter. I feared from the beginning that these people were not yet sufficiently enlightened for self-government; and that after wading through blood and slaughter, they would end in military tyrannies, more or less numerous. Yet as they wished to try the experiment, I wished them success in it. They have now tried it, and will possibly find that their safest road will be an accomodation with the mother country, which shall hold them together by the single link of the same chief magistrate, leaving to him power enough to keep them in peace with one another, and to themselves the essential powers of selfgovernment and selfimprovement, until they shall be sufficiently trained by education and habits of freedom to walk safely by themselves. Representative government, native functionaries, a qualified negative on their laws, with a previous security by compact for freedom of commerce, freedom of the press, habeas corpus, and trial by jury, would make a good beginning. This last would be the school in which their people might begin to learn the exercise of civic duties as well as rights. For freedom of religion they are not yet prepared. The scales of bigotry are not sufficiently fallen from their eyes to accept it for themselves individually, much less to trust others with it. But that will come in time, as well as a general ripeness to break entirely from the parent stem.

You see, my dear Sir, how easily we prescribe for others a cure for their difficulties, while we cannot cure our own. We must leave both, I believe, to heaven, and wrap ourselves up in the mantle of resignation, and of that friendship of which I tender to you the most sincere assurances.

TH: JEFFERSON

Adams to Jefferson

Montezillo February 3d. 1821

DEAR SIR

I have just read a sketch of the life of Swedenborg,[40] and a larger work in two huge volumes of Memoirs of John Wesley by Southey, and your kind letter of January 22d. came to hand in the nick of time to furnish me with a very rational exclamation, "What a bedlamite is man!" They are histories of Galvanism and Mesmerism [41] thrown into hotch potch. They say that these men were honest and sincere—so were the Wors[h]ipers of the White Bull in Egypt and now in Calcutta; so were the Worshipers of Bacchus and Venus; so were the worshipers of St. Dominick and St. Bernard. Swedenborg and Westley had certainly vast memories and immaginations, and great talents for Lunaticks.

Slavery in this Country I have seen hanging over it like a black cloud for half a Century. If I were as drunk with enthusiasm as Swedenborg or Westley, I might probably say I had seen Armies of Negroes marching and countermarching in the air, shining in Armour. I have been so terrified with this Phenomenon that I constantly said in former times to the Southern Gentlemen, I cannot comprehend this object; I must leave it to you. I will vote for forceing no measure against your judgements. What we are to see, *God* knows, and I leave it to him, and his agents in posterity. I have none of the genius of Franklin, to invent a rod to draw from the cloud its Thunder and lightning. I have long been decided in opinion that a free government and the Roman Catholick religion can never exist together in any nation or Country, and consequently that all projects for reconciling them in old Spain or new are Eutopian, Platonick and Chimerical. I have seen such a prostration and prostitution of Human Nature to the Priesthood in old Spain as settled my judgment long ago, and I understand that in new Spain it is still worse, if that is possible.

My appearance in the late convention was too ludicrous to be talked of. I was a member in the Convention of 1779, and there I was loquacious enough. I have harrangued and scribbled more than my share, but from that time to the convention in 1820 I never opened my lips in a publick debate. After a total desuetude for 40 years I boggled and blundered

40. By John Clowes, who wrote three works on Baron Swedenborg, published in 1799, 1806, and 1807.

41. Luigi Galvani, Italian physiologist, developed a theory of animal electricity, disputed by Alessandro, Count Volta. Frederick Anton Mesmer believed that an occult force within himself could influence others.

more than a young fellow just rising to speak at the bar. What I said I know not; I believe the Printers have made better speeches than I made for myself. Feeling my weakness, I attempted little and that seldom. What would I give for nerves as good as yours? But as Westley said of himself at my age, "Old time has shaken me by the hand, and parallized it."

What pictures of Monarchy, even limited Monarchy, have the trials of the Duke of York and the Queen of England held up to the astonishment, contempt and scorn of mankind.[42] I should think it would do more than the French and American revolutions to bring it into discredit. Indeed, all human affairs, without your philosophical and Christian mantle of resignation, would be deeply malancholy—even that friendship which I feel for you, ardent and sincere as it is, would be over clouded by constant fears of its termination.

JOHN ADAMS

Adams to Jefferson

Montezillo May 19. 1821

MY DEAR FRIEND

Must We, before We take our departure from this grand and beautiful World, surrender all our pleasing hopes of the progres of Society? Of improvement of the intellectual and moral condition of the World? of the reformation of mankind?

The Piemontese Revolution scarcely assumed a form; and the Neapolitan bubble is burst. And what should hinder the Spanish and Portuguese Constitutions from rushing to the same ruin? [43] The Cortes is in one

42. Frederick Augustus, Duke of York, was dismissed as commander-in-chief of the army for promoting officers who bribed his mistress, Mary Anne Clarke, to use her influence on their behalf. Queen Caroline, a princess of Brunswick, was the wife of George IV. They were married in 1795 when he was prince of Wales but their early separation had resulted from George's intimacy with Mrs. Fitzherbert. Although he broke with her in 1811, George never became reconciled with Caroline, who died soon after his coronation in 1821. Ernest L. Woodward, The Age of Reform (Oxford, 1938), 64-66.

43. In Naples a military mutiny in July 1820 had forced promulgation of a democratic constitution, but in March 1821 an Austrian invasion ended the new regime. A similar development took place in Piedmont in 1821 which was also crushed by Austria. The Spanish democratic constitution of 1812, restored in 1820, was overthrown by a French invasion and succeeded by a reactionary monarchy. Only in Portugal was the democratic constitution of 1820 maintained, in spite of the opposition of the Roman Catholic Church and insistence by Great Britain that the king be restored. Frederick B. Artz, Reaction and Revolution, 1814-1832 (N. Y., 1934), 152-60, 165-70; Oscar Browning, A History of the Modern World (N. Y., 1916), 112-17; Charles D. Hazen, Europe Since 1815 (N. Y., 1910), 49-50, 60-63.

Assembly, vested with the legislative power. The King and his Priests Armies Navies and all other Officers are vested with the Executive Authority of Government. Are not here two Authorities Up, neither Supream? Are they not necessarily Rivals constantly contending like Law Physick and Divinity for Superiority? Are they not two Armies drawn up in battle Array just ready for civil War?

Can a free Government possibly exist with a Roman Catholic Religion?

The Art of Lawgiving is not so easy as that of Architecture or Painting. New York and Rhode Island are struggling for Conventions to reform their Constitutions [44] and I am told there is danger of making them worse. Massachusetts has had her Convention: but our Sovereign Lords The People think themselves wiser than their Representatives, and in several Articles I agree with their Lordships. Yet there never was a cooler, a more patient candid, or a wiser deliberative Body than that Convention.

I may refine too much. I may be an Enthusiast. But I think a free Government is necessarily a complicated Piece of Machinery, the nice and exact Adjustment of whose Springs Wheels and Weights are not yet well comprehended by the Artists of the Age and still less by the People.

I began this letter principally to enquire after your health and to repeat Assurances of the Affection of your Friend

JOHN ADAMS

Adams to Jefferson

Montezillo August 20 1821

DEAR SIR

There are on the Journals of Congress some early resolutions for establishing a Nursery for the education of young men in military Science discipline and tactics; but paper money was so scarce that they never could afford to carry them into execution. When the idea was revived I do not remember; but it has been cherished under Jefferson Madison and Monroe and is now brought to a considerable degree of perfection. The late Visits of the Cadets to several States seem to have made the institution popular.[45]

44. New York held a constitutional convention and adopted a new constitution in 1821, but Rhode Island continued government under her colonial charter until 1840.

45. At a meeting of President Washington's cabinet, Nov. 23, 1793, according to TJ, "It was proposed to recommend the establishmt of a military academy. I objected that none of the specified powers given by the constn to Congress would authorize this. It was therefore referred for further considn and inquiry." "Anas," Ford, I, 269-70. In 1794 Congress established a School for Artillerists and Engineers at West Point, for military training only. During TJ's presidency a superintendent of the Academy was

Would not a similar establishment for the education of naval Officers be equally Usefull.[46] The public Opinion of the nation seems now to be favourable to a Navy as the cheapest and safest Arm for our national defence. Is not this a favourable moment for proposing a naval Accademy?

Floyd is gone! You and Jay and Carrol are all who remain.[47] We shall all be asterised very soon. Sic transit Gloriola (is there such a latin Word?) mundi.

JOHN ADAMS

Jefferson to Adams

Monticello Sep. 12. 21.

DEAR SIR

I am just returned from my other home, and shall within a week go back to it for the rest of the autumn. I find here your favor of Aug. 20. and was before in arrear for that of May 19. I cannot answer, but join in, your question, of May 19. Are we to surrender the pleasing hopes of seeing improvement in the moral and intellectual condition of Man? The events of Naples and Piedmont cast a gloomy cloud over that hope: and Spain and Portugal are not beyond jeopardy. And what are we to think of this Northern triumvirate, arming their nations to dictate despotisms to the rest of the world? And the evident connivance of England, as the price of secret stipulations for continental armies, if her own should take side with her malcontent and pulverised people? And what of the poor Greeks, and their small chance of amelioration even if the hypocritical Autocrat should take them under the iron cover of his Ukazes. Would this be lighter or safer than that of the Turk? [48] These, my dear friend,

appointed, but the type of education for which West Point is noted today was not begun until 1814 when Sylvanus Thayer became superintendent. Edward C. Boynton, *History of West Point* ... (N. Y., 1863), 186, 208, 217.

46. The United States Naval Academy was not established until 1845; George Bancroft, secretary of the navy, deserves chief credit for its founding. Russel B. Nye, *George Bancroft, Brahmin Rebel* (N. Y., 1945), 143-46.

47. William Floyd, of New York, signer of the Declaration of Independence. John Jay was not a signer. See above, TJ to JA, Jan. 21, 1812, above, 292 and n. 38.

48. The Northern Triumvirate consisted of Russia, Prussia, and Austria, authorized by the Congress of Vienna of 1815 to interfere in the internal affairs of the smaller nations to maintain the reactionary peace. The Greek war for independence against Turkey began in 1821 and was encouraged by the "hypocritical Autocrat," Tsar Alexander I of Russia, to embarrass the Turks. When war almost resulted between Russia and Turkey, Austria and Great Britain intervened to persuade the Tsar that it was bad policy to support revolutions. Nevertheless, Greek independence was proclaimed in Jan. 1822. Artz, *Reaction and Revolution*, 162-72, 207-8, 247-62, esp. 255.

are speculations for the new generation, as, before they will be resolved, you and I must join our deceased brother Floyd. Yet I will not believe our labors are lost. I shall not die without a hope that light and liberty are on steady advance. We have seen indeed once within the records of history a compleat eclipse of the human mind continuing for centuries. And this too by swarms of the same Northern barbarians, conquering and taking possession of the countries and governments of the civilized world. Should this be again attempted, should the same Northern hordes, allured again by the corn wine, and oil of the South, be able again to settle their swarms in the countries of their growth, the art of printing alone, and the vast dissemination of books, will maintain the mind where it is, and raise the conquering ruffians to the level of the conquered, instead of degrading these to that of their conquerors. And even should the cloud of barbarism and despotism again obscure the science and liberties of Europe, this country remains to preserve and restore light and liberty to them. In short, the flames kindled on the 4th. of July 1776. have spread over too much of the globe to be extinguished by the feeble engines of despotism. On the contrary they will consume those engines, and all who work them.

I think with you that there should be a school of instruction for our navy as well as artillery; and I do not see why the same establishment might not suffice for both.[49] Both require the same basis of general mathematics, adding projectiles and fortification for the artillery exclusively, and Astronomy and theory of navigation exclusively for the Naval students. Bezout conducted both schools in France, and has left us the best book extant for their joint and separate instruction. It ought not to require a separate professor.

A 4th. of July oration delivered in the town of Milford in your state gives to Samuel Chase the credit of having 'first started the cry of independance in the ears of his countrymen.' Do you remember anything of this? I do not. I have no doubt it was uttered in Massachusets even before it was by Thomas Paine. But certainly I never considered Samuel Chase as foremost, or even forward in that hallowed cry. I know that Maryland hung heavily on our backs, and that Chase, altho' first named, was not most in unison with us of that delegation, either in politics or morals, et c'est ainsi que l'on ecrit l'histoire ["and thus it is that history is written"]!

Your doubt of the legitimacy of the word *gloriola* is resolved by

---

49. In a special message of March 18, 1808, President Jefferson had advised Congress that the military academy was too limited in its subjects and recommended that it be transferred to Washington so that perhaps the Navy might have a part in it. Lipscomb and Bergh, eds., *Writings*, III, 471-72.

Cicero, who in his letter to Lucceius expresses a wish '*ut nos metipsi vivi gloriola nostra perfruamur* ["that we ourselves while living might enjoy our little bit of glory"].' Affectly. Adieu.

TH: JEFFERSON

Adams to Jefferson

Montizello 24 Septr. 1821.

DEAR SIR

I thank you for your favour of the 12 inst. Hope springs eternal. Eight millions of Jews hope for a Messiah more powerful and glorious than Moses, David, or Solomon, who is to make them as powerful as he pleases. Some hundreds of millions of Musslemen expect another Prophet more powerful than Mahomet who is to spread Islamism over the whole earth. Hundreds of millions of Christians expect and hope for a millenium in which Jesus is to reign for a thousand years over the whole world before it is burnt up. The Hindoos expect another and a final incarnation of Vishnu who is to do great and wonderful things, I know not what. All these hopes are founded on real or pretended revelation. The modern Greeks too it seems hope for a deliverer who is to produce them. The Themistoclese's and Demostheneses—The Plato's and Aristotle's The Solon's and Lycurgus'. On what prophecies they found their belief I know not. You and I hope for splendid improvements in human society and vast ameliorations in the condition of mankind. Our faith may be supported by more rational arguments than any of the former. I own that I am very sanguine in the belief of them as I hope and believe you are and your reasoning in your Letter confirmed me in them. As Brother Floyd has gone I am now the oldest of the little Congressional group that remain. I may therefore rationally hope to be the first to depart; and as you are the youngest and the most energetic in mind and body, you may therefore rationally hope to be the last to take your flight and to rake up the fire as father Sherman who always staid to the last and commonly two days afterwards used to say, "that it was his office to sit up and rake the ashes over the coals" and much satisfaction may you have in your office.

The Cholera Morbus has done wonders in St. Helena and in London. We shall soon hear of a Negociation for a second Wife. Whether in the body or out of the body I shall always be your friend.

The anecdote of Mr. Chase contained in the Oration delivered at Milford must be an idle rumour for neither the State of Maryland nor [any] of their Delegates were very early in their conviction of the necessity of Independence, nor very forward in promoting it. The old Speaker Tilghman, Johnson, Chase, and Paca, were steady in promoting resistance but after some of them Maryland sent one at least of the most turbulent Tory's that ever came to Congress.[50]

JOHN ADAMS

Jefferson to Adams

Monticello June 1. 22.

It is very long, my dear Sir, since I have written to you. My dislocated wrist is now become so stiff that I write slowly and with pain, and therefore write as little as I can. Yet it is due to mutual friendship to ask once in a while how we do? The papers tell us that Genl. Starke is off at the age of 93. Charles Thomson still lives at about the same age, chearful, slender as a grasshopper, and so much without memory that he scarcely recognises the members of his household. An intimate friend of his called on him not long since: it was difficult to make him recollect who he was, and, sitting one hour, he told him the same story 4. times over. Is this life?

> With lab'ring step
> To tread our former footsteps? pace the round
> Eternal?—to beat and beat
> The beaten track? to see what we have seen
> To taste the tasted? o'er our palates to decant
> Another vintage? [51]

It is at most but the life of a cabbage, surely not worth a wish. When all our faculties have left, or are leaving us, one by one, sight, hearing, memory, every avenue of pleasing sensation is closed, and athumy, debility and mal-aise left in their places, when the friends of our youth are all

50. Is TJ referring to Thomas Stone, who voted for independence but favored the peace negotiations with Lord Howe in Sept. 1776? Mary E. Fittro, "Stone, Thomas," *DAB*, XVIII, 84.
51. See Edward Young, *Night Thoughts on Life, Death and Immortality*, ed. by James Robert Boyd (N.Y., 1851), 157. TJ earlier quoted a portion of this poem in his letter to AA, Jan. 11, 1817, above, 504.

gone, and a generation is risen around us whom we know not, is death an evil?

> When one by one our ties are torn,
> And friend from friend is snatched forlorn
> When man is left alone to mourn,
> Oh! then how sweet it is to die!
> When trembling limbs refuse their weight,
> And films slow gathering dim the sight,
> When clouds obscure the mental light
> Tis nature's kindest boon to die!

I really think so. I have ever dreaded a doting old age; and my health has been generally so good, and is now so good, that I dread it still. The rapid decline of my strength during the last winter has made me hope sometimes that I see land. During summer I enjoy it's temperature, but I shudder at the approach of winter, and wish I could sleep through it with the Dormouse, and only wake with him in spring, if ever. They say that Starke could walk about his room. I am told you walk well and firmly. I can only reach my garden, and that with sensible fatigue. I ride however daily. But reading is my delight. I should wish never to put pen to paper; and the more because of the treacherous practice some people have of publishing one's letters without leave. L[or]d Mansfield declared it a breach of trust, and punishable at law. I think it should be a penitentiary felony. Yet you will have seen that they have drawn me out into the arena of the newspapers. Altho' I know it is too late for me to buckle on the armour of youth, yet my indignation would not permit me passively to receive the kick of an Ass.[52]

To turn to the news of the day, it seems that the Cannibals of Europe are going to eating one another again. A war between Russia and Turkey is like the battle of the kite and snake. Whichever destroys the other, leaves a destroyer the less for the world. This pugnacious humor of mankind seems to be the law of his nature, one of the obstacles to too great multiplication provided in the mechanism of the Universe. The cocks of the henyard kill one another up. Boars, bulls, rams do the same. And the horse, in his wild state, kills all the young males, until worn down with

---

52. TJ to Messrs. Ritchie and Gooch, May 13, 1822, thanking them for the paper "containing the arraignment of the Presidents of the United States generally, as peculators or accessories to peculation, by an informer who masks himself under the signature of a 'Native Virginian.'" The part relating to TJ was first published in the Baltimore *Federal Republican* "during the ferment of a warmly-tested election," and a copy was sent to him. He then explained to Ritchie and Gooch, editors of the Richmond *Enquirer,* how accounts owed him for his diplomatic service were still unpaid by the government after 1789 and how they were settled. Lipscomb and Bergh eds., *Writings,* XV, 365-70.

age and war, some vigorous youth kills him, and takes to himself the Haram of females. I hope we shall prove how much happier for man the Quaker policy is, and that the life of the feeder is better than that of the fighter: and it is some consolation that the desolation by these Maniacs of one part of the earth is the means of improving it in other parts. Let the latter be our office. And let us milk the cow, while the Russian holds her by the horns, and the Turk by the tail. God bless you, and give you health, strength, good spirits, and as much of life as you think worth having.

TH: JEFFERSON

Adams to Jefferson

Montezillo June 11th. 1822.

DEAR SIR,

Half an hour ago I received, and this moment have heard read for the third or fourth time, the best letter that ever was written by an Octogenearian, dated June the 1st. It is so excellent that I am almost under an invincible temptation to commit a breach of trust by lending it to a printer. My Son, Thomas Boylston, says it would be worth five hundred dollars to any newspaper in Boston, but I dare not betray your confidence.

I have not sprained my wrist, but both my Arms and hands are so over strained that I cannot write a line. Poor Starke remembered nothing, and talked of nothing, but the Battle of Bennington. Poor Thomson is not quite so reduced. I cannot mount my Horse, but I can walk three miles over a rugged rockey Mountain, and have done it within a Month. Yet I feel when setting in my chair, as if I could not rise out of it, and when risen, as if I could not walk across the room; my sight is very dim; hearing pritty good; memory poor enough.

I answer your question, Is Death an Evil? It is not an Evil. It is a blessing to the individual, and to the world. Yet we ought not to wish for it till life becomes insupportable; we must wait the pleasure and convenience of this great teacher. Winter is as terrible to me, as to you. I am almost reduced in it, to the life of a Bear or a torpid swallow. I cannot read, but my delight is to hear others read, and I tease all my friends most unmercifully and tyrannically, against their consent. The Ass has kicked in vain, all men say the dull animal has missed the mark.

This globe is a Theatre of War, its inhabitants are all heroes. I believe the little Eels in Vinegar and the animalcule in pepper water, I believe are quarrelsome. The Bees are as warlike as Romans, Russians, Britains, or Frenchmen. Ants or Caterpilars and Canker worms are the only tribes amongst whom I have not seen battles. And Heaven itself, if we believe Hindoos, Jews, and Christians, has not always been at peace. We need not trouble ourselves about these things nor fret ourselves because of Evil doers but safely trust the ruler with his skies. Nor need we dread the approach of dotage, let it come if it must. Thomson, it seems, still delights in his four stories. And Starke remembers to the last his Bennington, and exulted in his Glory. The worst of the Evil is that our friends will suffer more by our imbecility than we ourselves.

Diplomatic flickerings, it seemes, have not yet ceased. It seems as if a Council of Ambassadors could never agree.

In wishing for your health and happiness I am very selfish, for I hope for more letters; this is worth more than five hundred dollars to me, for it has already given me, and will continue to give me more pleasure than a thousand. Mr. Jay who is about your age I am told experiences more decay than you do. I am your old friend

JOHN ADAMS

Jefferson to Adams

Monticello June 27. 22.

DEAR SIR

Your kind letter of the 11th. has given me great satisfaction for altho' I could not doubt but that the hand of age was pressing heavily on you, as on myself, yet we like to know the particulars and the degree of that pressure. Much reflection too has been produced by your suggestion of lending my letter of the 1st. to a printer. I have generally great aversion to the insertion of my letters in the public papers; because of my passion for quiet retirement and never to be exhibited in scene on the public stage. Nor am I unmindful of the precept of Horace 'solvere senescentem, mature sanus equum, ne peccet ad extremum ridendus.' [53] In the present case however I see a possibility that this might aid in producing the very quiet after which I pant. I do not know how far you may suffer as I do, under the persecution of letters, of which every mail brings a fresh load. They are letters of enquiry for the most part, always of good will, sometimes from friends whom I esteem, but much oftener from persons whose names

53. "Set free an aging horse in a rational state lest he, being made sport of, make a complete fool of himself."

are unknown to me, but written kindly and civilly, and to which therefore civility requires answers. Perhaps the better known failure of your
hand in it's function of writing, may shield you in greater degree from
this distress, and so far qualify the misfortune of it's disability. I happened
to turn to my letter-list some time ago, and a curiosity was excited to
count those recieved in a single year. It was the year before the last. I
found the number to be 1267. many of them requiring answers of elaborate
research, and all to be answered with due attention and consideration. Take
an average of this number for a week or a day, and I will repeat the question suggested by other considerations in mine of the 1st. Is this life? At
best it is but the life of a mill-horse, who sees no end to his circle but in
death. To such a life that of a cabbage is paradise. It occurs then that my
condition of existence, truly stated in that letter, if better known, might
check the kind indiscretions which are so heavily oppressing the departing
hours of life. Such a relief would to me be an ineffable blessing. But yours
of the 11th. equally interesting and affecting, should accompany that to
which it is an answer. The two taken together would excite a joint interest,
and place before our fellow-citizens the present condition of two antient
servants, who having faithfully performed their 40. or 50. campaigns,
stipendiis omnibus expletis [after all their military duty had been com-
pleted], have a reasonable claim to repose from all disturbance in the
Sanctuary of Invalids and Superannuates. But some device should be
thought of for their getting before the public otherwise than by our
own publication. Your printer perhaps could frame something plausible.
C. Thomson's name should be left blank, as his picture, should it meet
his eye, might give him pain. I consign however the whole subject to your
consideration, to do in it whatever your own judgment shall approve, and
repeat always with truth the assurances of my constant and affectionate
friendship and respect.

TH: JEFFERSON

Adams to Jefferson

Quincy Montezillo July 12th. 1822

DEAR SIR

Yours of the 27th June is received with pleasure, for the free air of it
delights me.

Your number of 1267. letters in a year does not surprise me; I have no
list of mine; and I could not make one without a weeks research, and I do
not believe I ever received one quarter part of your number. And I very

much doubt whether I received in the same year one twelfth part; there are reasons enough for the difference.

I hope one day your letters will be all published in volumes; they will not always appear Orthodox, or liberal in politicks; but they will exhibit a Mass of Taste, Sense, Literature and Science, presented in a sweet simplicity and a neat elegance of Stile, which will be read with delight in future ages. I think that when a people turn out their old servants, either by legal suffrages or from complaisance to a vulgar opinion, they ought to grant them, at least, an outfit; for by making them conspicuous, and multiplying their acquaintances, they expose them to expences heavier than when in office. Your stationary bill alone for paper, Quills, Ink, Wafers, Wax, Sand and Pounce, must have amounted to enough to maintain a small family. I never can forgive New York, Connecticut, or Maine for turning out Venerable Men of sixty or seventy from the seats of Judgement, when their judgement is often the best.[54] To turn out such men to eat husks with the prodigal or grass with Nebuchadnezzar ought to be tormenting to the humanity of the Nation; it is infinitely worse than sa[y]ing "go up thou bald Head." For my part, my blindness and Palsy lay me under a necessity of neglecting to answer many letters, and other kind civilities which otherwise I should delight to acknowledge. I believe it will be best to brave it out; it will be impossible to conceal anything. I am your friend of forty seven Years Standing.

JOHN ADAMS

Adams to Jefferson

Montezillo October 15th. 1822

DEAR SIR.

I have long entertained scruples about writing this letter, upon a subject of some delicacy. But old age has over-come at last.

You remember the four Ships, ordered by Congress to be built, and the four Captains appointed by Washington—Talbot and Truxton and Barry etc. to carry an Ambassador to Algiers and protect our Commerce in the

54. In the new constitutions of Connecticut (1818) and New York (1821) age was a qualification for judges of the higher courts (the maximum was seventy and sixty respectively). This was not so in Maine, which JA may have confused with New Hampshire (age seventy under the constitution of 1792). Thorpe, ed., *Federal and State Constitutions*, I, 536-555; V, 2639-51; IV, 271-90.

Mediterranean. I have always imputed this measure to you; for several reasons.[55] First, Because you frequently proposed it to me while we were at Paris, negotiating together for peace with the Barbary powers. 2dly. Because I knew that Washington and Hamilton, were not only indifferent about a Navy, but averse to it. There was no Secretary of the Navy; only four heads of Departments. You were Secretary of State; Hamilton Secretary of the Treasury, Knox Secretary of War; and I believe Bradford was Attorney General. I have always suspected that you and Knox were in favour of a Navy. If Bradford was so, the majority was clear. But Washington, I am confident was against it in his judgment. But his attachment to Knox and his deference to your opinion, for I know he had a great regard for you—might induce him to decide in favour of you and Knox, even though Bradford united with Hamilton in opposition to you. That Hamilton was averse to the measure, I have personal evidence, for while it was pending, he came in a hurry and a fit of impatience, to make a visit to me. He said he was like to be called upon for a large sum of money to build Ships of War, to fight the Algerines and he asked my opinion of the measure. I answered him that I was clearly in favour of it. For I had always been of Opinion, from the Commencement of the Revolution, that a Navy was the most powerful, the safest and the cheapest National defence for this Country. My advice therefore was that as much of the Revenue as could possibly be spared, should be applied to the building and equipping of Ships. The conversation was of some length, but it was manifest in his looks and in his air that he was disgusted at the measure as well as at my opinion, that I had expressed.

Mrs. Knox, not long since, wrote a letter to Dr. Waterhouse,[56] requesting him to procure a Commission for her Son, in the Navy; that Navy, says her Ladyship, of which his Father was the parent, for, says she, "I have frequently heard General Washington say to my husband; the Navy was your Child." I have always believed it to be Jefferson's child, though Knox may have assisted in ushering it into the world. Hamilton's hobby was the Army. That Washington was averse to a Navy, I have full proof from his own lips, in many different conversations, some of them of length, in which he always insisted that it was only building and arming Ships for the English.

55. Congress authorized six frigates in 1794, including the *Constitution, Chesapeake,* and *Constellation.* The captains of the new Navy, chosen that year, were Joshua Barney, John Barry, Richard Dale, Samuel Nicholson, Silas Talbot, and Thomas Truxton. Barney declined to serve because he was put under Talbot, his junior. Edgar S. Maclay, *A History of the United States Navy from 1775 to 1901* (N. Y., 1901), I, 158-60. JA had asked these questions about the Navy in his letter of June 11, 1813, Chap. 9, n. 70, 328.

56. See TJ to JA, May 17, 1818, above, 523.

Si quid novisti rectius istis, Candidus imperti,
Si Non, his utere mecum." [57]

If I am in error in any particular, pray correct Your Humble Servt.

JOHN ADAMS

Jefferson to Adams

Monticello Nov. 1. 22.

DEAR SIR

I have racked my memory, and ransacked my papers to enable myself to answer the enquiries of your favor of Oct. 15. but to little purpose. My papers furnish me nothing, my memory generalities only. I know that while I was in Europe, and anxious about the fate of our seafaring men, for some of whom, then in captivity in Algiers we were treating, and all were in like danger, I formed undoubtingly the opinion that our government, as soon as practicable, should provide a naval force sufficient to keep the Barbary states in order, and on this subject we communicated together as you observe. When I returned to the US. and took part in the administration under Genl. Washington I constantly maintained that opinion, and in Dec. 90. took advantage of a reference to me from the first Congress which met after I was in office to report in favor of a force sufficient for the protection of our Mediterranean commerce, and I laid before them an accurate statement of the whole Barbary force, public and private.[58] I think Genl. Washington approved of building vessels of war to that extent. Genl. Knox I know did. But what was Colo. Hamilton's opinion I do not in the least remember. Your recollections on that subject are certainly corroborated by his known anxieties for a close connection with Great Britain, for which he might apprehend danger from collisions between their vessels and ours. Randolph was then Attorney General; but his opinion on the question I also entirely forget. Some vessels of war were accordingly built and sent into the Mediterranean. The additions to these in your time I need not note to you, who are well known to have ever been an advocate for the wooden walls of Themistocles. Some of those you added were sold under an act of Congress passed while you

57. "If you know anything more correct than these, candidly share them; if not make use of these with me."
58. "Report relative to the Mediterranean Trade," Dec. 28, 1790, Washington, ed., Writings, VII, 519-32.

were in office. I thought afterwards that the public safety might require some additional vessels of strength to be prepared and in readiness for the first moment of a war, provided they could be preserved against the decay which is unavoidable if kept in the water, and clear of the expence of officers and men. With this view I proposed that they should be built in dry docks above the level of the tide waters, and covered with roofs. I further advised that places for these docks should be selected where there was a command of water on a higher level, as that of the Tyber at Washington, by which the vessels might be floated out, on the principle of a lock. But the majority of the legislature was against any addition to the navy, and the minority, altho' for it in judgment, voted against it on a principle of opposition. We are now, I understand building vessels to remain on the stocks under shelter until wanted, when they will be launched and finished. On my plan they could be in service at an hour's notice. On this the finishing, after launching will be a work of time. This is all I recollect about the origin and progress of our navy. That of the late war certainly raised our rank and character among nations. Yet a navy is a very expensive engine. It is admitted that in 10. or 12. years a vessel goes to entire decay; or, if kept in repair costs as much as would build a new one. And that a nation who could count on 12. or 15. years of peace would gain by burning it's navy and building a new one in time. It's extent therefore must be governed by circumstances. Since my proposition for a force adequate to the pyracies of the Mediterranean, a similar necessity has arisen in our own seas for considerable addition to that force. Indeed I wish we could have a convention with the naval powers of Europe for them to keep down the pyrates of the Mediterranean, and the slave ships on the coast of Africa, and for us to perform the same duties for the society of nations in our seas. In this way those collisions would be avoided between the vessels of war of different nations, which beget wars and constitute the weightiest objection to navies. I salute you with constant affection and respect.

TH: JEFFERSON

Adams to Jefferson

Montezillo 2d. December. 1822

DEAR SIR

I have been deeply afflicted with the account of your accident. At first your Leg was broke—I shuddered, I feared that I should have no more letters from Montecello. Next came the account that it was only a small bone in the Arm. My hopes revived. The difference between the leg and the Arm was immense. To illustrate this difference, and for your consolation and amusement, I will give you an egotistical anecdote. When one of the Comets was here in our neighborhood I went out one evening into my garden to look at the wandering Star, with four or five Gentlemen. We returned through an alley over which my Men had placed a strong stake to prevent a peach tree from breaking down with its load of fruit. In the dark I blundered against this stake, broke its fastness—it fell and I with it on the sharp edge of a knot in it. I felt a sharp cut but thought it had only broke the skin. I scampered up and returned to the house with the other Gentlemen. My Daughter Smith cryed out, Sir, what has happened to you, your Leg is all bloody. I strip[p]ed off the stocking and low[!] a gash from half an inch, to an inch deep cut by the sharp knot, bleeding profusely. My Daughter cried out, bring me some Laudanum. I knew no better. Her Mother [who] always had an Apothecarys Shop in her closet instantly brought a Bottle. They poured a quantity of it into the wound and washed the neighboring flesh with it, [and] bound a bandage around it, but it produced an inflamation which cost me a confinement for two months. Several surgeons came to see me and all agreed that neither the genius nor experience of Philosophers, Physicians nor surgeons had hitherto invented any means of preventing the humours falling down into a wound in the Leg but by holding it up. They accordingly compelled me to hold mine almost perpendicularly, oftener lieing on my back on a Sofa oftener at an angle of forty five but never lower than an horizontal line. In this manner they made me vegitate for two months suffering continual twinges on the shin. The Bathes, tents and bandages and lotions I pass over. I verily believe that if nothing had been done to it but washing in warm water it would have been well in three days. You may console yourself with the hope that your Arm will soon be well; you will not be obliged to hold your arm up pointing to the skies.

If you cannot write yourself, pray the fair lovely and accomplished Miss Hellen Randolph [59] to write a line to inform me of your recovery. Your affectionate friend,

JOHN ADAMS

59. Ellen Randolph, TJ's granddaughter, the third daughter of Thomas Mann Randolph and Martha Jefferson Randolph.

Adams to Jefferson

Quincy February 10th. 1823.

DEAR SIR

Your Virginia Ladies have always been represented to me, and I have always believed it, as among the most beautiful, virtuous, and accomplished of their Sex. One of them has given me a most luxurious entertainment in a narration of her Visit to your Domicil.[60] Her description of the Mountain, the Palace, the Gardens, the vast Prospect, The lofty Mountains at a distance, The Capacious Valley between them, The Oceans of Fogg and Vapours appearing in the morning, Their dissipation with the rising Sun, and everything else, are painted in colours so distinct and lively that I seem to have as cleare an idea of the whole scene, as if I had led her by the hand, in all her rambles. Her account of the hospitality of the Family almost gave me a jealous and envious fit, as Swift says Popes Couplet gave him.[61]

But now to the point: This Lady says she saw in your sanctum sanctorum a large folio Volume on which was written libels, on opening which she found it was a Magazine of Slips of newspapers, and pamphlets, vilifying, calumniating and defaming you. I started as from a trance, exclaiming, what a dunce have I been all my days, and what lubbers my Children, and Grand Children, were, that none of us have ever thought to make a similar collection. If we had I am confident I could have produced a more splendid Mass than yours. I could have enumerated Alexander Hamilton, and Thomas Paine,[62] The two most extraordinary Men that

60. JA may have been referring to Mrs. Margaret Bayard Smith's account of her visit to Monticello in 1809. Gaillard Hunt, ed., *The First Forty Years of Washington Society, portrayed by the Family Letters of Mrs. Samuel Harrison Smith* ... (N. Y., 1906), 65-81.

61. "On the Death of Dr. Swift, 1731":

> In POPE, I cannot read a Line,
> But with a Sigh, I wish it mine:
> When he can in one Couplet fix
> More Sense than I can do in Six:
> It gives me such a jealous Fit,
> I cry, Pox take him, and his Wit.

Harold Williams, ed., *The Poems of Jonathan Swift* (Oxford, 1937), II, 555.

62. Hamilton printed his bitter denunciation of JA in *Letter from Alexander Hamilton, concerning the Public Conduct and Character of John Adams, Esq., President of the United States* (N. Y., 1800). Paine's attack on JA appeared in a series of articles entitled "To the Citizens of the United States and Particularly to the Leaders of Federal Faction," *National Intelligencer*, Washington, Nov. 1802, especially in Letter II (Nov. 22). Philip S. Foner, ed., *The Complete Writings of Thomas Paine* (N. Y., 1945), II, 912-18.

this Country, this Age or this World, ever produced. "Ridendo dicere verum quid vetat?" [63]

I most sincerely congratulate you on the recovery of your hand, and am your friend for this, and, I hope, and believe, for all future Worlds

J. ADAMS

Jefferson to Adams

Monticello Feb. 25. 23.

DEAR SIR

I recieved in due time your two favors of Dec. 2. and Feb. 10. and have to acknolege for the ladies of my native state their obligations to you for the encomiums which you are so kind as to bestow on them. They certainly claim no advantages over those of their sister states, and are sensible of more favorable circumstances existing with many of them, and happily availed of, which our situation does not offer. But the paper respecting Monticello to which you allude was not written by a Virginian, but by a visitant from another state; and written by memory at least a dozen years after the visit. This has occasioned some lapses of recollection, and a confusion of some things in the mind of our friend, and particularly as to the volume of slanders supposed to have been cut out of newspapers and preserved. It would not indeed have been a single volume, but an Encyclopedia in bulk. But I never had such a volume. Indeed I rarely thought those libels worth reading, much less preserving and remembering. At the end of every year, I generally sorted all my pamphlets, and had them bound according to their subjects. One of these volumes consisted of personal altercations between individuals, and calumnies on each other. This was lettered on the back 'Personalities,' and is now in the library of Congress. I was in the habit also, while living apart from my family, of cutting out of the newspapers such morsels of poetry, or tales as I thought would please, and of sending them to my grand-children who pasted them on leaves of blank paper and formed them into a book.[64] These two volumes have been confounded into one in the recollection of

63. "What forbids me to speak the truth by joking?"
64. See Constance E. Thurlow and Francis L. Berkeley, Jr., comps., *The Jefferson Papers of the University of Virginia. A Calendar* (Charlottesville, 1950), item 759: "Scrapbook of Songs and Poems. [1801 *et seq.*] 204 pp."

our friend. Her poetical imagination too has heightened the scenes she visited, as well as the merits of the inhabitants to whom her society was a delightful gratification.

I have just finished reading O'Meara's Bonaparte.[65] It places him on a higher scale of understanding than I had allotted him. I had thought him the greatest of all military captains, but an indifferent statesman and misled by unworthy passions. The flashes however which escape from him in these conversations with O'Meara prove a mind of great expansion, altho' not of distinct developement and reasoning. He siezes results with rapidity and penetration, but never explains logically the process of reasoning by which he arrives at them. This book too makes us forget his atrocities for a moment in commiseration of his sufferings. I will not say that the authorities of the world, charged with the care of their country and people had not a right to confine him for life, as a Lyon or Tyger, on the principle of self-preservation. There was no safety to nations while he was permitted to roam at large. But the putting him to death in cold blood by lingering tortures of mind, by vexations, insults, and deprivations, was a degree of inhumanity to which the poisonings, and assassinations of the school of Borgia and the den of Marat never attained. The book proves also that nature had denied him the moral sense, the first excellence of well organised man. If he could seriously and repeatedly affirm that he had raised himself to power without ever having committed a crime, it proves that he wanted totally the sense of right and wrong. If he could consider the millions of human lives which he had destroyed or caused to be destroyed, the desolations of countries by plunderings, burnings and famine, the destitutions of lawful rulers of the world without the consent of their constituents, to place his brothers and sisters on their thrones, the cutting up of established societies of men and jumbling them discordantly together again at his caprice, the demolition of the fairest hopes of mankind for the recovery of their rights, and amelioration of their condition, and all the numberless train of his other enormities; the man, I say, who could consider all these as no crimes must have been a moral monster, against whom every hand should have been lifted to slay him.

You are so kind as to enquire after my health. The bone of my arm is well knitted, but my hand and fingers are in a discouraging condition, kept entirely useless by an oedematous swelling of slow amendment. God bless you and continue your good health of body and mind.

TH: JEFFERSON

65. Barry Edward O'Meara, *Napoleon in Exile; or, A Voice from St. Helena*... (2nd edn., Philadelphia, 1822).

Adams to Jefferson

Quincy March 10th. 1823.

DEAR SIR.

The sight of your well known hand writing in your favour of 25. Feb. last, gave me great pleasure, as it proved your arm to be restored and your pen still manageable. May it continue till you shall become as perfect a calvinist as I am in one particular. Poor Calvins infirmities his rheumatism his Gouts and sciatics made him frequently cry out Mon dieu Jusque au quand. Lord how long! Prat once Chief Justice of New York always tormented with infirmities dreamt that he was situated on a single rock in the midst of the Atlantick ocean. He heard a voice—"Why mourns the bard Apollo bids thee rise, renounce the dust, and claim thy native skies."

The Ladies visit to Monticello has put my reader in requisition to read to me Simons travels in Switzerland.[66] I thought I had some knowledge of that country before, but I find I had no idea of it. How degenerated are the Swiss. They might defend their country against France, Austria, and Russia, neither of whom ought to be suffered to march armies over their Mountains. Those powers have practised as much tyrany and immorality as ever the Emperor Napoleon did over them or over the Royalists of Germany or Italy. Neither France Austria or Spain ought to have a foot of land in Italy.

All conquerors are alike. Every one of them. "Jura negat sibilata [i.e., sibi nata] nihil non arrogat armis.["] [67] We have nothing but fables concerning Theseus Bacchus and Hercules and even Sesostris, but I dare say that every one of them was as tyranical and immoral as Napoleon. Nebuchandnezzar is the first great conqueror of whom we have any thing like history and he was as great as any of them. Alexander and Cesar were more immoral than Napoleon. Zingis Kan was as great a conqueror as any of them and destroyed as many millions of lives and thought he had a right to the whole globe if he could subdue it. What are we to think of the crusades in which three millions of lives at least were probably sacreficed, and what right had St. Louis and Richard Coeur de Lion to Palestine and Syria more than Alexander to India, or Napoleon to Egypt and Italy. Right and justice have hard fare in this World, but there is a power above

66. Louis Simond, *Switzerland; or, A Journal of a Tour and Residence in that Country in the Years 1817, 1818, and 1819* ... (Boston, 1822).

67. "He denies that laws were made for him; he arrogates everything to himself by force of arms."

who is capable, and willing to put all things right in the end, et pour mettre chacun a sa place dans l'Universe and I doubt not he will.

Mr. English a Bostonian has published a volume of his expedition with Ishmael Pashaw up the river Nile.[68] He advanced above the third Cataract and opens a prospect of a resurrection from the dead of those vast and ancient Countries of Abyssinia and Etheopia. A free communication with India and the river Niger and the City of Tombuctou. This however is conjecture and speculation rather than certainty, but a free communication by land between Europe and India will e're long be opened. A few American steam boats, and our Quincy Stone Cutters would soon make the Nile as navigable as our Hudson Patomac or Mississippi. You see as my reason and intellect fails my imagination grows more wild and ungovernable, but my friendship remains the same. Adieu

JOHN ADAMS by proxy

Jefferson to Adams

Monticello. April 11. 23.

DEAR SIR

The wishes expressed, in your last favor, that I may continue in life and health until I become a Calvinist, at least in his exclamation of '*mon Dieu!* jusque à quand'! would make me immortal. I can never join Calvin in addressing *his god*. He was indeed an Atheist, which I can never be; or rather his religion was Dæmonism. If ever man worshipped a false god, he did. The being described in his 5. points is not the God whom you and I acknolege and adore, the Creator and benevolent governor of the world; but a dæmon of malignant spirit. It would be more pardonable to believe in no god at all, than to blaspheme him by the atrocious attributes of Calvin. Indeed I think that every Christian sect gives a great handle to Atheism by their general dogma that, without a revelation, there would not be sufficient proof of the being of a god. Now one sixth of mankind only are supposed to be Christians: the other five sixths then, who do not believe

68. George Bethune English, successively theologian, newspaper editor, and U. S. marine, was ordered on a cruise to the Mediterranean. In Alexandria he resigned his commission to become an officer in the Egyptian army and a Mohammedan. During 1820-21 he accompanied the son of the Pasha of Egypt to eastern Sudan and wrote one of the first descriptions of that country by a white man: *A Narrative of the Expedition to Dongola and Senaar* (London, 1822; Boston, 1823). Walter L. Wright, Jr., "English, George Bethune," *DAB*, VI, 165.

in the Jewish and Christian revelation, are without a knolege of the existence of a god! This gives compleatly a gain de cause to the disciples of Ocellus, Timaeus, Spinosa, Diderot and D'Holbach. The argument which they rest on as triumphant and unanswerable is that, in every hypothesis of Cosmogony you must admit an eternal pre-existence of something; and according to the rule of sound philosophy, you are never to employ two principles to solve a difficulty when one will suffice. They say then that it is more simple to believe at once in the eternal pre-existence of the world, as it is now going on, and may for ever go on by the principle of reproduction which we see and witness, than to believe in the eternal pre-existence of an ulterior cause, or Creator of the world, a being whom we see not, and know not, of whose form substance and mode or place of existence, or of action no sense informs us, no power of the mind enables us to delineate or comprehend. On the contrary I hold (without appeal to revelation) that when we take a view of the Universe, in it's parts general or particular, it is impossible for the human mind not to percieve and feel a conviction of design, consummate skill, and indefinite power in every atom of it's composition. The movements of the heavenly bodies, so exactly held in their course by the balance of centrifugal and centripetal forces, the structure of our earth itself, with it's distribution of lands, waters and atmosphere, animal and vegetable bodies, examined in all their minutest particles, insects mere atoms of life, yet as perfectly organised as man or mammoth, the mineral substances, their generation and uses, it is impossible, I say, for the human mind not to believe that there is, in all this, design, cause and effect, up to an ultimate cause, a fabricator of all things from matter and motion, their preserver and regulator while permitted to exist in their present forms, and their regenerator into new and other forms. We see, too, evident proofs of the necessity of a superintending power to maintain the Universe in it's course and order. Stars, well known, have disappeared, new ones have come into view, comets, in their incalculable courses, may run foul of suns and planets and require renovation under other laws; certain races of animals are become extinct; and, were there no restoring power, all existences might extinguish successively, one by one, until all should be reduced to a shapeless chaos. So irresistible are these evidences of an intelligent and powerful Agent that, of the infinite numbers of men who have existed thro' all time, they have believed, in the proportion of a million at least to Unit, in the hypothesis of an eternal pre-existence of a creator, rather than in that of a self-existent Universe. Surely this unanimous sentiment renders this more probable than that of the few in the other hypothesis. Some early Christians indeed have believed in the coeternal pre-existance of both the Creator and the world, without changing their relation of cause and effect. That this was the opinion of St. Thomas, we are informed by Cardinal Toleto, in these words 'Deus ab æterno fuit jam omnipotens, sicut cum produxit mundum. Ab æterno potuit producere mundum.—Si sol ab æterno esset, lumen ab æterno esset; et si pes, similiter vestigium. At lumen et vestigium effectus sunt efficientis solis et pedis; potuit ergo cum causâ æterna effectus co-æterna esse. Cujus sententiæ est S. Thomas Theologorum primus.' [69] Cardinal Toleta.

Of the nature of this being we know nothing. Jesus tells us that 'God is a spirit.' 4. John 24. but without defining what a spirit is 'πνευμα ὁ Θεος.' Down to the 3d. century we know that it was still deemed material; but of a lighter subtler matter than our gross bodies. So says Origen. 'Deus igitur, cui anima similis est, juxta Originem, reapte corporalis est; sed graviorum tantum ratione corporum incorporeus.' [70] These are the words of Huet in his commentary on Origen. Origen himself says 'appellatio ἀσωματον apud nostros scriptores est inusitata et incognita.' [71] So also Tertullian 'quis autem negabit Deum esse corpus, etsi deus spiritus? Spiritus etiam corporis sui generis, in suâ effigie.' [72] Tertullian. These two fathers were of the 3d. century. Calvin's character of this supreme being seems chiefly copied from that of the Jews. But the reformation of these blasphemous attributes, and substitution of those more worthy, pure and sublime, seems to have been the chief object of Jesus in his discources to the Jews: and his doctrine of the Cosmogony of the world is very clearly laid down in the 3 first verses of the 1st. chapter of John, in these words, ἐν αρχη ἦν ὁ λόγος, καὶ ὁ λόγος ἦν πρὸς τὸν Θεόν, καὶ ἦν ὁ λόγος. Οὗτος ἦν ἐν ἀρχη πρὸς τὸν Θεόν. Πάντα δι' αντοῦ ἐγένετο. Καὶ κωρὶς αὐτοῦ ἐγένετο οὐδὲ ἕν, ὅ γέγονεν.

Which truly translated means 'in the beginning God existed, and reason (or mind) was with God, and that mind was God. This was in the beginning with God. All things were created by it, and without it was made not one thing which was made'. Yet this text, so plainly declaring the doctrine of Jesus that the world was created by the supreme, intelligent being, has been perverted by modern Christians to build up a second person of their tritheism by a mistranslation of the word λογος. One of it's legit-

69. "God has been omnipotent forever, just as when he made the world. He has had the power to make the world forever. If the sun were in existence forever, light would have been in existence forever; and if a foot then likewise a footprint. But light and footprint are the effects of an efficient sun and foot; therefore the effect has had the power to be co-eternal with the eternal cause. Of this opinion is St. Thomas, the first of the theologians."

70. "God, therefore, to whom the soul is similar, in consequences of its origin, is in reality corporeal; but He is incorporeal in comparison with so much heavier bodies."

71. "The word ἀσωματον, among our writers, is not used or known."

72. "Yet who will deny that God is body, although God is spirit? Indeed He is spirit of His own type of body, in His own image."

imate meanings indeed is 'a word.' But, in that sense, it makes an unmeaning jargon: while the other meaning 'reason', equally legitimate, explains rationally the eternal preexistence of God, and his creation of the world. Knowing how incomprehensible it was that 'a word,' the mere action or articulation of the voice and organs of speech could create a world, they undertake to make of this articulation a second preexisting being, and ascribe to him, and not to God, the creation of the universe. The Atheist here plumes himself on the uselessness of such a God, and the simpler hypothesis of a self-existent universe. The truth is that the greatest enemies to the doctrines of Jesus are those calling themselves the expositors of them, who have perverted them for the structure of a system of fancy absolutely incomprehensible, and without any foundation in his genuine words. And the day will come when the mystical generation of Jesus, by the supreme being as his father in the womb of a virgin will be classed with the fable of the generation of Minerva in the brain of Jupiter. But we may hope that the dawn of reason and freedom of thought in these United States will do away [with] all this artificial scaffolding, and restore to us the primitive and genuine doctrines of this the most venerated reformer of human errors.

So much for your quotation of Calvin's 'mon dieu! jusqu'a quand' in which, when addressed to the God of Jesus, and our God, I join you cordially, and await his time and will with more readiness than reluctance. May we meet there again, in Congress, with our antient Colleagues, and recieve with them the seal of approbation 'Well done, good and faithful servants.'

TH: JEFFERSON

Adams to Jefferson

Quincy. Aug. 15th. '23

Watchman! what of the night!? Is darkness that may be felt to prevail over the whole world? Or can you perceive any rays of a returning dawn? Is the devil to be the "Lords anointed" over the whole globe? Or do you forsee the fulfilment of the prophecies according to Dr. Priestly's interpretation of them? I know not but I have in some of my familiar and frivolous letters to you told the story four times over, but if I have I never applied it so well as now. Not long after the denouement of the tragedy of Louis 16th. when I was vice-President, my friend the Dr. came to breakfast with me alone. He was very sociable, very learned and eloquent on the subject

of the French revolution. It was opening a new era in the world and presenting a near view of the millenium. I listened I heard with great attention
and perfect sang froid. At last I asked the Dr. do you really believe the
French will establish a free democratical government in France? He
answered; I do firmly believe it. Will you give me leave to ask you upon
what grounds you entertain this opinion? Is it from anything you ever
read in history—is there any instance of a Roman Catholic monarchy of
five and twenty millions at once converted into a free and rational people?
No, I know of no instance like it. Is there anything in your knowledge of
human nature derived from books or experience that any nation ancient
or modern consisting of such multitudes of ignorant people ever were or
ever can be converted suddenly into materials capable of conducting a
free government especially a democratical republic? No, I know of
nothing of the kind. Well then Sir what is the ground of your opinion?
The answer was, my opinion is founded altogether upon revelation and
the prophecies; I take it that the ten horns of the great beast in revelations, mean the ten crowned heads of Europe: and that the execution of
the king of France is the falling off of the first of those horns; and the
nine monarchies of Europe will fall one after another in the same way.
Such was the enthusiasm of that great man, that reasoning machine. After
all however he did recollect himself so far as to say, There is however a
possibility of doubt, for I read yesterday a book put into my hands by a
gentleman, a volume of travels, written by a french gentleman, in 1659,[73]
in which he says he had been travelling a whole year in England, into
every part of it and conversed freely with all ranks of people. He found
the whole nation earnestly engaged in discussing and contriving a form
of government for their future regulation. There was but one point in
which they all agreed and in that they were unanimous, that monarchy
nobility and prelacy never would exist in England again. The Dr. then
paused, and said, Yet in the very next year the whole nation called in the
King and ran mad with monarchy nobility and prelacy. I am no king
killer merely because they are kings—poor creatures they know no better
—they believe sincerely and conscientiously that God made them to rule
the world. I would not therefore behead them or send them to St. Helena
to be treated as Bonaparte was, but I would shut them up like the man in
the iron mask, feed them well, give them as much finery as they pleas'd

73. This volume may have been S[amuel] de Sorbière, *Relation d'un voyage en
Angleterre, où sont touchées plusieurs choses qui regardent l'état des sciences et de
la religion et autres matières curieuses* (Paris, 1664), translated as *A Voyage to England containing Many Things relating to the State of Learning &c.* (London, 1709);
or John Evelyn, *A Character of England as It was Lately presented in a Letter to a
Noble Man of France* (London, 1659), reprinted in *Harleian Miscellany*, 10 (1813),
189-98.

until they could be converted to right reason and common sense. I have nothing to communicate from this part of the country except that you must not be surprised if you hear something wonderful in Boston before long. With my profound respects for your family and half a centurys affection for yourself I am your humble servant.

JOHN ADAMS

Jefferson to Adams

Monticello Sep. 4. 23.

DEAR SIR

Your letter of Aug. 15. was recieved in due time, and with the welcome of every thing which comes from you. With it's opinions on the difficulties of revolutions, from despotism to freedom, I very much concur. The generation which commences a revolution can rarely compleat it. Habituated from their infancy to passive submission of body and mind to their kings and priests, they are not qualified, when called on, to think and provide for themselves and their inexperience, their ignorance and bigotry make them instruments often, in the hands of the Bonapartes and Iturbides to defeat their own rights and purposes. This is the present situation of Europe and Spanish America. But it is not desperate. The light which has been shed on mankind by the art of printing has eminently changed the condition of the world. As yet that light has dawned on the midling classes only of the men of Europe. The kings and the rabble of equal ignorance, have not yet recieved it's rays; but it continues to spread. And, while printing is preserved, it can no more recede than the sun return on his course. A first attempt to recover the right of self-government may fail; so may a 2d. a 3d. etc., but as a younger, and more instructed race comes on, the sentiment becomes more and more intuitive, and a 4th. a 5th. or some subsequent one of the ever renewed attempts will ultimately succeed. In France the 1st. effort was defeated by Robespierre, the 2d. by Bonaparte, the 3d. by Louis XVIII. and his holy allies; another is yet to come, and all Europe, Russia excepted, has caught the spirit, and all will attain representative government, more or less perfect. This is now well understood to be a necessary check on kings, whom they will probably think it more prudent to chain and tame, than to exterminate. To attain all this however rivers of blood must yet flow, and years of desolation pass over. Yet the object is worth rivers of blood, and years of desolation for what inheritance so valuable can man leave to his posterity? The spirit of the Spaniard and his deadly and eternal hatred to a Frenchman, gives me much confidence that he will never submit, but finally defeat this atrocious violation of the laws of god and man under which he is suffering; and the wisdom and firmness of the Cortes afford reasonable hope that that nation will settle down in a temperate representative government, with an Executive properly subordinated to that. Portugal, Italy, Prussia, Germany, Greece will follow suit. You and I shall look down from another world on these glorious atchievements to man, which will add to the joys even of heaven.

I observe your toast of Mr. Jay on the 4th. of July, wherein you say that the omission of his signature to the Declaration of Independence was by *accident*. Our impressions as to this fact being different, I shall be glad to have mine corrected, if wrong. Jay, you know, had been in constant opposition to our laboring majority. Our estimate, at the time, was that he, Dickinson and Johnson of Maryland by their ingenuity, perseverance and partiality to our English connection, had constantly kept us a year behind where we ought to have been in our preparations and proceedings. From about the date of the Virginia instructions of May 15. 76. to declare Independance Mr. Jay absented himself from Congress, and never came there again until Dec. 78. Of course he had no part in the discussions or decision of that question. The instructions to their delegates by the Convention of New York, then sitting, to sign the Declaration, were presented to Congress on the 15th. of July only, and on that day the journals shew the absence of Mr. Jay by a letter recieved from him, as they had done as early as the 29th. of May by another letter. And, I think, he had been omitted by the Convention on a new election of Delegates when they changed their instructions.[74] Of this last fact however having no evidence but an antient impression, I shall not affirm it. But whether so or not, no agency of *accident* appears in the case. This error of fact however, whether yours or mine, is of little consequence to the public. But truth being as cheap as error, it is as well to rectify it for our own satisfaction.

I have had a fever of about three weeks during the last and preceding month, from which I am entirely recovered except as to strength. Ever and affectionately yours

TH: JEFFERSON

74. In April 1776 Jay was elected to the New York Provincial Congress which met on May 14. In June he introduced a resolution demanding that the New York delegates to the Continental Congress consult the Provincial Congress before supporting independence. Jay was chairman of the committee to consider the Declaration when the New York Congress received its copy on July 9; and the committee recommended its adoption. Jay served as chief justice of New York until 1779 and did not resume his seat in the Continental Congress until Dec. 1778. George Pellew, *John Jay* (N. Y., 1890), 53-58, Chaps. III-IV.

Adams to Jefferson

Quincy September 18th. 1823.

DEAR SIR

With much pleasure I have heard read the sure words of prophecy in your letter of Sep. 4th. It is melancholy to contemplate the cruel wars, dessolutions of Countries, and ocians of blood which must occure, before rational principles, and rational systems of Government can prevail and be established. But as these are inevitable we must content ourselves with the consolations which you from sound and sure reasons so clearly suggest. Thes[e] hopes are as well founded as our fears of the contrary evils; on the whole, the prospect is cheering; I have lately undertaken to read Algernon Sidney on Government. There is a great difference in reading a Book at four and twenty, and at Eighty Eight, as often as I have read it, and fumbled it over; it now excites fresh admiration, that this work has excited so little interest in the literary world, As splendid an Edition of it, as the art of printing can produce, as well as for the intrinsick merit of the work, as for the proof it brings of the bitter sufferings of the advocates of Liberty from that time to this; and to show the slow progress of Moral phylosophical political Illumination in the world ought to be now published in America.

It is true that Mr. Jay, Mr. Dickinson, and Mr. Johnson, contributed to retard many vigorous measures, and particularly the vote of Independence untill he left Congress, but I have reason to think he would have concured in that vote when it was taken if he had been there. His absence was accidental. Congress on the fifteenth of May preceeding, as I remember had recommended to all the States to abolish all authority under the Crown, and institute and organize a new Government under the Authority of the People. Mr. Jay had promoted this resolution in New York by adviseing them to call a Convention to frame a New Constitution; he had been chosen a Member of that Convention, and called home by his Constituents to assist in it. And as Duane told me he had gone home with his Letter to Withe in his pocket for his Model and foundation, and the same Duane after the Constitution appeared asked me if it was not sufficiently conformable to my letter to Wythe.[75] I answered him I believed it would do very well. Mr. Jay was immediately appointed Chief Justice of the State,

75. JA to George Wythe, Jan. [?] 1776, "Thoughts on Government [1776]," *Works*, IV, 191, 193-200.

and obliged to enter immediately on the duties of his Office, which occasioned his detention from Congress afterwards, but I have no doubt, had he been in Congress at the time he would have subscribed to the Declaration of Independence. He would have been neither recalled by his Constituents nor have left Congress himself, like Mr. Dickinson, Mr. Willing, Governor Livingston and several others.

Nearly as I feel for the Spanish Patriots I fear the most sensible Men among them have little confidence in their Constitution which appears to me is modeled upon that in France of the Year 1789, in which the soverignty in a single assembly was every thing and the executive nothing. The Spaniards have adopted all this, with the singular addition that the members of the Cortes can serve only two years. What rational being can have any well grounded confidence in such a Constitution?

As you write so easy, and so well, I pray you to write me as often as possible, for nothing revives my spirits so much as your letters, except the society of my Son and his Family, who are now happily with me after an absence of two Years. I am Sir, with sentiments of affection and Respect Your Ancient Friend and humble Servant

JOHN ADAMS

Jefferson to Adams

Monticello. Oct. 12. 23.

DEAR SIR

I do not write with the ease which your letter of Sep. 18. supposes. Crippled wrists and fingers make writing slow and laborious. But, while writing to you, I lose the sense of these things, in the recollection of antient times, when youth and health made happiness out of every thing. I forget for a while the hoary winter of age, when we can think of nothing but how to keep ourselves warm, and how to get rid of our heavy hours until the friendly hand of death shall rid us of all at once. Against this tedium vitae ["weariness of life"] however I am fortunately mounted on a Hobby, which indeed I should have better managed some 30. or 40. years ago, but whose easy amble is still sufficient to give exercise and amusement to an Octogenary rider. This is the establishment of an University, on a scale more comprehensive, and in a country more healthy and central than our old William and Mary, which these obstacles have long kept in a state of languor and inefficiency. But the tardiness with which such works proceed may render it doubtful whether I shall live to see it go into action.[76]

Putting aside these things however for the present, I write this letter as due to a friendship co-eval with our government, and now attempted to be poisoned, when too late in life to be replaced by new affections. I had for some time observed, in the public papers, dark hints and mysterious innuendoes of a correspondence of yours with a friend, to whom you had opened your bosom without reserve, and which was to be made public by that friend, or his representative. And now it is said to be actually published.[77] It has not yet reached us, but extracts have been given, and such as seemed most likely to draw a curtain of separation between you and myself. Were there no other motive than that of indignation against the author of this outrage on private confidence, whose shaft seems to have been aimed at yourself more particularly, this would make it the duty of every honorable mind to disappoint that aim, by opposing to it's impression a seven-fold shield of apathy and insensibility. With me however no such armour is needed. The circumstances of the times, in which we have happened to live, and the partiality of our friends, at a particular period, placed us in a state of apparent opposition, which some might suppose to be personal also; and there might not be wanting those who wish'd to make it so, by filling our ears with malignant falsehoods, by dressing up hideous phantoms of their own creation, presenting them to you under my name, to me under your's, and endeavoring to instill into our minds things concerning each other the most destitute of truth. And if there had been, at any time, a moment when we were off our guard, and in a temper to let the whispers of these people make us forget what we had known of each other for so many years, and years of so much trial, yet all men who have attended to the workings of the human mind, who have seen the false colours under which passion sometimes dresses the actions and motives of others, have seen also these passions subsiding with time and reflection, dissipating, like mists before the rising sun, and

76. The first session of the University of Virginia was held during 1825-26.

77. *Correspondence between the Hon. John Adams, Late President of the United States, and the Late Wm. Cunningham, Esq., beginning in 1803, and ending in 1813* (Boston, 1823). William Cunningham, a distant relative of JA, had requested information of him which could be used against TJ as candidate for re-election to the presidency in 1804. JA's replies, characteristically frank, were written with the proviso that Cunningham would never publish them during JA's lifetime. But Cunningham died first, a suicide in May 1823, and his son immediately published the letters. Randall, *Jefferson*, III, 493. The son's purpose was to defeat J. Q. Adams in his campaigning for the presidency by casting aspersions on the character of the Adams family. J. Q. Adams recognized the purpose of the publication and regretted that such "venomous business" should have been introduced into the campaign. Charles Francis Adams, ed., *Memoirs of John Quincy Adams* (Philadelphia, 1875), VI, 176; Chinard, *John Adams*, 320-21, 342.

restoring to us the sight of all things in their true shape and colours. It would be strange indeed if, at our years, we were to go an age back to hunt up imaginary, or forgotten facts, to disturb the repose of affections so sweetening to the evening of our lives. Be assured, my dear Sir, that I am incapable of recieving the slightest impression from the effort now made to plant thorns on the pillow of age, worth, and wisdom, and to sow tares between friends who have been such for near half a century. Beseeching you then not to suffer your mind to be disquieted by this wicked attempt to poison it's peace, and praying you to throw it by, among the things which have never happened, I add sincere assurances of my unabated, and constant attachment, friendship and respect.

TH: JEFFERSON

Adams to Jefferson

Quincy 10th. November. 1823.

DEAR SIR

Your last letter was brought to me from the Post office when at breakfast with my family. I bade one of the misses open the budget; she reported a letter from Mr. Jefferson and two or three newspapers. A letter from Mr. Jefferson, says I, I know what the substance is before I open it. There is no secrets between Mr. Jefferson and me, and I cannot read it; therefore you may open and read it. When it was done, it was followed by an universal exclamation, The best letter that ever was written, and round it went through the whole table—How generous! how noble! how magnanimous! I said that it was just such a letter as I expected, only it was infinitely better expressed. A universal cry that the letter ought to be printed. No, hold, certainly not without Mr. Jefferson's express leave.

As to the blunder-buss itself which was loaded by a miserable melancholly man, out of his wits, and left by him to another to draw the trigger. The only affliction it has given me is sincere grief of the melancholly fate of both. The peevish and fretful effusions of politicians in difficult and dangerous conjunctures from the agony of their hearts are not worth remembering, much less of laying to heart.[78]

78. That the *Correspondence* between JA and Cunningham was published for political purposes directed against J. Q. Adams (a point disregarded by JA in the present letter) is borne out by the fact that several persons who put up money for the publication were later appointed as postmasters or collectors of customs by President Andrew Jackson. Adams, ed., *Memoirs of J. Q. Adams*, VI, 176n., VIII, 181.

The published correspondence is garbled. All the letters are left out that could explain the whole mystery. The vengeance against me was wholly occasioned because he could not persuade me to recommend him to the national government for a mission abroad or the government of a territory—services for which I did not think him qualified.

I salute your fire-side with cordial esteem and affection. J. A. In the 89 year of his age still too fat to last much longer

JOHN ADAMS

Adams to Jefferson

Quincy December 29th '23

DEAR SIR

I return your letter at your request signified by Gen. Dearborn, though it has been such a cordial to my heart. I feel much reluctance to release it. Since it has appeared in print it has been received with applause great and universal.[79] Our fellow citizens are determined to elect a President avec connaisance de cause, for the question has [been] in discussion in every nook in the United States for seven years. I should like to see an election for a President in the British empire or in France or in Spain or in Prussia or Russia by way of experiment. We go on pretty well, for we use no other artillery than goose quills, and our ink is not so deleterious as language and grape.

My old imagination is kindling into a kind of missionary enthusiasm for the cause of the Greeks.[80] My feelings go on with N. York, Pensylvania and Massachusetts, but after all they are feelings rather than reasonings. I confess that my information is not sufficiently extensive to forsee the result, but I comfort myself with the maxim of our friend Jebb, that no effort in favour of virtue is lost. I rely with confidence on the wisdom of our government to conduct us in the road of honour and the most probable path of safety. With the compliments of the season and with the

79. TJ to Henry Dearborn, Aug. 17, 1821, Lipscomb and Bergh, eds., *Writings*, XV, 329-30. Referring to JA, TJ wrote: "I am happy to hear of his good health. I think he will out live us all, I mean the Declaration-men...."

80. In his Seventh Annual Message to Congress, Dec. 2, 1823, President Monroe spoke on behalf of "the heroic struggle of the Greeks," just before he enunciated the "Monroe Doctrine." Richardson, ed., *Messages and Papers of the Presidents*, II, 217.

best wishes for your long continuance in life and health I remain your affectionate friend

JOHN ADAMS

Jefferson to Adams

Monticello July 11. 24.

DEAR SIR

My friend and correspondent of Richmond, Colo. Bernard Peyton will have the honor of delivering you this letter. He was a worthy officer of the late war, and now an equally worthy member of the mercantile body. Proposing to visit Boston, he has the natural ambition of being presented to the first of the revolutionary characters now living. I ask, of your friendship to give him a few moments of your time, the remembrance of which will to him be a gratification thro' life. I have pleasure in availing myself of every occasion of repeating to you the assurances of my constant friendship and respectful consideration.

TH: JEFFERSON

Adams to Jefferson

Quincy July 24th 1824

DEAR SIR

Mr. Benjamin Parker Richardson, a Grandson of a neighbour of mine, who has lived in harmony with me for almost eighty nine years, is very desirous of seeing the venerable Author of the Declaration of Independence, and as this is a virtuous curiosity which I always applaud and encourage in our young men, I have ventured to give him a line of introduction to you. A freedom which I have taken too often, especially as the reciprocity has always been on my side—never having received, as I recollect, in any one instance, a similar introduction from you.

I still breathe, which will not be long, but while I do I shall breathe out wishes for the welfare of mankind, hoping that they will daily become more deserving of it.

You are quite a young gentleman in comparison with your old friend

JOHN ADAMS.

Adams to Jefferson

Quincy November 15th. 1824

DEAR SIR

Your friend Professor Ticknor is bound upon a Tour in Virginia. Though he needs no introduction to you, he has requested a letter from me, and I cannot deny him. He carries his Lady with him, who is rich enough, and handsome enough, and amiable enough, and what can one say more? [81]

Is the present calm in the Political World to continue long or not? Our controversy will all be settled in a short time, and then we shall all submit like lambs. I hope the future Administration [82] will be as wise, as prudent, and as fortunate as the present, and then we shall all set down as quietly as Lambs.

Advanced fifteen days in my ninetieth year, I salute you as cordially as ever. I envy Mrs. Ticknor the pleasure of becoming acquainted with your family of Grand Daughters—my love to Mrs. Randolph.

You and I have been favored with a visit from our old friend General La Fayette.[83] What a wonderful Man at his Age to undergo the fatigues of such long journeys and constant feasts. I was greatly delighted with the sight of him and the little conversation I had with him.

France changes her King as easily as her glove.[84] His present Majesty, it is said, has commenced his reign by some very popular acts, and very wise ones, such as more freedom to the press, and unlimited Amnesty to all political offenders. Vale—

JOHN ADAMS

81. George Ticknor had married in 1821 Anna Eliot, daughter of the prosperous Boston merchant Samuel Eliot. Mr. and Mrs. Ticknor, accompanied by Daniel Webster, visited TJ in Dec. 1824. Ticknor found Mr. Jefferson "very little altered from what he was ten years ago, very active, lively, and happy...." Ticknor to William H. Prescott, Monticello, Dec. 16, 1824, Hillard, ed., *Life of Ticknor*, I, 348.

82. This proved to be the administration of J. Q. Adams, after the final decision in the election of 1824 was made in the House of Representatives.

83. At the invitation of President Monroe, Lafayette visited the United States during Aug. 1824–Sept. 1825. Symbol of victorious America of the revolutionary period, Lafayette was received everywhere with the wildest enthusiasm. He dined with Adams in Quincy on Aug. 29 and spent ten days with Jefferson at Monticello, Nov. 4-15, 1824. Edgar E. Brandon, ed., *Lafayette, Guest of the Nation...in 1824-1825* (Oxford, Ohio, 1944-57), I, 121, 129-30; III, 126-31, 137.

84. On the death of Louis XVIII in 1824, his brother Charles X, uncompromising reactionary, became king of France. He abdicated during the July Revolution of 1830.

Jefferson to Adams

Monticello Jan. 8. 25.

DEAR SIR

It is long since I have written to you. This proceeds from the difficulty of writing with my crippled wrists, and from an unwillingness to add to your inconveniences of either reading by the eyes, or writing by the hands of others. The account I recieve of your physical situation afflicts me sincerely. But if body or mind was one of them to give way, it is a great comfort that it is the mind which remains whole, and that it's vigor, and that of memory, continues firm. Your hearing too is good as I am told. In this you have the advantage of me. The dullness of mine makes me lose much of the conversation of the world, and much a stranger to what is passing in it. Acquiescence is the only pillow, altho' not always a soft one. I have had one advantage of you. This presidential election has given me few anxieties. With you this must have been impossible, independently of the question whether we are at last to end our days under a civil or a military government? I am comforted and protected from other solicitudes by the cares of our University. In some departments of science we believed Europe to be in advance before us, and thought it would advance ourselves were we to draw thence instructors in these branches, and thus to improve our science, as we have done our manufactures, by borrowed skill. I have been much squibbed for this; perhaps by disappointed applicants for professorships to which they were deemed incompetent. We wait only the arrival of three of the professors engaged in England to open our university.[85]

I have lately been reading the most extraordinary of all books, and at the same time the most demonstrative by numerous and unequivocal facts. It is Flourens' Experiments on the functions of the Nervous system, in vertebrated animals. He takes out the cerebrum compleatly, leaving the cerebellum and other parts of the system uninjured. The animal loses all it's senses of hearing, seeing, feeling, smelling, tasting, is totally deprived of will, intelligence, memory, perception etc. yet lives for months in perfect health, with all it's powers of motion, but without moving but

85. TJ sent his friend Francis Walker Gilmer abroad in 1824 to secure professors for the new University. In England he engaged Professors George Long (ancient languages), Thomas Hewett Key (mathematics), George Blaetterman (modern languages), Charles Bonnycastle (natural philosophy), and Robley Dunglison (anatomy). Herbert B. Adams, *Thomas Jefferson and the University of Virginia* (Washington, 1888), 111-18; Davis, ed., *Correspondence of Jefferson and Gilmer*, 113.

on external excitement, starving even on a pile of grain unless crammed down it's throat; in a state, in short, of the most absolute stupidity. He takes the cerebellum out of others, leaving the cerebrum untouched. The animal retains all it's senses, faculties and understanding, but loses the power of regulated motion, and exhibits all the symptoms of drunkenness. While he makes incisions in the cerebrum and cerebellum, lengthwise and crosswise which heal and get well, a puncture in the medulla elongata is instant death, and many other most interesting things, too long for a letter. Cabanis had proved, from the anatomical structure of certain portions of the human frame, that they might be capable of recieving from the Creator the faculty of thinking.[86] Flourens proves that the cerebrum is the thinking organ, and that life and health may continue, and the animal be entirely without thought, if deprived of that organ. I wish to see what the spiritualists will say to this. Whether, in this state, the soul remains in the body deprived of it's essence of thought, or whether it leaves it as in death, and where it goes? His memoirs and experiments have been reported on with approbation by a committee of the Institute, composed of Cuvier, Bertholet, Dumeril, Portal and Pinel. But all this you and I shall know, when we meet again in another place, and at no distant period. In the mean time, that the revived powers of your frame, and the Anodyne of philosophy may preserve you from all suffering, is my sincere and affectionate prayer.

TH: JEFFERSON

Adams to Jefferson

Quincy 22d January 1825

DEAR SIR

Your letter of the 8th has revived me. It is true, that my hearing has been very good, but the last year it has decayed so much, that I am in a worse situation than you are; I cannot hear any of the common conversation of my family, without calling upon them to repeat in a louder tone.

The presidential election has given me less anxiety than I, myself could have imagined. The next administration will be a troublesom one to whomso-ever it falls. And our John has been too much worn to contend much longer with conflicting factions. I call him our John, because when you was at Cul de sac at Paris, he appeared to me to be almost as much

86. See TJ to JA, March 14, 1820, above, 562.

your boy as mine. I have often speculated upon the consequences that would have ensued from my takeing your advice, to send him to William and Mary College in Virginia for an Education.

As to the decision of your Author, though I wish to see the Book I look upon it as a mere game at push-pin. Incision knives will never discover the distinction between matter and spirit, or whether there is any or not. That there is an active principle of power in the Universe is apparent, but in what substance that active principle of power resides, is past our investigation. The faculties of our understanding are not adiquate to penetrate the Universe. Let us do our duty which is, to do as we would be done by, and that one would think, could not be difficult, if we honestly aim at it.

Your University is a noble employment in your old Age, and your ardor for its success, does you honour, but I do not approve of your sending to Europe for Tutors, and Professors. I do believe there are sufficent scholars in America to fill your Professorships and Tutorships with more active ingenuity, and independent minds, than you can bring from Europe. The Europeans are all deeply tainted with prejudices both Ecclesiastical, and Temporal which they can never get rid of; they are all infected with Episcopal and Presbyterian Creeds, and confessions of faith, They all believe that great principle, which has produced this boundless Universe. Newtons Universe, and Hershells universe, came down to this little Ball, to be spit-upon by Jews; and untill this awful blasphemy is got rid of, there never will be any liberal science in the world.

I salute your fire side, with best affection, and best wishes for their health, wealth, and prosperity. Ever your friend

JOHN ADAMS

Adams to Jefferson

Quincy 23rd. January 1825.

MY DEAR SIR.

We think ourselves possessed or at least we boast that we are so of Liberty of conscience on all subjects and of the right of free inquiry and private judgment, in all cases and yet how far are we from these exalted privileges in fact. There exists I believe throughout the whole Christian world a law which makes it blasphemy to deny or to doubt the divine

inspiration of all the books of the old and new Testaments from Genesis
to Revelations. In most countries of Europe it is punished by fire at the
stake, or the rack or the wheel: in England itself it is punished by boring
through the tongue with a red hot poker: in America it is not much
better, even in our Massachusetts which I believe upon the whole is as
temperate and moderate in religious zeal as most of the States. A law
was made in the latter end of the last century repealing the cruel punishments of the former laws but substituting fine and imprisonment upon
all those blasphemers upon any book of the old Testament or new. Now
what free inquiry when a writer must surely encounter the risk of fine
or imprisonment for adducing any argument for investigation into the
divine authority of those books? Who would run the risk of translating
Volney's Recherches Nouvelles? who would run the risk of translating
Dupuis? but I cannot enlarge upon this subject, though I have it much
at heart. I think such laws a great embarassment, great obstructions to
the improvement of the human mind. Books that cannot bear examination certainly ought not to be established as divine inspiration by penal
laws. It is true few persons appear desirous to put such laws in execution
and it is also true that some few persons are hardy enough to venture to
depart from them; but as long as they continue in force as laws the
human mind must make an awkward and clumsy progress in its investigations. I wish they were repealed. The substance and essence of Christianity as I understand it is eternal and unchangeable and will bear
examination forever but it has been mixed with extraneous ingredients,
which I think will not bear examination and they ought to be separated.
Adieu

JOHN ADAMS

Jefferson to Adams

Monticello Feb. 15. 25.[87]

DEAR SIR
The people of Europe seem still to think that America is a mere garden
plat, and that whatever is sent to one place is at home as to every other.
The volume I forward you by this mail was found on Majr. Cartwright's
death, to have in his own handwriting an address for you altho' mis-
taking your Christian name. His friends having occ[asio]n to write to me

87. This letter is a draft in TJ's hand, in Jefferson Papers, Lib. Cong. See JA to TJ,
April 19, 1825, below, 610.

on another subject, and supposing we were but next door n[eigh]bors sent this vol. to N. Y. under my address, whence it has travelled post to this place, and must now travel back again and thence to the point to which it o[ugh]t to have gone at first.

I sincerely congratulate you on the high gratific[atio]n which the issue of the late election must have afforded you. It must excite ineffable feelings in the breast of a father to have lived to see a son to whose educ[atio]n and happiness his life has been devoted so eminently distinguished by the voice of his country. Nor do I see any reason to suppose the next adm[inistratio]n will be so difficult as in your favor of Jan. 22. you seemed to expect. So deeply are the principles of order, and of obedience to law impressed on the minds of our citizens generally that I am persuaded there will be as immediate an acquiescence in the will of the majority as if Mr. Adams had been the choice of every man. The scriblers in newspapers may for a while express their disapp[oint]m[en]t in angry squibs; but these will evaporate without influence[in]g the public functionaries, nor will they prevent their harmonising with their associates in the transaction of public affairs. Nights of rest to you and days of tranquility are the wishes I tender you with my affect[iona]te respects

Th: J.

Adams to Jefferson

Quincy 25th. Feby. 1825

DEAR SIR

Every line from you exhilarates my spirits and gives me a glow of pleasure, but your kind congratulations are a solid comfort to my heart. The good-natured and good-humoured acquiescence of the friends of all the candidates gives me a comfortable hope that your prediction may be fulfilled, that the ensuing administration will not be so difficult as in a former letter I had apprehended.

Here we have lost Eustace in whom the people appeared to be better united than under any former Governor, but we have a prospect now of a successor in Lincoln, in whom the people promise to be still more united; so that it is probable that this State will not be so troublesome to the National administration as it was some time ago.

I had not heard of the death of Major Cartwright. That gentleman has been an anxious and laborious writer against boroughs and borough-mongers for more than fifty years. He appears to have had an ardent love for liberty but he never understood the system necessary to secure it— One of those ardent spirits whose violent principles defeated all their benevolent purposes, of whom Horne Took was the most eminent and the great Greek scholar another.[88]

I look back with rapture to those golden days when Virginia and Massachusetts lived and acted together like a band of brothers and I hope it will not be long before they may say redeunt saturnia regna,[89] when I hope the world will hear no more of Hartford Convention or Virginian Armories.[90]

Have you read Genl. Smyth's Apocalypse? I wish he had read Dupuis. This Genl. Smyth appears to have an ardent, inquisitive head. I like him much for his curiosity. My old friend Randolph, whose fierce fire appears to have cooled down into a more moderate and dignified light and splendour, appears to have lost some of his animosity against me. He has not honoured me with a compliment for a year or two.

I wish your health may continue to the last much better than mine. The little strength of mind and the considerable strength of body that I once possessed appear to be all gone, but while I breathe I shall be your friend. We shall meet again, so wishes and so believes your friend, but if we are disappointed we shall never know it.

JOHN ADAMS

Adams to Jefferson

Quincy 19th April 1825

DEAR SIR

Mr. Charles Sigourney and lady, a respectable pair in Hartford, Connecticut, the Husband a Son of my old friend in Amsterdam, and the

88. Probably Richard Bentley (1662-1742), master of Trinity College, Cambridge, who was influential in the restoration of classical learning in Great Britain. *Dict. Nat. Biog.*, IV, 306-14.

89. "The golden age is returning."

90. The Virginian Armory was built in 1798 as a part of the regular program of state defense, but during the hysteria over the Alien and Sedition Acts the Federalists charged that Virginia had taxed its people to buy arms for use against the federal government. In the session of Congress, 1816-17, John Randolph of Roanoke made some loose remarks about Virginia's Armory in Richmond having been built "to resist, by force, the encroachments of the then Administration upon her indisputable rights." Professor Davidson has blasted the myth by pointing out that a program for defense was not new in Virginia in 1798 and that the Armory was authorized before the Alien and Sedition Acts were passed. Philip G. Davidson, "Virginia and the Alien and Sedition Acts," *Amer. Hist. Rev.*, 36 (1930-31), 336-42.

Wife a very conspicuous literary Lady,[91] have requested a line to you, as they are bound on a journey to the seat of your University and wish, I suppose, an apology for visiting Monticello.

I have lost your last letter to me, the most consolatory letter I ever received in my life.[92] What would I not give for a copy of it. Your friend to all eternity,

JOHN ADAMS

Adams to Jefferson

Quincy December 1st. 1825

DEAR SIR

I ought not to have neglected so long to write you an account of the delightful visit I received from Mr. and Mrs. Coolidge.[93] Mrs. C. deserves all the high praises I have constantly heard concerning her. She entertained me with accounts of your sentiments of human life, which accorded so perfectly with mine that it gave me great delight. In one point, however, I could not agree. She said she had heard you say that you would like to go over life again. In this I could not agree; I had rather go forward and meet whatever is to come. I have met in this life with great trials. I have had a Father, and lost him. I have had a Mother and lost her. I have had a Wife and lost her. I have had Children and lost them. I have had honorable and worthy Friends and lost them—and instead of suffering these griefs again, I had rather go forward and meet my destiny. I am, as ever, affectionately

JOHN ADAMS

91. Mrs. Lydia Howard Huntley Sigourney.

92. TJ to JA, Feb. 15, 1825, above, 608-9.

93. Joseph Coolidge, Jr., of Boston, married Eleanora Wayles Randolph, daughter of Thomas Mann Randolph and Martha Jefferson Randolph, on May 27, 1825. She was TJ's favorite granddaughter and he had the highest respect for Mr. Coolidge. TJ to Edward Everett, July 21, 1825, Lipscomb and Bergh, eds., *Writings*, XIX, 285; Zorn, *Descendants of the Presidents*, 49.

Jefferson to Adams

Monticello Dec. 18. 25.

DEAR SIR

Your letters are always welcome, the last more than all others, it's subject being one of the dearest to my heart. To my grand-daughter your commendations cannot fail to be an object of high ambition, as a certain passport to the good opinion of the world. If she does not cultivate them with assiduity and affection, she will illy fulfill my parting injunctions. I trust she will merit a continuance of your favor, and find in her new situation the general esteem she so happily possessed in the society she left.

You tell me she repeated to you an expression of mine that I should be willing to go again over the scenes of past life. I should not be unwilling, without however wishing it. And why not? I have enjoyed a greater share of health than falls to the lot of most men; my spirits have never failed me except under those paroxysms of grief which you, as well as myself, have experienced in every form: and with good health and good spirits the pleasures surely outweigh the pains of life. Why not then taste them again, fat and lean together. Were I indeed permitted to cut off from the train the last 7. years, the balance would be much in favor of treading the ground over again. Being at that period in the neighborhood of our Warm springs, and well in health, I wished to be better, and tried them. They destroyed, in a great degree, my internal organism, and I have never since had a moment of perfect health. I have now been 8 months confined almost constantly to the house, with now and then intervals of a few days on which I could get on horseback.

I presume you have recieved a copy of the life of Richd. H. Lee, from his grandson of the same name, author of the work. You and I know that he merited much during the revolution. Eloquent, bold, and ever watchful at his post, of which his biographer omits no proof. I am not certain whether the friends of George Mason, of Patrick Henry, yourself, and even of Genl Washington may not reclaim some feathers of the plumage given him, notable as was his proper and original coat. But on this subject I will not anticipate your own judgment.

I learn with sincere pleasure that you have experienced lately a great renovation of your health. That it may continue to the ultimate period of your wishes is the sincere prayer of usque ad aras amicissimi tui ["ever at the altars of your dearest friend"].

TH: JEFFERSON

Adams to Jefferson

Quincy 14th. January 1826

MY DEAR SIR

Permit me to introduce to your acquaintance a young Lawyer by the name of Josiah Quincy and with the title of Coll. being an Aid to our Governor. The name of Coll. Quincy has never I believe been extinct for over two hundred years. He is a Son of our Worthy Mayor of the City of Boston and possesses a character unstained and irreproachable. I applaud his ambition to visit Monticello and its great inhabitant, and while I have my hand in I cannot cease without giving you some account of the state of my mind. I am certainly very near the end of my life. I am far from trifling with the idea of Death which is a great and solemn event. But I contemplate it without terror or dismay, "aut transit, aut finit ["either it is a transformation, or it is the end"]," if finit, which I cannot believe, and do not believe, there is then an end of all but I shall never know it, and why should I dread it, which I do not; if transit I shall ever be under the same constitution and administration of Government in the Universe, and I am not afraid to trust and confide in it.

I have not the pleasure to see Mr. and Mrs. Coolidge as often as I wish—but I hear nothing of them but what is respectable and pleasing. I am as ever your friend

JOHN ADAMS

Jefferson to Adams

Monticello Mar. 25. 26.

DEAR SIR

My grandson Th: Jefferson Randolph, being on a visit to Boston, would think he had seen nothing were he to leave it without having seen you. Altho' I truly sympathise with you in the trouble these interruptions give, yet I must ask for him permission to pay to you his personal respects.

Like other young people, he wishes to be able, in the winter nights of old age, to recount to those around him what he has heard and learnt of the Heroic age preceding his birth, and which of the Argonauts particularly he was in time to have seen. It was the lot of our early years to witness nothing but the dull monotony of colonial subservience, and of our riper ones to breast the labors and perils of working out of it. Theirs are the Halcyon calms succeeding the storm which our Argosy had so stoutly weathered. Gratify his ambition then by recieving his best bow, and my solicitude for your health by enabling him to bring me a favorable account of it. Mine is but indifferent, but not so my friendship and respect for you.

TH: JEFFERSON

Adams to Jefferson

Quincy April 17th. 1826

MY DEAR SIR

Your letter of March 25th. has been a cordial to me, and the more consoling as it was brought by your Grandsons, Mr. Randolph and Mr. Coolidge. Everybody connected with you is snatched up, so that I cannot get any of them to dine with me—they are always engaged. How happens it that you Virginians are all sons of Anak? [94] We New Englanders are but Pygmies by the side of Mr. Randolph. I was very much gratified with Mr. Randolph, and his conversation. Your letter is one of the most beautiful and delightful I have ever received.

Public affairs go on pretty much as usual: perpetual chicanery and rather more personal abuse than there used to be. Messrs. Randolph and McDuffie have out-Heroded Herod. [95] Mr. McDuffie seems to be swallowed up in chivalry. Such institutions ought not to be suffered in a republican Government. Our American Chivalry is the worst in the World. It has no Laws, no bounds, no definitions; it seems to be all a Caprice. My love to all your family, and best wishes for your health

JOHN ADAMS.

94. Joshua 11:21.
95. Both John Randolph and George McDuffie in Congress were bitterly opposed to President J. Q. Adams's administration. McDuffie charged the President and his secretary of state, Henry Clay, with corruption in the electoral vote of 1824. Samuel F. Bemis, *John Quincy Adams and the Union* (N. Y., 1956), 41-42, 132-33.

INDEX

The index covers the introduction, text, and notes. Pages i-li, 1-282, are in Volume I; pages 283-614 are in Volume II.